Global Perspectives on Gender Equality

Routledge/UNRISD Research in Gender and Development

UNRISD is an autonomous agency engaging in multidisciplinary research on the social dimensions of contemporary problems affecting development. Its work is guided by the conviction that, for effective development policies to be formulated, an understanding of the social and political context is crucial. The Institute attempts to provide governments, development agencies, grassroots organizations and scholars with a better understanding of how development policies and processes of economic, social and environmental change affect different social groups. Working through an extensive network of national research centres, UNRISD aims to promote original research and strengthen research capacity in developing countries.

Current research programmes include: Civil Society and Social Movements; Democracy, Governance and Well-Being; Gender and Development; Identities, Conflict and Cohesion; Markets, Business and Regulation; and Social Policy and Development. For further information on UNRISD work, visit www.unrisd.org.

1. New Perspectives on Gender and Migration
Livelihood, Rights and Entitlements
Edited by Nicola Piper

2. Gendered Peace
Women's Struggles for Post-War Justice and Reconciliation
Edited by Donna Pankhurst

3. Global Perspectives on Gender Equality
Reversing the Gaze
Edited by Naila Kabeer and Agneta Stark with Edda Magnus

Global Perspectives on Gender Equality

Reversing the Gaze

Edited by
Naila Kabeer and Agneta Stark
with Edda Magnus

Routledge
Taylor & Francis Group
New York   London

First published 2008
by Routledge
270 Madison Ave, New York, NY 10016

Simultaneously published in the UK
by Routledge
2 Park Square, Milton Park, Abingdon, Oxon OX14 4RN

Routledge is an imprint of the Taylor & Francis Group, an informa business

Transferred to Digital Printing 2009

Typeset in Sabon by IBT Global

Library of Congress Cataloging in Publication Data
Global perspectives on gender equality : reversing the gaze / edited by Naila Kabeer, and Agneta Stark ; with Edda Magnus.
p. cm.
Includes bibliographical references and index.
ISBN 978-0-415-96349-7 (hardback : alk. paper)
1. Sex discrimination against women—Sweden. 2. Sex discrimination against women—Norway. 3. Sex discrimination against women—Cross-Cultural studies. I. Kabeer, Naila. II. Stark, Agneta, 1946– III. Magnus, Edda, 1976–

HQ1237.5.S86G56 2007
305.4209485—dc22   2007025880

ISBN10: 0-415-96349-4 (hbk)
ISBN10: 0-415-87450-5 (pbk)
ISBN10: 0-203-93838-0 (ebk)

ISBN13: 978-0-415-96349-7 (hbk)
ISBN13: 978-0-415-87450-2 (pbk)
ISBN13: 978-0-203-93838-6 (ebk)

The Expert Group on Development Issues (EGDI)

The Expert Group on Development Issues (EGDI) was an advisory body to the Swedish government from 1995–2007. The main task of the EGDI was to contribute to an increased understanding of global development processes and increase policy coherence for development. Serving as a channel of research findings into the heart of policy making, the group initiated and produced policy relevant studies on global development, including this study.

The Expert Group consisted of internationally renowned researchers and policy makers with extensive networks in the respective field. The research interests of the group, as well as approaches taken in EGDI studies, provided important perspectives on the Swedish policy for global development.

The EGDI and the EGDI Secretariat ceased to exist in May 2007.

For further information, please visit: www.egdi.gov.se

Contents

List of Figures

List of Tables

Foreword

The tendency in North–South research on social, economic, and policy issues has long been largely one-way. Researchers in the North have subjected the cultures, practices, and politics of the South and East to their telescopic gaze, interpretations, and analyses from a position of superordinate power in the global political order. In my travels as UN High Commissioner for Human Rights, the issue of the developed North constantly assessing developing countries by their yardstick came up quite often in discussions with women's groups. I confess it made me feel quite uncomfortable.

This volume provides a rather unique opportunity to reverse the gaze—to observe and examine gender-equality policies in two Nordic countries through the eyes of researchers from the South and East. This method is as uncommon as it is refreshing within the development field as well as within the specific field of gender studies. In fact, policy makers from donor countries have often been criticized for not paying enough attention to the ways in which various societies and cultures construct differences among women as well as between women and men. Such constructions relate to conceptions of womanhood and femininity, manhood and masculinity, as well as to other dimensions of social and gender equality. In light of this debate, this volume is an important contribution to the field of gender studies.

In 2004, the Expert Group on Development Issues (EGDI) initiated this study. The original idea was that inviting social scientists whose perspectives and experiences derive from developing and transitional countries and contexts to study Nordic policy approaches to gender equality would lead to new understandings, for policy makers and researchers in the Nordic countries as well as in the developing world. The researchers come from countries as diverse as Iran, Mexico, Hungary, and India. They discuss topics such as paid and unpaid work, sexuality, social policy, and motherhood. The authors conclude that the Nordic countries have come a long way in the area of gender equality. However, they also note that there is still a surprisingly large amount of work left to be done. For one thing, feminists in the two Nordic countries appear to have settled for a strategy of "do not disturb the men," meaning that women are expected to change themselves and their situations, while men do not have to change theirs. Issues of power, violence, and the management of multidimensional difference have, therefore, in comparison with the developing and transitional countries researched in this volume, entered the debate relatively late.

Comparisons between the Nordic countries and countries in the developing world render visible some important differences—as well as similarities—between them. Developing countries often suffer from problems due to colonial legacies, extremely diverse and heterogeneous populations, and economic hardships, while Nordic countries traditionally have had homogeneous populations (ethnically as well as in terms of income) and strong grassroots and political movements. These differences must be recognized and respected by politicians and policy makers when policies are formulated. This means that direct transference of blueprint approaches based on what has worked in Nordic countries should be avoided.

This volume can provide new perspectives on Nordic gender-equality policies, and the conclusions and suggestions presented can thus serve as an eye-opener for, and can contribute to, a richer and more open discussion among, researchers, politicians, policy makers, and feminists in the Nordic countries and elsewhere.

It is a timely publication, as we approach the 60th Anniversary of the Universal Declaration of Human Rights in 2008. I hope it will lead to other similar studies that reverse the gaze, and thereby help to promote a deeper understanding of how human rights need to be imbedded in the wider culture of countries and communities.

—Mary Robinson

Acknowledgments

HARIS GAZDAR

I am grateful to Naila Kabeer, Ayesha Khan, Agneta Stark, Ramya Subrahmanian, Irfan Khan, and an academic referee for comments on an earlier draft.

ELIZABETH JELIN

This report was prepared with the advice and assistance of Dr. Mabel Lopez Oliva, the prompt and efficient help of Edda Magnus in Sweden, and the guidance of Naila Kabeer. They deserve my gratitude. Swedish readers of the draft are gratefully acknowledged.

SHAHRA RAZAVI

I would like to thank Naila Kabeer, Barbara Hobson, and Diane Sainsbury for their useful comments on earlier drafts of this chapter, with the usual disclaimers. I would also like to thank Edda Magnus for excellent research assistance.

BEATA NAGY

My special thanks go to Agneta Stark and Naila Kabeer for their stimulating remarks, Ulrica Risso-Engblom for her patient and encouraging communication, and Edda Magnus for her continuous support in delivering the current literature on the Scandinavian countries. I should particularly like to thank all those who offered criticism or approval after lectures or seminar papers relating to this chapter.

RAMYA SUBRAHMANIAN

The author would like to acknowledge the valuable support, feedback, and advice provided by editors of the book and by two anonymous reviewers. Susanne Dodillet kindly helped with discussions and further references to the European literature. All limitations that remain are those of the author alone.

SEEMA ARORA-JONSSON

I would like to thank the women in Nayagarh who so generously shared their time and their thoughts with me as well as my co-researchers in Drevdagen, the women in the forum, from whom I learnt so much, about work and everyday life. Naila's encouragement to go ahead and write, and Ulrica's help with all practical matters were invaluable in making this chapter take shape.

SHIREEN HASSIM

I should like to thank Edda Magnus for her unparalleled research support in locating materials on Sweden.

BOLA AKANJI

My close working relationship with Prof Naila Kabeer and several leading voices on global gender research and advocacy facilitated my participation in this project. I wish to express my appreciation for the opportunity to collaborate with the EGDI. My special thanks go to Edda Magnus, the research assistant who supplied me with rich literature in my chosen topic and conducted interviews with key figures in Swedish Gender Statistics Unit. I also wish to thank Ulrica Risso-Engblom, who facilitated major areas of this collaboration as well as a special dissemination of my chapter at the CODESRIA Gender Symposium in Cairo in 2006.

FRANCISCO COS-MONTIEL

I would like to give thanks to Ulrica Risso-Engblom who provided very useful comments on earlier versions of this chapter. I would also like to thank Edda Magnus for key research assistance. I also particularly appreciate Naila Kabeer's encouragement and intellectual guidance and Jo Beall's unwavering support.

NAILA KABEER

I would like to thank Ulrica Risso-Engblom for all her help and support. I found it invaluable. I would like to thank Edda Magnus, who helped me track down various useful material on the Nordic situation. Hege Skjeie and Barbara Hobson provided helpful comments at various stages of the draft but are not responsible for any limitations of the final draft. Much of the reading for the chapter was carried out while I was the Kersten Hesselgren Visiting Professor at PADRIGU, University of Goteborg. I am grateful to the Swedish Research Council, who provided this opportunity. And finally, I would like to thank those who made comments and raised questions when I presented the ideas for this chapter at seminars at the University of Uppsala and Göteborg as well as to the reading group at the Institute of Social Science Trust, Delhi, where they told me that "pragmatism" was not a word that feminists in India generally liked to use about themselves.

AGNETA STARK AND NAILA KABEER, WITH EDDA MAGNUS

The editors would like to thank the EGDI for its support and Andrea Cornwall, Berit Olsson, Ann-Sofie Ohlander, Heba Handoussa, and Ulf Malmström for their comments on earlier drafts. They would also like to send their gratitude to the interns Alexandra Ahlmark, Moa Andrén-Nilsson, Andreas Wedner, Frida Hansson, and Therese Arnewing for their excellent assistance in the completion of this book.

1 Introduction

Reversing the Gaze

Naila Kabeer, Edda Magnus,
and Agneta Stark

THE RATIONALE FOR THIS BOOK

This book is the product of an experiment. It brings together scholars with firsthand knowledge and experience of developing/transition countries to reflect on approaches to gender equality in Norway and Sweden. The country experiences that are represented in the book are wide-ranging: Pakistan (Gazdar), Argentina (Jelin), Iran (Razavi), Hungary (Nagy), Mexico (Cos-Montiel), Nigeria (Akanji), South Africa (Hassim) and India (Subrahmanian; Arora-Jonsson). These are countries that have very little in common with the Nordic countries or indeed with each other. Nevertheless, the idea that there is value to be added, analytically and in policy terms, by a comparison between countries with very different historical trajectories, institutional configurations, and resource constraints is not entirely new. After all, a great deal of development assistance has consisted of attempts to transfer the lessons from experiences of advanced industrialised countries to the "south" and, more recently, to the transition economies of Europe. These attempts have been largely guided by the work of researchers and consultants who were drawn mainly from the donor countries and hence tended to interpret the realities of developing countries from the perspectives provided by their own values and experiences.

The contributions to this book represent a departure from this tradition. They offer assessments of Nordic achievements on gender equality from the perspectives of those who have long-standing professional and personal experience in developing countries. For these authors, participating in the project that gave rise to this book offered a refreshing opportunity to "reverse the gaze," to study what was achieved in two Nordic contexts from their own priorities and standpoints and to ask what can be learned from this comparison. Consequently, this book represents what they believe to be interesting or instructive about the Nordic experience rather than what different actors within the Nordic countries might consider to be the key issues. Some of the chapters draw out lessons in terms of what *could* be emulated from the Nordic experience; others focus on what should *not*. Still others focus on what was achieved in the Nordic context, how it was achieved, and what stands in the way of equivalent progress in their own countries. A number of the authors have focussed on earlier periods in the history of Norway and Sweden, when they were at a stage closer to those that prevail in many developing countries today, with a view to ascertaining how they overcame the constraints of the past to embark on the road to gender equality. Others focus on the contemporary period.

"CONTRASTING" COMPARISONS: THE NATURE OF THE ANALYTICAL CHALLENGE

A great deal of the comparative work on gender equality in the Organisation for Economic Co-operation and Development (OECD) context has been carried out within typologies of social policy regimes. Such typologies signal the differences in welfare approaches among the wealthy industrialised countries of the world. They point to different histories and institutional configurations, as well as differences in dominant ideologies about the relationship between the individual and the state and about gender roles within the family. Feminists have criticised and reworked this framework to accommodate the different models of the breadwinner and caregiver that prevail in the OECD context. Some have used child benefit packages as their main criteria (Bradshaw et al. 1993); others have added positions in the labour market, social security, and taxation systems (Lewis 1992); still others have focussed on the position of lone mothers (Kilkey and Bradshaw 1999; Hobson and Takahashi 1997). Their efforts suggest that countries are likely to be classified differently according to the criteria used (Lewis 1997).

However, even within this reworked version, the welfare regimes framework, taking for granted as it does that there is a discernible state commitment to welfare provision, is not particularly helpful in contexts where such a commitment cannot be taken for granted. And where markets remain partial and limited in their outreach, it is family, kinship, and community that underpin the search for livelihood and security and provide the main source of norms and values that govern people's lives. The social organisation of family, kinship, and community, and the societal norms and values which these generate, may have as much, and more, influence in explaining variations in gender equality in these contexts than state policies or legislation, particularly since policies and legislation often fail to be upheld in practice, a theme that recurs in the contributions to this book.

Table 1.1 helps to illustrate some of the differences between the countries being compared in this book. It reports on per capita income along with a number of widely used indicators of social progress, including measures of gender equality developed by the United Nations. For the purposes of our analysis, Korpi's distinction between basic "inequalities" and "elite inequalities" is a useful one (Korpi 2000). The first relate to the satisfaction of basic

Table 1.1 Human Development Indicators

Country	GDP per capita (PPP, US$)	HDI ranking (177 countries)	GDI ranking (136 countries)	GEM ranking[1] (75 countries)
Norway	38,454	1	1	1
Sweden	29,541	5	4	2
Hungary	16,814	35	30	41
Argentina	13,298	36	32	19
South Africa	11,192	121	92	18
Mexico	9,803	53	45	35
Iran	7,525	96	74	71
India	3,139	126	96	95
Pakistan	2,225	134	105	41
Nigeria	1,154	159	120	98

[1]GEM data for South Africa, India, and Nigeria is from other sources; see below
Source: UNDP (2006) Human Development Report 2006; GDP-, HDI- and GDI data for all countries collected in 2004; GEM data for Norway, Sweden, Hungary, Argentina, Mexico, Iran, and Pakistan collected in 20002004; GEM data for South Africa and India from UNDP (1999) Human Development Report 1999; data collected in 1995 for India and in 19981999 for South Africa, 102 countries were ranked; GEM data for Nigeria from UNDP (1996) Human Development Report 1996, data collected in 1995, 104 countries were ranked.

needs (mortality rates and life expectancy, health, literacy, and primary education), while the second relate to the extent to which professional women are held back by the glass ceiling, the percentage of women in cabinet, and so on.

The Human Development Index (HDI) focuses on overall achievements in basic health, education, and economic activity. The Gender-related Development Index (GDI) measures how countries are doing in terms of some of the basic dimensions of gender equality: wages earned (with controls introduced for differences in national income levels), life expectancy, and education levels attained. The Gender Empowerment Measure (GEM) is a composite of gender inequalities in earnings (removing the controls for differences in national income levels in the GDI measure), in professional, managerial, and technical occupations, and in parliamentary representation. It thus addresses some of the "elite" inequalities referred to earlier. It also offers partial insight into the nature of socioeconomic disparities in a country: countries that perform considerably better on the GEM index than on the GDI are also likely to be countries in which elite women have made important gains in the public domain but with little progress on the basic inequalities that affect poorer women.

A comparison of how the different countries perform on these indicators suggests a number of points. First of all, they show a broad association between per capita GNP and GDI, suggesting that countries improve their basic gender equality achievements with increases in their per capita income. The poor performance of developing countries can thus partly be attributed to their low levels of income. Second, however, they suggest that income is only part of the story. A number of countries are ranked far lower in terms of the GDI measures than their levels of per capita income would warrant. Nor is this deviation from the expected ranking a function of levels of income. Iran, South Africa, India, and Pakistan all fail to score a HDI or GDI rank commensurate with their per capita GDP ranking, but Iran and South Africa with higher levels of per capita income report much larger deviations. Nigeria, with lower levels of per capita income, does not deviate from the rank commensurate with its per capita income.

And third, how countries are ranked in terms of gender equality changes, often considerably, when the focus shifts to the GEM measure. This is less true for the Nordic countries, which perform as well on the GEM as they do on basic equality measures, suggesting that progress on equality is widespread in these societies. In other countries, the direction of the deviation between the two measures how they perform on second order relative to basic inequalities. Hungary performs better on basic equality measures than on second-order equality, a product perhaps of its very recent emergence from socialist-egalitarianism. While Iran is ranked much lower than some of the countries in the table—and, of course, considerably lower than Sweden and Norway, its ranking on the GEM is not that different from its GDI rank. While Argentina and Mexico are ranked above Iran for both indicators, they both perform far better on their GEM ranking than their GDI, indicative of the high levels of income and social disparities in these countries. Pakistan, too, at much lower ranks on both, performs better on the GEM index than on the GDI.

These shifts in how countries are ranked by different measures of gender equality mirror the differences in the ranking of countries within different typologies of welfare regimes. The problem with the welfare regime typologies, which focus largely on policy "inputs," is finding the appropriate set of policy indicators that will create meaningful categories among countries in terms of their approaches to gender equality, given the complexity of women's lives and their dual responsibilities within the home and marketplace. The problem with the UN gender equality measures, which focus on outcomes rather than policy inputs, is that it is possible for a country to perform well on certain indicators but poorly on others. This may reflect where the policy emphasis in a country is—there is a major push in developing countries on closing gender disparities in primary education, for instance, but less on addressing the causes of maternal mortality. It may also reflect the fact that, in highly stratified contexts, progress on the different dimension of gender equality varies across socioeconomic groups.

Clearly, measures like the GDI and GEM cannot capture all the multiple dimensions of gender equality, but they do serve to tell us that concerns about gender equality are likely to be different for countries at different levels of development. They are also different for men and women in different socioeconomic groups. The analytical challenge posed by the comparisons carried out in this book relate not only to different levels of development across which the comparisons are being carried out, but also to the vastly different histories, social formation, and value systems which are embodied in current gender equality outcomes. As Ellingsaeter points out in her comparison of Nordic countries:

> Politics and institutions are crucial in understanding the structuring of gender relations in society, but politics and their gendered outcomes are embedded in complex processes. Nations constitute different "historical packages" or unique constellations of factors . . . Both the formation of policies and the actual outcomes are conditioned by such configurations, that is by the economic, institutional and cultural settings in which they are embedded. (1998, 60)

If nations are seen to constitute different "historical packages" in the Nordic context to which her comments relate, the variations are likely to be even greater for the "north-south" comparisons with which this book is concerned. Faced with this challenge, the authors in this book have eschewed attempts to fit their analyses around existing or new typological approaches. Instead, they have taken as their organising framework the basic challenge of social reproduction common to all societies. This relates to how societies sustain, reproduce, and transform themselves over time and encompasses both the micro-level processes that sustain life and labour on a daily and generational basis as well as changes in the social relations of production and reproduction that govern these processes. The concerns with paid and unpaid work; marriage, parenthood, and sexuality; and literacy and education featured in the following chapters, together with an analysis of the politics and policies that promote greater equality in relation to these concerns, reflect this underlying framework. In the rest of this introduction, we highlight some key themes presented in these chapters.

STATE–SOCIETY RELATIONS AND THE CHALLENGE OF SOCIAL REPRODUCTION

The first of these themes relates to state–society relations in some of the countries covered. It is clear from the analysis contained in the book that while the main strides in the construction of "women-friendly" regimes in Norway and Sweden were taken in the post-war period, certain preconditions were in place which allowed such strides to be taken. Both countries had small and, till recently, relatively homogenous populations and histories of the twentieth century that have been dominated by social democratic governments and active labour movements. They also had high levels of organisation by women, in autonomous associations and within mainstream political parties and trade unions. These helped to create a national constituency for universalist policies, to socially embed values of equity and equality firmly within a shared cultural framework, and to provide a relatively hospitable environment for the struggle for gender equality.

This is in contrast to most of the countries with which comparisons are being made. Most of the latter have histories of colonisation which left lasting legacies of inequality. Their populations continue to be divided, not only by class but also by social identity: ethnicity and indigeneity in Nigeria and Mexico; race in south Africa; caste, religion, and language in India and Pakistan. In many of these contexts, these divisions have taken lethal forms. Ethnic differences have led to civil war in Nigeria and continue to fragment the experience of rights and citizenship; religion and caste divisions erupt into violence from time to time in the Indian subcontinent; race was the basis of state-sponsored violence in South Africa. In Mexico, indigenous groups have taken up armed struggle in pursuit of rights and recognition, while in Argentina the indigenous population was all but wiped out by European immigrants who regarded it as "empty territory" to be settled by them. The demise of socialism in Eastern Europe has allowed the emergence of social inequalities that had been hitherto suppressed, although Hungary has not been featured in the forefront of the resulting conflicts.

A unified constituency for women's advancement is clearly difficult to mobilise across such deep divisions. It is evident from the various contributions that barriers to such advancement have taken other forms as well. The extent of gender segregation of a society appears to be one important variable. Societies with a high degree of gender segregation, reflecting cultural norms of female seclusion within the domestic domain, tend to face a different set of barriers to gender equality than those where women are not confined to the domestic domain (Kabeer 2003). As the discussions in the book suggest, restrictions on their physical mobility curtails girls' capacity to attend school in Pakistan, women's capacity to take up paid work in the public domain in Iran (where the law requires husbands' permission), and opportunities for paid work in India.

The nature of the social formations that give rise to these basic inequalities is touched on at different points in the book, but the first three chapters, which take a historical perspective, deal most explicitly with the challenge of social reproduction in highly stratified contexts. Gazdar leads off with an analysis of the drive to universalise literacy in Sweden in the second half of the seventeenth century. He contrasts it with the failure of successive regimes in Pakistan to ensure the spread of literacy and the stark gender inequalities in basic education that persist in the country today.

His attempt to understand the factors behind these contrasting outcomes touches on a number of general themes which are relevant to later contributions. He comments on the capacity of the Swedish state to intervene in the lives of its citizens from a very early stage of the country's history to an extent that is unusual, not only from the perspective of Pakistan and some of the other countries discussed in the book, but also from the perspective of other advanced industrialised countries. Public life was far less gender segregated from an early period of Sweden's history than it was—and continues to be— in Pakistan, and the patriarchal household in Sweden enjoyed a far more limited "sovereignty." The church and state, firmly linked by the seventeenth century, were able to regulate individual behaviour across the population to an extent unimaginable in the context of contemporary Pakistan, where communities continue to be divided along "parochial" lines by kinship, caste, and so on, managing their own affairs and regarding the state with considerable suspicion. The "social engineering state" of the twentieth century was therefore a continuity, not a departure, from the country's history.

The question of the distance between state and citizen is crucial here. As Gazdar points out, distances are likely to be seen as far larger in countries that are economically polarised and socially stratified, as Pakistan is, compared to societies like those of Norway and Sweden, which largely share language, culture, and tradition. The state's ability to regulate the public life—and private behaviour—of its citizens appears to be a function of this distance. In Argentina, Jelin also describes a context where the state is separated from large sections of the country's population by both the physical distance implied by the urban/rural and centre/periphery distinction as well as the social distance of class and, to some extent, ethnicity. The failure of the ruling elites, closely aligned with the Church, to impose their views about family, sexuality, and reproduction led to the co-existence of parallel models alongside each other: the family of the urban middle class based on Catholic norms about male authority, wifely obedience, and indissoluble marriage bonds, on one hand, and the free conjugal unions and illegitimate offspring thath prevailed in the rural and frontier areas, on the other.

Despite the later democratisation of political life in Argentina, the Church continues to seek to hold back the forces of social change that are altering the choices available to women in their private lives. The persistent failures of the Argentine state to regulate the processes of social reproduction, that is, its role as "laggard" rather than "leader" in relation to social change, is contrasted with the pro-active role played by the Swedish state in anticipating and helping to shape the direction of social change as far as fertility behaviour and women's labour force participation were concerned.

Religion as a conservative force also features centrally in Razavi's account of the Iranian situation, but she provides a sobering reminder that the enforced "unveiling" and secularisation of society in pursuit of the dream of modernisation by the Pahlavi regime was as disenfranchising for many poorer rural women as the enforced veiling and Islamisation after the Iranian revolution proved to be for more educated professional women. Behind the half-hearted nature of the reforms carried out by the Shah was the widespread acceptance of the community's legitimate prerogative to set the limits of individual moral behaviour, particularly in relation to the preservation of female "modesty." Nor did his pursuit of modernisation include more than token gestures in the direction of the democratisation of society.

The Islamic Republic was able to close some of this distance between state and society because it expressed both the political aspirations of a vast majority of the people of Iran, who were largely unified in their rejection of the previous regime, as well as offering a model of society that was closer to the beliefs and values of the majority of the people. This allowed the Republic to effect some significant changes, including changes in the realm of gender relations, curtailing women's ability to hold public office, and prescribing their behaviour and apparel in the public domain. At the same time, the Islamisation of public space and the call to protect the Revolution against the invasion by Iraq gave women from lower income households far greater possibilities for public participation than had been available to them in the previous regime.

Subrahmanian's analysis is also premised on questions about the distance between the state and its citizens. It takes as its theme the criminalisation of the demand for commercial sex by Sweden—but not Norway—in response to the demands of its women's organisations. Sweden has sought to promote this approach in a variety of international forums, and a number of countries have followed suit. However, as Subrahmanian argues, such a measure is likely to play out very differently in the contexts of Sweden and India. Sweden is characterised by one of the world's most supportive welfare states, one that provides support to women's dual responsibilities in family and market and is also a major source of employment for women through the social services. Regardless of the extent to which states *should* intervene in the choices made by individuals or determine what constitutes a meaningful choice, it could be argued that the Swedish state does so in the context of guaranteeing alternatives to sex work as a means of securing one's living.

The same cannot be said in India. While it has had a less interrupted history of democratic politics than the other developing countries included in this book, and while the state has sought to promote some degree of social security for its citizens, its efforts have been both limited and uneven. The intersection of class, caste, and gender inequalities serves to create extreme forms of marginalisation, with women from poorer groups cut off from both market and state provision in their search for security. For many of these women, the sex trade offers one of the few livelihood options available. Despite the social stigma associated with sex work, it allows them a means of supporting themselves and their families in working conditions that are sometimes less exploitative and humiliating than the menial forms of domestic service or abusive marriages that may be their only alternatives. In a context where the state has not only failed to provide any kind of reliable safety net but has also perpetrated various forms of gender-based violence against women (custodial rape was one of the issues that galvanised feminist activism in recent decades), the criminalisation of sex workers or their clients offers little by way of improving the life prospects of these women. It may instead render them more vulnerable to predatory and corrupt police.

THE POWER OF DISCOURSE

A second underlying theme running through some of the chapters in the book relates to discourse as an example of a "power" resource for subordinate groups within a society. The Nordic experience helps to focus attention on some of the mechanisms through which women as a section of the population lacking the institutionalised power of the working class—"the politics of numbers and voting strength"—were able to mobilise around demands for a more "woman friendly" state (Hobson and Lindholm 1997). The construction of discursive strategies that allowed these demands to resonate for women across class barriers also served to galvanize allies outside their immediate ranks and proved a critical factor in their successes.

In the Swedish context, the discursive strategies of feminists largely took a "gender neutral" form, linking women's claims to the "master frames" (Snow and Benford 1992) of the Swedish social democratic culture of solidarity, democracy, and equality. Equality in the labour market was seen as the key to equality in other spheres, including great support for parenting responsibilities. In this, however, Sweden is probably an exception, even in relation to the other European countries. As Kabeer's chapter points out, it is the focus of Norwegian feminists on gender difference and on the values of motherhood as the bases for women's claims, that find more of an echo in developing country contexts. In the far more gender-differentiated social relationships that prevail in many of these societies, with the practice of female seclusion characterising a number of them, gender difference has been a far more common basis for women's claims.

An assessment of these rather different strategies for advancing women's claims for resources and recognition in the Nordic context prompted reflections not only on what is gained but also on what may be lost. Of all the countries discussed in this book, socialist Hungary probably came closest to the Swedish notion of equality based on equal participation in the labour market. However, as Nagy points out, socialist ideology constructed the male patterns of full-time, lifelong employment as the norm against which all citizens were required to perform, regardless of the fact that a significant percentage of women had additional child care responsibilities that men were not required to share. This was not a notion of equality with which the mass of women had struggled but a "forced emancipation" imposed by an undemocratic state. Nagy contrasts the struggle of Hungarian women to combine their child care and work responsibilities with little or no help from the state with the combination of part-time work, full protection, and support for parenting responsibilities that have allowed women in the Nordic countries to move in and out of the labour market without facing the prospect of impoverishment. It is clear from her discussion that Swedish and Hungarian notions of equality based on labour force participation, while superficially similar, result in very different labour market policies and patterns when feminists are able to play an active role in their interpretation.

While the Swedish focus on gender-neutral strategies within a wider social-solidaristic discourse won feminists allies beyond their immediate ranks and explains the extent and nature of the advances they made, the silencing of difference also served to suppress attention to the gender specificities of the experiences of men and women. As both Arora-Jonsson and Subrahmanian suggest in their chapters, it appears to have left little space for the more conflictual aspects of gender relations—male violence against women, for instance, or the capacity for women to organize *as women* around their own interests. Also reflecting on the neutrality strategy, Jelin argues that as maternal and paternal roles have not become interchangeable in practice, "difference" needs to be factored into the logic of equality which is based on a relational rather than an individual perspective: "the tension between gender equality and the acknowledgement of difference can only be approached through the recognition of their embeddedness in systems of social relations."

On the other hand, maternalism as a discursive strategy to promote women's claims has its own limitations. This point is made by Razavi: "Although maternalist politics has had contradictory and different outcomes in different countries, this form of claimsmaking shares an implicit acceptance that the rights women were claiming should come in return for certain pre-given responsibilities tied to traditionally ascribed gender roles." In Norway, for instance, maternalism was given a "radical" interpretation, and feminist movements in the early decades of feminist activism used the politics of gender difference and the value of motherhood to push for a series of measures that gave mothers a degree of economic independence through child-care allowances and the possibility of independent taxation. However, it also stood in the way of a unified resistance by women's groups to attempts by the Labour Party and the unions to curtail the rights of married women to employment. It also slowed down the provision of public child-care facilities in the Norwegian context until the wide-scale entry of women into the labour force led to changes in public policy on this front.

Along with an appreciation of the importance of discourse as a strategic resource, the Nordic experience is a reminder that the value of discourse as a mobilising or advocacy strategy does not occur in a vacuum. It is potent only when it has "narrative fidelity"—that is, it strikes a responsive chord with myths, beliefs, folklore, and so on that make up the existing culture (Snow and Benford 1992). In both Sweden and Norway, feminists developed their discursive strategies within the possibilities offered by prevailing cultural frameworks around identities of mother, worker, and citizen. Where hegemonic frameworks do not incorporate norms and values that are conducive to arguments for gender equality, feminist struggles are that much harder, and their gains are likely to be that much more limited.

This is exemplified in the book by the contrasting ways in which familial metaphors were used in the Nordic and the Argentine contexts. One of the most powerful and enduring metaphors of Nordic social democracy was the idea of the caring state as "the People's home" where all would be cared for and there would be no deprived or privileged members. The metaphor was intended to build support for social democratic parties beyond their immediate membership and to find neutral territory beyond class conflict. Its effect was to remove the symbolic barriers between public and private realms of citizenship (Hobson and Lindholm 1997). And while it had the potential to circumscribe women's influence within the home, in practice it was possible to use the promise of solidarity and equality to make claims around care, childrearing, and unpaid domestic work: the domain of the home and family, normally defined as the domain of the "private" in liberal political thought, emerged as the basis for the welfare state.

However, Jelin's account of the Argentine case shows that, in the absence of democratic institutions, the dissolution of the barriers between the public and private can be extremely dangerous—an intrusion into basic individual liberties. Here, the military government that took power in 1976 promoted the idea of the family as the basis of the natural social order and of family values as the foundation of Argentine identity. In addition, the metaphor of the "Grand Argentine family" was used for the nation as a whole, with "the Father-State having inalienable rights over the moral and physical fate of its citizens." Here, too, the distinction between public and private disappeared but what was on offer was a very different notion of state-as-family from that conveyed by the idea of People's Home. In the Argentine version, rebellious children and youth represented a potential threat to the nation-family, and only "good" children-citizens were truly Argentine. The military regime looked toward parents to control and discipline rebellious children, running frequent TV advertisements asking, "Do you know where your child is now?" The Argentine case reminds us that while a great deal of feminist mobilisation has been, and should be, around renegotiating the boundaries between public and private, the value of a "private" sphere has to be recognised as a critical precondition for individual freedom and a democratic society.

Familism as ideology lends itself to paternalist policies and politics based around the idea of the male breadwinner and patriarchal authority. It can equally give rise to maternalist discourses and strategies where claims are based on women's motherhood and the special values, strengths, and capacities this bestows on women. That the form taken by maternalist politics is contingent on the larger political context is also evident in the accounts of Iran and Argentina. In Iran, Islamist feminists have made imaginative use of religious discourse within the parameters permitted by a theocratic and patriarchal state to highlight the rights accorded to women by Islam, both as mothers and as wives in the domestic sphere as well as workers and political actors in the service of the Islamic state in the public sphere. They have succeeded in passing a law through Parliament which includes "wages for housework," although poor follow-up and the failure to back it up with public funds make it a symbolic rather than a substantive victory.

In Argentina, the centrality of the metaphor of the family in the discourse of the military dictatorship found a mirror image in its centrality in the discourse of the human rights opposition. The violations of human rights that the opposition denounced included crimes against families: kidnapping of people from their own homes to be tortured and "disappeared." Children were kidnapped, as were pregnant young women, for purposes of adoption by military personnel. Women in search of their lost children became the maternalist face of the human rights movement in Argentina, the Mothers of the Disappeared: their concerns for their own children merged with their concerns for all disappeared children.

Where an inhospitable political environment domestically curtails the discursive possibilities available to women's organisations, the global arena can be a source of alternatives. Indeed, "the global" appears to have become a strand in feminist politics in the later decades of the twentieth century across much of the world, including the Nordic countries. For the Nordic countries, their leading position in the UN league tables on gender equality has been a source of national pride, but as a number of Swedish feminists have noted, this has had the effect of contracting some of the space for critical reflections on the limits to what has been achieved. The demands by Iranian feminists for a greater role for women in the public and political domain has drawn strength from global feminist politics and from global discourses of women's rights, as promulgated through the UN World Conferences and International Conventions such as The Convention on the Elimination of All Forms of Discrimination Against Women (CEDAW). As Jelin notes, even the conservative military governments in Latin America were not untouched by new ideas circulating in the international arena in relation to legal rights, although they proved more willing to act on social than on political rights. In India, as Arora-Jonsson's chapter shows, international NGOs like Oxfam have brought new ideas and values about gender equality into grassroots programmes in some of the poorest areas of India and found a ready audience among many of the women, and some of the men.

The emphasis in the Beijing Platform on "gender mainstreaming" and sex-disaggregated statistics has had an effect on most of the countries discussed in this book, including Sweden and Norway. The requirement to report on progress on gender provided an impetus to re-examining their gender policies in the Nordic countries. Sweden had already declared its adoption of the mainstreaming approach by the early nineties as a logical outcome of a longer process of self-examination. In Mexico, on the other hand, the setting up of the gender mainstreaming machinery came in response to the government's search for international legitimacy rather than to the demands of the domestic women's movements—although the latter had been making these demands for some time. There was, consequently, considerable political distance between grassroots women's organisations and the machinery that was set up and little effort to set up mechanisms that would allow downward accountability.

However, the ability to draw on, and make discursive use of, alternative visions of family, work, and politics in environments where constituencies for gender equality are still in the process of being formed—as Akanji describes in the context of sub-Saharan Africa—is hampered by lack of information and advocacy skills. The Nordic comparison points to the importance of research and data as well as of advocates with the educational skills and political experience to make use of the data to make their case. In Africa, and in most Third World countries, such basic information is absent, as are the research capacity to collect it and the political will to fund it. Gender advocates in these countries must rely on scholars from outside and the consultancy studies funded by international donors to find the information they need—and such information is collected in response to imperatives that they may not share. Akanji is calling for something that had formed a core strategy in feminist mobilisation in the Nordic context: "to create an informed woman citizen who [understands] the policy debates and [can] influence the policy arena" (Hobson and Lindholm 1997, 485).

NETWORKS, ORGANISATION, AND WOMEN'S AGENCY

Women coming together around shared concerns have been an important impetus behind struggles for gender equality in different regions of the world. The extent and form of these collectivities is discussed explicitly in a number of chapters in this book and forms an implicit thread in others. It is a central theme in Arora-Jonsson's contribution based on her fieldwork in rural areas of India and Sweden. She found very different "levels of comfort" among women seeking to organise as women. Within the highly gender segregated—and unequal—social relations of rural Orissa, there appeared to be a natural logic to the idea of women coming together as women. However, while the women were initially organised by a nongovernmental development organisation to address issues of access to forest resources, these new associative forms allowed them to gain the confidence to enter less familiar domains of public action. In rural Sweden, on the other hand, where gender equality had been fought for through the institutionalised presence of women within the trade unions, political parties, and the media, the idea that women might want to organize autonomously appeared to generate a great deal of ambivalence, not only on the part of men, but also among the women themselves.

The history of Norwegian feminism was somewhat different where maternalist politics were used to demand women's right to be represented by women because of the common concerns of womanhood (Skjeie 1991). Not only did the idea of quotas for women in public life emerge earlier in Norway than Sweden, but there was a much stronger tradition of autonomous women's organisations. However, while the Nordic experience is often held up as an example of the successful use of quotas to increase women's representation, Hassim argues that there is no automatic relationship between women's electoral presence and progress on gender equality policies. The adoption of gender equality policies in the Nordic context reflected the longer process of constituency formation that lay behind the increased presence of women in public life. While quotas may help to "fast track" women's entry into the political domain in countries like South Africa and India, there is no automatic guarantee that this presence will translate into equally rapid progress on the policy front. The political inexperience of those who come into elected office purely through the quota route, the likelihood that they will not have any constituency to support them and to whom they are accountable, and their loyalties to the party that put them in office make it unlikely that they will have the commitment or the confidence to push for transformative policies. Indeed, Hassim argues that while gender quotas may increase the numerical visibility of women in politics, egalitarian gender policies may find greater support from sympathetic and progressive male allies.

Cos-Montiel's account also deals with the limits of transplanting apparently progressive administrative solutions to a context where women have mobilised at the grassroots level but have not cohered as an effective political constituency. In contrast to the systematic approach taken to gender mainstreaming in Sweden, he notes the piecemeal and half-hearted efforts evident in Mexico, where the setting up of a national machinery for women was a response to international imperatives. The failure to set up any bottom-up mechanisms that would allow grassroots women's groups to hold the government accountable for its performance merely reinforced the tendency of leadership of the women's machinery to see itself as beholden to the party leadership rather than answerable to the wider polity of women.

The range of contexts covered by this book helps to illuminate both the variety of different issues that make up women's concerns across the world and the diversity of political stances they bring to them. In South Africa, women have mobilised within the larger struggle against the apartheid regime. In Argentina, they have evoked the image of the Mother who seeks her own "disappeared" child and all other disappeared children as a counter to the image of the state as repressive Father put forward by the military regime.

Feminists in Mexico and India share the idea of founding a women's political party with feminists in Sweden and Norway. And while women mobilised in Sweden as the "Support Stockings" to put pressure on parties to put more women in power, the organisation of women in "self-help groups" through the livelihoods programmes of government and nongovernment organisations in the Indian context have allowed women in some states in India to come together formally for the first time and explore their common interests (Arora-Jonsson). Subrahmanian describes the growing activism of sex workers in India, among the most stigmatised of workers in the economy, and their forms of engagement with other civil society organisations in their struggle for rights and recognition, while Kabeer touches on the globalisation of workers' struggles with the globalisation of the economy. And while women have made relatively few gains in the labour market in Iran, Razavi notes that the spread of female education has helped to raise political awareness among the young generation of women. There is a greater willingness on the part of feminists with secular-socialist and Islamist politics in Iran to submerge some of their antagonisms in the face of the hardening gender politics of the state and to use women's journals as a forum for debating some of their differences.

The need to appreciate the implications of the diversity of ways in which women live their lives, formulate their priorities, and attain political consciousness is exemplified by Subrahmanian's discussion of the Swedish decision to criminalise the demand for prostitution. She points out that the Swedish position is premised on a denial of any agency on the part of women who become sex workers, a position that is challenged in the Indian context by both researchers and activists. As Stark points out, the views put forward by Subrahmanian around the issue of prostitution are likely to be viewed as provocative and controversial by Swedish feminists.

However, the reaction of Swedish feminists also came as a surprise to many of the authors of this book. Certainly the views that Subrahmanian puts forward would not command a consensus among feminists within a huge and diverse country like India itself or in the women's movements in other countries, but that is precisely the point. This is a highly contested issue and the idea that it could command a consensus, even among those interested in women's rights, is difficult to imagine. In a telling aside in her discussion of feminist struggles in Bangladesh, for instance, Huq (2005) relates how the eviction of sex workers from long-established brothels in urban Bangladesh drew a number of human rights and feminist organisations to their support. However, conflicting views about the nature of sex work itself meant that the alliance could only operate on the basis that this debate be postponed while the campaign was in force.

LESSONS LEARNED

The objective in putting together this comparative project was to explore some of the lessons that might emerge from the comparisons. However, the sheer differences in the contexts represented by Nordic and developing countries made it difficult to draw out any easy lessons that could be acted on within the near future. The direct "policy transfer model" which has been a strong strand in donor thinking does not find much support in the chapters in this book.

Akanji's chapter is one of the exceptions. She notes the early commitment to the collection of sex—disaggregated data in Norway and Sweden in response to demands from gender advocates and the uses made of this data in advocacy efforts. She contrasts this to the situation in many African countries where a vicious cycle exists: the absence of such data weakens gender advocacy efforts which, in turn, fail to secure commitment to generate such data in the future. The other exception is the chapter by Nagy. The Hungarian government has begun to show interest in the promotion of part-time work in recent years as a possible solution to unemployment and the gender gap in labour force activity. She suggests that the Nordic experience may offer important lessons as to the enabling measures that would allow part time work to act as a positive force for gender equality rather than a trap for women: these include child care, parental leave arrangements, and a greater focus on men's fatherhood roles.

Other chapters draw out more general lessons. Gazdar uses the history of the universalisation of literacy in Sweden to argue against the individualist demand-and-supply approach to educational provision of the World Bank, in favour of an approach that links the provision of education to a vision of the "imagined community" which informs the nation-building effort. A number of authors argue that administrative solutions to issues of gender inequality are unlikely to work without the additional effort necessary to link these solutions to a political constituency for gender equality. This is the gist of Hassim's discussion of political quotas in South Africa and Cos-Montiel's of gender mainstreaming machineries in Mexico. The contributions by Jelin and Razavi focus on the gap between state policy and ground-level social realities. Their message reminds us that if formal policies on gender equality have failed to translate into concrete outcomes in the absence of any genuine commitment on the part of the state, attempts by the state to regulate family, sexuality, and reproductive behaviour are likely to be equally futile if these policies do not speak to the reality of women's lives. Subrahmanian argues strongly against assuming that feminist politics around prostitution are context-independent. The decision to penalise the purchase of sexual services in a context where there is an effective welfare state is likely to play out very differently from contexts where such a state is not only weak but also an object of some suspicion on the part of feminists.

More generally, however, as the concluding chapters by the two co-editors of the book suggest, the value of this book lies in the opportunity it provides for examining Nordic approaches to gender equality from a perspective other than one that is normally taken. For Stark, the fact that the concerns and priorities of the contributors to the book do not necessarily converge with the views of the Nordic gender research community provides a lesson in the importance of standpoint in shaping the agenda and helps to challenge some taken-for-granted assumptions about what constitutes feminist priorities. By illuminating the magnitude of the challenges with which feminists have had to struggle in some other parts of the world, these contributions help to explain why questions of power came onto the feminist agenda far earlier in their struggles than they appear to have done in the Nordic countries.

For Stark, as one of the editors of the volume, another important point that comes of this project is the inward-turned nature of the Nordic debates. As she points out, important parts of debates among Nordic researchers are not available in English and appear to be targeted mainly at a Nordic audience. At the same time, references to research from outside the Nordic countries, with a heavy bias toward research published in English, are common in Nordic researchers' work: "This asymmetry could be interpreted as an indication that Nordic gender research tends to choose themes from and for a Nordic research agenda rather than from research topics and angles of interest to researchers from other parts of the world. A certain level of introversion could perhaps be traced in disseminating strategies in parts of Nordic gender research."

For Kabeer, the main lessons to be drawn from the Nordic experience lie in the strategies and processes which explained progress on gender equality policies rather than the policies themselves. And it is from the early years, when Nordic feminists were struggling to counter the taken-for-granted assumptions about gender relations, that there is most to be learned. Her contribution focuses on the role played by women's collective action and discursive strategies in advancing gender equality in the Nordic context. While both elements are also important in developing countries, she notes the different forms they take and the challenges they encounter. She also draws attention to some of the remaining—as well as newly emerging—forms of inequality in the Nordic context, particularly in a period of growing cultural diversity as a result of immigration from non-European countries. She suggests that the introversion within the Nordic gender research community commented on by Stark may explain the "epistemological blind spot" in Nordic feminism, that is, the failure to take on board the full implications of intersecting relationships of gender, class, ethnicity, and religion. For a Nordic audience, therefore, a book about the struggle for gender equality in Norway and Sweden written from the standpoint of scholars from the South may contribute to the longer term project of creating a space within Nordic society for alternative perspectives and for listening to the diverse voices of "the other."

REFERENCES

Bradshaw, Jonathan, John Ditch, Hilary Holmes, and Peter Vilhiteford. 1993. A comparative study of child support in fifteen countries. *Journal of European Social Policy* 3(4):255–71.

Hobson, Barbara, and Marika Lindholm. 1997. Collective identities, women's power resources, and the making of welfare states. *Theory and Society* 26(4)/August: 475–508.

Hobson, Barbara, and Meiko Takahashi. 1997. *The parent-worker model: Lone mothers in Sweden.* Stockholm: Stockholms Universitet: Sociologiska institutionen.

Huq, Shireen P. 2005. Bodies as sites of struggle: Naripokkho and the movement for women's rights in Bangladesh In *Inclusive citizenship: Meanings and expressions*, ed. Naila Kabeer, 164–181. London: Zed Press.

Kabeer, Naila. 2003. *Mainstreaming gender and poverty eradication in the Millennium Development Goals.* London: Commonwealth Secretariat.

Kilkey, Majella, and Jonathan Bradshaw. 1999. Lone mothers, economic well-being and policies. In *Gender and welfare state regimes*, ed. Diane Sainsbury. Oxford: Oxford University Press.

Korpi, Walter. 2000. Faces of inequality: gender, class and patterns of inequalities in different types of welfare states. *Social Politics* 7:127–91.

Lewis, Jane. 1992. Gender and the development of welfare regimes. *Journal of European Social Policy* 2:159–73.

Lewis, Jane. 1997. Gender and welfare regimes: Further thoughts. *Social Politics: International Studies in Gender, State & Society* 4:2, 160–77.

Skjeie, Hege. 1991. The uneven advance of Norwegian women. *New Left Review* 187:79–102.

Snow, David A., and Robert D. Benford. 1992. Master frames and cycles of protest. In *Frontiers in social movement theory*, ed. A. D. Morris and C. M. Mueller. New Haven, CT: Yale University Press.

United Nations Development Programme. 1996. *Human development report 1996.* New York: Oxford University Press.

United Nations Development Programme. 1999. *Human development report 1999.* New York: Oxford University Press.

United Nations Development Programme. 2006. *Human development report 2006.* New York: Palgrave Macmillan.

2 The Transition to Mass Literacy

Comparative Insights from Sweden and Pakistan

Haris Gazdar

INTRODUCTION

This chapter argues that comparing Sweden's transition to mass literacy with the experience of developing states such as Pakistan produces some useful insights into their respective historical processes of social development. The debate over education in Pakistan is currently dominated by a narrow "economics of education" perspective, which pays little attention to the role played by political and social motivations in literacy transitions elsewhere. Educational outcomes are framed in terms of supply and/or demand shortfalls, and solutions sought in terms of organisational and governance reforms, efficiency improvements, and community participation. The absence of "political will" to implement these reforms has often been identified as a constraint, but there has been little investigation into the social and political factors necessary for overcoming it.

This chapter examines the importance of ideological and political instrumentalism in the pursuit of a universalistic agenda. It notes the presence during Sweden's literacy transition of religious motivations, nation-building goals, and a universalising agenda, accompanied by the delegation of responsibility for achieving full literacy to community and parents. Similar notions of community responsibility deployed in contemporary Pakistan pay little attention to the fact that "community" here is constructed not with respect to geographical space but along lines of patriarchal kinship through which public and private is strongly gendered. The chapter comments on the challenges of cultural and ideological heterogeneity in the pursuit of mass literacy in Pakistan, but focuses primarily on the interaction between gender relations and the transition to modern citizenship in Sweden as well as in developing states.

WHAT MIGHT BE LEARNED?

Is it worthwhile, or even sensible, to compare the experience of gender equity and social development in Sweden with, say, Pakistan? What can one possibly learn from a comparison of outcomes so far apart from one another that they might as well be from different planets?

Life expectancy at birth in Pakistan in 2000 was 61 years; in Sweden this figure had been bettered before 1920 (Social Policy and Development Centre 2003; Statistics Sweden 2004). In Pakistan, female life expectancy was lower than male for all periods since records began, with the achievement of parity in the recent years. In Sweden, women have lived longer than men at least since the middle of the eighteenth century. Sweden achieved universal basic schooling for both males and females in the 1880s; in Pakistan around 56 percent of girls and 43 percent of the boys of primary school-going age were still not in school at the close of the twentieth century (E. Johansson 1977; World Bank 2002). Contemporary debates about gender equity in education in Sweden refer to the channelling of women students into specific professional careers, in Pakistan they are about girls having access to a functioning primary school.

There are, of course, countries and regions in the developing world—such as Sri Lanka and the Indian state of Kerala, to name but two—where comparison with the Swedish model might seem less contrived. But one could also quite easily substitute Pakistan for any number of developing countries and regions in Asia and Africa, and the comparison would still require some stretching of the imagination.

This chapter argues that the comparison between Sweden and countries like Pakistan is not only sensible and worthwhile, but might be quite useful for understanding the historical processes of social development in both countries. The main focus of this chapter is the Swedish "model" of the literacy transition.[1] This relates to a period spanning roughly two hundred years, from the middle of the seventeenth century up to the middle and late nineteenth century.

The Swedish experience is a neglected source of insight for the contemporary problem of literacy transition in a country like Pakistan.[2] The debate over education in Pakistan is dominated by a narrow "economics of education" perspective, supported in large measure by powerful organisations like the World Bank. This current orthodoxy pays little attention to the political and social motivations which have played a critical role in the literacy transition. Reference to the Swedish experience will help to reorient the debate.

At the same time, the historical comparison allows for a reinterpretation of the Swedish experience itself. In particular, the dominant account of Sweden's transition to mass literacy—if seen from a contemporary developing country lens—appears to take for granted the significance of two crucial characteristics of pre-literate Sweden: first, the limited "sovereignty" of the patriarchal household; and second, the existence of a proto-national community. Comparison with contemporary Pakistan will highlight not only the importance of these historical characteristics, but also the ways in which they are closely linked to one another.

CURRENT POLICY PARADIGM

The transition to mass literacy is, unquestionably, a key goal of economic and social development. Successive international protocols such as Education for All and the Millennium Development Goals have reaffirmed the importance of universal basic education as a minimal requirement for development. There are many countries, of course, that fall far short of full literacy or even universal basic schooling, and international organisations have been actively engaged in problem analysis and policy design.

The international policy debate on mass literacy in developing countries shifted around the 1980s from a cultural to an economic paradigm. The growing influence of the World Bank and other "economic" agencies over the likes of UNESCO and other "cultural" agencies was partly responsible for this migration. The emergence of the "human capital theory" and its adoption by the international system meant that now there was a clear synergy between the goals of economic growth and those of educational progress. It was acceptable—indeed, essential—for social sectors, and particularly education, to figure prominently in the World Bank programmes in developing countries.

While the interest in the social sectors and in education was welcome, one of its consequences was the domination of a narrowly focussed economics of education paradigm in addressing problems of the literacy transition. Educational outcomes, like all other phenomena, arose from an interplay of demand and supply factors. Individuals and households demanded schooling for children, and the government and the private sector supplied it. Shortfall—or the absence of universal school attendance—was due to insufficient demand and/or insufficient or inadequate supply. The appropriate policy response depended on where the constraint lay—in demand or supply factors.

Since the entry of World Bank was often premised upon an ongoing financial crisis, hugely increased financing of public education was not generally a serious policy option. Instead, the stress was on organisational changes within the education system, efficiency improvements, governance reforms, community participation, and various models of public-private partnerships. The absence of "political will" in implementing the required reforms was often seen as a constraint, but there were few serious attempts at understanding the political economy of a literacy transition. It was generally taken for granted that "political will" ought to exist, since investment in education had a manifest role in economic development, and governments were, presumably, interested in economic growth. The absence of "political will" was put down to rent-seeking interests within the state that blocked public good.

The question of what combination of social and political factors might overcome the "political will" constraint, has rarely, if ever, been asked. This question needs to be posed in a comparative historical perspective, with respect to countries that have, indeed, made the literacy transition. Sweden would be a prominent candidate for comparative analysis, if only because it was one of the first countries to have undergone this transition, having done so under conditions of technological backwardness and material poverty.

THE SWEDISH "MODEL"

There is an impressive body of literature, empirical and analytical, on the history of the literacy transition in Sweden.[3] This chapter reviews some of this literature, not only for what it highlights, but also for what is taken for granted. Two sources are of particular importance here as accounts of the literacy transition from around 1650 to the middle and late nineteenth century. E. Johansson's (1977) history of literacy, based on a careful consideration of historical records from the seventeenth and eighteenth centuries, has provided much of the data that has been used by subsequent authors. A second source is Boli's (1989) in-depth analysis of Swedish society, politics, and public debate, before and leading up to the introduction of mass public schooling in the mid-nineteenth century.

The story ends around the 1880s, when, by all accounts, there was virtually universal school attendance among children of primary school age, and school attendance ensured the attainment of the ability to read and write as well as basic numeracy. This was some forty years after the Swedish parliament passed a law making it mandatory for parish councils to establish public schools, and to ensure universal school attendance. The period between 1842 and the 1880s was one of steady expansion in public schools and improvements in their pedagogical standards, physical infrastructure, and management.

The story begins, according to E. Johansson (1977), with developments in the seventeenth century culminating in a Church Law in 1686 making it mandatory for all parents to ensure that their children were able to read the Bible. Lack of reading ability and knowledge of the Bible could lead to an adult being excluded from Communion and even marriage. The 1686 law was followed up with a system of annual public examinations in the village, where reading and Bible knowledge were assessed. Parish records of these examinations have, indeed, formed the basis of much of the historical data on reading ability in the seventeenth and eighteenth centuries.

E. Johansson's (1977) analysis of parish examination records, as well as other sources of data (such as information held for military recruits and convicts) led him to conclude that Sweden had achieved full literacy, for both women and men, by 1750. Literacy, however, was restricted to the ability to read, and to knowledge of the Bible. E. Johansson (1977) laid great emphasis on the distinctive histories of the spread of reading and writing in Sweden.

The compounding of reading and writing in contemporary definitions of literacy was the source of some confusion in interpreting Sweden's past. Data on writing ability—from census sources that allowed analysis of literacy trends from the early nineteenth century—dated the country's transition to full literacy to the 1870s. E. Johansson claimed, convincingly, that in Sweden the processes of acquiring reading and writing ability were entirely distinct, and hence it was understandable that there might be a lag of around 100 years between universal reading and writing.

Boli's (1989) main interest was in mass *schooling* rather than the ability to read or write. While using Johansson's data, he discounted the significance of literacy as the ability to read. For him it was the advent of mass public schooling in the nineteenth century, and social and political changes leading up to it, that demanded attention and explanation. Boli (1989) regarded the Bible-reading law and campaign as having explanatory value, but laid great emphasis on the institution of the pubic school as marking a qualitative change in society and politics. It was this shift, from a community based on households and the village, to a polity based on the citizenship of a state, which was the transition of historic significance.

These debates notwithstanding, it is possible to identify some of the key features of the Swedish experience of the transition to mass literacy. Whether or not "reading ability" constituted effective literacy of any type, there are some basic parts of the story on which there can be agreement.

First, religious motivations played a crucial role in the spread of literacy, or at the very least, the idea of literacy, in a poor and backward agrarian society. The Lutheran Protestant tradition in Sweden (and elsewhere) laid great emphasis on the individual's direct connection with God. The knowledge of religious texts in one's own language was a theological centre-piece of this movement, and was closely connected to its political content. It was not literacy or reading ability as such that was the objective, but the ability to read and comprehend religious texts in one's own language.

Second, the emphasis shifted toward nation-building goals in the nineteenth century, with a corresponding change of focus from home-based religious learning to school-based secular education. Boli (1989) discards a number of other instrumentalist theories—such as "social control," "group competition," and "modernisation"—as explanations for the emergence of mass schooling, in favour of the view that the public school came to be seen as an essential institution in the socialisation of citizens. His own preferred explanation, however, also favours the social instrumentalist motivation for schooling. While the ideological content of the debate on mass schooling was radically different from that of the earlier Lutheran Bible-reading campaigns, there was also an essential continuity. Both saw education of the masses as being of instrumental value for the achievement of the ideological and political goals of constructing particular types of communities—one a pious religious community, and the other a community of citizens.

Third, the mass education projects were universalistic in their aims. The objective was not just to expand Bible-reading or school attendance. The projects stressed exhaustive compliance as a goal in its own right. During the period of the Bible-reading project, writing ability was distributed unequally along the lines of class, region, rural or urban residence, and gender. In terms of reading ability, however, the various population segments converged in their achievement, until reading ability became universal.

Fourth, the role of the state or central authority was critical, but not comprehensive. The Bible-reading project assigned the responsibility of teaching to parents, while the central authority set up mechanisms for examinations and sanction. The mass schooling project required local parishes to establish schools. The central authority in this case set standards, provided curriculum guidelines, and established systems of examination and inspection. Subsidies were also made available to poor parishes to set up schools. While the onus of responsibility for providing education had shifted from the household to the local community, the central authority continued to play a supervisory rather than service-provision role.

Finally, and perhaps most importantly, the mass education projects in Sweden predated the modernisation of the economy. The literacy transition was not an outcome of economic growth, and it might have been a precursor. Even within Swedish society at any given moment in time, the introduction of the education project weakened the correlation between economic status and educational attainment.

Comparative analyses have shown that some of the key features of the Swedish "model" identified here have been present in various forms in other European as well as non-European societies. Sweden and the Nordic countries were pioneers in the transition to mass education, and they were recognised as such by other European countries in the nineteenth century. The pattern was repeated, perhaps with greater vigour and speed, in the twentieth century in a number of post-colonial and communist-ruled states around the world, where the literacy transition was telescoped into a fraction of the time taken by Sweden. The literacy transition was consciously posited as being instrumental to the wider ideo-political goal of "community construction"—in the shape of nation-building and creating citizens.[4]

The contrast between the Swedish "model" and the current development paradigm cannot be overstated. The Swedish "model" encapsulates, perhaps in its most pristine form, the process of social and political development that led to sustained "political will" for mass education. The experience of other industrial, post-colonial, and communist-led states that followed suit confirmed the primacy of projects of "community construction" in creating and sustaining political demand for mass education. Countries that have not made the literacy transition are left, however, with a policy framework that entirely ignores key lessons from Sweden and other successful cases. The blind spots concerning the ideological content and the political motivation behind mass education projects leaves the policy debate in these countries floundering in futile details such as "rent-seeking among education officials" or "the role of public-private partnerships."

THE PAKISTAN "MODEL"

Pakistan provides an instructive case study in the failure of education policy, and the evolution of the development paradigm with respect to schooling. A snapshot view of literacy and school attendance rates for different population segments is illustrative. In 1998–99, while the overall literacy rate was 43 percent, it was 27 percent for females and 17 percent for rural females (World Bank 2002).[5] By contrast, nearly three fourths of the urban males were literate. School enrolment rates, reflecting the current as opposed to the historic reach of the schooling system, indicated that the literacy deficit was likely to persist over time. Overall, only 50 percent of children aged five to nine were in school. Among girls, the proportion was 44 percent, and for rural girls it was 36 percent. By contrast, 67 percent of the urban boys were in school. In addition to gender and rural–urban residence, there was also considerable inequality in literacy and school participation among different income groups.

The low attainment and participation rates, and the slow pace of improvement, became the subject of active policy discussion in the early 1990s. This debate was kick-started by influential interventions from the international development community. Notable among these was an article by leading World Bank economist Nancy Birdsall (1993), which explicitly linked the education deficit with low growth rates. The publication of the UNDP's human development rankings, and Pakistan's poor standing compared to other low-income Asian and African countries, provided further cause for introspection.

The World Bank led the charge, and in the early 1990s a Social Action Plan (SAP) was formulated to address the gap between Pakistan's economic and social development. It was argued that a concerted effort was required to direct budgetary resources into the social sectors—mainly, education, health, and water and sanitation. While the World Bank-guided SAP failed to deliver on most of its projected targets, it did generate a great deal of interest, thinking, and analysis into problems of social development. The main "lessons" learned by the development agencies have remained influential beyond SAP and have guided subsequent policies and programmes. It is useful to provide a brief summary of the "lessons" learned on the expansion of basic education.[6]

"Demand" for schooling is constrained by low incomes and cultural factors, particularly for girls' schooling. There is evidence, however, that parents are increasingly "willing" to send their daughters to school. Given the presence of latent demand, the burden of explanation for low school participation rates must rest with the quantity and quality of schooling supplied.

While the government schooling system has expanded to provide quantitative coverage to most urban and rural communities, the quality of the schooling supplied varies greatly. Some government schools are completely ineffective or even harmful, while others function at a basic level.

There are serious governance issues in the management of the school system, and these issues are mostly related to rent-seeking behaviour on the part of the school administration, teachers, and other public employees. The electoral system fails to provide an adequate check, since strong patron-client interests dominate it. The solution is a combination of "community participation" and public-private partnerships to overcome the rent-seeking behaviour of government officials. Local communities need to be empowered to run schools and monitor the performance of teachers, and the private sector needs to be involved as a service provider.[7]

The "lessons" of the World Bank-led approach to education as human capital development had three crucial gaps. First, at the level of social relations, the easy reliance on "community participation" failed to take into consideration what might constitute "the community" in contemporary Pakistan. Notions of community, as will be shown here, are closely linked to modes of patriarchy in Pakistan. Second, the dominant development paradigm failed to take forward the question of "political will" to its logical next step: What type of political constituency might there be for universal schooling? Third, no questions were asked about the content of schooling, though these questions began to be raised in a prominent manner with reference to a different debate altogether.

COMMUNITY AND PATRIARCHY

"Community" as conceived by development planners, and particularly by the proponents of "community participation" turns out to be a highly problematic affair in Pakistan. The received notion of "community" is in terms of a self-contained village or urban settlement, with economic differentiation, to be sure, but with a collective identity and common interests. The "community" is presumed to be a repository of latent demand for schooling, including girls' schooling, and intermediary rent-seeking interests, such as those of patronage-based politicians or corrupt government employees, come in the way of realizing this latent demand.

Empirical researchers, however, are immediately confronted with not one but several robust and often competing notions of community and common interest, in rural and urban areas alike. Geographical location, moreover, is but one dimension of community identity, and quite often it is a relatively underprivileged one. Caste, kinship, tribe, ethnicity, and religious sects are all active markers of group identity, and are invoked on a routine basis in economic, social, and political interaction. In some instances the notion of a geographically self-contained village corresponds closely with one or some of these other sources of identity, and in other instances the geographical boundary is entirely irrelevant as a parameter of collective action.[8]

The multiple dimensions of community such as kinship, caste, tribe, and ethnicity tend to be nested in familial relations. In fact, kinship is the primary building block for families, social networks, and communities. The "community" may simply be a network of extended families, all linked to one another by blood ties, or it might be a broader coalition consisting of non-kinship-based alliances between smaller groups, which are in turn based upon kinship association. The model of the community, therefore, resembles more an extended family network, rather than a compact geographical village. The ties are literally reproduced through kinship relations.

There is a fundamental sense in which the parochial community is an extension of the patriarchal family. The division of space into the public and private spheres is highly gendered. The private sphere is where members of the family, male and female, can freely interact. The public sphere is the domain of males from across families and kinship groups. Females have only restricted access to the public domain, and that access too is regulated by the presence of males from their family. Non-family males have no access to the private domain. This gendered public–private division is not discrete but represents a continuum. The homestead is exclusively private, and the market might be exclusively public. But between the homestead and the market there are many other spaces that represent broader domains of association than the homestead—such as compound, locality, or village—which are accessible to women and men alike.

What is significant from a comparative perspective, however, is that the specific form that patriarchy takes in Pakistan and other similar (though not exclusively Muslim) societies is the gendered division of public and private spaces. The notion of *purdah* (literally *veil* or *curtain* marking the boundary of the female private sphere) is taken as a standard category in the analysis of patriarchy in these societies.[9]

A defining characteristic of a community is not necessarily the geographical area occupied by a group of residents, but social boundaries within which men and women may interact with various degrees of autonomy. Social distance is easily symbolised in terms of the level of access a male person will have to the private domain—with a close relative having complete access, and a distant associate being entirely excluded.

Communities are also extended patriarchies in the sense that they perpetuate themselves through marriage ties. Rules and preferences in marriage relations tend to reproduce kinship-based communities. Insiders and outsiders are defined in terms of whether it will be permissible or preferable to contract marriages with them.

Within this broad framework of extended patriarchies, it is possible to identify various types of parochial communities that are active in Pakistan. Some of these communities are akin to castes in the standard Indian sense. They consist of families belonging to the same caste, all of whom might share a common ancestry, share a similar level of social standing, and be roughly in the same economic class. There might be other castes residing in the same village, which might be in a subservient economic and social position to the dominant caste.[10] There are other communities residing in urban areas that are identified by their affiliation to particular religious sects.[11] These communities are closely bound by family ties, in addition to religious ideology. Their sense of exclusivity derives only partly from religious affiliation, and quite strongly from inter-family connections. The gendered division of space permeates these urban and apparently ideological communities in similar ways to the rural caste-based communities.

The existence of multiple atomised communities, based on caste, tribe, ethnicity, and religious denomination—all of which are cemented by patriarchal bonds of kinship—has posed serious problems for the "community participation" model preferred by development agencies for the promotion of social services. In fact, social segmentation implies that many of these communities already engage in community-wide collective action on a number of issues, including the provision of social services. The problem, therefore, is not the absence of collective action, but its proliferation along parochial lines. Groups that are powerful and well-organised tend to produce their own "public goods" or are able to appropriate state-provided "public goods" for their communities.

The unproblematic acceptance of "atomised communities" as agents of change raises two serious sets of issues in social exclusion.

First, the unreconstructed "community" is structurally linked to patriarchal familial norms, and a highly gendered division of space. Any model of change that fails to address this structural link implicitly accepts the perpetuation of gender inequity in the social, economic, and political domains for the foreseeable future.

Second, the prevalence of strong parochial communities implies that individuals and families who do not happen to belong to particularly powerful or well-endowed social networks might remain marginalised, unless there are conscious efforts to "bring them in." In fact, an individual's vulnerability to poverty in societies such as Pakistan is likely to be less a function of restricted access to human and financial capital than it is of restricted access to social capital.

POLITICAL CONSTITUENCY FOR UNIVERSAL SCHOOLING

One of the "lessons" of the World Bank-led approach in Pakistan is that the absence of "political will" is a constraint to the expansion of basic education. But this approach fails to query the possible sources of political demand for universal schooling. It is assumed that the demand (latent or manifest) for public schooling will come from parents, particularly those parents who are unable to afford to send their children to private schools. Political demand for schooling can be harnessed, according to this view, by empowering local communities in the management of schools. Experiments with School Management Committees and other similar exercises, however, have failed to make any discernible difference.

The only other constituency for schooling that is admissible in the current paradigm is that of economic managers who understand the importance of human capital in economic growth. What the World Bank-led approach fails to take into consideration, however, is the possibility that there might be political constituencies for *universal* schooling that have vested ideological or political interests in *universalism* as such, and not necessarily schooling in particular. The dominant paradigm privileges the notion of schooling as a contributor to individual or family advantage, at the expense of the idea of universal schooling as an instrument of societal consolidation or change.

THE CONTENT OF SCHOOLING

The content of schooling has been largely ignored in the World Bank-led approach, though there has been growing interest in this subject in recent years. This interest is partly motivated by the perception that Islamic religious seminaries, as well as the mainstream curriculum, promote an ideology of religious intolerance and glorify religious violence. Curriculum change and the regulation of religious seminaries have become key demands of foreign governments and development agencies.[12]

The interest in the content of schooling is driven by negative considerations—namely, concern about the harmful content of schooling and attempts at restricting this perceived harmful content. The belated understanding on the part of government and development agencies that a negative ideological project of community construction had been underway has not as yet led to the acknowledgment of the need for a "positive" ideological project. Rather, there is a complacent assumption that it is possible to have an ideologically neutral education system geared to the needs of producing human capital.

The project of constructing a national community using the mass schooling system never quite recovered from the rude shock it received in the immediate aftermath of Pakistan's emergence from British colonial rule in 1947. A national conference on education was convened in November of that year, just three months after the creation of the state. This conference started with enthusiastic debates on the necessity for promoting a post-colonial national vision. It quickly got bogged down in an intractable debate over the "national language," and the mandatory medium of instruction in schools. Conference participants from East Bengal and Sindh—two provinces of Pakistan with their own languages and developed literary traditions—successfully resisted the imposition of Urdu as a mandatory medium of instruction (Government of Pakistan 1947).

This conference was a sobering reminder, if one was needed, of the complicated problem of creating a unified nation-state out of diverse ethno-linguistic communities. After further ham-fisted and violent attempts at language imposition, the state's attempts at ideological nation-building through education remained restricted to the introduction of shallow, reactionary, and xenophobic rhetoric in the curriculum.

LESSONS FROM SWEDEN AND PAKISTAN

The policy debate on mass education in Pakistan can gain much from the Swedish historical experience.[13] As shown above, Sweden's history of the literacy transition, with its emphasis on universal education as an instrument for community construction, provides a very useful perspective on the gaps in current policy thinking in Pakistan. The historical comparison also draws attention to a number of instructive parallels and contrasts.

DEMAND–SUPPLY OR PULL–PUSH FACTORS

A persistent feature of Pakistan's educational deficit is the inequality between sexes, economic classes and rural and urban locations. Analysis of historical data on both reading and writing achievement in Sweden reveals that similar inequalities existed there prior to the onset of the education projects. E. Johansson (1977) classified factors influencing educational outcomes as "pull" and "push" impulses, respectively. "Pull" factors correspond to the spontaneous demand for education on the part of individuals and families. As "push" factors Johansson identifies "systematic pedagogical measures irrespective of regional and social differences" (E. Johansson 1977, 8). This represents not just the "supply" of schooling in the passive sense, but social and political activism on the part of the state or other public bodies.

In the absence of strong push factors, the pull factors dominate, and educational outcomes are likely to be determined by the interplay of demand and supply conditions. This clearly is the case in contemporary Pakistan. Those who tend to be better educated are the wealthy, the males, and people in urban localities. The wealthy have greater purchasing power, males are more active in the labour market, and urban people have easier access to schooling facilities.

What is striking, however, is that these very patterns of inequality were present in Sweden prior to the arrival of the push factors. It is interesting to note that the two historically distinct sets of push factors—the Bible-reading project of the late seventeenth century, and the mass schooling project of the mid-nineteenth century—both reveal identical patterns of progress. Before the application of the push factors associated with the Bible-reading project, there were significant inequalities in the reading ability of men and women, and residents of well-connected and remote parishes. These differences eroded as the Bible-reading project progressed. While reading ability was increasing and becoming steadily more equal through this period, writing ability remained stagnant. Moreover, the traditional gender and urban–rural inequalities in writing ability persisted until the start of the mass schooling project.

RELIGIOUS REFORM—HISTORICAL PARALLELS

The importance of the Lutheran Protestant movement in Sweden and in other countries of northern Europe in the expansion of mass education draws attention to the role of religious reform movements in other countries. Even those like Boli (1989), who dispute the significance of the Bible-reading project in advancing mass education, acknowledge the role played by the Church in laying the basis for individual agency. What was particularly significant in this regard was the stress in the Lutheran movement on the believer's individual piety and unmediated access to God, and the use of local languages.

Religious reform movements with similar aims have existed, and succeeded, to varying degrees in the history of Islam in the region comprising Pakistan.[14] Two strands are particularly significant. First, the Sufi movement, spanning a period of around seven centuries culminating in the flowering of local languages and folk music in the late seventeenth/early eighteenth centuries, defined to a great extent the indigenous religious discourse of Punjab and Sindh—the main constituents of modern-day Pakistan. The Sufi tradition developed anti-clerical positions, and stressed the use of local languages in the place of received texts in Arabic and Persian. The theological content of these movements was mystical rather than pious, however, and they eschewed formal organisation in favour of devotional association.[15]

The second strand, that in many ways was in direct theological opposition to the Sufi movement—though being of a later vintage—were the formalist revivalist movements that emerged from the eighteenth century onwards. These revivalist movements—which continue to spawn yet new waves of reformers and theologians—attempted to formalize the practice of the Islamic faith, and to "recover" it from the mystical excesses of the Sufis. The revivalists are rationalist in their approach to ritual and, like the seventeenth-century Lutherans, espouse a compact sense of community. They lay great emphasis on the knowledge and observance of a "pure" Islamic faith by Muslims as individuals. Like the Lutherans, the revivalists have been at the forefront of religious education campaigns and have established both religious seminaries as well as temporal schools with additional religious instruction. They are strong supporters of the idea of using education and schooling for the instrumental goals of community construction—in their case the community in question is made up of "pious" and "practicing" Muslims.[16]

It is interesting to note that the types of religious and theological impulses that are thought to have contributed to mass education (and then social development) in Sweden have been present in various forms in Pakistan. Two of the essential features of the Lutheran movement—stress on individual knowledge of religion and piety, and the use of local languages—were present in different (sometimes opposing) strands of religious currents in Pakistan. Moreover, the "Islamic revivalists" of present-day Pakistan have much in common with the Lutherans of seventeenth-century Sweden.

GENDER NORMS BEFORE THE PROJECTS

There are two striking features of seventeenth-century Sweden, however, that the comparison with Pakistan throws up in sharp relief. First, the historical evidence indicates that even before the Bible-reading project, and well before the mass schooling project, public life was already less gender-segregated in Sweden than it is in contemporary Pakistan. Second, the construction of a national polity in Sweden was a far less challenging proposition because of the pre-existence of a shared culture and mythology.

The two main sources of historical evidence cited in this chapter—E. Johansson (1977) and Boli (1989)—make only passing reference to the position of girls and women with respect to education. What can be gleaned from the historical material, however, is that the Bible-reading project applied equally to women and men. Public examinations and parish records routinely refer to girls and women in the same vein as boys and men. Females were examined and evaluated by the clergy, as were men, and Johansson finds that according to the grades given for reading ability, women frequently not only read as well as men, but also generally had a higher grade for "understanding." This was due to the fact that it was the women of the household who mainly taught children to read, and women also functioned as teachers for children of other families. The responsibility for learning to read was placed with the patriarchal household, but the parents (frequently mothers) were equally accountable for females and males within the household. Not surprisingly, when the "push" factors began to dominate the "pull" factors, the gap between male and female reading ability narrowed quickly.

Female schooling was already an accepted goal in the early nineteenth century, some forty years prior to the institution of mass public schooling. This period, which saw a rapid increase in the number of private schools, also witnessed the establishment of many schools for girls (Boli 1989). Interestingly, the tradition of women teaching children in the home continued into the schools. From the beginning of public schooling, the overwhelming majority of primary teachers were women. Already in 1859 specific seminars for women who wanted to be secondary school teachers were created. At the turn of the century, female secondary school teachers were nearly as many as male (Florin and U. Johansson 1991).

By the middle of the nineteenth century, while women were not recognised as full citizens, they were already participating autonomously in various social and political movements. In his discussion of various social movements of the mid-nineteenth century, Boli makes almost passing reference to the fact that women, particularly from the working classes, constituted two thirds of the membership of the "free-church" movement and a considerable proportion of the temperance movements. With respect to mass schooling, "both in the grass-roots movement and the 1842 statute girls were deemed self-evident candidates for citizenship" (Boli 1989, 232). There was little support in the Swedish parliament in 1847 for separate schooling for boys and girls (Boli 1989).[17]

The comparison with Pakistan—where the public school system remains divided along gender lines even at the primary level—illustrates the significance of these passing observations about women's participation in public life and about girls' schooling in historical Sweden.

Scholars of Swedish social history have been rightly exercised by the transformation in the structure of society from one based around a state-church-household axis[18], and a polity consisting of hierarchically ordered Estates, to a political society made up of autonomous individual citizens. What is most remarkable from the Pakistani comparative perspective, however, are the limitations of sovereignty enjoyed by the patriarchal household even in the period prior to the Bible-reading project.

In fact, the available evidence for pre-eighteenth-century Sweden (or even northern Europe) suggests very different patterns of patriarchy from those observed in contemporary Pakistan. Yalom's (2001) account of the gradual transformation in northern Europe of the marriage rite from being a private to a public event identifies the church as a persistent transgressor into the domain formerly held by the family.[19] Studies in historical demography also provide insights into the structure of households and communities in "traditional" Scandinavia. Hanssen's (1978) work on selected parishes in Scania finds, for example, that the "farmstead"—often shared by two unrelated peasants, and including a large number of non-kin "inmates"—rather than the kinship-based family, defined the normal mode of cohabitation.[20]

In Swedish history, the seventeenth and early eighteenth centuries are characterised as a period of "an increasingly strong nation state . . . [when] . . . the Church was more firmly linked to the state . . . [and where] . . . the state's endeavour to impose social discipline and a religiously based ideology extended to the entire population" (G. Andersson 2001). The idea that the clergy and the state were powerful enough, in the seventeenth century, to legislate, regulate, and sanction the behaviour of individuals within the patriarchal household clearly defined limits to the agency of the patriarch.[21] However, there were exceptions; for example, husband and wife had the right to carry out corporal punishment on their servants and children up until the twentieth century, and husbands could use corporal punishment against their wives until 1858 (Ohlander 1994). Bonds of kinship appeared to be relatively unimportant in the way households and communities were organised. The boundaries between the public and private domains were weakly operational—even in comparison with contemporary Pakistani society. Seen from this perspective, the later transformations in the Swedish social structure appear more as continuity and less as disjuncture.

PRIOR NOTION OF COMMUNITY AND POLITY

The preceding section explored the relationship between community and patriarchy in contemporary Pakistan. The two categories were found to be closely interconnected—with the patriarchal family as the basic building block, and kinship relations as the cement. The Swedish model of constructing a polity premised on citizenship, and the role of mass public schooling as an instrument, envisages a national community of autonomous individuals bound together by a common national culture. Comparison between the two indicates common features as well as significant historical differences.

The contemporary aim of attaining universal schooling in societies like Pakistan can be characterised as a problem of not one but several literacy transitions. National statistical data show that while some groups, such as rural females, are virtually illiterate, others, such as urban males, are close to full literacy. Aggregate data conceal, however, that there are acute inequalities along the lines of caste and social grouping. It is not unusual for primary data to reveal full literacy among some, and complete illiteracy among other kinship- or caste-based social groups residing within the same locality. Social exclusion on the basis of parochial community also implies a high degree of access for insiders. Moreover, parochial communities act as peer reference groups, thus influencing attitudes to schooling.[22]

In many cases the process of attaining "universal" schooling within the group is not dissimilar, at the micro-level, to that of achieving universal schooling across the national community. This is most aptly illustrated with reference to religious-sect-based communities in Pakistan. As mentioned earlier, these communities, although conspicuously based on ideological affiliation, are effectively bound together through a network of social and familial relations.

It is common practice for such communities to provide for their own exclusive denominational schools and to ensure the attendance of all children. Peer group pressures are also strong, and lagging behind in education can place a family at a severe disadvantage in finding suitable marriage partners within the community. It is not surprising, therefore, that such communities enjoy "universal" basic education within the group. In these communities, the patriarchal household's sovereignty is limited in ways similar to the seventeenth-century Swedish household facing the Church Law of 1686.[23]

It is clear, of course, that the Lutheran Bible-reading project was denominational and not national in its outlook. E. Johansson (1977) cites historical data from Finland, which then was part of the Swedish realm, to show that there was a wide gap between the reading ability of Lutherans and Greek Orthodox in that country, which was only overcome by the institution of mass public schooling.

In the Swedish realm as whole, the parochial and denominational community corresponded, from the outset, quite closely with the polity or national community of a modern state. Besides exceptions—the Finnish population, the Saami communities in the north, and the former Danish region of Skane—people who shared a similar language, culture, and tradition almost exclusively inhabited the state's territory. The experience of the exceptional communities is also instructive. Particular efforts were made—and resistance encountered—for the "Swedification" of the Skane. These efforts included the establishment of special educational facilities, and other measures, with "nation-building" as an explicit goal (Lindmark 1995). The Saami-speaking communities in the north presented further issues both for the church's Bible-reading project as well as for the establishment of universal schooling by the modern nation-state (Anderzén 1996). These exceptional cases simply highlight the remarkable homogeneity, a priori, of the proto-national community in eighteenth-century Sweden. They suggest strong resemblance between sources of political will behind the Swedish model and latter-day nation-building projects in post-colonial countries.[24]

CONCLUDING REMARKS

The two extremely divergent cases examined in this chapter appear to have some important parallels as well as contrasts, both equally useful sources of insight. A Swedish historical perspective on Pakistan helps to identify significant blind spots in the current (World Bank-dominated) policy debate on universal basic schooling. This debate needs to be more attentive to the problem of finding and constructing political constituencies for *universalism* rather than simply assuming there is an active constituency for public schooling.

The Pakistani perspective on the Swedish model is equally instructive. It favours the observation that Sweden—even in the seventeenth century—was a society where the patriarchal family enjoyed only limited sovereignty. The transformation from a state-church-family nexus to a citizenship-based polity in the nineteenth century, let alone the advances of the modern welfare state in the twentieth century, ought to be assessed in the light of this observation.

The processes associated with the limited sovereignty of the patriarchal family are both historically specific and complex. Some of the impulses that in retrospect appear to signify individual agency would easily fall under the label of "religious extremism" in our times. Other factors, such as the prior cultural homogeneity of Swedish society, are neither available on demand nor particularly desirable attributes for contemporary cosmopolitan societies.

The patriarchal family was relatively weak to begin with in Sweden, unless, of course, we adopt a very broad definition of the patriarchal family that sees the entire proto-national community as an extended family. Such large extended families are active in contemporary Pakistan in the shape of kinship groups and religious sects, and have achieved intra-sect universalistic outcomes of sorts. These outcomes fall far short, of course, of universal achievements for all citizens.

The challenge, therefore, is to reduce the power of the patriarchal family (and extended families) and to break down the gendered division of public and private spaces. The state is the obvious instrument for achieving such goals. It also needs to be understood, however, that social structures (even extended patriarchal families) can provide protection to individuals by blunting some of the more repressive and predatory impulses of the state machinery. The political legitimacy of the state is critical, therefore, in marking the difference between repression and development.

Perhaps the inevitable "lesson" of a historical comparison of this type is that the development paradigm ought to pay more attention to history. Developing countries like Pakistan will do well to look beyond the simplistic "economics of education" view that dominates current policy thinking. Sweden and other developed societies, moreover, need to take their own experiences more seriously while intervening in development debates.

NOTES

1. The word "model" is used as shorthand to refer to the stylised but widely accepted account of Sweden's history of transition to mass literacy.
2. Pakistan, incidentally, will be used as shorthand for regions with broadly similar conditions. Large swathes of northern India (including the states of Uttar Pradesh) will easily answer to similar descriptions.
3. While much of this literature is in Swedish, there are valuable summaries as well as detailed reviews of literature available in English. See, for example, Lindmark (1997, 2003), I. Andersson (1986), and Richardson (1963).
4. See Glen Peterson (1997) on communist China. Turkey provides an interesting example of nation-building in a non-communist political system. It is worth quoting from Ziya Gök Alp, an influential authority on the development of Turkish nationalism, and himself a leading Turkish nationalist: "Nation is not a racial, ethnic, geographical, political or voluntary group or association. Nation is a group composed of men and women who have gone through the same education, who have received the same acquisitions in language, religion, morality, and aesthetics" (Kirisci 1998, 234).

5. Figures cited in this paragraph are based on data from the Pakistan Integrated Household Survey 1998–99, analysed in World Bank (2002).
6. A useful example of a comprehensive statement by the World Bank on this issue is World Bank (1996). A fuller commentary on this and related documents is available in Gazdar (1999).
7. The former led to the creation, at the stroke of a pen, of thousands of "School Management Committees", and the latter led to experiments such as "voucher schemes" and "adopt-a-school programmes" (World Bank 1996).
8. For field-based insights on this question, see Gazdar (2002).
9. Examples of empirical work on the women's mobility and the gendered division of space include Khan (1999) and Weiss (1992). Khan (2000) argues that the *burqa* (veiled gown) was a compromise reached within the Muslim community between the outright prohibition of women from the public space, and their full admission as equals. Also see Gazdar (2002a) for an understanding of gendered spaces as being linked to the construction of local communities, and collective actions at various levels.
10. Field-based insights are available in Gazdar (2002b).
11. Prominent examples are communities such as the Aga Khan Ismailis, and the Bohras, mostly resident in Karachi. On the former, see Daftary (1998). On the latter, see Engineer (1993) and Blank (2001).
12. The most recent manifestation of this interest is the passage of a law in the U.S. Congress requiring the American Secretary of State to regularly report on the progress of secularisation in the educational system of Pakistan, as a condition for the continuation of economic aid and concessions. See, for example, Alan K. Kronstadt (2004).
13. Features of the Swedish model can also be found in subsequent experiences of literacy transition in other countries.
14. Strictly speaking, cross-cultural and inter-temporal comparisons of "religion" need to be prefaced by the qualification that we are simply highlighting the significance, in different settings, of coherent systems of faith.
15. The rendering of Islamic religious themes in local languages was popularised in the Indus basin region by seventeenth- and eighteenth-century poets such as Bullhe Shah, Sachal Sarmast, and Shah Latif Bhitai, who combined anti-clericism with the promotion of local languages. The use of the poetical form might be seen within the context of a developed oral but underdeveloped literary tradition in these languages. Literary work and high culture were produced in the more exclusive (in class terms) foreign languages, such as Persian and Arabic.
16. On the influential revivalist movement of the late nineteenth century, see Metcalf (2004).
17. However, effective segregation between boys' grammar schools and girls' secondary schools continued at the post-compulsory level (U. Johansson and Florin 1993).
18. On the Lutheran model of the *Haustafel*, see Lindmark (1995).
19. Yalom's (2001) account does not have a specific treatment of Sweden or the Nordic countries, but does examine in some detail the doctrine and influences of Lutheran Protestantism on prevailing patterns of patriarchy.
20. The editors of the collection of studies on historical demography, including Hanssen's paper, find that "a simple family structure with only parents, unmarried children, and perhaps some servants living together has been predominant in large parts of Western Europe at least since the sixteenth century" (Åkerman et al. 1978, 107).
21. Temporal as well as religious courts effectively pursued liabilities of men and women as individual albeit unequal legal agents (G. Andersson 2001) within a centralised system of judicial authority.

22. Empirical analyses of school participation in Pakistan and India routinely yield caste as a key correlate of schooling status independently of household wealth and other characteristics. See, for example, Gazdar (2002c).
23. Engineer's (1993) critique of the Bohra community provides interesting insights into essentially civil means of social control—very similar to those mentioned in the historical Swedish material.
24. These examples also suggest historical antecedents to contemporary problems of assimilating non-ethnic Swedish communities into the "Swedish model."

REFERENCES

Åkerman, Sune, Hans Christian Johansen, and David Gaunt, eds. 1978. *Chance and change: Social and economic studies in historical demography in the Baltic area.* Vol. 52 of *Odense University Studies in History and Social Sciences.*

Andersson, Gudron. 2001. Gender as symbolic capital?: Women and property in the seventeenth and eighteenth centuries. In *Guises of power: Integration of society and legitimisation of power in Sweden and the low countries ca. 1500–1900,* eds. M. Ågren et al., 23–31. Uppsala: Opuscula Histiorica Upsaliensia.

Andersson, Inger. 1986. *Reading and writing: An analysis of texts for the general reading and writing instruction 1842–1982.* Umeå: University of Umeå, Akademiska avhandlingar vid pedagogiska institutionen.

Anderzén, Sölve. 2003. Language, literacy, and religion: Popular education in the Torne Laplands, 1744–1803. In *Religious education in history: Confessional and inter-confessional experiences,* ed. D. Lindmark, 93–103. Umea: Kultureus Frontlinjer.

Birdsall, Nancy. 1993. Underinvestment in education: How much growth has Pakistan foregone? *The Pakistan Development Review.* 32(4); Winter):453–92.

Blank, Jonah. 2001. *Mullahs on the mainframe: Islam and modernity among Daudi Bohras.* Chicago: University of Chicago Press.

Boli, John. 1989. *New citizens for a new society: The institution of mass schooling in Sweden.* Oxford: Pergamon Press.

Daftary, Farhad. 1998. *A short history of the Ismailis: Traditions of a Muslim community.* Princeton, NJ: Markus Weiner Publishers.

Engineer, Asghar Ali. 1993. *The Bohras.* Delhi: Vikas.

Florin, Christina, and Ulla Johansson. 1991. Education as female strategy: Women graduates and state grammar schools in Sweden 1870–1918. *Journal of Thought* 26, nos. 1 and 2.

Gazdar, Haris. 1999. Policy failure, political constraints and political resources: Basic education in Pakistan. Working Paper 5, Asia Research Centre, London School of Economics.

Gazdar, Haris. 2002a. The politics of gender: Borders and boundaries. *NGORC Journal* (September). www.ngorc.org.pk (accessed January 7, 2002).

Gazdar, Haris. 2002b. *A qualitative survey of poverty in Pakistan.* Background paper for the World Bank's Pakistan Poverty Assessment 2001. mimeo, Poverty Reduction and Economic Management Unit, The World Bank, Washington DC, and Collective for Social Science Research, Karachi.

Gazdar, Haris. 2002c. Who missed school: Caste in rural Pakistan. Paper presented at the annual conference of the Econometric Society (Asia Pacific), Lahore University of Management Sciences, Pakistan, December.

Government of Pakistan. 1947. *Report of the First National Conference on Education,* November 1947, Ministry of Interior (Education Division),. Government of Pakistan.

Hanssen, Börje. 1978. The Oikological approach. In *Chance and change: Social and economic studies in historical demography in the Baltic area*, eds. Sune Åkerman, Hans Christian Johansen, and David Gaunt (Vol. 52 of Odense University Studies in History and Social Sciences). Odense: Odense University Press.

Johansson, Egil. 1977. *The history of literacy in Sweden in comparison with some other countries*. Educational Reports Umeå No. 12. University of Umeå and Umeå School of Education. Umeå, Sweden.

Johansson, Ulla, and Christina Florin. 1993. "Where the glorious laurels grow . . .": Swedish grammar schools as a means of social mobility and social reproduction." *History of Education* 22(2): 435–453.

Khan, Ayesha. 1999. Mobility of women and access to health and family planning services. *Reproductive Health Matters* 7(14): 39–48.

Khan, Ayesha. 2000. *Rhetoric and reform: Feminism among Indian Muslims— 1900–1940*. Lahore: ASR Publications.

Kirisci, Kemal. 1998. "Minority/majority discourse: The case of the Kurds in Turkey. In *Making majorities: Constituting the nation in Japan, China, Malaysia, Fiji, Turkey, and the United States*, ed. Dru C., 227–248. Gladney. Stanford, CA: Stanford University Press.

Kronstadt, Alan K. 2004. *Education reform in Pakistan*. Congress Research Service Report for Congress, December 23, 2004, http://fpc.state.gov/documents/organization/40145.pdf.

Lindmark, Daniel. 1995. *Instruction, education, enlightenment: Currents in Swedish popular education before the era of compulsory schooling*. Umeå: Umeå University.

Lindmark, Daniel. 1997. Frontlines between traditionalism and modernity: Popular revivalism challenging official reading culture in 19th century Upper Norrland. In *Puritanismen och Lättsinnet*. Kulturgräns Norr 6. Umeå: Kultureus Frontlinjer.

Lindmark, Daniel. 2003. Literacy, text, practice and culture: Major trends in the Umeå history of education research group 1972–2002. In *Religious education in history: Confessional and interconfessional experiences*. Umeå: Umeå Universitet, Institutionen för litteraturvetenskap och nordiska språk, Kungälv.

Metcalf, Barbara Daly. 2004. *Islamic revival in British India: Deoband, 1860–1900*. Oxford: India Paperbacks.

Ohlander, Ann-Sofie. 1994. *Women, children and work in Sweden 1850–1993*. Swedish Government Official Reports 38:17

Peterson, Glen. 1997. *The power of words: Literacy and revolution in South China, 1945–95*. Vancouver: UBC Press.

Richardson, Gunnar. 1963. *Kulturkamp och Klasskamp [Cultural Struggle and Class Struggle]*. Göteborg: Akademiförlaget.

Social Policy and Development Centre. 2003. *Social development in Pakistan— Annual review 2003*. Karachi: Social Policy and Development Centre.

Statistics Sweden. 2004. *Women and men in Sweden 2004—Demographic analysis and gender equality*. Stockholm: Statistics Sweden.

Weiss, Anita M. 1992. *Walls within walls: Life histories of working women in the old city of Lahore*. Boulder, CO: Westview Press.

World Bank. 1996. *Improving basic education in Pakistan: Community participation, system accountability, and efficiency*. Report, World Bank Resident Mission, Islamabad, Pakistan.

World Bank. 2002. *Pakistan poverty assessment 2001*. Washington, DC: The World Bank, Poverty Reduction and Economic Management Unit.

Yalom, Marilyn. 2001. *A history of the wife*. New York: Harper Collins.

3 Gender and the Family in Public Policy

A Comparative View of Argentina and Sweden

Elizabeth Jelin

INTRODUCTION

In his recent discussions about the future of the welfare state, Esping-Andersen analyses the "three pillars" of welfare: markets, families, and governments. He then compares European countries in terms of which of the three is the main source of welfare, and how other pillars have to absorb "pillar-failures": families and/or governments compensating for market failures; families and markets compensating for governmental failures; governments, and less often markets, absorbing family failures. "Where neither is capable of substituting for 'failure' in the two others, this is when we encounter an acute welfare deficit or crisis" (Esping-Andersen 2002, 12). In this model, the Scandinavian welfare system is characterised as being unique in its emphasis on the government pillar and its active "de-familiarisation" of welfare responsibilities. According to the author, this has been done with two aims in mind: to strengthen families by unburdening them of obligations, and to enhance individual independence and, I would add, gender equality. The general idea behind the model is to provide ample care services, and through them to solve (or at least lessen) the "incompatibility problem," namely, the tension that women face between their responsibilities toward their children and being able to pursue a work career.

Many issues are involved in welfare agendas. The key question refers to who is responsible for the well-being of the members of a social group (be it a small group or a national community)? If gender equality is a goal, and traditional gender differences are de-naturalised, how is care to be managed and socially distributed? In a broader comparative perspective, the issue concerns the specific models of family and maternal/paternal roles that allow for, foster, or hinder the goal of gender equality. A related question is the role that public policy and legal provisions can play in promoting change toward the desired goal. Certainly, family models existing in a society at a given time are the product of historical social, cultural, economic, and political developments. Purposive public policies can affect family forms; in turn, the range of public policies is conditioned by the prevailing and ideal family forms. And both of them—public policies and family forms—have a direct and indirect effect on gender relations and gender equality.

In this chapter, the Swedish history of family and family policy will be looked at, to understand how models of the family evolved over time, and the impact of family policy in shaping options and alternatives for men and women will be examined as well. The questions asked about Sweden are presented in an implicit dialogue with the experience of South America, especially of Argentina.[1] It is, in a sense, a selective comparative history, presenting first some of the main features of the history of family policy in Argentina, then looking at Sweden.

At first sight, the two stories are absolutely different, to the point where it is hard to think that we are dealing with the same institution and the same issues. Yet there is a comparative thread in the stories, one that suggests that there is no single or simple solution to the challenges that gender roles in the family pose to an ideal of gender equality. The contrasting ways in which the two societies define and approach these challenges illuminate the complexity and paradoxical nature of the issue at hand.

The comparative framework implicit in the chapter can be seen in a few significant features. A first thread refers to the role of ideas and "moral entrepreneurs" in shaping policy (Becker 1963). The contrast is between the Swedish situation, where the political will of certain social actors (mostly women) to foster gender equality has led to legal changes that then influenced social practices, and the South American one, where the strength of political actors with conservative and patriarchal views (including foremost but not solely the Catholic Church) deters changes and new options in social practices. As a consequence, the temporal relationship between changes in law and policy on one hand, and prevailing family practices on the other, shows opposite patterns: legal and policy interventions tend to mold social practice in Sweden, while changes in social practices more often precede and clash with legal provisions and public policies in South America.

Another general underlying issue refers to the different approaches and understandings of "gender equality." The contrast is between policies that are based on "gender neutrality" and those based on recognizing (and reinforcing) gender differences (based on a gender hierarchy or even on a view of "equal but different"). To bring out the tensions in each of the models, the concluding section frames the comparison of the contrasting cases in the recurrent "paradoxes" that women "have to offer" (Scott 1996).

A CONCEPTUAL NOTE ON THE FAMILY

The family is a social institution anchored in biologically based universal human needs: sexuality, reproduction, and daily subsistence (based on co-residence in households). Its members share a social space defined by kinship relations, conjugality, and parental ties (Jelin 1998). It is a social organisation, a microcosm of relations of production, reproduction, and distribution, with a power structure and strong ideological and affective components. There are collective tasks and interests, but members have also their own interests, rooted in their own location within production and reproduction processes. Of special interest for this chapter is the way gender relations are established in the conjugal couple, and the way responsibilities linked to paternity and maternity are socially defined.

Family relations are the basic criteria for the formation of households and the performance of tasks linked to biological and social reproduction in everyday life. In the Western modern paradigm, ties within the family are expected to be based on affection and mutual care, yet they also involve instrumental, strategic, and interest-based considerations, both in everyday life and in longer intergenerational perspectives.

As a social institution, the family involves the pattern of legitimised sexuality, marriage, conjugality, and fertility. It also involves issues of divorce and separation, as well as the intergenerational transmission of social and economic capital (inheritance). Formal rules embodied in law, and common sense norms that often contradict the law, are at the same time a reflection of and a guide for social practices.

The family is never an isolated institution, but rather part and parcel of wider societal processes, including the productive and reproductive dimensions of societies, cultural patterns, and political systems. Households and family organisations are linked to the labour market and the organisation of social networks; sociodemographic trends such as fertility rates, divorce rates, and processes of aging are part of wider social and cultural processes as well as subject to public policy; and as a basic societal institution, the family is enmeshed in issues of basic cultural values and in political processes.

Given the fact that census and survey information usually is based on households, there is a tendency to identify the family with the household. In general, population statistics are based on household counts. For many purposes related to everyday life and the satisfaction of basic needs such as food and shelter, households are an appropriate unit of analysis. However, for analysing the dynamics of family and kinship ties, especially at times of high divorce rates and of diversified migratory patterns, one has to put special emphasis on the lack of correspondence between households and families. Under such conditions, family responsibilities and obligations can be met by members who do not share a household. Love and care can be exchanged on a nondaily basis. And these are issues that will have to be raised to fully understand contemporary family trends.

Furthermore, an often-neglected dimension of the theme involves the symbolic and ideological significance of the family. By "naturalizing" a certain type of family, other forms are stigmatised, and those who push for greater choice in living arrangements (or sexual orientation) can then be seen as abnormal or subversive. In fact, although seldom taken as a research theme in itself, the belief system and the political presence of family and kinship bonds is a highly significant phenomenon of public life.

THE FAMILY IN ARGENTINA

The South American subcontinent was colonised by Spain and Portugal, introducing Catholicism as the basic normative parameter. Canonical principles were prevalent in colonial times, and only gradually did civil law and lay principles evolve. At the time of independence and the formation of the national state (during the nineteenth century), the countries in the region adopted a patriarchal conception of the family, inherited from their French, German, and Spanish models. In the Civil Codes of Argentina (1869), Chile (1855), Brazil (1916), and Uruguay (1868), legislation on the family included the right of the man (*pater familias*) to decide about his wife and children and the duty of obedience of women toward their husbands and fathers. Women were not full citizens; they were not legally competent but defined as dependent, unable to conduct public activities on their own. Catholic norms prevailed both regarding the marriage bond—considered undissolvable—and regarding sexuality and virginity. The patriarchal principles were clearly established in law: women were subject to their husbands' decisions in many areas of life, and the father had legal rights over his children.

It is important to note, however, the fragility of the law in this area. During the nineteenth and early twentieth centuries, the legal and judicial systems of the region were very weak, and social practices could be quite far off from legal principles. The judicial apparatus was not developed enough to be able to supervise and guarantee the implementation of the emerging law over the full territory of the emerging nation-states. In fact, there were at least two coexisting family models: the Catholic one (as the ideal norm in cities and middle classes), and a pattern of free conjugal unions and "illegitimate" offspring, especially in rural and frontier areas (Moreno 2004). In both, women were subordinate and dependent on men.

Equality of men and women before the law was a gradual and incomplete struggle all along the twentieth century. In Argentina, a 1926 law sanctioned the equal civil rights between men and women, both single and married. Yet equality was not granted to married women until 1968, when the law established equal property rights and their full civil capacity. There are still some legal provisions in need of change to guarantee total equality.

The influence of the Catholic Church regarding family norms in the region has been significant, although with differences by country.[2] From early on, especially in Argentina and Chile, there have been recurring conflicts regarding family norms between, on one hand, the hierarchy of the Catholic church and its civil allies, who were trying to keep the legal system as close as possible to the views about the family sustained by the Church, and, on the other, progressive and liberal social actors who pushed for legal changes.

Legislation about separation, divorce, and the formation of new unions, provision of contraceptive devices and sexual education in public institutions, and mothers' rights vis-à-vis their children, among other themes, were (and still are) subject to public debate. The result has been a sharp discrepancy between social patterns of behaviour and legal frameworks. Since the power of Catholic conservative actors was more significant among political elites, this affected primarily formal provisions. Social patterns in everyday life of much of the population were following other principles. Therefore, social change took place earlier and was more widespread than legal changes. Marital separation and new nonmarried unions, the use of contraceptives, fertility decline, and illegal abortions are clear indications of patterns of change in social behaviour that took place in spite of legal prohibitions.

In Argentina, civil marriage was introduced in 1888, yet the legal recognition of divorce had to wait almost 100 years (until 1987). In practice, informal separations and new not-formalised conjugal unions were widespread and socially accepted much earlier. *Patria potestad* only changed in 1985, allowing for shared paternal and maternal rights over children. Also, equality of rights between children of married couples and out-of-wedlock children was only introduced at that time (1985). Finally, with the Constitutional reform of 1994, international treaties became part of the constitutional text, thus recognizing the rights of children, the denunciation of all forms of discrimination against women, and the recognition of basic human rights.

The issue of reproductive rights and national policies linked to reproductive behaviour merit some attention. The elites of the nineteenth century saw in European immigration the way to solve the population deficit of the country. This hegemonic perspective was to change in the 1930s, when immigration policies became much more restrictive, while fertility rates were reaching their lowest point in Argentine history. The new perspective was clearly pro-natalist, and called for active social policies fostering larger families. In the 1960s, while U.S.-sponsored policies for Latin America called for fertility control to slow down population growth in the region, Argentina was the exception: both the Catholic and nationalist right (based on moral and geopolitical considerations) and the left (based on anti-imperialist stands) opposed active policies of population control.

These policy debates—including also the link between population policy and development plans—had concrete effects on the lives of actual people. In 1974 a presidential decree was introduced to control the marketing of contraceptive devices, and public health activities geared to fertility control were forbidden. This policy had a clear social stratification effect: women who could afford private medicine had access to specialised modern reproductive control knowledge and services; the others, that is, poor women, were left out of family planning public services. Thus, many women end up undergoing illegal abortions to interrupt unwanted pregnancies, performed in clandestine clinics. Although there are no reliable statistics, several studies show that abortion is a common practice (estimates vary between 335,000 and 500,000 abortions per year) (Ramos et al. 2001; Checa and Rosemberg 1996, among others).[3]

In spite of the lack of adequate long-term social policies regarding reproductive health and reproductive rights, fertility rates have consistently been declining in the country. In fact, Argentina represents an exception in Latin America because of its very early decline in fertility, beginning in the last decade of the nineteenth century.[4] This decline can be linked to the process of secularisation of its population, which implied an early process of urbanisation and an increase in educational levels for both men and women. The ideology of family progress through educational and occupational mobility took hold easily among European immigrants and native middle classes. In that paradigm, there was a widespread aspiration to regulate fertility in order to achieve a small family size. The interesting fact is that this early demographic transition began way before modern contraceptive devices were developed.

By the end of the overseas massive immigration period (1930), the country showed a dual population model: "modern" immigrants and urban middle classes on one hand, and traditional patterns of fertility (high, nonregulated fertility) in the rest of the population. Internal rural-to-urban migration in the following years, coupled with vigorous economic growth and redistributive policies of the Peronist government (1946–1955), led to a decline in fertility differentials between urban middle and working classes. The total fertility rate remained constant until 1980, and continued its slow descending trend afterwards. Estimates for 2000–2005 are 2.4 children per woman. Yet regional and class differentials are still very large: while total fertility in the city of Buenos Aires for 2000–2005 is 1.47 children, the comparable figure for the province of Misiones is 3.34 (INDEC 2001, 2003).

Since the return to democratically elected governments in 1983, the opening of the public sphere to new social actors (such as the human rights and the feminist movements) led to a new framework for the interpretation of the issue of reproductive health: the framework of reproductive rights. This new paradigm took hold in many social groups in the country, although not necessarily among government officials and public policies. The demands raised by the feminist movement and governmental commitment to comply with the Action Plans of various international conferences and treaties established the bases for the recognition of reproductive rights, providing legitimacy to initiatives for the definition of policies in this field. Yet, although Argentina ratified international treaties dealing with the rights of women, it aligned itself with the Vatican in international fora when issues of population control and reproductive rights were discussed (in the Cairo Population Conference, in the Beijing Women's Conference). There was much public debate and feminist mobilisation about these issues in the 1990s. Political confrontations regarding reproductive rights legislation and regarding the legalisation of abortion are ongoing.

Regarding education, free and mandatory lay public education was established in the 1870s. Although the coverage of public schools throughout the country did not follow automatically, school attendance increased and illiteracy started to decline, both among men and women. By the 1930s, there was practically no gender differential in illiteracy rates and in primary school enrolment. During the 1950s and 1960s, women equalled men in secondary school attendance. By the 1990s, there were more women than men enrolled in higher education. The picture is not one of total educational equality, however. Women have higher drop-out rates at all levels of the educational system, and they are concentrated in certain gender-typed careers, although there is a trend toward wider choices and feminisation of some professions (medicine, for example).

In the prototype of the patriarchal nuclear family, a gender division of labour is well entrenched: the father-husband-provider role of the adult male is coupled by the mother-housewife-caretaker role of the adult female. But Argentine reality has been always very far from this model with respect to women's responsibilities—not so in terms of male authority and power. Rural and urban working-class women—especially the young and unmarried—have always been engaged in productive activities: in domestic service, as textile and garment workers, and as family helpers on farms. Since early on, middle- and upper-class women also entered the professional and white-collar world. Urbanisation and modernisation implied an initial decline in the women's labour force participation during the first half of the twentieth century. Around 1950, participation rates of women reached their lowest point, then began to grow, slowly and steadily. For the country as a whole, 23 percent of women were in the labour force in 1947, 25 percent in 1970, and 27 percent in 1980, to then increase significantly.[5] In the 1990s, with increasing unemployment and poverty for both men and women, participation rates for women continued to grow. Yet, as a result of neoliberal economic restructuring, unemployment, underemployment, and poverty affected about half of the population, both men and women. Thus, the increase in the labour supply of women during the 1980s and 1990s does not reflect a reaction to new opportunities but rather an adaptive behaviour to cope with neoliberal adjustment and crisis.

The significant fact for the analysis of the family is that the increase in labour force participation included married women and even those with small children at all educational levels (Wainerman 2003). Yet this was not accompanied by state policies regarding working mothers' rights or childcare provisions. Issues of incompatibilities between maternal duties and responsibilities were, to a large extent, left to be handled by the family, kinship, and neighbourhood networks, and—for higher income groups—the market (especially through hired domestic help).

The ideal model of the single-male-provider nuclear family persisted for most of the twentieth century. School textbooks conveyed this naturalised image of family life up until the 1980s, presenting girls playing "mothers" with their dolls while boys played "jobs" with their trucks and tools; mothers cleaning and preparing food while fathers worked and came back home in the evening. Only in the 1990s did textbooks incorporate other family models besides the complete nuclear one: women who work, and boys and girls sharing the same games (Wainerman and Heredia 1991).

Actual reality of family and household responsibilities shifted considerably in the last two decades. Among households with female spouses ages 20 to 60 in the metropolitan area of Buenos Aires, the single-male-provider household declined from 74.5 percent to 54.7 percent between 1980 and 2000, while two-provider households increased form 25.5 percent to 45.3 percent. This shift took place in households at all stages of family life: with and without small children. Also, it is more common among the upper and lower socioeconomic strata than among the middle ones (Wainerman 2003).

Another important trend regarding family formation is the clear increase in cohabitation and its expansion from backward rural areas to urban and middle-class populations. Cohabitation and consensual unions has existed since early times as a popular practice, at times followed after some years by civil or religious marriage. This practice began to decline with the process of urbanisation and modernisation, to experience a reversal in the last decades. Cohabitation without formal marriage represented seven percent of all unions in 1960, increasing to 18 percent in 1991 (Torrado 2003, 268). There are two variants: consensual unions as an initial stage, to be followed by a legal union (mostly when children are born), and as an alternative to the legal bond. While the incidence of consensual unions is highest in the poorest regions of the country (in 1991 they represented 32.5 percent of all unions in the North-eastern region), the change in the city of Buenos Aires is impressive: 1.5 percent in 1960, 13.6 percent in 1991, and 21 percent in 2001.

Lower marriage rates and higher cohabitation rates indicate that the major change has been in marriage as an institution. At the same time, there has been an increase in divorce rates.[6] This set of phenomena has been interpreted as an indication of weakening or even a crisis in the conjugal couple. Yet, the prevalence of couples as the preferred living arrangement has not decreased. In fact, when considering the quality of the bonds, decreased marriage rates and higher divorce rates can also be seen as indications of (especially for women) an increasing freedom to exit unsatisfying relationships and of a process leading toward the constitution of new family forms.

FAMILISM AND MATERNALISM

All along modern history, "familism" and "maternalism" have been very strong, even within the ranks of progressive groups. The family is the key social institution within which the role of the mother is always enshrined. In no place can the political centrality of the family be seen more clearly than in the recent tragic history of dictatorship and the activism of the human rights movement.

As is well known, in the midst of deep political conflict and widespread political violence, a military coup took place in Argentina in March 1976. The military government defined itself as the saviour of the nation, following its duty to bring back peace and order where chaos and "subversion" were destroying the "natural" Argentine values and institutions. The reference to the traditional family was paramount in the framing of the military coup. First, it defined society as an organism constituted by cells (families). In this way, it linked social structure to a biological origin, naturalising family roles and values. The military developed a massive campaign to consolidate family unity, justified by the place of the family in the natural social order. The metaphor of the family was used for the nation as a whole, the Father-State having unalienable rights over the moral and physical fate of its citizens. The image of the nation as the "Grand Argentine Family" implied that only the "good" children-citizens were truly Argentine. Official discourse represented citizens as immature children in need of strong paternal authority. There was no room for citizens with rights, for human beings with personal autonomy. The military regime had to be helped by other "minor" parents, in charge of controlling and disciplining the rebellious adolescents. State-sponsored advertisement on TV would ask: "Do you know where your child is now?" urging parents to reproduce *ad infinitum* the policing and controlling that the military were carrying out. The distinction between public life and private family disappeared (Filc 1997).

At the same time as they claimed to defend the traditional patriarchal family, the military implemented a systematic policy of clandestine repression. The policy to handle the political conflict and to wipe out the existing armed political groups included widespread kidnappings of people from their own homes, to then be tortured and *disappeared* (Calveiro 1998). Young children were also kidnapped with their parents, and pregnant young women were kept alive until giving birth. With changed identities, the children were appropriated by military personnel and others linked to their ranks. Estimates of the number of disappearances vary up to 30,000; estimates of surviving kidnapped children with false identities reach 500 (of which about 80 cases have been solved).

Right from the beginning of this repression, relatives of detained and disappeared persons organised themselves to denounce kidnappings and demand information and redress. The organisations created at that time were marked by kinship ties.[7] In the political context of dictatorship, political organisations and labour unions were suspended, and thus relatives were the only ones who could voice their grievances.

Mirroring the military regime, which used the family as a central metaphor, familism became and remained the central image of the discourse and practices of the human rights movement. This movement denounced crimes against the family, projecting at the same time an image of the "good child" and of "normal" family life. The paradigmatic image is that of the mother, symbolised by the *Madres de Plaza de Mayo*, who leaves her "natural" private realm of family life to invade the public sphere in search for her kidnapped/disappeared child. The Mother challenges the powerful, expressing family mandates linked to caring and protecting. What is significant here is that they enter the public sphere not as metaphors or symbolic images of family ties, but grounded in actual kin relations.

This public emergence of family ties in political life has wider cultural significance. It implies a reconceptualisation of the relationship between private and public life. In the image that the human rights movement conveys to society, the family link to the victim is the essential justification and legitimacy for action. For the justice system, it is actually the only one: only relatives are considered "affected" in the demands for reparation. The Mothers may have generalised their maternity, with the slogan that all the disappeared are the children of all the Mothers. Yet the primary importance of kinship ties creates a distance between those who are the carriers of "truth" of personal and private suffering and those who are ready to mobilize politically for the same cause but with no direct kinship ties to victims. With such criteria, justification for public participation seems to be stratified, with family ties being more "legitimate" in the public view than citizenship and political concerns.

THE SWEDISH FAMILY IN PERSPECTIVE

Up until the beginning of the twentieth century, Sweden was a poor rural country, with considerable male emigration to America. In the mid 1800s, women were active participants in the rural household economy—in milk husbandry and in the fields. They were also economically active in textile mills and in the nascent industries. And they were in charge of households and of child-care chores. Yet Swedish women were not legally competent. In 1845, women gained the same inheritance rights as men, and in 1858 full adult status at age 25 was legally recognised, but only for single women (Swedish Government Official Reports 1994).

Improvements in access to education during the second half of the nineteenth century led to new professional opportunities for women (the traditional ones, such as nurses, school teachers, and the like). Yet the pattern of a clear legal and practical distinction between single and married women deepened: gainful employment was for single women, and marrying (especially in the middle classes) meant withdrawing from work. Marriage involved subordination to the husband and losing legal rights. Cohabitation without marriage emerged as an alternative, especially among urban working-class populations.

The situation of working mothers and the hardship and hazards for children made clear the incompatibility entailed in trying to combine productive and reproductive roles of women. The first public policy oriented toward the protection of motherhood was a Labour Safety Act in 1900, which prohibited women engaged in an industrial occupation from working for the first four weeks after giving birth. This mandatory leave was not accompanied by any payment, thus taking for granted the existence of a family with a husband provider, which was not necessarily the rule. In 1912 the leave was increased to six weeks of unpaid mandatory leave, and only in 1931 was a Maternity Benefit Law passed, justified as an attempt to lower infant mortality by fostering breast feeding, given that the prevailing image made mothers morally responsible for the death of their babies. In the 1930s, lone mothers were granted the same general benefits as married mothers (Hobson and Takahashi 1997), justified mostly in terms of the high infant mortality. During all this period, the laws did not take into consideration the other responsibility of women, namely that of financial support of their children (Ohlander 1991).

At the beginning of the century, a concern for the decline in the marriage rate led to legal changes. Divorce was introduced in 1915, and a new Marriage Code in 1921. In order to foster marriage and motherhood, the new law assured women the continuance of their legal competence after marriage, allowed married women to own property, and established that joint property rules would apply when marriages were dissolved (Dahlberg and Taub 1992). These three principles are still in place in Sweden today.

In spite of the changes in the marriage code, the father was still the sole legal guardian of his children. This provision was altered in 1949 when the Code of Parents was adopted and both parents became the legal guardians of children born within marriage. Regarding names, women had to take their husband's family name, and the children took the father's name. These rules were changed in 1963, when women could retain their maiden names upon marriage, and in 1982, when the law became that children had their mother's last name unless there was a declaration that the father's name should be given (Dahlberg and Taub 1992).

In sum, during this early period, there was a growing recognition of the gender inequalities involved in the marriage contract. State intervention led to the recognition of some rights of women within marriage, but did not involve the full abandonment of the patriarchal model. Regarding motherhood, there was recognition of women's responsibilities as mothers for the well-being of their children, but no legal recognition of women's responsibilities for the financial maintenance of themselves and their children. The tension between these responsibilities and the recognition of women's citizenship rights was, and continued to be, at the core of the whole history of family policy in the country.

THE PROCESS OF CHANGE, 1930–1960

The rise to power of the Social Democrats in 1932 generated changes in the political scenario. The Social Democrats pushed for a minimum standard of living for all, with special emphasis on children. A key turning point was the publication, in 1934, of the book *The Population Crisis* by Alva and Gunnar Myrdal (Bonniers 1934). Up until the 1930s, family policy had been framed by concerns regarding maternity, breast-feeding and child care; now the issue was to be interpreted in the framework of a Population Policy.

The ideology of the housewife and the husband-provider was still very strong, especially in labour unions and among conservatives. Two fronts opened up against these conservative views: on one hand, radical Marxist theorists claimed that the issues of reproduction had to be solved within the productive sphere; on the other, more pragmatic politicians looked for a solution in positivistic "social engineering." For them, gender issues were amenable to economic measures, and social policy should be a prophylactic family policy managed through economic incentives. Informality in sexual relations had to be legalised in marriage, and the promotion of higher fertility required state action. For this aim, they claimed, families should get subsidies, housing help, and pensions for children. Women should get additional help through paediatric clinics, fertility clinics, day-care and child-care centres.

Concern over low birth rates was addressed by unmistakably pro-natalist government policies. Such policies were to advance simultaneously three different lines of work: first, the promotion and protection of families, the "normal" site for child rearing (ideally four children per couple); the provision of services to help women in their household and caring responsibilities; and the encouragement of measures to improve the participation of women in education and the labour force.[8]

Swedish feminists, however, placed their demands firmly within the interpretive frame of citizenship. The mother and caregiver figure was not a sufficient basis for demands, insofar as women saw themselves also as workers and citizens. They saw work as a basic citizenship right, pushing for the double recognition of married women's right to work and working women's right to marry (Hobson and Lindholm 1997, 488–92). The tension women faced between work and marriage was at the centre of policy discussions (Frangeur 1998).

The government's preoccupation with population issues led to the creation, in 1935, of a Special Population Commission. A key issue was the attempt to restrict the right of married women to work, rooted in the rise of unemployment due to the Depression: by 1934, nine bills prohibiting the employment of married women had been introduced in Parliament. Opposition from women's groups ensued, and finally a resolution was adopted declaring that women's rights to professional training were integral to their full and equal civil rights. It took five years of work by the Special Committee for Married Women's Work to produce a final report. The report recognised that female workers were indispensable in the textile, shoe, and clothing industries and in the Swedish economy. It also dismissed the arguments about the threat to home and family posed by married women workers. In 1939, a law was passed that banned sacking women on the grounds of their marital or maternal status. The bill also gave women the right to three months of maternity leave without penalty of job loss. Mothers, including single mothers, were entitled to free health care, and maternity insurance benefits were increased (Frangeur 1998; Hobson and Lindholm 1997).

Pro-natalist views did have an impact in the realm of reproductive rights. One area of conflict was regarding abortion. Social Democratic and other women were promoting abortion legislation, and pro-natalist ideas were put forth as arguments against such laws (Ohlander 1991). Finally, and after much debate and struggles, advertising and selling contraceptive devices was legalised in 1938, and a law was introduced allowing abortion for ethical, medical, and eugenic reasons, but not on request.

Regarding measures in support of marriage and family formation, in 1937 credit for the newly wed became available (to foster earlier marriages), as did rent subsidies. Maternity relief provisions in 1937 granted a modest benefit to all mothers, and in 1947 child allowances were introduced. Both of these benefits were paid directly to mothers, giving women a limited, though real, leverage within the family. Yet it also meant that the responsibility of caring for children continued to be in the hands of mothers, with no participation of fathers.

All these measures, however, did not drastically change the situation for women. Although their rights as workers were equal to those of the men, and married women were legally autonomous, legislative change was not accompanied by public policies that would effectively allow women to develop themselves as workers on an equal footing with men (Hirdman 1998). The formal recognition of the double role of women—worker and housewife—was not accompanied by policies that would allow women to freely choose where and how to work, or to solve the problem of the daily care of children.

In sum, during the 1930s Swedish women's organisations were able to push for "policies that became the core of social citizenship in the Swedish welfare state: maternity leaves and job security; protection of married women's right to work; income maintenance policy for solo mothers; universal maternal health-care" (Hobson and Lindholm 1997, 498). In this way, women's issues took centre stage: as producers of children, as consumers of modern services, and as substitute mothers (as child-care workers) in a fully modern society, but not necessarily as equal citizens in actual practice. Sweden still had a large middle class that maintained the ideal of the father-provider, mother-housewife. Furthermore, as Hirdman suggests, the formula of "women's dual role" (workers before marriage and after the first years of child care, homemakers when children were small) was presented as a solution to the gender conflict. "The result, however, corresponded well with the explicit divisions of the dual-role theory giving women a kind of half-person status both in the labour market and in the political life" (Hirdman 1998, 40).

ACTIVE POLICIES, 1960–1990

In the 1960s, "a new normative, gender contract was formulated stating the individuality of men and women, in the family as well as in society" (Hirdman 1998, 41). This was the turning point for the presentation and promotion of the model of the dual-breadwinner family. The concept of gender equality was developed and placed on the political agenda by a diverse group of people "who might be called the 'gender equality people'" (Florin and Nilsson 1999, 11–15) Thus, the 1960s saw a new articulation of the "gender conflict" (Hirdman 1998), which had a legislative answer in the 1970s, and further policy effects in the 1980s.

The recognition of an ideal of gender equality and the individualistic understanding of this notion required considerable policy changes. First and foremost, equality in the labour market had to be accompanied by significant changes in family and domestic responsibilities. Political ideology and political will had to converge with labour market demands for new workers as the economy was growing, on one hand, and with the workings of a political system and political parties that had to respond to constituencies' demands, on the other. Furthermore, in the construction of a social and legal system based on men and women being independent workers, child care became a key social issue in the governmental agenda. Thus, legal reform and social policy responded to the need to break with the family model based on sole maternal responsibility for the well-being of the children (Scheiwe 2003).

Policies oriented toward equality multiplied: maternity leave was transformed into parental leave insurance in 1974. This entitled both father and mother to 90 percent of their usual income for a period of time (first six months, later 12 months), but left the decision of who would take the leave, and for how long, in the hands of couples. The complementary reform implied access to quality child care. At the same time, rights to maintenance were reduced, reflecting the view of women as autonomous and independent human beings.

Marriage was again the focus of discussion within this new paradigm. Divorce rates were rising, and marriage rates declining. New legal changes vis-à-vis the family were introduced in 1987, recognizing the individual's right to choose his/her lifestyle, while at the same time favouring marriage. The new Marriage Code is couched in gender-neutral language. It does not presume different roles for men and women, nor does it provide different rules for men and women, yet it involves some provisions to protect the "economically weaker spouse" (which is usually the woman). In Dahlberg and Taub's interpretation, by formulating these corrections in gender-neutral terms, "it has risked losing sight of the sex-based nature of women's continuing subordinate position" (1992, 139).

The equality ideology influenced many other measures (including pensions, taxation, sexuality, and custody). Yet, in most areas, this equality principle had to be amended in the same direction of protecting the "weaker spouse," which in fact involves a recognition that both parts are not always equal nor independent, but rather interdependent and partners in an unequal relationship.

In general, the legal regulation of marriage was weakened considerably. Rights and responsibilities of partners of marital and cohabitation agreements are left to individual discretion, providing some protection to the "weaker partner." What is much more regulated is parent–child relations: changes adopted in the 1970s and 1980s pertain to parental leave as well as to child custody provisions. Parents have shared responsibility for the children during marriage since 1949, and since the early 1980s they have shared responsibility after divorce (if the parents were not married, it is assumed that the mother is the guardian unless parents apply for joint custody). Divorced parents determine what the rules of their custody will be. Although in this case the law is again based on equality and is gender-neutral, and is always concerned with the well-being of the child, there were and are tensions and contradictions, because in reality, inequalities exist. As Dahlberg and Taub conclude,

> The overall impact of these reforms of women's interests is far from clear. On the one hand, the preference for joint custody in conjunction with making the custodial mother responsible for its smooth operation ... imposes severe constraints on women's autonomy. At a minimum, this requires her to maintain the continuous contact necessary for making arrangements for visitation. Often such contacts allow the man to manipulate her. On the other hand, an expanded, functional relationship between father and child lightens the mother's load. (Dahlberg and Taub 1992, 146–47).

THE DUAL-BREADWINNER MODEL IN ACTION

Balancing work and family is the centre of different models of state intervention through public social policy. The way the state intervenes has different implications for gender equality and family models: "the cash benefit for childcare schemes encourage the gender-differentiated family; childcare services facilitate the dual-earner model; while parental leave legislation encourages dual-earning and care-sharing parenthood" (Leira 2002,

4). Swedish policy took a clear stand, preferring the latter, in contrast to Argentina (and in general, the Latin American countries) where there is very little active policy—because an assumption of the "natural" maternal role of women persists.

Women's labour force participation has increased steadily, reaching 79 percent in 2003, when men's economic activity rate was 84 percent. and by 2002, 47 percent of households had a cohabiting couple (Statistics Sweden 2004). In these households, it is very likely that the dual-breadwinner model is a reality. Yet behind these figures, inequalities persist and new ones have emerged. The labour market is stratified: women work much more often than men in part-time jobs, and having young children makes for a clear pattern of female part-time work: 52 percent of working women aged 20 to 64 with three children, the youngest one being 1 to 2 years old, were part-time workers, compared to 33 percent of the total female working population. Furthermore, job segregation persists, reflecting the traditional division of labour: women are the large majority of nurses, secretaries, and educators of young children, while men work in industry, in economics, and in technology (Statistics Sweden 2004).

Quality state-sponsored child care was a cornerstone of the gender equality ideal. The 1975 National Preschool Act established that local authorities had to include child care among their public services. In 1975, 17 percent of children ages one to six were enrolled in child-care centres, rising to 52 percent in 1985 (Bergqvist and Nyberg 2002). In 2002, 67 percent of children ages 1 to 5 were enrolled in municipal day-care centres, and 10 percent were in privately managed centres (Statistics Sweden 2004, 36).[9] Yet the municipal child-care staff remains almost totally female, indicating that child care—be it at home or in public day-care centres—is clearly women's responsibility.

From a theoretical perspective, perhaps the most significant step toward the replacement of the patriarchal family for one based on gender equality is the recognition and promotion of the paternal role. This is clearly an area where commitment to change requires active state intervention. Since very early in the twentieth century, Swedish policy has tried to formalize the rights and obligations of biological fathers toward their children. In the 1970s, the financial obligations of fathers were transformed to include care obligations (based on the rationale that this is in the best interests of children). Joint custody, paternal leave, and the "daddy month"—which obliges fathers to take parental leave or forfeit the leave—were established toward active fatherhood, coupled by strong publicity campaigns and information packets fostering fathering (Bergman and Hobson 2002).

This parental leave model, by de-naturalising mother's role and by allowing for father's child care on an equal footing, "serves the demands of social reproduction over those of production . . . Inclusion of fathers among those entitled to care for children reformulates the work–family issue as a concern of both parents and a matter for welfare state intervention" (Leira 2002, 76).

However, gender-neutral parental leave (leave beyond the "daddy month") continues to be basically taken by mothers. Fathers take leave for very short periods of time. Thus, in 2003, 43 percent of the insured persons claiming parental allowance were males, but they accounted only for 17 percent of the total number of days taken (Statistics Sweden 2004, 38).

The likelihood that fathers will take the voluntary parental leave varies according to socioeconomic conditions. In their study of parents of children born in 1994, Sundström and Duvander report that half the fathers used some days of parental leave. They show that fathers are more likely to take the leave among families with higher incomes, and that it is father's earnings (more than mother's) that impacts on the probability of taking the leave. Also, the situation at work of father and mother (tenure, rewarding or unrewarding jobs) influences the practice. The authors conclude that parents' decisions about whether to share the parental leave should be seen as the outcome of two important bargaining and adjustment processes. First, the decision involves bargaining between the mother and the father about how long the mother's leave should be. Father's parental leave seems simply a residual. Second, the father also has a bargaining process at work, which factors in possible negative reactions (Sundström and Duvander 2002, 443).

Since the dual-breadwinner model became established, there is also a trend toward decreased family stability, with women taking the initiative for divorce, as well as reports of increasing health problems for women, particularly related to stress. In a study of parents of 5-year-olds, "home stress" defined as stress experienced in connection with responsibilities for home and family, including family conflict, was reported more often among women than among men. When asked about their preferences, parents want greater job flexibility in working hours and shorter working hours in order to be able to combine work and family roles (Björnberg 2000).

This parental leave model may also affect gender equality in the labour market. The expectation of long leave periods may make young women less attractive to prospective employers, putting women at a disadvantage in terms of careers and job opportunities. On the other hand, insofar as the paid leave presupposes prior employment, it may involve more attachment to the labour force on the part of women and a high rate of return to work. In a longer term perspective, it is clear that the right to share parental leave has not changed the primary child-care role of the mother, and the gendered nature of the labour market suggests that expectations about men's responsibilities still centre on the idea that work and family are separate spheres, "that norms associated with masculinity should dominate and that the most trusted and loyal workers should be men" (Haas and Hwang 1999, 45).

State policies have nevertheless affected the organisation of families and households, as well as the organisation of everyday life. There seems now to be no major incentive for legal marriage, a fact that is related to the individualisation of social policies and benefits, and there are now three parallel social institutions: married couples living together, non-married cohabiting couples, and the newer phenomenon of "living apart together" (LAT) relationships (Trost and Levin 2004). Fertility is the result of individual desires and negotiations within couples, with access to all reproductive health services and rights needed to fulfill such desires.

The future of the role of direct state intervention in family organisation, however, is unclear. The expansion of the welfare state during the second half of the twentieth century was anchored in a growing economy, a growing labour demand that could absorb the expanding supply of women workers, and in a state that could increase social spending accordingly. The 1990s witnessed a reversal of these long-term trends: economic recession resulted in increasing unemployment; growing public deficits led to cuts in social policy budgets; the political change in government implied the defeat of Social Democracy and the introduction of neoliberal ideas by the Conservative political parties. Cuts in expenditures in 1996 involved decreasing parental leave provisions from 90 percent to 75 percent of wages. Although there is no decline in the number of children covered by public day-care centres, the quality of services may have suffered. This is leading to upper income families demanding private household workers and in-house child care (Winkler 1998; Berqvist and Nyberg 2002). There are also initiatives to privatise social services, including provisions for mothers to stay at home to take care of children.

In such a context, one key issue is whether the gender equality model is sustainable under conditions that do not match full employment and continuous economic growth. Employers' policies regarding work and family may become more important than formal rights mandated by the government, and stiffer competition may lead to a backlash: "General policies aimed at forcing employers to make work and family easier to reconcile could in fact produce more unequal conditions for women if employers see more risks than advantages in hiring women as employees" (Björnberg 2000, 73).

CONCLUDING REMARKS

Swedish history during the later part of the twentieth century is a clear case of visibility, recognition, and promotion of women's rights. This historical development is not random, but the result of the convergence of various factors over time: economic conditions, the demands of women's organisations, changes in cultural patterns, and a variety of political forces. Political parties, labour unions, women's groups, and other actors (including intellectuals and journalists) played a role in the development of this story of the promotion of gender equality. Perhaps the peculiar Swedish feature is the critical role played by the state: from early on, there was a strong government commitment to gender equality policies, and relatively little open opposition to feminist demands, especially in the more recent periods.

It is clear also from this story that family legal provisions and public policy were key mechanisms for bringing about greater gender equality. Since the 1970s, the active promotion of gender equality led to the development of the dual-breadwinner family model. The "equal status contract" (Hirdman 1998) implies greater autonomy of women, the same obligation for men and women to work to support their children, rights and obligations within the family being equally distributed (sharing housework and childcare), expectations that men and women will have the same standard of living, and the like.

State commitment to issues of gender equality is seen also in the studies and reports that the government produces in this area. Interestingly, there is a Parliamentary decision ruling not only that statistics be disaggregated by sex, but also that they "reflect gender issues and problems in society" (Statistics Sweden 2004, 9). The systematic nature of data collection allows for monitoring, analysis of advances, and identification of areas where gender equality is still wanting, such as the double burden on women and the emerging concern around high levels of domestic and sexual violence.

The contrast in the political agenda for family policy between Sweden and Argentina (and other Latin American countries) is striking. In Sweden, the focus of debate is around the quality of child care in public institutions and about the ways to foster greater participation of fathers in the upbringing of children. The rationale combines concerns for gender equality and ideas about the well-being of children. Basic issues regarding reproductive health and reproductive rights, as well as equality in citizenship rights, seem to have already been solved. Throughout the twentieth century, the state was a proactive force called in to foster policies to change family structure and forms. Undoubtedly, changes in State policy were the result of social struggles, where women committed to a feminist agenda used a variety of strategies—inside and outside political parties—to affect results.

The agenda in South America is quite different. In fact, in Argentina and other South American countries, the efforts of women are still to "denaturalise" the patriarchal family and to gain recognition of women's basic civil rights. The struggle against the principles of the Catholic Church and its civilian allies has been a constant feature of the history of these efforts, and that struggle is still going on. Now that legalisation of divorce and shared *patria potestad* have been secured in law, pending issues relate to reproductive rights, the legalisation of abortion, and the recognition of homosexual relationships. Furthermore, in times of the dismantling of the welfare state and the rise of neoliberal policies, there is no political room to ask for state provision of child care facilities, maternal and paternal leaves, and the like.

In matters related to the family and "familism," the state itself has become one of the arenas of confrontation between social and political actors. The bases for a broad consensus on these matters are weak or even nonexistent, and thus the possibilities of consistent policy and action are limited. The strongest policy advocates are still the Catholic Church and its conservative powerful allies. Yet, as the recent experience of the human rights movement shows, "familism" and "maternalism" are very strong components of the basic interpretive framework prevalent in everyday life and in the public arena.

In contrast to the political continuity of democratic politics in Sweden, political instability was the mark of the second half of the twentieth century in South America. The succession of military and civilian governments surely implies oscillations and back-and-forth movements in governmental policies. In the longer term, however, the trend has been toward a slow yet increasing liberalisation of family law and increasing legal recognition of women's rights. In her comparison between Argentina, Brazil, and Chile, Htun (2003) shows that patriarchal and conservative military dictatorships could effect change in some legal matters. Without public debate, through the formation of small official commissions of experts to advise them on legal matters, these dictatorships opened a window of opportunities for the incorporation of international trends and new ideas circulating in legal circles. Issues dealt with under military regimes were couched in technical legal terms—property rights of married women, or full civil capacity of women. Other issues, those more entrenched in conservative Catholic ideas, such as divorce, abortion and reproductive rights, rights of nonmarried conjugal partners, or recognition of same sex couples, could emerge into open discussion only under civilian governments. In all these matters, the struggles to change legal provisions usually follow, rather than anticipate, informal social practices and norms. Yet, even when public opinion is in favour of change, the progressive proposals may fail in Congress and policy decisions because of the strength of conservative actors, the difficulties in forming coalitions backing reform, and the limited salience that such family issues have in the priority list of many political actors.

A further, more substantive and normative comment, is needed. Swedish family law is couched in gender-neutral language, assuming—and through this intending to foster—equality among partners. Yet realities are different. First, it is women who bear and breast-feed babies, involving features and tasks that cannot be couched in gender-neutral terms. Second, even in a society that has taken gender equality as its priority, and has promoted policies in this direction for more than thirty years, the preferences and incentives of men and women regarding their families, especially the care of their offspring, is still highly differentiated. Women and men still see the maternal role as "natural," and seem to conceive being replaced by men as "giving up" a natural motherhood role. Thus, maternal and paternal roles do not seem to be interchangeable—a realisation that calls into question the ideal of "gender neutrality." The question then arises as to how to introduce such differences and inequalities in an equality driven framework or paradigm.[10]

In Latin America, law provisions and actual reality take for granted the existence of gender differences (and implicitly or explicitly, of a gender hierarchy), and the efforts of feminists and progressive forces are geared to decrease inequalities and attain recognition of women's rights. Motherhood and maternality are very strong values in Latin America (the Catholic view of motherhood is important here, reinforced by other discourses, including some trends within feminism).

Thus, taking the more extreme recognition of gender differences in Latin America and the silenced recognition (covered by the use of gender-neutral language) in Sweden, is gender neutrality the appropriate route for gender equality? How can we combine the logic of equality with a logic of recognition of differences (Fraser 1997; Minow 1990)? How can we deal with the tension between women as mothers and carers of others vis-à-vis their full and equal citizenship? It seems to me that the tension between gender equality and the recognition of difference can only be approached through the recognition of women's and men's embeddedness in systems of social relations, and less so in individualistic frameworks.

This brings us back to the initial considerations about welfare regimes. Sweden represents a case of the individualisation of benefits and of the "de-familisation" of welfare. The result is, undoubtedly, more equality than in other societies, which are loaded with traditional and-not so-traditional gender hierarchies and inequalities. Yet there may be costs to this option: Does individualisation imply solitude and lack of community ties and bonds? How can familism, mutual responsibilities, and affection be combined with respect and consideration of individual rights and wishes? The tensions between individualisation and a sense of community, as that between equality and difference, are some of the challenges we still face.

NOTES

1. While the focus is on Argentina, the main trends in family policy analysed in the chapter are shared by other countries in the region.
2. The history of the positions of the Church in Argentina, Brazil, and Chile vis-à-vis family norms, especially divorce, abortion and gender equality, is discussed by Htun (2003).
3. Maternal death due to induced abortion is extremely high in the country. In 1993, it was estimated that 29 percent of maternal deaths in the country were due to complications of induced abortions (Ministerio de Salud y Acción Social 1995).
4. In 1895 the rate was seven children per woman; in 1914 it declined to 5.3, reaching 3.2 in 1947 and leveling off at that rate until 1980 (Torrado 2003).
5. Figures for 1991 indicate a rate of 36 percent, yet because of changes in measurement techniques, figures are not totally comparable (Wainerman 2003, 60).
6. Divorce (and the legal capacity to remarry) became legal in Argentina only in 1986. Before that, *de facto* separations and new conjugal bonds involved not marriage but consensual unions. The law was followed by a "boom" in divorces and a sharp increase of marriage rates, involving mostly the legalization of *de facto* conditions.
7. The first was *Familiares de Detenidos y Desaparecidos por Razones Políticas* (Relatives of detained and disappeared for political reasons), followed by

Madres de Plaza de Mayo (Mothers of Plaza de Mayo) and *Asociación de Abuelas de Plaza de Mayo* (Association of Grandmothers of Plaza de Mayo).
8. The contrast with the pro-natalist policies in Argentina, especially the prohibition of free contraceptive services in 1974, is striking.
9. There are some discrepancies in the data presented in that report. Compare p. 36 and p. 37.
10. These issues are present in the Code of Parenthood and its gender-neutral provisions. Looking at the provisions for visiting rights, Dahlberg and Taub conclude: "The 'sexual contract' of Sweden today is thus a male-centred right to take care of or have access to his own children and, via the children, contact with and even control over their mother" (Dahlberg and Taub 1992, 149).

REFERENCES

Becker, Howard S. 1963. *Outsiders: Studies in the sociology of deviance.* New York: The Free Press.
Bergman, Helena, and Barbara Hobson. 2002. Compulsory fatherhood: the coding of fatherhood in the Swedish welfare state. In *Making men into fathers: Men's masculinities and the social politics of fatherhood*, ed. Barbara Hobson, 92–123. Cambridge: Cambridge University Press.
Bergqvist, Cristina, and Anita Nyberg. 2002. Welfare state restructuring and child care in Sweden. In *Child care policy at the crossroads*, eds. Michel Sonya and Mahon Rianne, 287–308. New York: Routledge.
Björnberg, Ulla. 2000. Equality and backlash: Family, gender and social policy in Sweden. In *Organizational change and gender equality: International perspectives on fathers and mothers in the workplace*, eds. Linda Haas, Philip Hwang, and Graeme Russell, 57–75. Newbury Park, CA: Sage.
Calveiro, Pilar. 1998. *Poder y desaparición: Los campos de concentración en Argentina* [*Power and disappearance: Concentration camps in Argentina*]. Buenos Aires: Colihue.
Checa, Susana, and Martha Rosemberg. 1996. *Aborto hospitalizado: Una cuestión de derechos reproductivos, un problema de salud pública* [*Hospitalized abortion: A reproductive rights issue, a public health problem*]. Buenos Aires: El Cielo por Asalto.
Dahlberg, Anita, and Nadine Taub. 1992. Notions of the family in recent Swedish law. *International Review of Comparative Public Policy* 4:133–153.
Esping-Andersen, Gösta. 2002. Towards the good society, once again? In *Why we need a new welfare state*, ed. Gösta Esping-Andersen, 1–24. Oxford: Oxford University Press.
Filc, Judith. 1997. *Entre el parentesco y la política: Familia y dictadura, 1976–1983* [*Between kinship and politics: Family and dictatorship, 1976–1983*]. Buenos Aires: Biblos.
Florin, Christina, and Bengt Nilsson. 1999. 'Something in the nature of a bloodless revolution . . .' How gender relations became gender equality in Sweden in the nineteen-sixties and seventies. In *State policy and gender system in the two German states and Sweden 1945–1989*, ed. Rolf Torstendahl, 11–17. Uppsala: Opuscula historica Upsaliensia.
Frangeur, Renee. 1998. Social democrats and the woman question in Sweden: A history of contradiction. In *Women and socialism, socialism and women: Europe between the two World Wars*, eds. Helmut Gruber and Pamela Graves, 425–449. New York: Berghahn Books.
Fraser, Nancy. 1997. *Justice interruptus: Critical reflections on the "postsocialist" condition.* New York: Routledge.

Haas, Linda, and Philip Hwang. 1999. Parental leave in Sweden. In *Parental leave: Progress or pitfall*, eds. P. Moss and F. Deven, 45–68. NIDI/CBGS Publications, Vol. 35. Brussels: The Hague.

Hirdman, Yvonne. 1998. State policy and gender contracts: The Swedish experience. In *Women, work and the family in Europe*, eds. Eileen Drew, Ruth Emerek, and Evelyn Mahon, 36–46. London: Routledge.

Hobson, Barbara, and Marika Lindholm. 1997. Collective identities, women's power resources, and the making of welfare states. *Theory and Society* 26:475–508.

Hobson, Barbara, and Meiko Takahashi. 1997. The parent-worker model: Lone mothers in Sweden. In *Lone mothers in European welfare regimes: Shifting policy logics*, ed. Jane Lewis, 121–139. London: Kingsley Publishers.

Htun, Mala. 2003. *Sex and the state: Abortion, divorce, and the family Under Latin American dictatorships and democracies*. Cambridge: Cambridge University Press.

Instituto Nacíonal de Estadística y Censos [National Statistics and Census Institute]. 2001. *Censo Nacional de Población*. Buenos Aires: INDEC. Available at www.indec.mecon.ar/nuevaweb/cuadros.

Instituto Nacíonal de Estadística y Censos [National Statistics and Census Institute]. 2003. *Comunicado de Prensa. Encuesta Permanente de Hogares*. Buenos Aires: INDEC. Available at www.indec.mecon.ar/nuevaweb/cuadros.

Jelin, Elizabeth. 1998. *Pan y afectos. La transformación de las familias*. Buenos Aires: Fondo de Cultura Económica.

Leira, Alaug. 2002. *Working parents and the welfare state: Family change and policy reform in Scandinavia*. New York: Cambridge University Press.

Ministerio de Salud y Acción Social [Ministry of Health and Social Affairs]. 1995. *Estadísticas vitals—Información básica*. Buenos Aires: Ministerio de Salud.

Minow, Martha. 1990. *Making all the difference: Inclusion, exclusion and American law*. New York: Cornell University Press.

Moreno, José Luis. 2004. *Historia de la familia en el Río de la Plata [Family history in the area of the River Plate]*. Buenos Aires: Sudamericana.

Ohlander, Ann-Sofie. 1991. The invisible child? The struggle for a Social democratic family policy in Sweden, 1900–1960s. In *Maternity and gender policies: Women and rise of the European welfare states, 1880–1950*, eds. Gisela Bock and Pat Thane, 60–72. New York: Routledge.

Ramos, Silvina, Mónica Gogna, Mónica Petracci, Mariana Romero, and Dalia Szulik. 2001. *Los médicos frente a la anticoncepción y el aborto, ¿una transición ideológica? [Physicians facing contraceptives and abortion: An ideological transition?]* Buenos Aires: Centro de Estudios de Estado y Sociedad [Center for the Study of the State and Society].

Scheiwe, Kirsten. 2003. Caring and paying for children and gender inequalities: Institutional configurations in comparative perspective. *Journal of Family History* 28(1):182–198.

Scott, Joan W. 1996. *Only paradoxes to offer: French feminists and the rights of man*. Cambridge: Harvard University Press.

Statistics Sweden. 2004. *Women and men in Sweden. Facts and figures 2004*. Stockholm: Official Statistics of Sweden.

Sundström, Marianne, and Ann Zofie Duvander. 2002. Gender division of childcare and the sharing of parental leave among new parents in Sweden. *European Sociological Review* 18(4):433–447.

Swedish Government Official Reports. 1994. *Women, children and work in Sweden 1850–1993* (Report for the International Conference on Population and Development in Cairo, 1994). Stockholm: Ministry for Foreign Affairs.

Torrado, Susana. 2003. Historia de la familia en la Argentina moderna (1870–2000) [History of the family in modern Argentina (1870–2000)]. Buenos Aires: Ediciones de la Flor.

Trost, Jan, and Irene Levin. 2004. Scandinavian families. In *Handbook of world families*, eds. Bert Adams and Jan Trost, 347–363. London: Sage Publications.

Wainerman, Catalina. 2003. La reestructuración de las fronteras de género [Restructuring gender frontiers]. In *Familia, trabajo y género: Un mundo de nuevas relaciones [Family, work and gender: A world of new relations]*, ed. Catalina Wainerman. Buenos Aires: UNICEF—Fondo de Cultura Económica.

Wainerman, Catalina, and Mariana Heredia. 1991. *¿Mamá amasa la masa? Cien años de los libros de lectura de la escuela primaria [Mom kneads the dough? One hundred years of reading books for primary schools]*. Buenos Aires: Universidad de Belgrano.

Winkler, Celia. 1998. Mothering, equality and the individual: Feminist debates and welfare policies in the USA and Sweden. *Community, Work and Family* 1(2):149–166.

4 Maternalist Politics in Norway and the Islamic Republic of Iran

Shahra Razavi

INTRODUCTION

In the context of a highly authoritarian and theocratic state in Iran, women's rights have been framed within an Islamist normative discourse, not only by religious and state authorities, but also by some advocates of women's rights, dubbed "Islamist feminists" (Yeganeh and Tabari 1982; Afshar 1998).[1] Such strategies have attracted considerable controversy, almost since the immediate aftermath of the Iranian revolution in 1979. Some observers have underlined the ways in which Islamist feminist strategies have enabled women not only to derail the claim that feminism and gender equality are Western paradigms, but to break the male monopoly on interpreting Islamic texts (Hoodfar 1999). Others have been more sanguine about such strategies and their outcomes, underlining the patriarchal nature of Islamic teaching and scripture and its incompatibility with feminism and gender *equality* (Afkhami 1994; Moghissi 1994).

More recently, attention has been drawn to the maternalist thrust in Islamist women's advocacy. In post-revolutionary Iran, it is claimed, motherhood has provided a legitimate discursive space for the contestation of women's rights and the grounds for women's inclusion in the public sphere (Gheytanchi 2001). Yet questions have also been raised about the serious limits of such discursive strategies given their proclivity to reinforce traditional gender roles and undermine women's economic citizenship (Moghadam 2005).

Norway has also seen, historically at least, the presence of religious forces in politics, deeply embedded notions of gender *difference* in the political culture, and women's relatively low levels of workforce participation (at least by regional standards) prior to the 1980s. The influence of the Christian People's Party has been noted as a factor that can partly account for Norwegian "exceptionalism" within the Nordic context (Leira 1992). A related and much-remarked feature of Norwegian feminist politics lies in the strength of maternalist strands in women's mobilizations. In contrast to Sweden, maternalist concerns were strongly present in Norwegian women's mobilizations in the pre-World War Two period and had a lasting impact on its welfare policies.

This chapter compares and contrasts the ways in which women's movements in Norway and Iran have intersected with the policy establishment. Yet the two scenarios—early twentieth century Norway and present-day Iran—are not easily comparable. One is a Protestant majority country that became secularized in the twentieth century and later went on to institutionalize women's public roles and political representation within a social democratic set-up. The other is a predominantly Muslim country that witnessed the resurgence of political Islam and the fusion of religion and state in the form of a theocracy in 1980.

The label *maternalist* covers very different realities as far as women's-rights strategies are concerned. In Iran, maternalism has been used as a springboard for women's rights advocacy because this has been the only discursive opportunity on the horizon, rather than as a framing device for creating women's political identities. The juxtaposition of the two scenarios provides useful insights into the political constraints that have rendered women's-rights activism in Iran ineffective given the emasculating effects of state authoritarianism.

The Norwegian trajectory is helpful for drawing attention to the chasm that often separates state policies and the legal edifice, on one hand, and social practices, on the other. These are particularly useful insights for the Iranian context where, despite state repression and a highly patriarchal legal structure, women and young people continue to subvert many of the Islamization measures promulgated by the state. Eight years of war with Iraq (1980–1988), more than two decades of economic recession and impoverishment, and changing aspirations have propelled large numbers of women into the public domain. Iranian society and its gender order are being transformed in fundamental ways by women acting as their own change agents, through coping strategies, spontaneous movements of civil resistance, as well as sporadic collective efforts. Not only are women increasingly present in the educational establishment, in formal and informal politics, as well as through productions of art and culture, they are also gaining a toehold in the world of paid work, albeit under conditions that remain far from adequate and in the context of economic recession and mass impoverishment. Hence, what the Islamist state has attempted to achieve through its draconian laws and policies must not be mistaken for social reality, which tends to be far more diverse and on many issues, especially those pertaining to gender relations, light-years ahead of the thinking among political elites.

NORWAY: THE "WOMEN-FRIENDLY" WELFARE STATE[2]

After the 1997 elections in Norway and the coming to power of a centrist minority coalition, a controversial "cash-for-care" reform was put in place. The cash benefit had conflicting objectives, but the main stated aim of the reform was to improve parents' opportunities to provide good childcare.

This was to be achieved through three channels: first, by allowing families to give more time to care for their own children; second, by giving families real freedom of choice regarding the form of care they want for their children (unpaid, private, informal, public); and third, by facilitating a just distribution of state subsidies to families with children regardless of how child care is arranged (Ellingsaeter 2003). The left opposition was strongly opposed to the reform and argued that it would lead to serious setbacks for gender equality, both in the labour market and in the family as only mothers, especially those with limited labour market resources, would reduce their participation in paid work.

The reform came at a time when mothers' employment rates had reached an all-time high, taking the lead among Scandinavian countries, and in many ways appeared to sit uncomfortably alongside the "dual-breadwinner family" promoted in the 1980s and 1990s by expanding public provision of child care and putting in place parental leave schemes. Yet this controversial reform is also a reminder of the strong maternalist tradition that dominated social policy in the "housewife era" of 1920s and 1930s and continued to structure welfare reforms well into the 1960s and 1970s.

EARLY WELFARE MEASURES: THE 1920S AND 1930S

Maternalism was clearly present in the nationalism of the early twentieth century, through which women were galvanized in large numbers. Tensions around Norway's forced political union with Sweden after the Napoleonic wars reached the brink of war before the union was dissolved in 1905. Women's mobilization for independence transformed the organizational base of the suffrage struggle from a small association into a mass movement, which included both socialist and nonsocialist women. Many organizations that came together around Nationalism with a reformist agenda mobilized nonsocialist women as members, and many of them espoused a gender ideology celebrating women's difference, domesticity, motherhood, and moral purity. Together, reformers argued that for Norway to be truly civilized and independent, it must demonstrate a sense of responsibility for all its citizens, including women and children, and women in turn had a duty to bring up children and secure the future of the nation (Sainsbury 2001).

During the first two decades of the twentieth century, Norwegian women made remarkable gains: they won universal women's suffrage in both national and local elections in 1913; rights to paid maternity leave in 1909; and insurance rights for married women in 1915 (whereby wives received maternity benefits and free medical treatment irrespective of their labour market status). The controversial Child Welfare Act of 1915 gave equal paternal inheritance rights and the right to the father's name to children born out of wedlock (making unmarried mothers less vulnerable) and provided a small maternity benefit for single mothers. Following this, and in a similar spirit, in 1919 the Oslo City Council introduced special pensions ("mothers' pension") for all single mothers with children under the age of 15, whether divorced, widowed, unmarried, or separated; the "mothers' pension" was located outside the poor relief system and was funded through taxation (Leira 1993; Skrede 1998; Seip and Ibsen 1991).[3]

Some of these reforms raised controversies within the women's movement. While many women's groups supported some form of aid to single mothers and their children, dissention over moral issues (Who is a deserving mother?) and inheritance rights prevented a broad coalition of women's groups (Sainsbury 2001). Both proposals were actually launched by a cross-gender alliance on the left, and a strong element of control in the pension scheme betrayed the moralistic attitudes of even the Labour representatives who struggled against conservatives to include all poor single mothers in the pension scheme regardless of their marriage status. To protect the municipality from being "invaded" by single mothers, a 15-year residence requirement was imposed, and to protect the taxpayer against misuse of the scheme a system of control of clients was introduced to screen out "bad mothers" (Seip and Ibsen 1991, 43).

Both the gains and the controversies surrounding some of these reforms (especially the Child Welfare Act), also led to a more unsavoury outcome: growing rifts were appearing between different groups of women, across both ideological and class lines. The controversies revolved around a wide range of issues, including the scope and aim of suffrage, body rights, women's economic rights (protective legislation), and the rights of unmarried women. The growing dissention undercut the possibilities for forging alliances in the 1930s when, after a period of radicalization of working-class politics, the Norwegian political scene became less polarized. It was also at this time that the unfavourable economic climate of depression and high unemployment threatened married women's employment.

While in Sweden the 1930s produced cross-class alliances among women's groups in defence of married women's employment, developments in Norway took a different turn. In 1925, when Sweden introduced a law that granted women almost the same rights as men to employment in the civil service, Norway introduced the "curtail decision" on married women's employment opportunities (Sörensen and Bergqvist 2002). While this piece of legislation may not have produced a massive impact on women's employment (given the relatively small numbers of married women in employment), there is consensus in the literature that it had enormous ideological and symbolic implications in terms of supporting a male breadwinner model.

In Norway during the 1920s and 1930s, energies were being spent on the proposal for a "mother's wage"—or "child allowances," as the system was called after 1930s. There was much debate among the rank and file of the women's movement, but the majority thought that wages for mothers should make it possible for women to stay at home; it was seen as remuneration for their unpaid work. There was also near consensus that the "wage" or supplement should be paid directly to the mother, regardless of the labour market status of the father. This, apparently, was a view shared by both socialist and nonsocialist women.

The Commission set up to explore the proposal delivered its report in 1937, and the majority recommended universal allowances paid to the mothers in families with more than one child and financed through taxation. The bill did not, however, go to Parliament until after the Second World War, and the form it finally took was quite different, although it remained universal in reach. It was child centred or family centred, rather than mother centred: "the mother had receded to the background" (Seip and Ibsen 1991, 56), even though the allowance was still to be made through her. Moreover, the allowance could not be seen as a mother's wage; it was too small as a source of income and had to be supplemented by other sources of income. Nevertheless, indicative of the maternalist politics that had given rise to the idea of a "mother's wage," and the interests that it had come to create, when the Treasury proposed to modernize the allowance in 1970 by converting it into a tax rebate, it met with strong opposition and had to be dropped (Seip and Ibsen 1991).

"THE SCHIZOPHRENIC PERIOD":[4] 1945–1970

Even though the political climate became less hostile to married women's employment in the first 25 years after the Second World War, the vision underpinning public policy vis-à-vis women remained ambiguous and ambivalent, with "one policy for the mothers and another for the daughters" (Skrede 1998, 186). Social policy continued to regard women mainly as mothers and wives, but significant efforts were made to increase girls' access to education in the context of the democratization of educational opportunities. Married couples' rights to separate taxation (which favours married women's labour force participation) were introduced as early as 1959, but women's right to paid employment was seen by policy makers as an individual's "freedom of choice." In other words, the responsibility for the reconciliation between paid work and family tasks was considered to be a private matter. For much of the 1960s and 1970s, child-care provision was left mainly to private institutions and informal arrangements. Many mothers with young children entered the labour force before public child care became available, as was the case in Sweden (Skrede 1998), but in Norway, when public childcare was eventually introduced, it was conceived of as part-time and concerned with the socialization of children, rather than explicitly with reconciling women's needs for work and care.

While married women's employment in Norway lagged behind other Scandinavian countries, processes of social change driven by women as change agents ultimately seem to have led to changes in public policy in the 1980s that concentrated on granting women equal access to both education and paid employment within a highly gender-segregated labour market (Skjeie 1991). Girls' and women's access to education and to new contraceptive methods gave women both the possibility of controlling their own reproduction and aspirations for greater financial independence.

It is nevertheless important to underline the continued divisions within the women's associations, well into the 1970s, on the question of day care and mothers' employment. Some of those advocating day care continued to see it more as "relief for the home-based mother, not as a service for the employed one" (Leira 1992, 131). The issue that seems to have united women's groups and associations was that of women's right to be represented by women within politics ("group representation") based on the argument that women hold *different* values and have *different* interests—rather than making their demand on the basis of individuals' right to equal, nondiscriminatory treatment (Skjeie 1991).

There was no such clear unity among women on the issue of childcare. Indeed, Leira claims that women's agency played a minor role in the policy process around childcare in Norway. From the mid-1980s onwards, however, the increased participation of young mothers in paid employment and pressure from the new feminist movement fuelled the political demands for more supportive state policies. Such pressure ensured that the demands for a more active role on the part of the state vis-à-vis "care-and-career politics" were gradually incorporated into both party politics and state policies, witnessed by several extensions of the publicly financed parental leave period and an increase in state subsidies to promote childcare centres (Skjeie 1991, 1993).

WOMEN, THE FAMILY, AND THE STATE IN IRAN

Taking a leap from Norway to Iran, we are confronted with a radically different historical trajectory. Yet there are insights to be gained by placing the two scenarios side by side. How women's movements have intersected with mainstream politics to make claims in these two diverse contexts that nevertheless share the weight of conservative and religious forces and social sentiments provides interesting contrasts. What are the issues that have brought the different streams of the women's movement together, and those that have divided them? If class politics and socialist/nonsocialist rifts have been the main dividing lines in Norway, in Iran the modernist/traditionalist or secular/religious rifts—which may overlap, but do not neatly coincide, with social class—have been among the most divisive.

In both contexts, women's movements have struggled hard with questions of women's public and private roles in their own ranks as well with other political actors, and have at different times put forward proposals to support women in their roles as wives and mothers. However, unlike Norwegian maternalists in the inter-war period, Iran's Islamist feminists are products of the late twentieth century and its global feminist politics. While they have demanded "wages for housewives"—with far less efficacy than their Norwegian counterparts—they are far more outspoken in their advocacy of a greater public role for women, with regard to political participation in particular. And yet what made the Norwegian maternalists more effective in seeing their proposals through into the policy process was their ability to bridge divides within the women's movements, and make strategic alliances with organized labour and left-leaning parties, within a largely *democratic and less polarized political context*. This is indeed the very point made by Helga Hernes (1987) in her discussion of the "women friendly" Scandinavian states: that by moving into employment and public life, women become actors in the making of policies that affect them.

THE POLITICIZATION OF THE "WOMAN QUESTION"

Over the past century, the "woman question" has been a contested terrain within which women have been used as a symbol of "modernity" and "progress" by the secularist elites, or a hankering for cultural authenticity (increasingly identified with Islam) by their critics (Najmabadi 1991). Iran was never a formal colony, but the meddling of foreign powers—Russia and Britain prior to the Second World War and the United States thereafter—has had far-reaching ramifications for internal power struggles and competing notions of what constitutes "a good society" and of women's place within it.

The forced unveiling of women by Reza Shah in 1936, the granting of female suffrage by his son Mohammad Reza Shah (hereafter, the Shah) in 1963, the promulgation of family reform legislation in the 1960s and 1970s, and the appointment of women as judges and members of cabinet were all highly significant moments in the country's attempt to usher in an era of modernity and "progress," and to catch up with the developed world. Likewise, the forced veiling of women by the new Islamic regime in 1980, the scrapping of the Family Protection Act, the barring of women from the judiciary, and the gender segregation of public life have all been part of the attempt by the revolutionary state to reject that modernity and to search for, and reinstate, an "authentic" Islamic past, even if in practice this has amounted to a different, albeit Islamist, modernity (Adelkhah 2000).

And yet, as Najmabadi (1991) argues, there have also been continuities between these different historical moments and paradigms. Two in particular stand out. First, the modernity that was crafted by the monarchs in Iran was half-hearted: a new criminal code, for instance, was drafted in the 1930s largely on the basis of European codes, while the civil code which included family laws and inheritance rights remained Islamic (Paidar 1995, 109). In the 1960s and 1970s further reforms, more bold in many respects, were put in place and indeed the family laws of this period were the "flagship" of the state's modernization policy (Paidar 1995). However, despite consecutive legislation, the family laws still only scratched the surface of male–female inequality within the domain of marriage, family, and kinship, and "the law still concentrated on curbing the excess of male power in the family rather than fundamentally shifting it" (Paidar 1995, 157).

Underpinning these half-hearted reforms was a common acceptance of the legitimacy of the community's prerogative to set the limits of individual moral behaviour, often summarized in terms of the preservation of female "modesty" as a desirable female characteristic (Najmabadi 1991). While there were many attempts to extend the reach of the modernist state to rural and remote areas of the country, and women were targeted for literacy, health, and family planning programmes, the actual reach and capacity of the state at the local level was limited. By 1978, the rural female literacy rate was still no more than 17 percent, and the maldistribution of medical services between urban and rural areas meant that health indicators remained far below what the country's income level would have allowed. While social insurance coverage was widened in the 1970s, workers outside the formal state and private sectors were not reached, and women only comprised 4 percent of the primary insured workers (Messkoub 2005).[5] The inadequacy of redistributive mechanisms meant that for the vast majority of women in rural areas, as well as in many urban centres, it was ultimately the family and kin that offered the little social protection they ever experienced.

A second significant source of continuity between these different historical moments has been the authoritarian and repressive nature of the state, and its patronage of women's groups and movements. In some ways similar to the nationalist era in Norway, the Constitutional era[6] in Iran had witnessed a flowering of women's associations, societies, and journals, raising both nationalist demands as well as more gender-specific ones, such as female education and the modernization of motherhood, and creating the opportunity for women to organize and establish a woman's movement (Paidar 1995). The space that was created for women's activism—albeit in the context of a weak state and foreign intervention, as well as indifference and hostility on the part of the Constitutionalists to the demands of women's advocates—was soon to disappear, as Reza Khan came to power in 1921 through a military coup (and later declared himself the King of a new dynasty).

In the mid-1930s, all independent women's journals and societies were closed while at the same time the state took over the implementation of the very reforms that women activists had been calling for through their journals, such as the opening up of schools for girls, encouraging female employment in the expanding state bureaucracy, and discarding of the veil. Such authoritarian trends, and the subordination of the "woman question" into the cause of state-building, were reinforced in the subsequent era. An important factor from the 1960s onwards was the political economy of oil, which made it possible for the state to become progressively more detached from, and less accountable to, social groups and forces.[7]

The restriction of all autonomous spaces of feminist activism, and their wholesale absorption into the State/Party apparatus, was a distinct feature of this period. The Woman's Organization of Iran (WOI) became the umbrella organization advocating women's rights, dissolving and absorbing other organizations and societies that had gone before it. WOI was founded under the presidency of Princess Ashraf (the Shah's sister) and the vice presidency of the Queen Mother. While it was staffed by many dedicated women's rights advocates and feminists of upper and middle-class backgrounds, and promoted many innovative policies, very little effort was made to effectively engage with and represent the concerns of grassroots women, to bridge the deep chasm that was emerging between the official modernist orientation and policies of the centre and the realities of women's lives in many low-income households and communities. This was a constant source of criticism by the opposition (whether left, liberal, secular, or religious) directed at the state discourse and policy on women's emancipation. Much of WOI's energies instead were spent convincing the Shah of the necessity of the reforms it was proposing, and projecting a modernist image for the regime internationally.

GENDER RESTRUCTURING UNDER THE ISLAMIC REPUBLIC

The developments under the Islamic Republic have been highly contradictory. The Islamist movement that captured state power in 1979 based its grievances against the monarchy and the United States, and its own system of government (the "governance of the jurisprudence" or *velayat faqih*) on a highly patriarchal, if not misogynous, interpretation of Islam. The transition to the Islamic Republic then led to the total moralisation of the "woman question" (Najmabadi 1991) that went hand-in-hand with a powerful critique of modernist attempts at transforming society. Women who had been singled out by the opposition (both secular and Islamist) as symbols of decadence and crass consumerism under the monarchy were to bear the brunt of subsequent social and gender restructuring or "purification" (Paidar 2001). Many regressive measures were put in place, such as the forced imposition of the veil, the expulsion of women from the judiciary and higher echelons of bureaucracy, the forced segregation of schools and universities, and heightened violence against women, both domestic and public. Under these repressive conditions it became extremely difficult for women activists with a secular orientation (like their male counterparts) to be openly engaged in any political activity inside the country. Many went into exile, and those who remained were silenced.

However, both the Islamisation of the public sphere and the social mobilisations of the revolutionary era were powerful forces that propelled large numbers of low-income women from traditionalist backgrounds out of the confines of their homes and into the public arena—a development that was beyond the control of any one group or political force and with long-lasting social consequences, even if thus far their access to any form of lasting institutional power has been limited.

It is worth remembering that the revolutionary Islamist ideology was itself an amalgamation of ideas, which included demands for social justice taken from left-leaning organizations such as the Tudeh Communist Party and the Marxist guerrilla organizations, laced with a strident critique of neocolonialism, which was perceived not merely as an economic project but as a deeply cultural undertaking aimed at subverting colonized nations by depriving them of their authentic cultural heritage ("cultural imperialism"). This was also a discourse that was gendered: crass consumerism and pornography were seen as the imported tools that turned women into "sex objects" and "Western dolls" and ultimately undermined the entire nation.[8]

The aspirations for equality and social justice found their way into the Constitution of the Islamic Republic, even if they were subsequently watered down in social and economic policies. But it was the search for "cultural authenticity" in a world that was perceived to be polarized and divided into the colonizers and the colonized, reinforced through Iraq's invasion of Iran in 1980 with implicit support from Western powers, which remained at the forefront of the Islamic Republic's sense of identity for decades to come—an identity which impinged most closely and intrusively on the lives of women.

At the same time, the creation of separate male and female spaces and the donning of *hejab* (head cover) in educational establishments, offices, and indeed all public spaces allayed the fears of traditionalist families regarding women's presence in public life. Meanwhile, the revolution was experienced very differently by women who were secular upper and middle class compared to those who were from more traditionalist and working-class backgrounds (Bahramitash 2003). Iranian society is highly stratified—across region, social class, as well as the secular/religious divide, which cannot be collapsed into social class, insofar as many affluent merchants who have benefitted hugely from the economic conditions and policies over the past two decades also follow traditionalist lifestyles, and many middle-class families who have suffered great economic privation since the early 1980s are secular in orientation and lifestyle. This secular and impoverished middle class remains voiceless in current Iranian politics.

A few simple statistics can help capture the contradictions unleashed by two decades of revolutionary Islamic rule. The Islamic Republic lowered the minimum age for marriage of girls from 16 years to 9 years—a highly controversial move, which effectively sanctioned child marriage. And yet, the mean age at first marriage for women before the Revolution was 19.7 years (1976); twenty years later it had gone up to 22.4 years (Statistical Centre of Iran 2003). Female literacy, which was 35.6 percent in 1976, rose to 80 percent in 1999 (and for rural women it rose from 17.4 percent to 62.4 percent), and by 2001 more than 50 percent of university students were women (UNESCO 2004; see Figures 4.1 and 4.2).[9] Education has had a privileged position because it is viewed by the regime as a vehicle for disseminating its ideology, and school curricula were rapidly changed to beef up the Islamic content (Mehran 1991; Hoodfar 1998). Nevertheless, the social implications of the mass entry of young women into universities across the country have been potentially enormous but remain under researched.[10]

The eight-year war with Iraq, with its enormous toll on male lives, was no doubt an important factor that mobilized women into a wide range of public roles: to staff the mass kitchens and laundries that serviced the war front, to serve as nurses in military hospitals, and to take up civilian profiles in government offices (Najmabadi 1991). "Contrary to the initial assault against day-care, for instance, as an imperialist plot to separate mothers from children, good childcare centres were now projected as a social necessity so that the mother could perform her services with a peace of mind" (Najmabadi 1991 69). But the war was not the only factor. As in many other countries in the region, especially those dependent on the export of primary commodities and oil, the Iranian economy was in deep recession for much of the 1980s and 1990s. With high rates of male unemployment and underemployment and the erosion of the "family wage," the male breadwinner model has come under increasing strain. Inevitably, there has been greater recognition within the regime of the need for women to play a more active public role. The official data points to a slight increase in female economic activity rates. But the data also indicate a relative decline in women's share of the industrial labour force and a distinct increase in their share of the "service sector"—a catch-all category for all kinds of informal work which

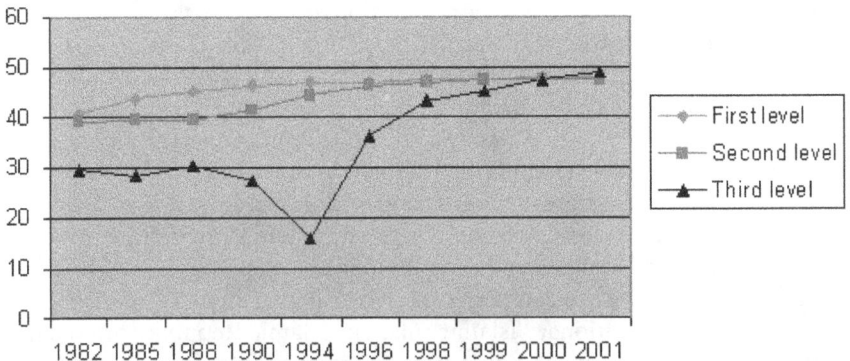

Figure 4.1 Percentages of girls' educational enrollment by level.

Source: UNESCO Institute for Statistics. Global Education Digest 2004. Montreal. http://millenniumindicators.un.org/unsd/cdb/cdb_series_xrxx.asp?series_code= 25550.

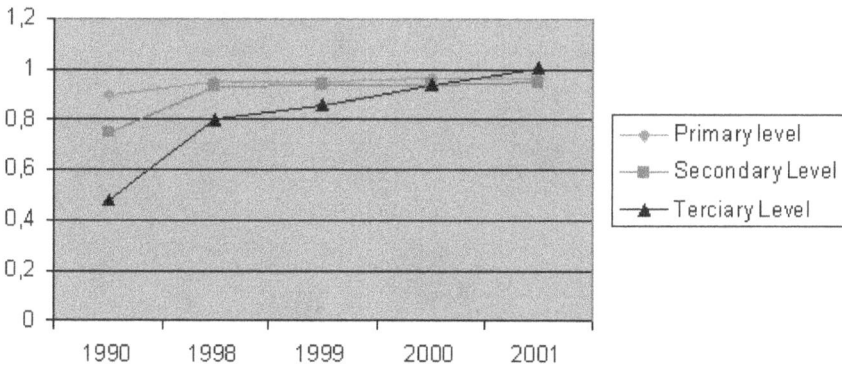

Figure 4.2 Girls to boys ratio of educational enrollment by level.

Source: Global Monitoring Report 2003/2004. *Gender and Education for All: The Leap to Equality* (Paris: UNESCO Publishing, 2003).

is likely to include many forms of badly remunerated work (see Figure 4.3 and Table 4.1).

At the same time, the expansion of primary health facilities to the remotest corners of the country, to attend to births and to mother and child health, has brought about significant improvements in maternal mortality and in infant mortality and child health (see Figure 4.4). As Hoodfar (1998) rightly remarks, in contrast to the provision of basic education, which is designed to primarily benefit the regime by cultivating its ideological vision, improving universal access to basic health services has been the main avenue through which the regime has communicated its commitment to the poor. By 1998 the government had also introduced and carried out one of the most efficient family planning programmes in the developing world; this

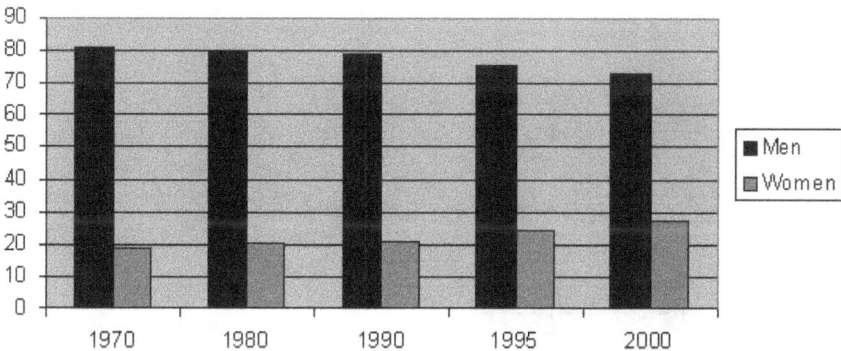

Figure 4.3 Percentages of economically active population by sex.

Source: Economically Active Population, 1950–2010, fourth edition, diskette database (Geneva: International Labour Organization, 1997).

Table 4.1 Percentages of Economically Active Population in the Islamic Republic of Iran by Industry Groups and Sex, 1970–1990 (ILO Estimates)

Industry Groups	Sex	1970	1980	1990
Agriculture, hunting, forestry	Men	77.82	73.91	72.14
	Women	22.18	26.09	27.86
Industry	Men	77.49	86.80	83.27
	Women	22.51	13.20	16.73
Manufacturing	Men		75.94	72.01
	Women		24.12	27.99
Services	Men	90.57	80.59	81.14
	Women	9.43	19.41	18.86
Total	Men	80.95	79.60	78.76
	Women	19.05	20.40	21.24

Source: *Economically Active Population, 1950–2010,* fourth edition, diskette database (Geneva: International Labour Organization, 1997).

represented yet another major ideological u-turn for a government whose ideologues were among the most strident critics of family planning (Hoodfar 1998).

The widespread availability of contraception, falling fertility rates, and women's increasing access to education (at all levels, including tertiary) are making it increasingly likely that women of different social classes will seek paid work and greater financial autonomy. Women's share of civil service

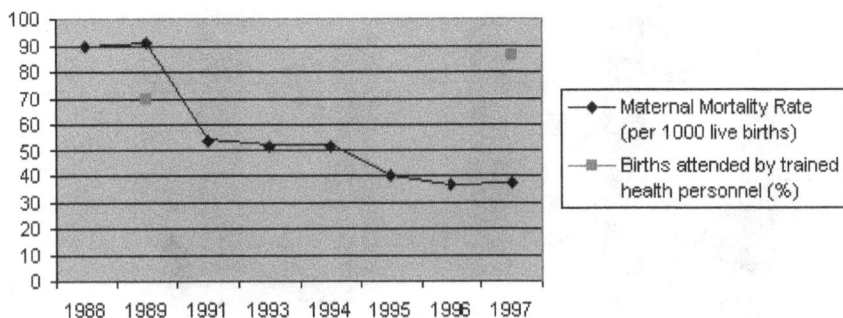

Figure 4.4 Selected women's health indicators.

Source: *Human Development Report of the Islamic Republic of Iran, 1999* (Tehran: United Nations and Islamic Republic of Iran, Plan and Budget Organization, 1999).

employment, for example, has grown from 30 percent in 1986 to 38 percent in 1996, which may be linked either to the rising educational attainment of women and/or the downgrading of the public sector and gravitation of men into the supposedly more lucrative private sector. Predictably, the jobs obtained by women are not necessarily at high levels: in the late 1990s they had a mere six percent presence in administrative and managerial positions (Moghadam 2004).

While both economic circumstances and the war with Iraq were important elements in breaking down the forced domesticity that was promulgated by the Islamic regime in its most doctrinaire years, the changing landscape of feminist politics was the other underestimated element in this evolving scenario.

ISLAMISM AND REFORMISM: CONTESTED VISIONS OF A NEW GENDER ORDER

Islamist positions vis-à-vis women's social roles and debates around the tensions between women's domestic roles (as wives and mothers) and their social responsibilities and rights in an Islamic order have been far from homogeneous. Broadly speaking, three main positions can be identified (Najmabadi 1991).

The first strand of thinking, highly influential in the early years after the revolution when women were purged from the public sector and the judiciary, is the "traditionalist" (Mir-Hosseini 1999) perspective of the conservative clerics who have had their tentacles extending deep into the key centres of power and decision making, and indeed the Spiritual Leader himself who holds vast veto powers. These men hold relatively rigid views of women's roles based on essentialised gender attributes. Women are seen as caring and nurturing, but also sexualised beings capable of inflicting chaos and confusion if not sufficiently controlled. The veil and segregation are deemed necessary to tame the dangers of female sexuality and to maintain social order and harmony. It is therefore imperative that women maintain the "hearth and the home" while the public world of politics and commerce is purified of their presence.

The second perspective, more in tune with Iranian realities, insofar as it recognized at least that women were already present in the public life, was that of the governments of Moussavi and Rafsanjani. They argued that the veil and segregation were necessary in order to facilitate women's active public presence—be it in the world of work, in schools and universities, or in collective mobilisations of various kinds, *especially* the huge "voluntary" effort that drew on women's labour for the war. This was the new revolutionary and Islamist womanhood that appealed to a younger generation of women from low-income traditionalist backgrounds who had been active in street demonstrations during the revolution and who aspired to go to the university and to work now that the public sphere had been purified. It was ultimately this perspective that became dominant (Najmabadi 1991).

A third perspective emphasized both the *rights* and the responsibilities of women. Its proponents include a diverse group of "Islamist feminists" who gained increasing prominence throughout the 1980s and 1990s, as well as some notable clerical authorities who have provided innovative readings of Islamic texts—the phenomenon of "dynamic jurisprudence" that is elaborated by Mir-Hosseini (1999).[11]

The "Islamist feminists" have emerged from the heart of the Islamic Republic. Many of them are connected through kinship and marriage networks to elite politics. In other words, they are the "insiders" who have come to accept "feminist" positions in response to some of the early doctrinaire measures adopted by the new state. Many of these women had a different understanding of Islamic womanhood and were shocked to see that the government they had supported was proceeding to put into effect such draconian measures (Yeganeh and Tabari 1982). With the secularists marginalized and silenced, they found themselves as the critics of the new government, giving voice to some of the many grievances that women felt.

A wide range of views and positions are represented by this group, with some simply acting as "cheerleaders" of the Islamic Republic, while others candidly criticize the state for failing to meet its obligations to grant women their Koranic rights (Afshar 1998). The more critical advocates of women's rights have complained through women's journals and other media that women's "voices are not heard," that they are being "pushed aside" when it comes to public appointments, that women are being used "as extras to build up the crowd to give legitimacy to the demonstrations," and have repeatedly drawn attention to women's absence and marginalisation in the centres of decision making (Afshar 1998, 42–3), even under the Presidency of Khatami. These women have advocated for divorce laws that are based on women's autonomy, choice, and economic security, and custody laws that are based on the best interests of the child and the mother.

They have defended women's public presence (after all, they themselves were operating in the public domain) and have focused their efforts on highlighting the rights that Islam accorded to women, both in their domestic roles as mothers and wives, *as well as* in the public realm as workers, political actors, and law-abiding and faithful citizens. Some of them are critical of the forced imposition of the veil (Davoudi-Mohajer 2005). Their aim is to ultimately reinstate the woman-friendly aspects of Islam, which they claim have been overlooked over the centuries by masculinist readings of Islamic holy texts.

Their defence of women's rights is not usually articulated in the language of "liberty" or "equality" (which would come too close to suggesting gender sameness) but through a careful balancing of "entitlements" and "duties," and the complementarity of gender roles. While Islamist women have had a marginal presence in the Parliament, they were nevertheless responsible for reversing many of the early Islamisation measures (on child custody, quotas for women in universities), as well as putting forward some new pieces of legislation, dubbed "maternalist" (Gheytanchi 2001; Moghadam 2005). The latter includes the much-cited *ojratolmesl* (wages for housework), which was passed by Parliament in 1992. Dismayed at how women could be easily divorced without just compensation, and using religious idiom, Islamist women activists argued that "in Islamic tradition wives have no duties to their husbands beyond being faithful, and are not required to work in their husbands' homes, to the extent that women are not even obliged to breastfeed their children without payment from their husbands. Therefore, since all women do in fact work in their husbands' homes, they are entitled to the fruit of their labour" (Hoodfar 2000, 311). Although the law may have given women some additional benefits and increased the cost of divorce to men, it remained a toothless piece of legislation with no follow-up and no public funds allocated to it. Moreover, this entitlement is due only to wives who are deemed to be not at fault in the case of divorce (Moghadam 2006).

Further measures were to make the payment of women's dowry (*mahr*) in cases of divorce payable in real terms (that is, adjusted for inflation), finally ratified by the Parliament in 1996, and including in every marriage contract the stipulation of certain conditions and rights by wives, which effectively shifts the burden to the groom who must then negotiate to remove the clauses with which he disagrees (Hoodfar 1999).

These advocates have been able to speak to those in power by being anchored in Islamic idiom and law, which gives them the necessary legitimacy and "insider" status to be policy advocates for women. But it is also likely that they resonate with women from lower income and traditionalist backgrounds in a way that secular feminists may never have done. "They expose injustices suffered by women in the name of creating a 'just' Islamic society, and invite the public to be the judge. The language used is often simple, marked by everyday religious concepts and metaphors, and usually in the context of real life stories" (Hoodfar 1999, 32–3). But such discursive strategies can act as a double-edged sword: in a society that has become so sharply divided on the role of religion in politics, the very use of Islamic idiom is likely to alienate many younger women who have come to hold different views about Islam and its role in society, as well as many secular feminists who are reluctant to use the Islamist discourse (Moghadam 2006).

These divisions are reflected in feminist politics. Even when Islamist advocates have struggled for issues such as women's rights with respect to divorce or child custody, alliances with secular feminists are rare. For Islamist women's rights advocates operating within the highly constrained and repressive political climate in Iran, such an overture would risk delegitimation. But the distrust and suspicion has been mutual, as many secular feminists, especially in the diaspora, continue to find the label "Islamic feminism" a contradiction in terms.

However, a different politics seems to be unfolding in the pages of a much-cited women's magazine published in Iran, *Zanan* (Women). *Zanan* has broken new ground by publishing the writings of women's rights advocates from very diverse political and ideological persuasions. Through its editorials it has introduced individual woman's "autonomy" and "choice" into the Islamic discourse on women's rights, thereby "opening up new discursive space for conversations between secular and Islamic feminists in Iran" (Najmabadi 1999, 65).[12] Some observers see this as the dawn of a new kind of "pragmatic feminism" in Iran, and argue vehemently for feminists of different persuasions to overcome their authoritarianism and sectarianism and to build bridges, make alliances, and engage in issue-oriented coalition politics (Paidar 2001).

COMPARATIVE INSIGHTS

The two countries analysed in this chapter do not provide the basis for a comparative study in the strict sense of the term: the economic, political, and social scenarios are too diverse to allow such an endeavour. I have therefore used the term "comparative" in a much looser sense, to see what insights can be gleaned from one context for the other.

The first point that stands out is the insidious ways in which state authoritarianism weakens women's movements and their capacities to articulate and debate gender interests. With the exception of a few short democratic interludes, the Iranian state, in its different authoritarian incarnations, has seriously undermined women's efforts in coming together through autonomous organisational forms. In the Constitutional era—parallel to the turn-of-the-century mobilisations of women's groups in Norway—women's groups were able to flourish, and a wide spectrum of positions coexisted and conversed side by side inside women's journals and societies. While in Norway these diverse positions were able to join forces (despite their differences) and push through certain reforms, in Iran pluralism was cut short by the heavy hand of the modernising state and subsumed into a single state-directed project of "women's emancipation"—a development that has seen its mirror image under the Islamic Republic. We catch only a glimpse of such exclusionary dichotomies in Norway in the 1920s, when the Labour Party briefly joined the Communist International and abandoned reformism, and Labour women in turn abandoned all efforts at alliance building with bourgeois women's groups.

A second striking contrast that emerges is the emancipatory potential of women's labour force participation and the ways in which it has enabled and facilitated political agitation on the part of women (via political parties) for social policy transformations. It is on this basis that Moghadam (2005) highlights the strategic importance of women's economic citizenship in the Iranian and broader regional context.

It would be foolish to deny the need for public policies that can generate decent employment conditions for women (as well as for men), especially in the Iranian context where a new generation of highly educated women are entering the labour force each year but finding few sustainable employment options. The incapacity to generate decent employment is indeed a conundrum that many countries face—low rates of economic growth and "jobless growth" being problems that currently afflict a wide range of countries.

However, the urgency of economic policies that can generate growth and employment should not detract from the equally urgent and strategic task of rendering state–society relations more democratic, and the state less prone to patronizing autonomous women's groups and movements. It is here that the strength of the democratic struggles in which the women's movement has engaged in Iran needs to be located. In the absence of a political space that allows public discussion around issues of gender equality, even if economic conditions were to facilitate women's mass entry into the labour force, it would be very difficult for women's interests (with respect to wages, working conditions, and social welfare) to find their way into state and corporate agendas.

In effect, labour market entry became a gender-enabling process in Norway precisely because there was a democratic institutional space to allow women's interests to find their way into the policy process, albeit at the cost of institutionalising those interests within state and corporatist bureaucracies. In the absence of a wider democratic space, however, labour force entry may not only fail to translate into an emancipatory movement, but it can be experienced very negatively by women themselves as yet another demand on their already overstretched time and energy. Hence, for the mass entry of women into the workforce to become an enabling one for gender equality, a democratic civil society is a necessary precondition. It is for this precise reason that feminist movements have so consistently insisted on the need for autonomous spaces for women's organizations and movements: "only in this way can women's interests find a separate, distinct and recognized articulation, and respond to the wishes and concerns of a female constituency" (Molyneux 1996, 46).

The third insight that emerges from the analysis is the complexities of maternalist ideologies, and the different forms they can take. Maternalism provides a useful conceptual lens through which to illuminate the ways in which women in very different contexts use the language of motherhood to legitimize their political activism and to advocate for better conditions and social support for women. Although maternalist politics has had contradictory and different outcomes in different countries, this form of claims-making shares an implicit acceptance that the rights women were claiming should come in return for certain pre-given responsibilities tied to traditionally ascribed gender roles. An equal rights agenda, by contrast, tends to be less closely tied to the performance of responsibilities, or, even if there is an implicit acceptance of certain responsibilities, these are not often tied to given gender roles. This acceptance of traditional gender roles has rendered maternalist movements and demands controversial. The protean character of maternalism also lent itself to subtle shifts from "a vision of motherhood in the service of women to one serving the needs of paternalists" (Koven and Michel 1993, 5).

In the case of Norway, with the coming together of a strong mass movement of women, maternalist discourses were able to register significant gains in the first two decades of the twentieth century: the right to maternity leave as part of the health insurance act; insurance rights for married women irrespective of their labour market status; and equal paternal inheritance rights and the right to the father's name to children born out of wedlock. This was perhaps the most "radical" moment of maternalism, to use Koven and Michel's (1993) distinction between radical and conservative varieties. There were, however, certain costs attached to this particular strategy and ideology, and these became particularly evident in the 1930s, when legislation was passed to curtail married women's employment. The privileging of gender difference, and women's roles as mothers and carers, opened certain doors but also closed others. Hobson (2006) describes such mechanisms as boundary making: certain forms of claims-making are recognized while others are shaded out.

In the case of Iran, the gains are clearly more elusive and could be more accurately described as "damage control." This is in part due to the fact that those who have been advocating maternalist policies have not had the connections to, and support of, organized movements of women—as maternalists in Norway did. But they have also had to operate in an environment that is hostile to gender equality, with different organs of the revolutionary state taking it upon themselves to restructure the social and gender order.

However, an appreciation of what maternalist politics was about in Norway, particularly in the 1920s and 1930s, also serves to underline the thoroughly modern character of Islamist women's movements in Iran. Norwegian maternalism was centrally about claiming rights for women as mothers in return for certain predetermined duties that women had to perform (as mothers, wives, and careerpersons). While Islamist feminists may have struggled for wages for housework and protective labour legislation, they have been particularly adamant about the need for women to assume more visible public roles. While this reflects the current state of feminist politics globally (and the fact that these women are not immune to global discourses of women's rights), it is also in response to the attempts that the traditionalists have made time and again to push women into the domestic sphere. Maternalism, therefore, does not seem to capture the totality of Islamist feminist positions, which are also about claiming for women a larger and more equal public presence and role. Islamist feminist politics and strategies have in fact had a more extensive reach than the "maternalism" label conveys. In other words, women's-rights activists have used maternalist arguments and Islamic law as springboards for their advocacy because these have been the only legitimate discursive opportunities available to them.

The fourth, and a critically important, insight is about processes of social change and how they can shape expectations and demands, even over a very short space of time. The sequence of developments in Norway, whereby social change was proceeding at a much faster pace than policy, is one that reverberates very strongly with the Iranian scenario. Not only do we see "one policy for the mothers and another for the daughters" (Skrede 1998, 186) in present-day Iran, a remark that was made in relation to Norwegian social policy in the 1940s, but it is equally true that women are the main change agents while policy seems to be lagging behind years, if not decades. This becomes evident in the way women have seized and run with the few openings that are available to them, despite the patriarchal legal edifice. As one-observer notes: "The Islamic Republic has not opened the gates. Women are jumping over the fences" (Moghissi 1994, 183).

Finally, while feminist politics in Norway in the 1980s may have been shaped by developments in neighbouring Sweden, it is striking how the "woman question" in Iran has been contested in the twentieth century, either explicitly or implicitly, in relation to what is widely perceived as *a* hegemonic "Western" model—whether in the attempt by modernizers to emulate it, or by their critics to reject it and search for an "authentic" model of womanhood in "tradition" and Islam. As Kandiyoti (1991) aptly remarks, neither of these can be understood without a consideration of the global context within which the modern nation-state operates.

It is at once inescapably clear that the question of national identity and how it impinges on women's comportment and autonomy has become so central to the political debate in Iran, especially over the past twenty-five years, that questions of redistribution and accumulation have receded to the background. This is indeed one of the blind spots in the ongoing debates about democracy and reform that the reformist movement has been able to thrust onto the political agenda, and women's rights advocates are not immune to it. Hard-liners, reformists, and feminists are debating democracy, citizenship, and the role of religion in politics with scant attention to questions of economic strategy, redistribution, and the role of social policy— the questions that were central to the construction of social democracy in Norway and Sweden. It is not surprising, therefore, that feminist demands for employment and child care that were central concerns in Norway and Sweden are at best marginal to feminist debates in contemporary Iran.

One of the reasons for the defeat of the reformists in the 2005 presidential elections was precisely their failure to present a credible agenda for combating economic and social deprivation and respond to popular concerns and anxieties about increasing inequality, poverty, and insecurity. The more "fundamentalist" elements in the regime were able to exploit these anxieties with their populist revolutionary rhetoric. Whether the reform movement, and the feminist currents within it, will be able to recuperate from this defeat and present a programmatic alternative to the old and vacuous revolutionary slogans of social justice that are premised on a deeply patriarchal gender order, remains to be seen.

APPENDIX:TABLES AND FIGURES ON WOMEN IN THE ISLAMIC REPUBLIC OF IRAN

NOTES

1. There is no consensus in the literature on whether Islamist advocates of women's rights can be called "feminist."
2. It is important to add the proviso that this is an outsider's reading of Norwegian history, based on selected secondary literature.
3. This support system served as a model for other municipalities and became the model for national legislation later in the 1960s (Skrede 1998).
4. This is the phrase used by Kari Skrede (1998) to describe the period.
5. A larger proportion of women would have been beneficiaries as wives and daughters of male breadwinners who were primary members of the insurance programme.
6. The movement for Constitutionalism, which gathered force around the turn of the century (1890–1910), embodied demands for justice, state accountability, and a constitution to replace absolutism.
7. There is a vast literature on "rentier states" for oil-based economies; for an early analysis of "petrolic despotism" in the case of Iran, see Katouzian (1981).
8. Ali Shariati, who was impressed with the Algerian Liberation Movement and other Third World liberation struggles, and who was familiar with Western philosophy and existentialism in particular, was the most influential thinker of this genre, modernising and radicalizing Islam for a younger generation of Iranian women and men in the 1960s and 1970s. His thinking was deeply influenced by the writings of Frantz Fanon. He died in exile in 1977, two years before the Iranian revolution.
9. It is important to point out, however, that *real* social spending *per capita* has gone down since the Revolution due to the decline in GDP in the 1980s, spiralling inflation, and high population growth (see Messkoub, 2005, for data).
10. The competitive nature of the examination for university entrance (the *concours*) often means that applicants have to accept offers from universities even in far-flung corners of the country away from their families and homes. The implications in terms of housing arrangements (both dormitories provided by universities, as well as private arrangements whereby groups of young girls live communally) and lack of parental supervision are noticeable features of urban life in smaller Iranian towns and cities.
11. The proponents of this alternative reading, who are clerical authorities, argue that the rules of *shari'a* with respect to gender concerns are time and place sensitive—hence the label "dynamic jurisprudence." "We believe that since the subject [women's situation] has changed, the framework of civil laws must change too. Our current civil laws are in line with the traditional society of the past, whereas these civil laws should be in line with contemporary realities and relations in our own society" (Ayatollah Yusef Sane'I, cited in Mir-Hosseini 1999, 160). These proponents are censored by the regime.
12. For an elaboration of the multiple ways in which *Zanan's* interpretive work has broken new grounds in Islamic approaches to women's rights, see Najmabadi (1999) and Paidar (2001).

REFERENCES

Adelkhah, Fariba. 2000. *Being modern in Iran.* New York: Columbia University Press.

Afkhami, Mahnaz. 1994. Women in post-revolutionary Iran: A feminist perspective. In *In the eye of the storm: Women in post-revolutionary Iran*, eds. Mahnaz Afkhami and Erika Friedl, 5–18. London: I. B. Tauris.

Afshar, Haleh. 1998. *Islam and feminisms: An Iranian case study.* (Women's studies at York). Basingstoke: Macmillan Press.

Bahramitash, Roxana. 2003. Myths and realities of the impact of political Islam on women. *Development in Practice* 14(4):508–20.

Davudi-Mohajer, Fariba. 2005. *Hich E'teqadi be Hejabe Ejbari Nadaram [I Do Not Believe in Forced Veiling]*. http://www.emrouz.info (accessed March 8, 2005).

Ellingsaeter, Anne Lise. 2003. The complexity of family policy reform: The case of Norway. *European Societies* 5(4):419–42.

Gheytanchi, Elham. 2001. Civil society in Iran: Politics of motherhood and the public sphere. *International Sociology* 16(4):557–76.

Hernes, Helga Maria. 1987. *Welfare states and woman power: Essays in state feminism.* Oslo: Norwegian University Press.

Hobson, Barbara. 2006. The evolution of the women friendly state: Opportunities and constraints in the Swedish welfare state. In *Gender and social policy in a global context: Uncovering the gendered structure of "the social,"* eds. Shahra Razavi and Shireen Hassim, 151–172. Basingstoke: Palgrave.

Hoodfar, Homa. 1998. *Volunteer health workers in Iran as social activists: Can "governmental non-governmental organizations" be agents of democratisation?* (Occasional Paper No. 10). Women Living Under Muslim Law (WLUML).

Hoodfar, Homa 1999. *The women's movement in Iran: Women at the crossroads of secularization and Islamization.* (The Women's Movement Series No.1). Grabels Cedex, France: Women Living Under Muslim Law (WLUML).

Hoodfar, Homa. 2000. Iranian women at the intersection of citizenship and the family code: The perils of Islamic criteria. In *Gender and Citizenship in the Middle East*, ed. Suad Joseph. New York: Syracuse University Press.

Kandiyoti, Deniz. 1991. Introduction. In *Women, Islam and the state*, ed. Deniz Kandiyoti, 1–21. Philadelphia: Temple University Press.

Katouzian, Homa. 1981. *The political economy of modern Iran: Despotism and pseudo-modernism.* New York: New York University Press.

Koven, Seth, and Sonya Michel. 1993. Introduction: Motherworlds. In *Mothers of a new world: Maternalist politics and the origins of welfare states*, eds. Seth Koven and Sonya Michel, 1–42. New York: Routledge.

Leira, Arnlaug. 1992. *Welfare states and working mothers: The Scandinavian experience.* Cambridge: Cambridge University Press.

Leira, Arnlaug. 1993. The "woman-friendly" welfare state? The case of Norway and Sweden. In *Women and Social Policies in Europe*, ed. Jane Lewis, 49–71. Aldershot: Edward Elgar.

Mehran, Golnar. 1991. The creation of the new Muslim woman: Female education in the Islamic Republic of Iran. *Comparative Education Review* 35(2):194–210.

Messkoub, Mahmood. 2005. Constitutionalism, modernization, and Islamization: The political economy of social policy in Iran. In *Social policy in the Middle East and North Africa*, eds. Massoud Karshenas and Valentine Moghadan, 190–220. Basingstoke: Palgrave.

Mir-Hosseini, Ziba. 1999. *Islam and gender: The religious debate in contemporary Iran.* New Jersey: Princeton University Press.

Moghadam, Valentine. 2004. *Women's livelihood and entitlements in the Middle East: What difference has the neoliberal policy turn made?* (Background paper for UNRISD Report, *Gender Equality: Striving for Justice in an Unequal World*). Geneva: United Nations Research Institute for Social Development.

Moghadam, Valentine. 2005. Gender and social policy: Family law and women's economic citizenship in the Middle East. In *Social policy in the Middle East and North Africa*, eds. Massoud Karshenas and Valentine Moghadan, 221–253. Basingstoke: Palgrave.

Moghadam, Valentine. 2006. Maternalist policies versus women's economic citizenship? Gendered social policy in Iran. In Gender and Social Policy in a Global Context: Uncovering the Gendered Structure of "the Social." eds. Shahra Razavi and Shireen Hassim, 87–108. Basingstoke: Palgrave.

Moghissi, Haideh. 1994. *Populism and feminism in Iran: Women's struggle in a male-defined revolutionary movement*. London: Macmillan Press.

Molyneux, Maxine. 1996. *State, gender and institutional change in Cuba's "special period": The Federacion de Mujeres Cubanas* (Research Paper No. 43). London: Institute of Latin American Studies.

Najmabadi, Afsaneh. 1991. Hazards of modernity and morality: Women, state and ideology in contemporary Iran. In *Women, Islam and the State*, ed. Deniz Kandiyoti, 48–76. Philadelphia: Temple University Press.

Najmabadi, Afsaneh. 1999. Feminism in an Islamic republic: Years of hardship, years of growth. In *Islam, Gender, and Social Change*, eds. Yvonne Yazbeck Haddad and John Esposito, 50–84. Oxford: Oxford University Press.

Paidar, Parvin. 1995. *Women and the political process in twentieth-century Iran*. Cambridge: Cambridge University Press.

Paidar, Parvin. 2001. Gender of democracy. The encounter between feminism and reformism in contemporary Iran. Programme on Governance, Democracy and Human Rights, Paper No.6, Geneva: United Nations Research Institute for Social Development.

Sainsbury, Diane. 2001. Gender and the making of welfare states: Norway and Sweden. *Social Politics* 8(Spring):113–43.

Seip, Anne-Lise, and Hilde Ibsen. 1991. Family welfare, which policy? Norway's road to child allowances. In *Maternity and gender policies. Women and the rise of the European welfare states, 1880s–1950s*, eds. Gisela Bock and Pat Thane, 40–59. London: Routledge.

Skjeie, Hege. 1991. The uneven advance of Norwegian women. *New Left Review* 187:79–102.

Skjeie, Hege. 1993. Ending the male political hegemony: The Norwegian experience. In *Gender and party politic*, eds. Joni Lovenduski and Pippa Norris, 231–262. London: Sage Publications.

Skrede, Kari. 1998. Shaping gender equality—The role of the state: Norwegian experiences, present policies and future challenges. In *Comparing Social Welfare Systems in Nordic Europe and France*, Vol. 4, 169–199, Copenhagen Conference. Paris: MIRE-DREES.

Sörensen, Kerstin, & Christina Bergqvist. 2002. Gender and the social democratic welfare regime: A comparison of gender-equality friendly policies in Sweden and Norway. *Work Life in Transition*, Vol. 5. Arbetslivsinstitutet: National Institute for Working Life.

Statistical Centre of Iran. 2003. Population Statistics. http://www.sci.org.ir (accessed July 1, 2005).

UNESCO. 2004. *EFA monitoring report: The quality imperative*. Paris: United Nations Educational, Scientific and Cultural Organization.

Yeganeh, Nahid, and Azar Tabari. 1982. *In the shadow of Islam*. London: Zed Press.

5 Challenging the Male Norm of Employment
Evidence from Sweden, Norway, and Hungary

Beata Nagy

INTRODUCTION

This chapter looks at some of the characteristics of women's and men's employment in Sweden, Norway, and Hungary to investigate the meaning of the "male norm of employment" and to assess some of the tools available for challenging it. Both Norway and Sweden have taken a series of policy initiatives in the last decades which, at different levels, attempt to support women in the labour force and redistribute domestic and reproductive responsibilities as part of this process. This chapter reviews some such initiatives in an attempt to measure the extent of their effectiveness. Reflecting on some apparent limitations of these initiatives to gender equality goals—as well as on some successes—and placing these alongside recent Hungarian initiatives to promote fertility through supporting women's dual roles, the chapter draws out some conclusions on the contexts of policy processes and the "enabling conditions" for challenging the male norm employment model.

The expression "male norm" of employment is increasingly used in sociological, feminist, and policy literature without any reference to theoretical frameworks. In this chapter, the term refers to a model of work and life arrangements in which wage-earning activity is expected to be full-time and lifelong, interrupted at the most for a short time for childbirth. The model demands a high level of commitment to work, and a personal life relegated to the background. It also tacitly endows women with responsibilities relating to child care. Women are expected to work in a flexible way in order to reconcile family and employment, while men are expected to participate only minimally in reproductive work. In the workplace, women are nevertheless required to work as if they were men, according to "male" rules and expectations (Wajcman 1998). Cockburn (1991) suggests that men have an active interest in maintaining this model of employment and often resist attempts to change it. Women are required not to change the model, but to be assimilated into it because assimilation "[is] the price of acceptance. You can't be equal *and* different" (Cockburn 1991, 13). It remains the case throughout the world that "the most powerful organizational positions are almost entirely occupied by men, with the exception of the occasional bio-logical female who acts as a social man." (Acker 1990, 139) Women who do not want to or cannot follow this employment pattern, and who take time out of employment to raise children, often find themselves on the "mommy track" (Hochschild 2001) on their return to work, where career prospects are significantly smaller, where opportunities for accessing responsibility at work are reduced, and where they are treated in distinct ways.

In Hungary, this male model of employment remains rarely questioned and is very much the norm. Women find few opportunities to deviate from this model, and deviation carries its own risks. Work performance is evalu-ated on male terms, in which work is expected to take priority over private life, and women's special experience—due to their special responsibilities in reproductive and domestic work—is barely taken into account. Both women and men are expected to work life-long and full time, with no concessions to family and domestic responsibilities.

As in other socialist countries, in Hungary much lip service has been paid to women's issues, and women's full-time labour market participation was considered the major indicator of emancipation (Gal and Kligman 2000). The ideology of socialist emancipation developed a gender regime based on Engels's theory of women's slavery within the household from which they should be liberated through socialising all reproductive duties (Engels 1982). Particularly in the first period of socialism, the emphasis was on the fundamental sameness of the genders, and attempts at women's emancipa-tion were focused on assimilation to the masculine norm. In the second period of socialism, gender differences were also recognised and acted upon, but in terms which left women's responsibility for social reproduction intact, and with the intention of "helping" women achieve the male norm, rather than challenging it. Combinations of paid work and child care became more widely accepted than in the earlier period, and the welfare regime around reproduction—paid maternity leave, and day-care facilities—was extended. Gradually, large numbers of women entered the labour market and worked full time, but the issue of equal divisions of household labour remained totally silent. Asztalos-Morell (1999) comments cryptically that "It was more tolerated under state socialism in Hungary to criticise the system, than to criticise men's power over women" (p. 363).

Hungary arrived at nearly balanced participation in the labour market between men and women some years ago, and on the face of it these par-ticipation rates appear similar to those achieved in Sweden and Norway. However, the different trajectories to these rates have produced significant differences in patterns of employment. A notable example is the widespread existence of part-time work opportunities in Sweden and Norway, in which women are heavily concentrated. In Hungary, by contrast, part-time work barely exists as an employment option for women or men, and the share of those employed in any kind of flexible or non-full-time situations is insignificant.

This chapter proceeds by investigating the meaning of this situation more closely, and assessing how far the mechanism of part-time work has influenced the "male norm" employment scenario.

PART-TIME WORK

Although employment rates of men and women appear at first sight to be almost balanced in Hungary as well as in Sweden and Norway—with women making up 44 to 48 percent of the labour force in all three countries—a closer examination of overall employment rates, disaggregated by gender, reveals an obvious and stable gender gap of 12.5 percent in postsocialist Hungary, much larger than the gap in either Sweden or Norway (see Table 5.1).

At the same time, part-time employment rates are much higher in Norway and Sweden than in Hungary for both women and men, but most significantly so for women. In Hungary in 2003, for example, only about 2 percent of men's work was part-time, and around 5 percent of women's work, while in Sweden over 20 percent and in Norway over 30 percent of women's employment was part time (see Table 5.2).

The low levels of part-time employment in Hungary are reflected in many other post-socialist countries—in the Czech Republic women's part-time employment is 5.3 percent; in the Slovak Republic it is 3.6 percent[2] (OECD 2004, 310)—and there are several reasons for it. Financial burdens for employers relating to social and health security benefits have historically been the same for part-time and full-time employees, making part-time

Table 5.1 Employment/Population Ratio (Persons Aged 15–64 Years, Percentages)

Men	1990	1999	2000	2001	2002	2003	2004	2005
Hungary	...	62.6	62.7	63.0	62.9	63.4	63.1	63.1
Norway	78.6	82.1	81.7	81.0	80.2	78.8	78.4	78.3
Sweden	85.2	74.8	76.1	77.0	76.3	75.6	75.0	...
Women	*1990*	*1999*	*2000*	*2001*	*2002*	*2003*	*2004*	*2005*
Hungary	...	49.0	49.6	49.8	49.8	50.9	50.7	51.0
Norway	67.2	73.8	74.0	73.8	73.9	72.9	72.7	72.0
Sweden	81.0	70.9	72.2	73.5	73.4	72.8	71.8	...

Sources: OECD Employment Outlook 2004, Table B, p. 294; and OECD Employment Outlook 2006, Statistical Annex, Table B, pp. 249–250.

Table 5.2 Part-Time[1] Employment as a Proportion of Employment

	Men					Women				
	1990	*2000*	*2001*	*2002*	*2003*	*1990*	*2000*	*2001*	*2002*	*2003*
Hungary	...	1.7	1.7	1.7	2.1	...	4.7	4.0	4.3	5.1
Norway	6.9	8.7	9.1	9.2	9.9	39.8	33.4	32.7	33.4	33.4
Sweden	5.3	7.3	7.3	7.5	7.9	24.5	21.4	21.0	20.6	20.6

Source: OECD Employment Outlook 2004, Table E, p. 311.

workers considerably more expensive for employers. Part-time work is generally seen as a substantial privilege in Hungarian companies as a result of these costs (Nagy 2004). Meanwhile, in the context of low wage rates generally in Hungary by European standards, few employees can afford the wage cut implied by part-time work.

Low levels of part-time opportunities are accompanied by an absence of flexible working arrangements in the labour market in general. Working hours are very rigid, and most employers believe employees would misuse flexibility, resulting in under-performance. These factors together mean that labour force participation requires assimilation to a relatively rigid version of the male norm, leaving women—and men—little room for manoeuvre in integrating or rebalancing work and domestic lives.

The government, however, has become interested in promoting part-time work recently, as it is seen as offering potential solutions both to working-age economic inactivity—which grew dramatically to some 40 percent after the transition in the 1990s—, and to closing the labour force gender gap. Hungarian employment policy now treats female employment again as an economic and social priority, particularly regarding young mothers' return to the labour market. In 2004, employers' payment obligations for part-time workers were reduced, and the lump-sum health-care contribution was abolished for women part-time workers in receipt of child-care allowance, child benefit, or caregivers' fees. Recipients of the child-care allowance can now take on part-time employment after the child turns one year old, and since January 2005, employers hiring persons returning from parental leaves have been entitled to a 50 percent reduction on social security contributions (Implementation 2005, 10).

Although it remains too early to evaluate the outcomes of these new initiatives, the stage is clearly set for a substantial rise in part-time employment opportunities. The pertinent gender-equality question thus becomes: can a part-time work model in Hungary challenge the relatively rigid male norm of employment? What lessons do the Swedish and Norwegian experiences of high levels of part-time work offer us?

THE SWEDISH AND NORWEGIAN EXPERIENCES

The Nature of Part-time Work

In Sweden and Norway, part-time employment significantly contributed to the spread of female employment up until around 1990, when part-time opportunities were generally exploited by former housewives and young mothers. As shown in Table 5.2, part-time employment rates have remained steady since the millennium, and relatively high in both countries, remaining for men at around 9 and 7.5 percent in Norway and Sweden, respectively, and over 30 percent and 20 percent, respectively, for women. However, Table 5.3 suggests that the characteristics of part-time workers began to change during the 1990s, with young people starting to form the majority of part-time workers, and the significance of full-time work increasing among mothers.

This suggestion is confirmed by later accounts: according to the Swedish Labour Force Survey 2003, 62.5 percent of employed men and 82.4 percent of employed women under 20 worked part-time, whereas this ratio is much lower for the whole 16–64 age group (10.5 percent and 39.9 percent, respectively; SCB 2003, 23). In Norway, similar trends are evident: it is now young men and overwhelmingly young women who work part-time (see Figure 5.1).

Short and Long Part-time

This scenario is somewhat complicated by a distinction in Swedish literature and statistics into short and long part-time work. Short part-time means between 1 and 19 hours a week, while long part-time means between 20 and 34 hours a week. Full-time work consequently means at least 35 hours a week. While 51 percent of women and 73 percent of men between 20 and 64 years work full time, nearly all part-time workers fall into the "long part-time" category: only four percent of women and two percent of

Table 5.3 Women's/Men's Part-Time Employment by Age 1996, Sweden

Age Cohort	Proportion (%) Among All Employed Men	Proportion (%) Among All Employed Women
16–24	24.5	51.4
25–54	5.6	35.7
55–64	18.9	47.5
All (16–64)	9.3	38.9

Source: Xu, 1997, p. 20.

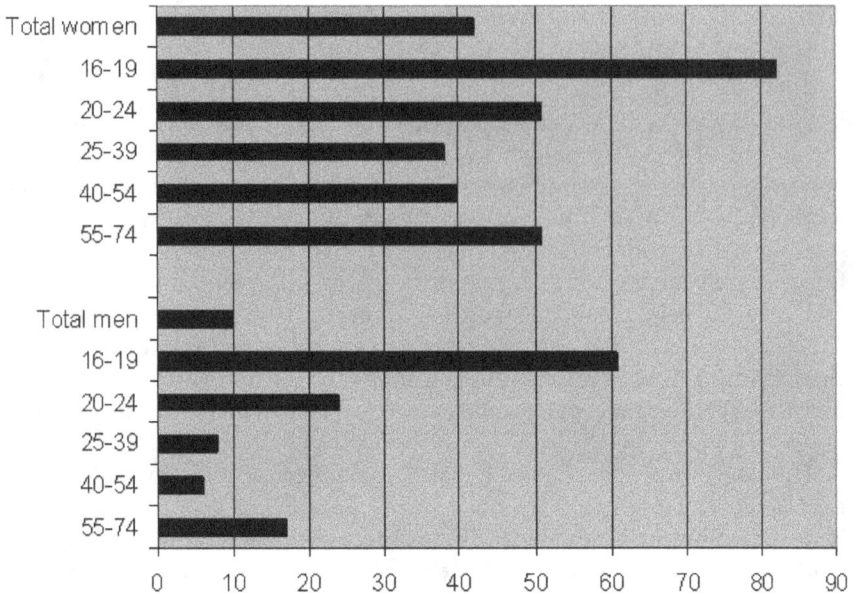

Figure 5.1 Part-time employees by age and gender, 2002 (%).

Source: Håland and Daugstad 2002.

men aged 20–64 work short part-time (SCB 2004, 43). In Norwegian surveys, a further different classification is used: part-time work means 1–36 hours a week, with the exception of persons working 32–36 hours who classify themselves as full-time employed. Full-time work is 37 hours and over, together with these cases (SN/AKU 2004). OECD data, on the other hand, reflects the categorisation of part-time work as meaning 1–29 hours a week. Stark and Regnér (2002) point out that this has in some cases led to exaggerations of the differences between countries in the incidence of part-time work.

Nevertheless, what remains clear is that long part-time jobs are dominant in Sweden and Norway, and especially significant for women. Although there persists a widespread belief that the public sector is the main provider of these jobs, recent Swedish data suggests that the private sector is in reality an equally significant part-time work employer for women (see Table 5.4).[3] Table 5.4 shows that the public sector of local government and state employment provided 338,400 short and long part-time jobs to women in 2003, while the private sector provided 322,500.

Based on calculations derived from Table 5.4, Table 5.5 clearly demonstrates the outstanding significance of long part-time work for women, while also suggesting that if the OECD definition of part-time work were used—that is, with an upper limit of 30 hours per week, the high ratio of Swedish female part-time workers could substantially diminish.

Table 5.4 Employed Women Distributed by Sector and Working Time per Week (1,000 Persons), Sweden[4]

Women	State Employment	Local Government, County Council	Private	Total
1–19 hours (short part-time)	2.7	37.9	85.9	126.7
20–34 hours (long part-time)	16.1	281.7	236.6	534.6
35–39 hours (full-time)	10.2	154.0	178.4	342.7
40 hours (full-time)	82.7	391.1	454.0	928.1
Total	111.6	864.6	954.9	1,932.1

Source: SCB, 2003, Table 10.

Men's employment data (Table 5.6) show that the overwhelming majority (90 percent) of male employees works full time (i.e., 35 hours or above) and usually work more than 40 hours a week, and most work in the private sector (81.3 percent). The public sector plays an insignificant role in men's employment, and both sectors are only marginal providers of male part-time jobs.

Thus women and men in Sweden, despite public policy designed to enable women to enter the workforce on an equal basis with men, nevertheless appear to have different work patterns, with the public sector and private sector acting equally to provide female part-time work, mostly of a "long" nature. Men's presence in the public sector, meanwhile, is insignificant, and they rarely have part-time jobs. The majority typically work 40 hours a week.

Table 5.5 Employed Women Distributed by Sector and Working Time per Week (%), Sweden

Women	State Employment	Local Government, County Council	Private	Total
1–19 hours (short part-time)	2.4	4.4	9.0	6.6
20–34 hours (long part-time)	14.4	32.6	24.8	27.7
35–39 hours (full-time)	9.1	17.8	18.7	17.7
40 hours (full-time)	74.1	45.2	47.5	48.0
Total	100.0	100.0	100.0	100.0

Source: Calculations on the basis of the previous table.

Table 5.6 Employed Men Distributed by Sector and Working Time per Week (1,000 Persons), Sweden

Men	State Employment	Local Government, County Council	Private	Total
1–19 hours (short part-time)	1.9	8.8	48.7	59.6
20–34 (long part-time)	7.3	23.6	94.9	126.1
35–39 (full-time)	16.5	24.1	212.3	253.4
40– (full-time)	96.1	170.0	1,175.1	1,442.1
Unknown	0.4	1.0	4.5	5.9
Total	122.2	227.6	1,535.5	1,887.1

Source: SCB, 2003, Table 10.

Successes and Evidence of Gaps

Part-time work is well known for its potential traps of low pay, minimal benefits, and low career prospects. However, it also offers a model for minimising social exclusion by offering continuous attachment to working life through periods in which full-time work is not possible or desirable—for instance, when children are young. When opportunities for training arise in conjunction with part-time work, it can increase career prospects and can also be a link to full-time employment. People out of employment altogether face more serious problems than part-time workers in "catching up" with skills and competencies. The role of the welfare state in adding to or offsetting women's disadvantages in the labour market is a hotly debated one in the Nordic context. While it has brought women into very specific segments of the labour market, these are secure and well-paid jobs and have resulted in lower gender pay differentials relative to the international picture.

There is some evidence that the Scandinavian models have avoided some potential traps of part-time work. In Sweden, part-time work is not connected exclusively to lower prestige jobs, and part-time workers are also well protected: they usually have stable and permanent work contracts, and social security. Consequently, they are relatively well integrated into the labour market (Ellingsæter 1998). There is also substantial mobility out of part-time work (Sundström 1999), partly because an institutional guarantee has been in place since 1979 allowing young parents to reduce their working time by ten hours a week until the child turns eight, at which point they are entitled to return to full-time, and perhaps partly because of the relatively small difference between long part-time and full-time working hours.

However, there is also evidence that women in Sweden and Norway "still do not participate in the labour force on the same terms as men" (Xu 1997, 1).

The profile of different work patterns for women and men discussed previously provides some indication of this, but there are also others. One is that part-time work is not always the result of a free choice. Xu (1997) finds that more Swedish women are willing to work full time than actually do, and a recent Norwegian Labour Force Survey found that "The number of under-employed, i.e. part-time employees who want to work more hours, went up from 97,000 to 109,000 from the first quarter of 2004 to the first quarter of 2005" (SN/AKU 2005). Further indications are the continued existence of a degree of labour market gender segregation in Sweden and Norway, and notable glass ceilings for women.

Horizontal Labour Market Segregation

Table 5.7 shows that in 2003 gender segregation—here based on a classification of 350 occupation types—remains quite strong in Sweden, with over 70 percent of women grouped into women-dominated occupations.

Horizontal labour market segregation generally places women in the "secondary segment" of a dual-level labour force (Barron and Norris 1976). The differences between the two segments are significant, and include pay levels, job security, required skill levels, career opportunities, and labour turnover rates. The frequently observed secondary position of women in the labour market is determined by several factors, such as the level and type of education, women's double burden of reproductive and "secondary" wage earning work, and their (perceived) lower commitment to the labour force. The notion of "secondary" earning, rooted in taxation and social welfare systems "built on the image of the man as the breadwinner and the woman

Table 5.7 Occupational Segregation, 2003 (%), Sweden

Percentage Distribution and Numbers in 1,000s		
Occupations with	*Women*	*Men*
90–100% women, 0–10% men	27	2
60–90% women, 10–40% men	44	12
40–60% women, 40–60% men	14	13
10–40% women, 60–90% men	13	40
0–10% women, 90–100% men	2	33
Total, percent	100	100
Number	1,976	2,139

Source: Labour Force Survey, SCB, 2004, p. 57.

as the dependent or secondary earner" (ILO 1996, 4), itself reinforces the bias faced by women attempting to enter and retain positions in the "first segment" of the labour market on male terms.

Glass Ceilings

Labour market segregation commonly operates vertically as well as horizontally, with one manifestation of segregation reinforcing the other. Women—who usually work in female-dominated, segregated jobs—are badly represented in the upper levels of management in business life. Table 5.8 shows that Sweden and Norway are no exceptions, not even equalling the EU average of women in leadership positions in the top 50 companies in each country[5], though showing a higher-than-average presence of women in decision-making bodies.

Melkas and Anker (2003) find that women "are either members in bodies that have restricted power, or lower-level managers" in Nordic countries, and that glass ceilings follow occupational segretational lines: "It is easier for women to reach top positions in the public sector than in the private sector, and in female-dominated fields and occupations" (Melkas and Anker 2003, 27). Data from Europe in general suggests that this situation has little to do with education levels: according to International Standard Classification of Occupations (ISCO) categories, women occupy 30 percent of management positions, but more that 50 percent of higher education places.

Table 5.8 Women and Men in Decision-Making Positions in the Top 50 Companies

	Norway	Sweden	Hungary	EU Average
Female heads of higher decision-making bodies (%)	2	0	4	2
Male heads of higher decision-making bodies (%)	98	100	96	98
Female members in higher decision-making bodies (%)	18	17	13	10
Male members in higher decision-making bodies (%)	82	83	87	90
Female CEO (%) (Daily executive body)	2	2	9	2
Male CEO (%) (Daily executive body)	98	98	91	98

Source: *Women and Men in Decision Making 2004.*

MEN'S WORK

A further, less visible sign of the persistence of the male norm of employment is the continued focus in research and data collection on women's work behaviour, with relatively little questioning of changes in men's role. Kitterød and Kjeldstad (2002) point out that men's and especially fathers' employment have not been studied systematically despite the emergence of active fathering and new fathers' roles in Scandinavian countries, implying that it is women's activity that needs systematic and permanent investigation and evaluation.

POLICY AND WORK PATTERNS IN HUNGARY

Women's relatively low labour force participation rates in Hungary are partly due to high inactivity since the transition, which presents a serious social and economic problem. Those excluded are often relatively poorly educated—a problem that affects particularly the older generation. Meanwhile, those who are unemployed or who cannot work full time or to the male norm face the risk of social exclusion.

The labour market in Hungary also shows signs of profound occupational and vertical gender segregation (see Table 5.9), although there are some signs that segregation is decreasing in some areas: "The gender gap in the occupational structure has decreased by a large amount in the case of young people: in the early nineties, the difference was as high as 70

Table 5.9 Occupational Segregation, 1999 (%), Hungary

Occupations	Individual Jobs' Distribution within the Total Group	Employed Women's Distribution within the Total Group
90–100% women, 10–0% men	11.0	35.7
60–90% women, 40–10% men	19.0	34.2
40–60% women, 60–40% men	16.0	17.2
10–40% women, 90–60% men	27.0	11.7
0–10% women, 100–90% men	27.0	1.2
Total, percent	100.0	100.0
N	617	1,726,700

Source: Frey 2002, p. 24.

percent, while after 2000 it was 59 percent." (Bukodi 2006, 26). Research since the mid-1990s has underlined the existence of glass ceilings, and—like in Sweden—the links between the two segregation mechanisms: women make their careers more often in feminised fields, and reach the second level of management in the supportive branches of the organisation (Nagy 1999).

A wide range of measures and benefits have been in place for some time to support those combining work and family, including family allowance, maternity leave, child-care leave, child-care allowance, child-care fee, and tax credits, but uptake of these benefits is profoundly gendered. Time allowances for maternity and child-care leave are generous but are a double-edged sword: in the absence of part-time work opportunities, they discourage women from an early return to the labour market, hence eroding their labour market integration. Women with three or more children can use a combination of benefits to stay at home for as long as nine years.

Social policy also provides for men to stay at home with small children on child-care allowance, but uptake of this provision is very low: according to the 2000 Labour Force Survey, 10 percent of women but only 0.03 percent of men of working age were away from the labour market temporarily on subsidised child-care allowance (Frey 2002, 17). This is often a rational economic decision: where men's earning is significantly higher than women's, their absence from work would produce a financial disadvantage to the family. But women's weakened labour market integration due to child care reinforces the situation in which women are less likely to earn as much as men.

A more recent introduction of five days paid holiday for fathers when a child is born—which doesn't threaten labour market integration—seems to have been more widely taken up and welcomed. My recent research suggests that employers also do not openly oppose this change, and some are very proud of their male colleagues taking part in this work. However, there is little expectation that it will increase fathers' involvement in child care, either in the short or in the long term.

So what are the prospects for the entry of part-time work opportunities in Hungary? Labour markets in Scandinavia and in Hungary remain in some ways different—although they share common features, and some common gender differential trends. The historical processes by which they have arrived at their contemporary labour situations have also been different. The following section draws out some features of the Nordic experience that may have provided the "enabling conditions" in which part-time work can represent a positive force for gender equality rather than a trap for women, and briefly reviews the extent to which these conditions are in place in Hungary.

ENABLING CONDITIONS FOR CHALLENGING
MALE EMPLOYMENT NORMS

The Cultural Framework

Although much research has been conducted on changing gender relations and roles in Scandinavian countries, the social forces behind these changes are often presented less distinctly than the measures themselves. Research on active fathering, for example, tends to take for granted that there was an inherent social need to implement this idea (Bergman and Hobson 2002). Juxtaposing the Nordic situations with Hungary, however, suggests a need to look carefully at the social contexts in which policy for redistributing reproductive labour is implemented. From a central European viewpoint, it seems that attitudes to the notion of gender equality may be deeply significant in shaping employment norms.

The notion of equality in general, and gender equality in particular, has been a central plank of the Swedish welfare state and receives widespread social acceptance. Not only have men been significant advocates of this principle, but feminists have been able to turn employment issues into demands for public services to support reproduction and changing family roles. As von Otter notes (2004, 59): "The gainful employment of women and its consequences have resulted in demands for public services, new roles within the family, and, not least, have required working life to be organised with equality and fairness in mind. In addition, we expect to be able to combine the needs of the private sphere with full-time work.

In Hungary, by contrast, prevailing attitudes to employment and gender roles have in some ways regressed since the transition from state socialism. International Social Survey Programme data from 1988, 1994, and 2002 suggest that while in 1998 mainly men had very traditional attitudes to gender roles, by 1994 women's views had become more similar to these, not less (Tóth 1995). The 2002 survey showed some signs of positive attitudes to changing gender roles, although, significantly, young men's opinions (aged 18–26) lag behind other groups regarding gender equality (Blaskó 2005).

Similar results have emerged from other kinds of surveys: in a 1991 survey asking "What is more important in your life: the family and private life or work and job?" no Hungarian women chose the "work and job" option (Pongrácz 2002). In later work, Pongrácz (2006) found that nearly 80 percent of respondents agreed that home and children are more important for women than work, although work is also important, and over 70 percent agreed that "it is the husband's responsibility to earn money to support his family and [the] wife's task is to perform household work." Interestingly, however, only 23 percent agreed that "for men, work must be more important than family" (Pongrácz 2006, 73–78).[6]

Part of the explanation for these attitudes, and in particular for the apparent increase in women expressing "traditional" attitudes to gender roles, lies in the trajectory of women's engagement with the labour market during the socialist period. The "gender regime" during the early years of socialism advocated forced emancipation as a political priority, and female employment was seen as a primary indicator of this. Women were pulled out of the household and integrated into the labour force with some aggression, and in the absence of substantive support to their domestic responsibilities, which remained largely unchanged.

Against this backdrop, and in a formulation which suggests fatigue with the burden of full-time employment and reproductive work, the role of the housewife has gained legitimacy in the post socialist period (Tóth 1995; Blaskó 2005). Despite this, there remains a strong pressure on women to work. Pongrácz reports that over 90 percent of respondents to the previously mentioned survey also thought that women are obliged to work to safeguard the livelihood of the family (Pongrácz 2006). Relatively few can actually afford to stay at home.

Trenchant resistance to gender equality is also revealed in research on attitudes to women's leadership. Recent research on gender equality in local government found that while women made up the majority of both subordinates and leaders in this research site, female leaders enjoy limited acceptance, and doubts from colleagues concerning their professional competence (Baumann 2005). These findings bear out Wajcman's (1998) more general suggestion that women can easily be "punished" by withholding social influence when they manage to climb career ladders by espousing the male norm.

Feminist Responses to Fertility Issues

Further factors influencing how part-time work may challenge gendered employment norms seem to relate to the state's diagnosis of the relationship between fertility and work, and the ability of gender advocates to turn declining fertility rates—which prevail in much of Europe, for example—into a successful feminist public policy issue. In Hungary, for instance, demographic decreases over recent years have not raised public discussions on the topic of the gender division of labour, but rather strengthened the traditional view that socialist emancipation and modernisation worked against family values (Pongrácz 2006). In the post-socialist period there was a new belief that women's withdrawal from paid work could contribute to increasing fertility levels—an expectation which manifestly has not been fulfilled, given that today Hungary's fertility rate is among the lowest in Europe, in a group with a number of other post-socialist countries (see Table 5.10).

Evidence for a relation between low women's employment levels and higher fertility rates remains thin elsewhere also. Table 5.10 shows no clear correlation between women's employment rates and fertility rates, although

Table 5.10 Female Employment Rates and Total Fertility Rates in the European Union, 2004

	Employment Rate	Total Fertility Rate
Ireland	56.5	1.99
France	57.4	1.90
Finland	65.6	1.80
Denmark	71.6	1.78
Sweden	70.5	1.75
United Kingdom	65.6	1.74
Netherlands	65.8	1.73
Luxembourg	50.6	1.71
Belgium	52.6	1.64
EU25	55.7	1.50
Cyprus	59.0	1.49
Austria	60.7	1.42
Estonia	60.0	1.40
Portugal	61.7	1.40
Malta	32.8	1.37
Germany	59.2	1.36
Italy	45.2	1.33
Spain	48.3	1.32
Greece	45.2	1.29
Hungary	50.7	1.28
Lithuania	57.8	1.26
Slovenia	60.5	1.25
Latvia	58.5	1.24
Slovakia	50.9	1.24
Poland	46.2	1.23
Czech Republic	56.0	1.22

Sources: Figures for employment (women aged 15–64 years) are from Indicators 2005, Key indicator 2; Total fertility rate from Eurostat 2006; Ranked here by total fertility rate/employment rate.

it is notable that of the eight countries with high fertility rates (over 1.7), five—Denmark, Netherlands, Finland, Sweden, and the UK—also have high female employment rates (over 60 percent).

As Shapiro (2005) points out, declining fertility rates have given different countries different messages. As with employment issues in general, Swedish feminists were able to seize the moment of domestic concerns around fertility rates to claim legitimacy for policies helping women to reconcile work and family life, and to encourage men to do likewise. Ohlander (1994) notes that, despite economic difficulties during the 1980s, Sweden's birth rate remained stable at a relatively high level, and she attributes this to cultural as well as structural factors, including initiatives such as day-care centre development since the 1970s and a parental leave system that incorporated return-to-work guarantees. In countries where women have lower levels of social guarantee to return to the labour market and lower levels of available child-care facilities, they appear to be less willing to have more children (Del Boca et al. 2003) This pattern is typical of countries with low fertility rates, such as Italy, Spain, and Greece.

Thus it seems likely that both social norms and social policy shape women's employment patterns and influence the number of children desired and born. But what kind of policy works? Hungary continues to belong to a group of countries where parental leave provisions have not halted declining birth rates, and where fertility/parenthood has a sharper effect on women's employment than in nearly all other European countries (Indicators 2005).

The Content of "Supportive Policy"

Female employment levels across Europe are influenced deeply by the national social policy on parental leave and child-care provision. Sweden and Norway represent two rather different models of combining these welfare options, but with broadly similar results in terms of women's employment rates (Table 5.1). Proportionately more women work part time in Norway, however, than in Sweden (Table 5.2). Meyers and Gornick (1999) note that these two countries adopted different "breadwinner models" during the 1980s, which translated into public policy, namely, extensive parental leave accompanied by child-care facilities in Sweden,and generous parental leave along with less extensive child care for children under three in Norway (Ellingsæter 2003).

Parental leave policy has a long history in Sweden. Introduced in 1974— the first gender-neutral programme in the world—it was initially a six-month leave at a 90 percent compensation level. It included a strong financial incentive for young women to enter the labour market before childbirth, because leave entitlement was connected to 180 days of health insurance before the birth. At the same time it offered great flexibility in order to combine the earner and the carer roles (Sundström and Duvander 2002). Nyberg adds that child-care facilities were slower in coming because the "dual-earner/dual-carer" model—embodied in the gender-neutral parental leave programme—drew women into paid work, which subsequently created a demand for child care: "Swedish mothers entered the labour market long before there was enough public childcare" (Nyberg 2004, 8).

Norway's gender equality model, reflected in its welfare system, has emphasised valuing motherhood as a basis from which to claim support for women in their two roles, but nevertheless promotes a dual-earner system. This system is embodied in its parental leave system introduced in 1977, and extended in the 1990s to 52 weeks with 80 percent wage compensation or 42 weeks with 100 percent wage compensation. Ellingsæter (2003) identifies a "family policy dualism" in this model, which she sees as introducing a level of ambivalence into the women's situation, and perhaps explains Norwegian women's slower integration into the labour market and the fact that "Norwegian mothers return later to work after giving birth and motherhood often leads to a reduction of work hours" (Ellingsæter 1998, 63).

In 1998/99 Norway launched the "cash for care" reform, which entitled the parents of small children to choose between using public child-care facilities or receiving a monthly payment equivalent to the costs of those facilities (approximately 400 Euro in 2003). The reform generated much debate, with opponents emphasising that it could lead to a more uneven household division of labour among young parents and was likely to support the traditional family models in which young mothers stay at home to take care of young children. However, the change was less dramatic that these predictions suggested. Ellingsæter reports that although the majority of parents claim the payment, "few use it to reduce their time in paid work" (2003, 426), and the ratio of "stay-at-home" mothers actually decreased, remaining at not more than 10 percent of mothers with small children in 2003 (2003, 434).

Thus "good" policy seems to consist of child-care and parental-leave arrangements, but—importantly—flexibility in how these can be used and interpreted. However, a further distinguishing feature of the Nordic models has been a focus—from the early years of policy development around women's work—on increasing men's responsibility for reproductive work.

A Focus on Fathers

In Sweden and Norway, massive and unquestionable incentives have been integrated in social policy in order to make men and fathers interested in family life and reproductive work. This issue had emerged as early as the late 1950s in Sweden, when, according to Bergman and Hobson, gender inequality was already "attributed to both women's lack of participation in paid work and men's lack of participation in carework" (2002, 104). During the 1960s the focus on altering parental roles intensified, and the dual-earner/dual-carer model developed, explicitly including the notion of the care-giving father and based on an invocation of family solidarity (Ohlander

1994). The modification of gender roles was largely seen as a question of re-education and socialisation: with re-education for parents, and the de-emphasis on full-time work for men, men would devote more time to family and parenting, and new forms of masculinity would emerge (Bergman and Hobson 2002).

In Norway, the emphasis on fathers' participation in family work came later in the 1990s, following a focus in the 1970s and 1980s on helping women to reconcile paid work and family care (Kitterød and Kjeldstad 2002, 1). Both countries have since the 1990s, however, introduced specific initiatives casting fathers as carers: in Norway the "father's quota" was introduced in 1993 and a time-account scheme in 1994; and in Sweden the "daddy month" was introduced in 1995. The Norwegian fathers quota introduced in 1993 consisted of 4 weeks of the parental leave time, reserved for the father and not transferable to the mother. In 1994 the "time account" was created, to enable parents to divide the parental leave time in a flexible way, using an upper limit of parental leave as they wished, for instance reducing daily work hours (working 60 percent and taking 40 percent out of the time account), or dividing weeks between parents. The rules are fairly complex for this account. The fathers' quota still applied.

The Swedish daddy month consisted of 30 days of parental leave which could be taken at any time until the child reaches the age of eight or completes the first school year (Riksförsakringsverket 2004, 13). The length of the leave and rates of compensation have changed several times during the last ten years, and the daddy month was expanded to 60 days in 2002 (SCB 2004, 6).

This initiative has resulted in some gradual changes. Before the introduction of the daddy month, 50 percent of fathers did not use any leave entitlement before the child was four years old (Nyberg 2004, 14). It remains the case that not all fathers take up their parental leave entitlement, but the proportion of those that do is increasing, as shown in Table 5.11. Sundström and Duvander (2002) observe, however, that while the number of leave takers has increased, the average number of days they take has decreased and they attribute this to greater uptake by less motivated fathers.

There are three groups of fathers who take parental leave more frequently than average: fathers who are less educated than their partners; well-educated fathers; and men in female dominated jobs. Married fathers use the parental leave more frequently than cohabiting fathers (Sundström and Duvander 2002).

Thus, while the introduction of parental leave systems directed at men has made incremental changes to the division of reproductive work, and no doubt has bolstered the development of vision around new roles for fathers, the evidence suggests that there remain some challenges. Men's response to the leave benefit has been somewhat ambivalent, and men and women continue to take the total of 480 days parental leave asymmetrically. They also tend to take the leave at different life cycle stages of the children: women

Table 5.11 Percentage of Fathers Among All Parental-Leave Users:
Fraction of All Benefit Days Used by Fathers and Average Days
Used by Fathers Who Took Leave, 1974–1998

	Fathers' Use of Parental Leave Measures as		
	Percent of All Leave Users	*Percent of All Benefit Days*	*Days per Father (Average)*
1974	2.8	0.5	n.a.
1977	7.0	2.2	n.a.
1987	24.5	7.3	27.1
1990	26.1	7.7	32.9
1993	27.0	10.1	39.5
1994	28.1	11.4	39.5
1995	27.9	9.6	34.3
1996	31.1	10.6	30.5
1997	30.9	9.9	28.0
1998	32.4	10.4	27.4
1999	36.2	11.6	27.1

Source: Sundström and Duvander. 2002, p. 437.
For the period 1987–1999, part-time days have been recalculated into full-time days, but not for the earlier period.

typically take it during the first 12 months after giving birth, whereas men typically take it when the child is between 11 and 15 months (Nyberg 2004).

My earlier discussion has suggested that, in contrast to Nordic countries, gender roles in Hungary are firmly entrenched in a "traditional" framework, in which women are understood to be entirely responsible for domestic and reproductive work. Gender equality in contemporary Hungary is viewed with some suspicion—given the nature of emancipatory initiatives during the socialist era—and this perhaps explains the very low uptake of father's entitlements to parental leave. Nevertheless, it remains noteworthy that while Hungarian women put in, on average, more hours on domestic work than Swedish and Norwegian women, hours of domestic work by Hungarian, Swedish, and Norwegian men appear remarkably similar. Table 5.12 shows not only this, but also that employment reduces women's time in domestic work significantly more in Hungary than in Sweden or Norway—although

Table 5.12 Time Spent on Domestic Work (Hours and Minutes per Day) 1998–2002

	Hungary	Sweden	Norway
Women aged 20–74	4:57	3:42	3:47
Employed women	3:54	3:32	3:26
Women living with partner with youngest child aged 7–17	5:24	3:58	3:43
Men aged 20–74	2:39	2:29	2:22
Employed men	2:09	2:23	2:12
Men living with partner with youngest child aged 7–17	2:44	2:34	2:28

Source: Eurostat, 2004 (on the basis of Tables 1.1–1.4, 6.3).

their overall hours remain higher. The *difference* between domestic labour hours for women and men, however, remains higher in Hungary than in the Nordic countries.

CONCLUSIONS

This discussion has sought to bring into focus why Hungarian initiatives to support women in employment seem to have had little impact on work culture, or on the expectation that "work" means full-time and lifelong, for women or for men. It has also sought to explore whether the Nordic models of widespread long part-time work (for women) combined with supportive policies around parental leave, child care, and drawing fathers into child-care responsibilities provide examples of systems that could challenge male-oriented Hungarian employment structures. The Hungarian data suggest that changes in the labour market policy are not enough to change the traditional beliefs about women's and men's "real" jobs. Even those women who are well placed in the labour market and who contribute the bulk of family income are not exempt from the demand of household responsibilities, and household responsibilities create a vicious cycle of women's relatively low integration into the labour market, lower career prospects when they enter it, and low impact on the male evaluation structures that dominate it.

The comparison between Hungary and the Nordic countries draws attention to the fact that unless emancipatory provisions are rooted in the society's expectations, confirmed by the civil society, and focus on men's changing roles, only a very contradictory and restricted type of emancipation can be realized. It also suggests that political willingness to support both employers and employees to achieve gender equality—absent in Hungary, despite the rhetoric—was a significant feature of the changes in gender roles and relations that Nordic countries have been able to bring about.

Certain features of the Nordic system and methods for its development may offer real possibilities in Hungary. One is the conscious promotion of a dual-earner/dual-carer model through work at all levels of society and particularly with employers. A second feature is the "daddy month" initiative, which could easily be adapted to Hungarian contexts, and which includes an implicit penalty to families in which fathers are unwilling to take on child-care work.

Nevertheless, these features need be recommended only with some caution. It appears to be the case, in spite of the decades of social engineering in Nordic countries, that women continue to have quite different work patterns from men, with many working long part-time hours, and they continue to meet with glass ceilings in professional life. Moreover, they also continue to bear the main responsibility for managing family life in Sweden and Norway, as they do in Hungary.

Several questions thus remain unanswered, notably whether employment will ever be degendered in the absence of substantively equal distributions of domestic work. Swedish women's part-time work, which has been a significant tool in the challenge to male employment norms, was until recently a sector largely catered to by the state. For Hungary important questions remain around who would be responsible for the supply of part-time jobs in a context where the state has radically shrunk and the focus for development is on the private sector.

NOTES

1. Part-time employment refers to persons who usually work less than 30 hours per week in their main job. Data include only persons declaring usual hours.
2. Although in Poland it reaches 16.8 percent (OECD 2004, 310).
3. The Swedish Statistical Office sent the latest data on part-time employment in Sweden directly to us—that is, the basis of the calculations was neither an official publication nor an online database. (The data provider was Gunilla Widlund.)
4. Tables 5.4 and 5.5 contain only the data of employees, thus excluding employers with or without employees and unpaid family workers. Consequently, these data refer to 94.9 percent of women and 70.1 percent of men, because women are more often employees compared to men, who are relatively often employers.
5. According to the EU definition, "Top 50 companies are defined as the companies that are quoted on the national stock exchange and that have the highest market capitalisation. Market capitalisation is defined as the market price of an entire company, calculated by multiplying the number of shares outstanding by the price per share' (*Women and Men in Decision Making 2004*)
6. It should be noted that the phrasing of questions in these surveys presupposes to some extent women's commitment to the family, and are therefore at risk

of considerable bias, but the surveys nevertheless probably paint a broadly accurate picture.

REFERENCES

Acker, Joan. 1990. Hierarchies, jobs, bodies: A theory of gendered organizations. *Gender and Society* 4(2):139–158.

Asztalos-Morell, Ildikó. 1999. *Emancipations's dead-end roads? Studies in the formation and development of the Hungarian model for agriculture and gender (1956–1989).* Acta Universitatis Upsaliensia 46. Uppsala: I. A. Morell.

Barron, David R., and Geoffrey M. Norris. 1976. Sexual divisions and the dual labour market. In *Dependence and exploitation in work and marriage,* eds. S. Allen and D Barker, 47–69. London: Longman.

Baumann, Fruzsina, ed. 2005. *Nemek esélyeg enlőség egy önkormányzatnál* [Gender awareness at local governments]. Budapest: Budapesti Szociális Forrásközpont.

Bergman, Helena, and Barbara Hobson. 2002. Compulsory fatherhood: The coding of fatherhood in the Swedish welfare state. In *Making men into fathers,* ed. B Hobson, 92–124. Cambridge: Cambridge University Press.

Blaskó, Zsuzsa. 2005. Dolgozzanak-e a nők? A magyar lakosság nemi szerepekkel kapcsolatos véleményének változásai, 1988, 1994, 2002 [Should women work? The changing attitudes of the Hungarian population on gender roles, 1988, 1994, 2002]. *Demográfia* 2–3:159–186.

Bukodi, Erzsébet. 2006. Women's labour market participation and use of working time. In *Changing roles: Report on the situation of women and men in Hungary 2005,* eds. I Nagy, T Pongrácz, and I. Gy Tóth, 15–43. Budapest: TÁRKI.

Cockburn, Cynthia. 1991. *In the way of women: Men's resistance to sex equality in organizations.* London: Macmillan.

Del Boca, Daniela, Sylvia Pasqua, and Chiara Pronzato. 2003. *Analyzing women's employment and fertility rates in Europe: Differences and similarities in Northern and Southern Europe.* http://www.iser.essex.ac.uk/epunet/2003/docs/pdf/papers/pronzato.pdf (Accessed April 20, 2005).

Ellingsæter, Anne Lise. 1998. Dual breadwinner societies: Provider models in the Scandinavian welfare states. *Acta Sociologica* 41:59–73.

Ellingsæter, Anne Lise. 2003. The complexity of family policy reform: The case of Norway. *European Societies* 5(4):419–43.

Engels, Friedrich. 1982. *A család. a magántulajdon és az állam eredete* [The origin of the family, private property, and the state]. Budapest: Kossuth.

European Commission Employment and Social Affairs DG. 2005. *Indicators for Monitoring the Employment Guidelines, 2004–2005 Compendium* http://europa.eu.int/comm/employment_social/employment_strategy/indic/compendium_jer 2004_en.pdf (updated April 15, 2005).

Eurostat. 2004. *How Europeans spend their time: Everyday life of women and men. Data 1998–2002.*

Eurostat. 2006. *A statistical view of the life of women and men in the EU25.* News release 29/2006, March 6, 2006. http://epp.eurostat.ec.europa.eu/pls/portal/docs/PAGE/PGP_PRD_CAT_PREREL/PGE_CAT_PREREL_YEAR_2006/PGE_CAT_PREREL_YEAR_2006_MONTH_03/3-06032006-EN-BP1.PDF (Accessed June 20, 2006).

Frey, Maria. 2002. Nők és férfiak a munkaerőpiacon [Women and men in the labour market]. In *Szerepváltozások. Jelentés a nők és férfiak helyzetéről 2001,* eds. I Nagy, T Pongrácz, and I. Gy Tóth. Hungary: TÁRKI.

Gal, Susan, and Gail Kligman. 2000. *The politics of gender after Socialism: A comparative historical essay.* Princeton, NJ: Princeton University Press.

Håland, Inger, and Gunnlaug Daugstad. 2002. The gender-divided labour market. *Statistical Magazine of the Statistics Norway.* http://www.ssb.no/english/magazine/ (Accessed April 20, 2005).

Hochschild, Arlie. 2001. *The time bind: When work becomes home and home becomes work.* New York: Holt.

ILO. 1996. *World of Work Magazine.*, No. 17, September/October 1996. http://www.ilo.org/public/english/bureau/inf/magazine/17/women.htm (Accessed November 25, 2004).

Implementation. 2005. *Light update of the first Hungarian National Action Plan on Social Inclusion (NAP/incl) 2004–2006.* June 2005 Budapest.

Kitterød, Ragni Hege, and Randi Kjeldstad. 2002. More full-time work for mothers—less long hours for fathers: A labour force survey analysis of Norwegian parents 1991–2000 Working Paper 21, presented at the Conference of European Statisticians, Geneva.

Melkas, Helinä, and Richard Anker. 2003. *Towards gender equity in Japanese and Nordic labour markets: A tale of two paths.* Geneva: International Labour Organization (ILO).

Meyers, Marcia K., and Janet C. Gornick. 1999. Public childcare: Parental leave and employment. In *Gender and welfare state regimes,* ed. Diane Sainsbury. Oxford: Oxford University Press.

Nagy, Beata. 1999. Women's career. In *The changing role of women: Report on the situation of women in Hungary 1997,* eds. K Lévai and I Tóth. Hungary: TÁRKI.

Nagy, Beata. 2004. *Hungarian companies' equal opportunity policy* (Research paper). http://www.policy.hu/nagy

Nyberg, Anita. 2004. *Parental leave: Public childcare and the dual earner/dual carer model in Sweden* (Discussion paper). Peer Review Programme on the European Employment Strategy, Parental Insurance and Childcare. April 19–20. Stockholm. http://peerreview.almp.org/pdf/sweden04/disspapSWE04.pdf

OECD. 2004. *Employment outlook.* http://www.oecd.org (Accessed October 25, 2004).

OECD. 2006. *Employment outlook 2006: Boosting jobs and incomes* (Statistical Annex). http://www.oecd.org (Accessed January 4, 2007).

Ohlander, Ann Sofie. 1994. *Women. children and work in Sweden 1850–1993.* Swedish Government Official Report 38, Ministry for Foreign Affairs, Stockholm, Sweden.

Pongrácz, Marietta. 2002. A család és a munka szerepe a nők életében [The role of family and job in women's life]. In *Szerepváltozások. Jelentés a nők és férfiak helyzetéről 2001,* eds. Idlikó Nagy, Marietta Pongrácz, and Tóth István Györgi. Hungary: TÁRKI.

Pongrácz, Marietta. 2006. Opinions on gender roles: Findings of an international comparative study. In *Changing roles. Report on the situation of women and men in Hungary 2005,* eds. Idlikó Nagy; Marietta Pongrácz; and Tóth István Györgi. Hungary: TÁRKI.

Riksförsakringsverket [National Social Insurance Board]. 2004. *Social insurance expenditure in Sweden 2001–2004: Who gets the money and how is the insurance financed?*

SCB. 2003. Labour Force Survey. Statistics Sweden. http://www.scb.se

SCB. 2004. *Women and men in Sweden: Facts and figures 2004.* Statistics Sweden. http://www.scb.se

Shapiro, Judith. 2005. *Feminist paradox or feminist stalemate? Lessons from the linked Swedish construction of gender and fertility.* Manuscript

SN/AKU. 2004. *Labour force survey 2004.* http://www.ssb.no/english/subjects/06/01/aku_en/tab-2005-02-02-06-en.html (Accessed June 20, 2006).

SN/AKU. 2005. *Labour force survey 2005*. http://www.ssb.no/english/subjects/06/01/ aku_en/ (Accessed June 20, 2006).

Stark, Agneta, and Åsa Regnér. 2002. *In whose hands? Of work. gender. ageing and care in three EU-countries*. Linköping: Department of Gender Studies.

Sundström, Marianne. 1999. *Part-time work in Sweden—An institutionalist perspective*. www.suda.su.se/SRRD/srrd138.doc (Accessed October 29, 2004).

Sundström, Marianne, and Ann-Zofie Duvander. 2002. Gender division of childcare and the sharing of parental leave among new parents in Sweden. *European Sociological Review* 18(4):433–447.

Tóth, Olga. 1995. Attitűdváltozások a női munkavállalás megítélésében [Changing attitudes on women's employment]. *Szociológiai Szemle* 1:71–86.

von Otter, Casten. 2004. *Swedish working life—Searching for a new regime*. Stockholm: Arbetslivsinstitutet.

Wajcman, Judy. 1998. *Managing like a man: Women and men in corporate management*. Cambridge: Polity Press.

Women and Men in Decision Making. 2004. (Database—Social and economic domain) http://europa.eu.int/comm/employment_social/women_men_stats/out/ measures_out438_en.htm (Accessed October 25, 2004).

Xu, Jia. 1997. Sex discrimination in the Swedish labour market: Present situation and legal practices. Working Paper 5, Institutet för Social Forskning, Stockholm, Sweden.

6   Sexual Politics and Social Policy
Swedish Policy Reviewed

Ramya Subrahmanian

INTRODUCTION

Why does Sweden, given its global standing as a leader in promoting gender equality, follow a policy approach to dealing with prostitution that seems to be at odds with evolving approaches in countries in the South, and elsewhere, especially in its Nordic neighbours and other regions in Europe? This is the central question that this chapter addresses. The state's gender equality project has extended to the criminalisation of the purchase of sexual services of prostitutes based on the view that prostitution is an aspect of patriarchy and hence is detrimental to women's gender interests. The emphasis on prostitution as patriarchy is made by imposing penalties only on the [male] client and the intermediary—the punter and the pimp—and not on the seller of the service, the prostitute. To an external observer, this policy approach seems at odds with developments elsewhere that increasingly recognise sex workers' agency as a mediating variable in determining policy responses to sex work and trafficking.

This approach to the incorporation of sexual politics into the social policy framework of the Swedish state—that is, addressing the rights of women to control their bodies and the place of commoditised sexual labour in relation to these rights—merits attention for two principal reasons. First, it signals an approach to social policy that sees the state playing a decisive role in determining a normative position on the commodification of female sexual labour. Second, it signals the state's role in determining what livelihood options are acceptable for citizens, a role made possible by its commitment to protecting the welfare of its citizens through economic and social safety nets.

A noteworthy feature of the Swedish position on prostitution is that the state's authority to define the public position derives from consensus evolved through democratic processes, such that political debate in the public political arena and the representation of women in large numbers have in fact shaped it. The Swedish case demonstrates the powerful coming together of historical and contemporary forces and a shift from dealing implicitly with "body politics" [e.g., policies relating to motherhood] to a more explicit regulation of the female "body" in the context of prostitution. The chapter examines dimensions of this shift and offers some reflections on the applicability in other contexts of the ideas that ground it.

An underlying issue that is addressed concerns the implications of an increasing recognition that women's agency is a mediating variable in policy response to issues of sex trafficking and sex work.[1] In many European countries, a combination of predominantly pragmatic policymaking—recognising the resilience of the sex industry over centuries—and the influence of feminist activists who argue for a greater appreciation of female agency, has influenced the development of a "shades of grey" approach to sex work. This recognises that not all women are necessarily exploited by sex work, and that the role of public policy is to help deal with the worst excesses and abuses associated with it, such as coercion and violence. In Germany, where a law was passed in 2001 approving prostitution as a regular profession, prostitutes are differentiated in public policy into "groups with differing grades of involvement," thereby, for example, distinguishing those who sell sex for financing drug addiction to those who sell sex as "professionals." In contrast to Sweden, Germany views the biggest problems of prostitutes as the stigma that is attached to their profession, and sees this policy position as reflecting general public acceptance of prostitution as a legitimate occupation (Dodillet 2004). Such calibrated approaches to prostitution entail making the trade visible, and regulating it, as opposed to abolishing it and decrying its existence.

These debates are now global, but they have particular salience for fledgling social policy approaches in developing countries. To explore the social policy dimensions of the issue of sex work, I contrast the statist approach to tackling prostitution in Sweden, based on a welfare state with a firm commitment to gender equality, on one hand, with multiactor struggles in India, on the other, where sex workers seek to earn their livelihood with dignity in the absence of social safety nets and meaningful economic choices, and given high levels of gender inequality. In India, growing evidence of widespread trafficking of women and children for sexual and other labour has raised debates about the links between trafficking and prostitution, and the distinctions between voluntary and forced migration in a context of widespread poverty and economic marginalisation. In a country with no universal safety-net provision, limited focus through law or policy on employment rights for women, and a continuing role played by communities in terms of mutual support, debates on the link between sexual rights and social policy are not strongly developed, and public policy in this area seems doomed to failure in the absence of the ability of the state to guarantee universal basic needs.

Further, in contexts where female labour has long been treated as without value apart from the reproductive function, the commodification of women's sexual labour has in some situations transformed perceptions of the value of women as contributors to household domestic income, giving those women enhanced status within their communities (Shivdas 2003). This complicates the reading of "prostitution" only in terms of an exploitative practice, and demands engagement with wider issues such as: how choices and opportunities are shaped in the context of the large-scale experience of poverty, what access women have to these choices and opportunities and on what terms, how changing economic structures impel mobility and hence migration, and how these forces may combine to offer or deny women the means to lead their lives with some dignity and security. The juxtaposition of the Swedish and Indian cases helps to question whether the Swedish approach to prostitution/sex work may over-simplify complex sets of choices for women, and invisibilise the possibility that prostitution may in many cases offer women an exit option from other oppressive experiences—such as an oppressive marriage or domestic violence—that is, it offers a means of survival in contexts where options are a luxury.

The Swedish case, however, remains the main focus of analysis in this paper, in keeping with the theme of this volume. The Swedish approach to prostitution is explained by a model of social welfare that attaches much importance to gender equality, accompanied by a political discourse that has historically emphasised the importance of inclusiveness and consensus as a basis for social policy development. The wider metaphor for this project, encompassing both the policy and the politics, is of course the "People's Home" (*Folkhemmet* in Swedish), an ideological concept of a society that includes all people in the state, and in which the needs, interests, and security of the lower and middle classes are met, not just those of the elite. In relation to prostitution, however, the policy project of the People's Home appears to be paradoxical: while an engine of gender equality has been women's identity as workers, and a focus on labour, this does not extend to an acceptance of prostitution as a form of work or employment like any other.

Regarding the "protection" that the Swedish State accords prostitutes (criminalising the buyer but not the seller of sexual services), it is notable that the policy has received widespread support from within the feminist community in Sweden as well as from the public. While there is some dissent, the overall impression drawn from the literature on the passage of the legislation is of broad consensus that the Swedish approach is the "right" one, and is in keeping with its reputation as the leading guardian of women's right to equality (Svanström 2004).

The feminist satisfaction with the state's position can be largely explained by the preoccupation in Swedish feminism with the limitations of the Swedish welfare model, particularly in addressing issues relating to women's bodily integrity. The prevalence of violence against women, particularly within the home and domestic relationships, is argued to uncover deep structures of resistance to gender equality in Sweden, and the continuing power that men wield over women through its exercise. Taken as a clear articulation of the operation of power in society, the continuing prevalence of domestic and sexual violence in Sweden is seen to constitute a blot on the otherwise impressive progressive political project that gender equality in Sweden is recognised to represent to the world. Both external and internal commentators have thus drawn attention to this issue, focusing on the role of the women's movement in shaping (or not) the policy space and discourse on violence, and the ways in which constructions of the family, particularly the rights of the child, continue to determine the ways in which femininity and masculinity are constructed.

The condemnation of both gender-based violence and prostitution within the mainstream of Swedish feminism indicates that the two phenomena—women's sale of their sexual services and the physical abuse perpetrated on women by men with whom they are often in intimate relationships—are seen as similar, that is, as forms of male violence against women and girls. Both prostitutes and women experiencing violence are seen as "victims" needing protection from the state. In this chapter, I am less concerned with exploring the ideological and normative dimensions of this conflation—particularly the link between bodily integrity and sexuality. Instead, I am interested in understanding *how* this conflation has arisen, and what it says about the relationship between women's bodies and social policies in Sweden. The juxtaposition of these two themes—violence and prostitution—draws its orientation from the broader international feminist arena, where the issue of sexual violence does indeed elicit unanimous condemnation whilst the issue of prostitution/sex work is the subject of great contestation in terms of perspectives on women's bodily rights and sexual integrity, with significant policy consequences.

"WHAT SORT OF FREEDOM IS IT TO CHOOSE TO SELL YOUR BODY?"[2] PROSTITUTION POLICY IN SWEDEN

In 1998 it was estimated that there were 2,500 women in prostitution who worked through a variety of *modus operandi* in Sweden, of whom 650 were street prostitutes. This number is considered to be fairly small, especially in contrast to countries like the Netherlands (Kilvington et al. 2001). An estimated 125,000 men purchased sexual services each year in Sweden,[3] and 10–13 percent of Swedish men were estimated to have bought sex from women prostitutes (Boëthius 1999). Trafficking is also seen as a growing problem. Immense borderlines, especially in the more inaccessible parts of northern Scandinavia, visa freedom with the Baltic States, and the use of the Internet have made trafficking harder to control (IAF 2001).

The Evolution of an Approach

Despite being considered a "liberal" society—for example, marriage has historically drawn on diverse traditions, most of which acknowledged pre-marital sex and recognised cohabitation as a form of marital alliance—the

Swedish policy approach to prostitution is abolitionist. Purchase of sexual services is seen as incompatible with the traditions and values of Swedish society. In 1998, purchase of sexual services was legislated as an imprisonable criminal offence.

In 1993, a Commission was constituted which investigated the growth and change in the sex industry and submitted its report in 1995. Prostitution was argued to be a degradation of women and a form of violence against women (Gould 2002, 443). Gould attributes the perspectives of the Commission to growing concerns about the growth of the sex industry, particularly in terms of political and economic change in Eastern Europe. In the context of Sweden's emphasis on non-exploitative gainful employment, there was resistance to seeing prostitution as a part of the mainstream labour force and to espousing the liberalism evident in countries such as the Netherlands. While the "neo moralism" of this approach was denounced in particular quarters, the tenor of the public and policy debates was firmly abolitionist. Although several women activists and politicians were keen to only penalise the punters, and succeeded in ensuring that this was enshrined in the law, the overall abolitionist approach was supported in most feminist quarters (Gould 2002, 207).

The 1993 Commission found its roots in a longer history of political and civil debates on the issue of prostitution, driven by increasing concerns about violence against women being articulated by women's movements. A Commission had been set up in 1981 as a response to women's movements' criticisms of an earlier commission on sexual offences that had sought to soften rape charges and reduce penalties.[4] Commissioner Hanna Olsson[5] stated in the report that prostitution was not a "woman question," but rather one of human dignity (Svanström 2004, 227). Yet, the report did not suggest criminalisation, arguing that this would increase the stigma associated with prostitution, and in all possibility drive it underground. Instead measures that were proposed focused on criminalising the (male) purchaser of sexual services, placing strictures on landlords not to rent properties used for prostitution, creating positive material incentives to enable prostitutes to leave this line of work, and also banning public pornographic shows. Parliamentary and wider debates on the report found general support for the proposals, particularly the move not to criminalise prostitutes, while criminalising their clients.

The construction of prostitution in these debates and subsequent statements surrounding the enactment of a government bill in 1982 had three particular features: one, the problem was framed as a societal one, not particularly about either men or women, but about the relationship and imbalance of power between them; two, it built on a widespread view that the commercialisation of sexuality was not to be encouraged or indeed was to be condemned outright; and three, it placed prostitution within an analytical framework of gender relations, and recognised patriarchy as the wider problem. The framing of the issue as not about women alone, but about society more widely, was the basis on which men, as clients and pimps, were brought into the debates on prostitution.

Furthermore, the social welfare state was posited as an alternative to prostitution. When the law came into force, some media ran sob stories: What about the prostitutes who could no longer make a living? Naturally, prostitutes will lose income, but the idea is that social welfare will help them find other occupations that do not involve humiliation and oppression (Boëthius 1999, 5).

The debates revealed nontolerance for any approach to prostitution that allowed for the possibility of prostitution as the outcome of the exercise of choice, however limited, and posited the state's support and patronage through the social welfare system as the appropriate counterpoint to the exploitation and abuse that was assumed to go hand-in-hand with prostitution. The moral condemnation of the exploitation of women that was considered to define prostitution received backing, or rather was made possible, by the policies of a paternalistic welfare state.

While these initial debates flirted with the idea of criminalising the client, the 1982 law prohibited public pornographic shows but went no further. However, Svanström (2004, 233) notes that between 1983 and 1993, over fifty bills were proposed, thirty of which advocated the criminalisation of the client. The 1993 Commission was set up both to investigate the prevalence of different types of prostitution (homo- and heterosexual) and to propose solutions to tackle them, including the question of the effectiveness of criminalisation as a measure. This Commission proposed criminalisation of both the prostitute and the client—arguing that one could not be punished and the other let off. Dissenters from this Commission argued that the proposal did not address the patriarchal structures that resulted in women prostituting themselves. The issue of male power over women would be glossed over if the prostitute were criminalised alongside the client. Reactions in the media supported the view that women were the victims and that punishing them would not be appropriate. The final bill proposed by the government in 1998 accepted many of the arguments made and proposed criminalisation of only the client (Svanström 2004, 235).

The proposal put forth in 1998 for *Kvinnofrid* (Violence Against Women Act) was greeted with great debate, both within Parliament and outside of it. Svanström (2004) notes gender differences within some of the parties, where women members were more in favour of criminalising just the buyers. Those in favour of the proposal argued that as much of sex work was already underground, it was important to legislate in a manner that would decrease demand for services. The law enacted in 1999 went ahead and criminalised only the buyer, with penalties of fines or imprisonment for up to six months. Criminalisation was seen as an adjunct approach, with a central focus on providing counselling and support services to buyers[6] (IAF 2001). The "discourse of distinctions" (Westerstrand 2002) was rejected[7] and all forms of prostitution were seen as a social problem (Kilvington et al. 2001).

It could be argued that the active presence of women in politics, and of coalitions of women across party lines, was what drove the passage of the bill. In 1994, Swedish voters placed more women in Parliament than anywhere else in the world, with 41 percent of Riksdag members being female (Boëthius 1999). Boëthius points out that: "As women storm into the political arena, something extremely interesting occurs: what has been seen as 'natural'—such as prostitution—is suddenly being questioned" (1993, 3).

Impact of the Law

As Svanström (2004) notes, the passage of the Kvinnofrid law has not marked the end of the debate. A significant reason for this is that the issue of whether the sex trade has declined as a result of the act is not yet resolved. Although the Rikskriminalpolisen report (2004, 22) suggests that the sex trade has declined significantly as a result of lower demand, with significant knock-on effects on trafficking,[8] it also acknowledges that cross-border methods of disturbance of networks for prostitution ". . . will hardly lead to the disappearance of the sex trade." Writing in the newsletter of the International Abolitionist Federation (IAF 2001), Sjögren and Petterson (2001, 10) claim that the first visible effect was that street prostitution in the biggest Swedish cities declined dramatically as a result of police actions. Although numbers went up again after a time, they remained lower than previously (see also Socialstyrelsen 2003; Kilvington et al. 2001). They also note changes in methods as the sex trade has adapted to the law's enforcement, with more mobile phones being used, and more women falling out of contact with the outreach workers of IAF, and possibly hence also of the State. Further, they note that prostitutes themselves have varied opinions of the law—some carry on as before, whilst others see the law as an opportunity for change.

Mechanisms for enforcing the law include counselling as well as police enforcement. A common national coordination mechanism is in place for prostitution and violence, and a National Centre set up for dealing with violence against women has prostitution included within its remit (IAF 2001). Anti-trafficking initiatives are coordinated by the police to enable cooperation with cross-border police and authorities in other countries (Rikskriminalpolisen 2004). Sjögren and Pettersen (2001) note that while the police were given funds to cover their extra duties in enforcing the legislation, social work institutions received no extra funds to deal with prostitution. Given the difficulties of reaching both clients and prostitutes who continued in the sex trade despite the law, both social workers and the police have found it difficult to have a comprehensive effect. For example, social workers in a project that provides counselling to prostitutes' clients found that they were not attracting more clients than they were prior to the law's enactment. For the police, male clients are less likely to come forward to report on pimps and profiteers, as they can be legally implicated in the process (Östergren 2004).

The irony with the law is that while it was designed to "protect" prostitutes by not making it illegal for them to offer sex, prostitutes have been possibly exposed to greater harm in the course of their "legal" activities. This is a theme that Petra Östergren[9] develops in her substantial critique of the Swedish policy. Aside from pointing out the lack of representation of the voices of prostitutes in the whole debate in Sweden, most of whom she claims oppose the law, she notes that sex workers have become more vulnerable, been forced to turn to deceit in order to rent premises, and also in some cases forced into street work as a result of the ban on procurement.[10] This is compounded by their fear of turning to the police as they are worried that they will be forced to complain formally about their clients. The overall decline of street prostitution has also reduced the chances for women to network, which prevents them from sharing information about dangerous or violent clients. She reports that sex workers face greater competition as a result of a decline in customers, which forces them to engage in forms of sexual activity that they otherwise may refuse. Overall, reduction in the control of sex workers over their trade has been damaging to them. These reports are supported by reports on the implementation of the law by official enforcement agencies (see, for example, Socialstyrelsen 2003).

While the law's intention was to cut down demand, allowing prostitutes to then turn to the social welfare state, reality has not followed the policy model's expectations. Östergren reports that many sex workers do not think that what they do is wrong, and feel that the law has the far worse effects of stigmatising them and making them view the state as opposed to their interests. She notes that according to the law, the women are neither criminals nor the victims of criminals, which makes their position in courts of law highly ambiguous when they are called upon as witnesses against their clients. What the Swedish law does is confer a status of *social* victimhood on prostitutes (through arguing that they are the victims of patriarchy) rather than *criminal* victimhood, which places them at the receiving end of continuing stigmatisation of their profession, and without rights when they appear in courts of law.[11]

In the contested debates around prostitution in Sweden, the famous pragmatism of the Swedish policy approach seems somewhat absent. Instead, the debates have seen the characterisation of those in favour of the decriminalisation of prostitution as "libertarian," believing in free choice, and ignoring the "systemic oppression and subordination of females by males and men's eroticization of females as objects for their sexual pleasure" (Ekberg 2002). Westerstrand (2002, 55) criticises opponents of the legislation for choosing "a fragmented individually-oriented view that obscures the complexity of the issues and the gender political dimensions." Such a polarisation is not surprising, characterising as it does much of the international debate on prostitution.

A final point to make here is that criticisms of decriminalisation policies seem equally applicable to criminalisation policies—at least as far as some of the Swedish literature has revealed. For example, D'Cunha (2002, 38–39) lists the following limitations of decriminalisation policies:

- greater product, service, and market expansion and diversification, and newer, more brutal or bizarre forms of exploitation;
- the difficulty of controlling the industry once it has been normalized;
- the lack of attention to the structural forces that have conditioned women's entry into prostitution and the perpetuation thereby of a vicious cycle, where opportunities for developing "reciprocal, equal, just, and empowering relationships" between women and men are undermined and the grounds laid for more girls to enter the trade;
- women in legalised brothels are likely to be subjected to even greater controls by their pimps.

Each of the preceding issues has been argued in Sweden to occur despite criminalisation.[12] The one exception is D'Cunha's (2002, 38) observation that decriminalisation indicates sanction for "an exploitative and oppressive institution that has emerged from the historical vulnerability and subordination of women." In that sense, the biggest advantage of the Swedish policy approach is, arguably, that it has consolidated a majority view about the undesirability of prostitution on Swedish soil, and indirectly reflected a move toward commitment to gender equality based on an analysis of male power. Even so, the reasons for this development in Sweden merit attention, and an effort is made in the next section to highlight factors that may explain this shift.

SOCIAL POLICY FOR "SOCIAL VICTIMHOOD"?

As argued at the outset of this chapter, there is a linking of gender-based violence and prostitution suggested in some of the advocacy around feminist struggles to address bodily integrity in Sweden. Both violence and prostitution share a tendency to attract generalised stereotypes, which often are used to construct static notions of "victimhood." Accounts relating to both survivors of violence as well as sex workers often suggest that excessive dependence—on male relationships or on drugs—mark their common experience of male power. Sex workers are, by and large, assumed to have experienced some form of violence at the hands of men.[13]

A wider limitation of the protective approach is the faith demanded in the state's management of a gender-equitable social order. Such a paternalistic policy approach can restrict spaces for women to come forward and articulate the violations of their rights. Gender equality as a "discursive truth" in Swedish policy (Elman 2001) first resisted efforts to provide evidence of flaws in the social democratic project in the form violence, and second, when this neglect was corrected, created a paradox where announcing abuse is seen as a sign of vulnerability not strength. Women who are strong—"the strong victim"—provide a counter-image to the "vulnerable victim"—that is, "the prosecution requires the victim's willingness to cooperate but the withdrawal of the cooperation indicates that the victim is frightened and that the case should indeed be prosecuted" (Elman 2001)

An approach to gender equality that emphasises women's victimhood at the hands of patriarchy may result in an overemphasis on women's vulnerability to the detriment of allowing the women who are the subjects of violence and prostitution to script policy responses to their situation. Much recent Swedish feminist writing refers to patriarchy to explain why, despite the advancement of several rights for women and a measure of economic security afforded by the state, women still experience violence, or resort to selling their sexual services to men. Westerstrand unites the two strands by promoting an approach that "sees violence as a life context for men and women" and also "sees prostitution as a gender-cultural arena" or a site where relations between women and men are reproduced within a patriarchal framework of power and control (2002, 55).

Insisting that both violence and prostitution should be seen solely in terms of larger gender regimes of ideas and norms, and by declining to allow that an individually oriented perspective may also be appropriate in determining policy, Westerstrand argues that prostitutes are not the "legitimate interpreters of the sex trade," but rather "everyone is responsible for taking a stance on the existence of the sex trade" (2002, 55.). Equally, she argues, any argumentation based on the rights of women over their bodies and what they do with them cannot be considered acceptable (2002, 53). Implicit in Westerstrand's argument are the views that the experiences of both women in prostitution and women who are in violent relationships can be analysed within an overarching framework of patriarchal gender relations, and that both categories of women are deserving of state protection. The complexities in difference between women who experience violence and those who sell their services are, by and large, overlooked—or when addressed, not seen as sufficient to merit a delinking of the two issues in terms of policy discourse.

FROM MOTHERHOOD TO PERSONHOOD TO PARENTHOOD—UNDERLYING CURRENTS IN SWEDISH SOCIAL POLICY

Four features of the debates and policy actions on prostitution and gender-based violence have been raised in this chapter thus far. First, in the current phase of Swedish policy discourse, protection of women who are "bodily" vulnerable is treated as a measure of gender equality, moving on from a focus on labour and employment rights. Second, this reflects correction of a history of policymaking that is considered to have been largely gender-neutral in its approach to gender equality (Eduards 1991). Third, this could to a great extent reflect the high levels of women in Parliament, and the articulation of their voices, with external feminist allies, on issues that continue to affect women in Sweden. Fourth, in keeping with traditions of policy development in Sweden, the approach continues to be paternalistic, casting women as requiring protection, and strongly normative, potentially discouraging the subjects of such policy initiatives from voicing their opinions and experiences.

However, I argue that a further part of the explanation rests in the particular development and articulation of "personhood" in Swedish welfare and gender equality policy. Despite shifts from motherhood to a gender-neutral worker, women's personhood is still associated strongly with reproductive responsibilities. The partial success of paternity leave policies in influencing the division of labour, and the continuing positioning of women within the labour market as mostly part-time and lower-paid workers are issues treated at length elsewhere in this book. However, gains made by women have enabled them to retain a fair degree of autonomy by replacing dependence on men with dependence on the state.

The origins of the Swedish welfare and gender equality approaches were based on motherhood and had roots in the foundation of social democracy and the vision of a classless society represented by the People's Home. Arguing for bimodal career patterns for women, encompassing both work as well as motherhood, the Swedish welfare model supported both motherhood and flexibility from employers.[14] Lewis and Åström (1992) argued that therein lay the seeds of the distinctive Swedish approach to women's welfare: emphasising both equality as well as difference, on terms that privileged motherhood rather than women themselves. In the 1960s and 1970s, the shift was toward emphasising a dual-breadwinner family model, building this into the social insurance system. Economic and labour market policy thus was oriented toward a notion of personhood that recognised individual rights as well as gender-based identities, particularly in relation to motherhood. Through this "bimodal" understanding of women's claim to equality, the Swedish model is seen as offering important implications for discussing women's social citizenship elsewhere, particularly regarding how both equality and difference arguments have been used (Lewis and Åström 1992).

However, the normative (masculinist) underpinnings of citizenship have not been fully challenged. First, citizenship for women requires both recognition of "personhood" (an individual's independent claim to rights as a human being) as well as a strong welfare model that backs political citizenship. The gender equality model of the Swedish state is premised on the welfare state; however, the full employment model that underpins the welfare state means that those who benefit most are those who work full-time all their lives—"men, in other words" (Eduards 1991, 174). A high proportion of women work, but on different terms than men—nearly half work part-time, and continue to have primary responsibility for children, and women generally still earn less than men for similar work. "Equal status policies have not succeeded in changing these well-established narrow social definitions of what is useful work and productivity, and have thus been of little value in the struggle for a less sex-segregated society" (Eduards 1991, 174).

Second, the focus on children's welfare has brought new dimensions to both the state's relationship with the family unit, whether defined by marriage or not, with implications for gender relations that may compromise women's independence and autonomy. Parenthood has become a new mode through which the state regulates the family, with policies that particularly strengthen the rights of women (as mothers), such as the payment of subsidies to mothers and not fathers. Florin and Nilsson (1999) associate this concern with the effects of greater gender equality—rising levels of divorce and the increased tendencies for people to cohabit rather than marry may have put concerns for children's welfare on the radar of government policy. A spate of government investigations were instituted in the mid-1970s, putting children's welfare centre-stage in the social policy arena. Sweden's ratification of the UN Convention on the Rights of the Child also played a role, as reflected in legislation for children's protection such as the law against hitting children.

The construction of children as central to the project of gender equality underlies Swedish family policy "which presupposes shared parenting and a high degree of parental co-operation post-separation/divorce"[15] (Eriksson 2002). The ensuing focus on fatherhood through the lens of gender equality, argues Eriksson (2002), results in the impact of violent fathers on the child's well-being being subordinated to the right of the child to be raised by both parents, regardless of the relationship between the parents. For example, a controversial amendment to the law governing custody and visitation rights made in 1995 places a woman who does not actively support her child's contact with its father at risk of losing custody of the child. That is, family policy becomes particularly interventionist at the point when the family unit breaks down. The policy is based primarily upon the notion of the child's right to a close contact with both (biological) parents, as the aim of Swedish welfare reform has been to enable both parents to take part in the everyday care of children (Eriksson 2002, 9).

However, the privileging of joint custody (even if against the will of one parent), could result in difficulties for women where the father has a history of violence toward his partner. Elman (1996) found that women in shelters for battered women were still obliged to entitle their spouses to equal rights over the child. In cases where this meant disclosing the address where the women were staying, even shelter organizations could be penalised for colluding with women unwilling to disclose this information (Elman 1996). Further, this also made abused women think harder about leaving their spouses, as the children would anyhow be obliged to maintain a relationship with their father. The presumption is that a violent husband is not necessarily a violent father, with the burden resting on the woman to prove otherwise. Dahlberg and Taub (1992, 149) argue that the legal codes on parenthood suggest that: "the sexual contract of Sweden today is thus a male-centred right to take care of or have access to his own children, and via the children, contact with and even control of their mother."

These two examples—the normative construction of personhood through the social welfare model, and the possible impact on gender relations through the regulation of child welfare—are used to highlight the difficulties of crafting a gender equality model that can both grant "personhood" and at the same time recognise the complex web of emotions and power that constitute interpersonal relationships. The Swedish response to prostitution reflects the complexity of these issues, yet gives rise to solutions that deny those involved their "personhood," by imposing a status of social victimhood and not making room for prostitutes themselves to exercise their voices in the public debate or in the implementation of the policy response.

On a more practical level, the reliance on the state as an alternative to those interpersonal relationships that result in abuse and exploitation experienced by women may need to be called into question, and may also explain why the law on prostitution has not fully had the desired effect. As the welfare state rolls back, there may be a question of how far it can be the provider for all, both materially and in terms of covering the choices that people may want to make. Further, as Kilvington et al. (2001) have pointed out, policy discourses need to recognise the impact of transnational migration on the state–citizen relationship. The issue of prostitution is not a matter merely to be resolved for Swedes by Swedes. The presence of women of different races and nationalities in the Swedish sex trade, with their own stories and struggles, requires perspectives on the Swedish state's responses to global patterns of labour movements and a more global citizenry.

A counterview reflects on the changing circumstances of young women and children in the context of globalisation, economic distress, and the decline of the state in many parts of the world, and argues that the changing nature of the sex industry needs to be understood (Kilvington et al. 2001). Such an approach emphasises the importance of a "third way," between the routes of abolition and regulation, to allow sex workers to organize themselves so that some sex workers are not driven underground either by being compelled to register to enjoy state benefits, or by the criminalisation of their clients. Drawing on experiences from the United Kingdom and Germany, they argue that allowing localised action on the part of sex workers and support workers, alongside a recognition that many sex workers may be migrants whose vulnerability forces them to hide from authorities, may offer more pragmatic options to address the issue. This means placing at the centre of efforts a concern for the well-being of sex workers, regardless of normative and moralistic considerations that may be a part of public debate. Some of these issues are elaborated in the next section.

EMPHASISING VOICE IN THE ABSENCE
OF CHOICE: AN INDIAN CONTRAST

The focus on Sweden's policies on prostitution and gender-based violence has raised the following points. The shift from implicit to explicit regulation of women's bodies has been, first, a natural development of the policy trajectory that has emphasised consensus-based social policy with a strong emphasis on social engineering as a necessary role of the welfare state. Second, it has been in keeping with Sweden's strong self-perception as well as an external perception of Sweden as a champion of women's rights and gender equality. Third, it has been influenced by the strength of the feminist movement, particularly as a force operating within the political system.

Yet, the Swedish state in its attempt to shape gender equality has taken on a particular approach which appears to deny the agency and voice of those women it seeks to protect. Is this approach a model for the rest of the world? While many would welcome a state that protects its citizens from exploitation, it is not clear in this case whether the policy has been entirely successful. As noted earlier, there is a concern that through criminalisation, the whole phenomenon has been driven underground, hence preventing the state from protecting those it seeks to protect. This risk explains policies elsewhere in Europe which have chosen to decriminalize sex work with a view to more effective regulation. Further, how relevant can this policy approach be in a context where poverty and constrained economic opportunities remain a deep concern? The importance of disaggregating the phenomenon to unpick differences in circumstances of those who undertake sex work, and to acknowledge differences in the degree of agency that women may exert to come into or leave the trade on their own terms, is not reflected in the Swedish discussion. In this section, we consider briefly some of the issues that arise from exploring the issue of sex work in the Indian context.

Sex work in India is hard to measure and has its roots in diverse economic and sociocultural phenomena. A Government of India (1998) report on the issue identifies several drivers and variations, including: forcible abduction and kidnapping; induction through family members or brothel owners and pimps; traditional social caste or tribal groups who, on losing their traditional livelihoods such as performing or music, push their womenfolk into sex work; traditional cultural practices such as the ritual dedication of young women to temples, a form of prostitution under the guise of "marriage" to the God; women in economic distress on account of widowhood, abandonment, or separation from the family; and those women who work on the fringes of the sex industry, such as bar dancers who may or may not be sex workers.

Data on sex work and trafficking is hard to gather. A compilation of statistics from diverse sources by the Coalition Against Trafficking of Women (CATW) shows that in 1996 there were an estimated 10 million sex workers in India. An estimate (undated) of trafficking suggests that between 5,000 and 7,000 women and girls from Nepal are trafficked into Indian brothels, joining the estimated 200,000 to 250,000 women from that country already present. Cross-border trafficking from Bangladesh is also a large-scale phenomenon. In the context of widespread migration more generally, a number of distinctions become important for policy purposes: first, between coerced migration and voluntary migration, and second, between trafficking and prostitution.[16]

Formulating a single policy position in the face of such scale and complexity is clearly a challenge. A large-scale study[17] recently conducted by the National Human Rights Commission in India concluded that addressing the vulnerability of women in the sex trade and who are trafficked is a critical basis for formulating policy. For instance, they note that addressing the vulnerability of migrants is critical for dealing with trafficking, as many are lured by traffickers with promises of jobs. Similarly, marriage is another incentive used to get women to move to cities (NHRC 2004).

These economic and social vulnerabilities are such that a single protective approach is unlikely to work. Many attempts to "rescue" girls from brothels and rehabilitate them through state-sponsored economic schemes fail spectacularly because most state and NGO interventions do not or choose not to understand sex workers' own motivations and desires, even where the latter are unhappy about their choice of trade:

> . . . while state interventions sought to either rescue and rehabilitate, or incriminate the women, and non-governmental initiatives attempted to rescue, protect and empower the women, the women themselves were preoccupied with pursuing their livelihood, devising ways to gain social acceptance and resisting the intrusion of outsiders. (Shivdas 2003, 174)

In addition to questions about the feasibility of a single approach in the context of diverse motivators and opportunities for sex workers, there are also issues about diverse normative worlds within which sex work is defined. Sex work may be considered more acceptable in some social settings than it is in a policy domain dominated by particular elites from particular social groups holding particular worldviews:

> The emphasis in trafficking discourses about the pretexts under which women, mostly young girls, get trafficked by strangers and also the implication that ethnic minority women are more likely to be trafficked become problematic as other key issues in the trafficking of women get ignored. Recognition of family collusion in trafficking is often unacknowledged by such representations because the imagery is mainly about a male stranger who lures innocent women and girls for sale in Indian brothels. Other issues such as the women's knowledge and agreement to migrate for sex work, the role of frequent comers and the

remittance from sexual labour that benefit the women's families do not find a place in these discourses. (Shivdas 2003, 13)

These diverse perspectives, circumstances, and dimensions render any approach that would seek to impose one way of judging or analysing sex work both undesirable and unviable. Two cases from recent times are discussed briefly in the next section to elaborate this point.

PERSPECTIVES FROM SEX WORKERS IN CALCUTTA, INDIA[18]

Findings from a recent study from Calcutta, India (Bandyopadhyay et al. 2004) offer a lens on prostitution and trafficking from the experience of those women who have been sold, exchanged, or lured under false pretexts to the brothels of the city, in a context of poverty and livelihood deprivation. The workplace—whether a household where they worked as domestic labour or an informal manufacturing unit—was often a site of sexual harassment, where their physical labour was exploited in that they often received little or no wages. For some, boyfriends with whom they had left home brought them to the sex industry; some women chose to become sex workers when they left home based on information from neighbours who had been sex workers. The study highlights the role of multiple layers and levels of networks of informants who influence or aid women's journeys from the home to the outside world. It also reveals the complex web of decisions that women make in the process of working out their choices and strategies. While for many the entry into the brothel may not have been a matter of choice, engagement with other sex workers enabled them to find practical ways out of their trafficked situation. Importantly, a constraint to their exit options was the stigma associated with having been in the sex trade—for many this removed the options of returning home where they feared rejection from their families and community. Where women had actually left relationships, there was fear of returning to a violent husband. By uncovering the motivations and thought processes of women in the sex trade about moving on and beyond their positions as trafficked women, the study helps dispel a founding myth of trafficking—that it confers a form of permanent victimhood on women.

According to the study, women identified the local police, local petty criminals, brothel owners, and local politicians as oppressive forces. Support was sought from the state, or from other community networks. However, state interventions that see trafficked women as victims in need of "rescue" often do more harm than help in the course of their raids aimed at removing women from brothels. Placed in rehabilitation centres run by the state, trafficked sex workers are often at further danger of being harassed and exploited within the remand homes.

In the absence of state interventions that offer a meaningful (or less exploitative or abusive) alternative to the world of the sex trade, women rely strongly on each other to provide alternatives. In Calcutta, this has taken the shape of a sex workers' forum, an organized attempt by sex workers to regulate the trade and their working conditions. The Durbar Mahila Samanway Committee (Durbar) in 1999 established three self-regulatory boards aimed at ending exploitation in the sex industry by setting business norms for the conduct of the sex trade. Taking a strong stand against trafficking, the organization rejects any form of sex work that is based on coercion or deception. As an organization representing sex workers and defending their rights, the focus is on "restoring a degree of control to the trafficked individual"; conviction of the trafficking agent is seen as a matter for the state. Thus focus is placed on ensuring that no trafficked woman or child is recruited as a sex worker within the sex trade. Drawing on their own networks of sex workers, the forum is able to gain confidential and accurate information about the movements of women and children and gain access to these women. Unable to trust those who offer "rescue" for trafficked women, the forum acts as an intermediary between sex workers and the world that seeks to "save" them yet stigmatises them and their experiences.

This quick sketch is intended to highlight a few key issues that arise when looking at issues confronting sex workers in the global south. For women entering the sex trade in Calcutta, as elsewhere, the journey was a culmination of a quest for some form of change in their lives. While the journey to the brothels may not have in most cases been a matter of choice, handled as they were by a range of male and female intermediaries, the quest for change invariably came from either situations of familial breakdown, marital or relationship conflict, or a search for economic opportunities. Within the narrow world of choices in a context of poverty and deprivation, the situation in brothels was not always as bad as or worse than what they faced at home in terms of coercive sexual relationships and subordination.

A further point that the study makes is that the lives of women who are trafficked are not devoid of relationships. The world of the sex trade becomes an all-important resource given the stigma placed on them and their livelihood by external actors. Approaches that are abolitionist may underestimate the effects that such extreme positions may have in consolidating rather than dislodging the relationships that constitute the sex trade.

A final point concerns the form through which women choose to express themselves and deal with their "victimhood." The inability of women to place faith in the state has seen the evolution of new forms of organization. Durbar is one such example, where women have initiated their own systems, but involve others on their boards to represent more "mainstream" society. The work of Sangram, an NGO working in Maharashtra state on peer education in HIV/AIDS, has given rise to a collective of women in prostitution called VAMP, which is independently registered. Members of VAMP arbitrate community disputes, lobby with the police, help women access government programmes, and develop leadership potential. VAMP has also interacted with local policy makers to demand better-quality condoms and better medical treatment, and has placed a call to address trafficking on the South Asian Association for Regional Cooperation (SAARC) agenda (Point of View 1997).

Women's collective action is also increasingly evident as a strategy to counter domestic and other forms of gender-based violence. An example is *Nari Adalats* (Women's Courts) and *Mahila Panchs* (Women's Councils). These are forums where women can find justice that is accessible, respectful toward them, and inexpensive. These forums, initiated by women, enabled a public face-to-face arbitration in violence cases, bringing together both sides involved in domestic violence disputes. The central point of their actions, similar to Durbar, is to focus on the woman herself; strengthen her position, her self-confidence, and her ability to make decisions; and devise solutions to her problems.

The contrast with the Swedish context, where reliance on machinery of the state to implement laws and the simplification of what is a very complex set of issues are the outcomes of a particular trajectory that has been pursued over time, is striking. In contrast, the emergence of the Indian state from a context of colonialism, as well as the struggle to move social structures forward from feudal social relations through the infrastructure and values of democracy, among others, are relatively nascent. Alternatives to the state become more meaningful for groups for whom citizenship is denied because of the stigma associated with what they do, and whose access to the state is mediated by layers of intermediaries belonging to community and other social networks; and where the state is itself in the process of defining its rules, norms, and procedures. The state becomes only one, albeit a critical, agency that women turn to in order to struggle for justice. This point is highlighted in the next brief case study, the recent struggle of "bar dancers" in the state of Maharashtra to resist the state's intention to close down dance bars on the grounds that they are a "breeding ground" for prostitution.

Bar Dancers' and the Struggle Against the State

A recent decision in Maharashtra state to ban[19] dance bars, where young women dance for the entertainment of their customers, mostly to popular film songs, has met with widespread resistance from both bar owners and the dancers. Newspaper reports on the issue, which has dominated headlines in the city and elsewhere, quote senior government ministers as decrying the bars as a site where women are exploited and young men engage in crime (BBC News 2005). The state has an estimated 1,500 dance bars, employing 100,000 women.

Findings released from a study by a number of women's organizations, however, challenged assumptions that all bar dancers offer sexual services in addition to their dance entertainment, and that the women are trafficked into the bars (The Hindu 2005). Interviews with 153 women working in fifteen dance bars in Mumbai revealed that 89 percent of the women came from outside the city, and many from different states in India. The average age of the women was between 21 and 25 years, and the majority of the women had entered the profession through other members of the family. In that sample, all the women barring one said they preferred to work in the bars despite the stigma attached to the job, as they had insufficient education to qualify them for other jobs. While a few admitted to offering sexual services, many said they were only dancers. Another study (Kale, cited in Seshu 2004), also based on interviews with bar dancers in the state, revealed, however, that in addition to waiting on tables and dancing, the sale of sexual services was expected of the women. This study concluded that the presence of young women from various parts of the country and beyond suggested trafficking and migration as related phenomena. This study also revealed that most of these women are from the underprivileged, lower castes or minority communities. Despite the disputes over whether bar dancers do offer sexual services or not, the state government's move has met with resistance from both bar owners and bar dancers. A series of raids conducted by the police led to a massive demonstration by 30,000 bar dancers on August 20, 2004 (Seshu 2004). Although the protests were aimed at highlighting several issues—including the "hypocrisy" of the state where both police and politicians are alleged to make profit out of informal taxes levied on bar owners—it is clear that despite the conditions under which the women work, the decision to either close down or "regulate" the business was not agreeable to the women themselves. The bar dancers' protests have led to the incipient formation of a union, led by the "Womanist Party" a recently registered women's political party. The union, the "Bharatiya Bar Girls Union," is aimed at strengthening the women's position within the industry, while also recognising the vulnerabilities they face in the course of their work. Seshu notes that the range of issues that the Union is seeking to tackle includes actions to loosen the control of bar owners over the women, as well as ensuring regular medical check-ups, HIV/AID awareness, encouraging regular savings, and familiarizing the women with sex workers' unions across the world.

The question of "choices" is highlighted by Roy (2005), who reports that in the wake of the decision to close dance bars, agents are receiving more demand than before for opportunities to go to bars and brothels in the Gulf States. She notes that "excess supply" is halving the money that agents are offering the women. Many of the young women she interviewed are either the sole wage-earners in their families, or sought work in the bars as a result of family economic crisis. Many of them are not interested in alternative vocational training being offered to them because of the lower potential incomes in these alternative trades—such as applying *mehndi* (henna) or cooking—and the income that will be foregone in the course of learning new skills.

Both of the cases referred to here demonstrate the difficulties of intervention, where there is a need both for an overarching analytical approach to gender equality, while at the same time recognizing the richness and diversity of women and men's experiences, needs, interests, choices, and aspirations. Thus, an important medium for intervening in "social problems" that have negative outcomes on women is to work directly with women themselves, thus recognizing their unequal status, while at the same time developing their inner resources to overcome the situations with which they are confronted. As Shah et al. (2002, 23) note, "a rights-based approach acknowledges the agency of adult women and respects their choices, trying to offer a range of real alternatives for informed choice."

CONCLUSION

This chapter has sought to look at why Sweden, departing from developments in neighbouring and other countries, has since 1999 taken an abolitionist approach to prostitution. I have chosen to make my surprise at this development explicit, thereby making my position on the issue also explicit. Yet, the aim is not to join the chorus of critique from outsiders on this issue; the intention has rather been to use this development as a way of exploring how it may be explained as one in consonance with a history and trajectory of policy in Sweden. In a sense, I sought to explain to myself why this development should not be seen as surprising, reflecting as it does several features of Swedish models of gender equality—first, a tendency to paternalism and reliance on the state; second, a backlash against the politics of pragmatism and gender-neutrality, resulting in a swing away from pragmatism toward radical perspectives on Swedish society; and third, a policy approach that seeks to retain its identity in the face of many global changes that make gender equality policies more complex, particularly in relation to "body politics," thereby, paradoxically, underestimating the need for Swedish policymaking to recognise that the concept of "protection" needs to transcend older state–citizen models and recognise the diverse choices and influences operating on Swedish territory.

Yet what the review of literature on the issue uncovers is that bringing together violence and prostitution under one overarching ideological approach to gender equality represents a moral struggle on the part of a majority of actors of Sweden who retain an ideological distaste for sex work. While this ideological distaste is shared by many global actors, pragmatism combined with a recognition of the complexity of choices and trade-offs in a global order marked by inequalities of all forms have allowed for approaches to sex work that are open to the possibility of regulating it, and conferring some social and economic rights to those in the sex trade. Given the difficulties of crafting an approach to gender equality, and recognising the vast strides made by Sweden to push for greater social equality and gender equality, there is a sense here that with the issue of prostitution, Swedes may have finally found the limits to the social engineering project that the Swedish welfare state represents.

The differences in constructions of personhood between the Nordic and Indian contexts appear relevant. The community as a mediating site in India stands out in relation to the Nordic experience, where, as Niemi-Kiesiläinen (2001) suggests, the approach is communitarian in the sense that people share many common values and have a strong sense of solidarity—"but rely on the state to organize societal functions rather than on private initiative in communal life," In India, on the other hand, different forms of identity continue to be privileged in policy terms over gender, and women thus face challenges in terms of both state as well as community for the construction of their personhood. If family, state, and market are seen as the foundational pillars of the welfare state (Esping-Andersen 1990), then it is no surprise that the transferability of Nordic models to the developing country context is questioned; the role of community as a key player in the shaping and realising/practising of rights is particularly pertinent in states where institutions of modernity are still in the process of being constructed.

A second dimension of comparison in this chapter, therefore, refers to the role of the state in shaping and legitimating rights claims and the role and strategies of the women's movement (and other social movements) in expanding the categories of rights that women are to claim. While in India the regulatory power of the state is weak, particularly in terms of enforcing rights claims made by women (and other disadvantaged groups), the state continues to be an important site for the feminist project. This has an impact on the strategies of the women's movement, which has to both attack the state as well as cooperate with it (Gandhi and Shah 1991). Reforming the state in order to ensure that it serves better as an upholder of gender justice has therefore been an integral aspect of feminist activism, as has building trust in state institutions so that women are able to bypass community institutions and take refuge in more broadly defined entitlements when required. In many instances, as in the case of sex workers, this can cause contradictory or paradoxical motions in their struggle for rights.

The lack of state capacity and institutions has also meant that women's movements in India have focused on building alternative institutions for women. These alternative institutions (whether in the form of women's self-help groups or new forms of collective association) have also pointed to the salience of community (or non-state spaces) as a regulatory site. This is another area where differences are worth exploring. For instance, sex workers in Calcutta have focused on self-regulation as a means to combat trafficking, setting up their own organizations, rather than relying on external actors as discussed previously. Alternative forms of mobilisation also include using folk and local cultural media to reconstruct women's struggles for respect and dignity. In Sweden, a highly developed and proactive state and a history of strong support for the welfare state by feminists and women politicians has resulted in the lack of space for women who do not feel embraced by the paternalistic state to create their alternatives. Eduards (1997) suggests that this is changing, and that more women in Sweden are dissatisfied with the state and are creating their own networks.

While I noted at the outset the apparent paradox of the Swedish approach in empowering women through recognising and promoting their opportunities as workers, whilst more recently moralising about one aspect of that work—commercial sex work—the contrast with the Indian case raises questions about the regulation of "work." The informality of labour markets in India—both legal as well as illegal—means that for women the exploitation of different workplaces may have little relevance in terms of the choices they make. Family structures may be as exploitative and abusive of women's sexual services as those in the commercial market. Where neither family nor state can be relied upon, women's own spaces to organize in a way that best meets their needs are critical.

NOTES

1. The use of different terminology in referring to sex work needs to be briefly addressed here. While use of the terms "sex work" and "sex worker" is prevalent in the rest of the world, reflecting the growing demand for rights for those in the sex trade who have long been at the receiving end of derogatory treatment from society and state, "prostitution" and "prostitute" seems to be the preferred official terminology in Sweden. My preferred usage is the former, which is reflected in the text that follows.
2. Conservative politician quoted in Gould 2002, 206.
3. Also reported in a Reuters article cited in Coalition Against Trafficking of Women (CATW) website: *Factbook on Global Sexual Exploitation: Sweden,* http//:www.Uri.edu/artsci/wms/Hughes/Sweden.htm (accessed October 25, 2004).
4. The Sexual Crimes Report of 1971 enraged feminists with its view that rapists could be merely fined if it was deemed that their crime was "less than serious" (Boëthius 1999, 3). Furthermore, the report suggested that the state be involved as little as possible in people's sexuality, and did not refer to prostitution at all. A major focus of the public protest and debates was to disband the report and appoint a new Reporting Committee. This point is recorded as a turning point in more recent Swedish history, bringing both prostitution and violence under the spotlight.
5. Hanna Olson was the Secretary of the Prostitution Report, and at that time a section head at the Swedish National Board of Health and Welfare (Boëthius 1999).
6. An approach followed also in the legislation prohibiting drug use.
7. In contrast with the Netherlands, for example, where a distinction is drawn between forced and voluntary prostitution (Kilvington et al. 2001).
8. The report notes that through interrogations with women as well as interception of telephone calls, it appears that traffickers and pimps have found it difficult to find purchasers of sex for the women (Rikskriminalpolisen 2004, 38).
9. Petra Östergren is a Swedish writer and social commentator with a Master's degree in Social Anthropology.

10. Anyone profiting from the sale of sexual services by another is subject to the law. This includes, of course, pimps, but also landlords of properties hired for sexual services.
11. Though, as Kilvington et al. (2001, 85) point out, women involved in cases in Sweden are not required to appear in court when their clients are being tried, to preserve their anonymity.
12. Kilvington et al. (2001) point out the complexities of appropriate policy responses, arguing that both liberal/regulatory and abolitionist approaches have particular negative effects on sex workers/prostitutes, in terms particularly of driving the phenomenon underground.
13. This is a general assumption associated with sex work, but is not easily substantiated. Violence when experienced is not necessarily from clients, but may be from partners.
14. See Lewis and Åström (1992) for a detailed discussion.
15. Rights to divorce in Sweden have never been particularly contested, although procedures for formalising divorce may have been convoluted.
16. The Government of India's position as reflected in a report (1998) clearly recognises that all trafficking is not for prostitution. This is in contrast with the Swedish position which views international trafficking and internal prostitution as connected (Dodillet 2004).
17. The study covered 4,006 respondents in 13 States and Union Territories, including women who had been trafficked into prostitution, brothel owners, traffickers, clients, and trafficked children rescued by police officials.
18. I draw here on the case study by Bandyopadhyay et al. (2004), which in turn draws on findings of a recent research study with the Durbar Mahila Samanway.
19. The bill authorising the ban was passed in the Maharashtra Assembly on July 22, 2005. It provides for three years' imprisonment and a penalty of Rs. 200,000 (U.S.$4,650. at the time of writing) for those violating the ban.

REFERENCES

Bandyopadhyay, Nandinee et al. 2004. "Streetwalkers show the way": Reframing the debate on trafficking from sex workers' perspective. *IDS Bulletin* 35(4).
BBC News, March 30, 2005. http://news.bbc.co.uk/2/hi/south_asia/4394277.stm (accessed June 28, 2005).
Boëthius, Maria-Pia. 1999. *The end of prostitution in Sweden?* Swedish Institute. www.sweden.se (accessed October 25, 2004).
Dahlberg, Anita, and Taub, Nadine. 1992. Notions of the family in recent Swedish law. *International Review of Comparative Public Policy* 4:133–53.
D'Cunha, Jean. 2002. *Legalizing prostitution: In search of an alternative from a gender & rights perspective.* Seminar on the dffects of legalisation of prostitution activities—A critical analysis, Stockholm, November 5–6 (pp. 28–46).
Dodillet, Susanne. 2004. *Cultural clash on prostitution: Debates on prostitution in Germany and Sweden in the 1990's.* Paper presented at the first Global Conference on Sex and Sexuality, Salzburg, October 14.
Eduards, Maud. 1991. The Swedish gender model: Productivity, pragmatism and paternalism. *West European Politics* 14(3):166–81.
Eduards, Maud. 1997. Interpreting women's organizing. In *Towards a new democratic order? Women's organizing in Sweden in the 1990s,* ed. G. Gustaffson, 11–25. Stockholm: Publica.

Ekberg, Gunilla. 2002. *The international debate about prostitution and trafficking in women: Refuting the arguments.* Seminar on the effects of legalisation of prostitution activities, Stockholm, November 5–6.

Elman, R. Amy. 1996. *Sexual subordination and state intervention: Comparing Sweden and the United States.* Providence, RI: Berghahn Books.

Elman, R. Amy. 2001. Unprotected by the Swedish welfare state revisited: Assessing a decade of reforms for battered women. *Women's Studies International Forum,* 24(1):39–52.

Eriksson, Maria. 2002. Men's violence, men's parenting and gender politics in Sweden. *NORA* 10(1):6–15.

Esping-Andersen, Gösta. 1990. *The three worlds of welfare capitalism.* Princeton, NJ: Princeton University Press.

Florin, Christina, and Bengt Nilsson. 1999. Something in the nature of a bloodless revolution: How new gender relations became gender equality policy in Sweden in the nineteen-sixties and seventies. In *State policy and gender system in the two German states and Sweden 1945–1989,* ed. R. Torstendahl, 11–77. Uppsala: Historiska institutionen.

Gandhi, Nandita, and Nandita Shah. 1991. *The issues at stake: Theory and practice in the contemporary women's movement in India.* New Delhi: Kali for Women.

Gould, Arthur. 2002. Sweden's law on prostitution: Feminism, drugs and the foreign threat. In *Transnational prostitution: Changing global patterns,* ed. A. Gould. Thorbek and Pattanaik. London: Zed.

Government of India. 1998. *Report on the Committee on Prostitution, Child Prostitutes and Children of Prostitutes and Plan of Action to Combat Trafficking and Commercial Sexual Exploitation of Women and Children.* New Delhi: Ministry of Human Resource Development, Department of Women and Child Development.

The Hindu. 2005. Bar girls were not trafficked into Mumbai. June 15. http://www.hindu.com/2005/06/15/stories/2005061511010300.htm (accessed June 28, 2005).

IAF. 2001. Prostitution in the Nordic countries. Special issue, *Newsletter of the International Abolitionist Federation,* August.

Kilvington, Judith, Sophie Day, and Helen Ward. 2001. Prostitution policy in Europe: A time of change? *Feminist Review* 67:78–93.

Lewis, Jane, and Gertrud Åström. 1992. Equality, difference, and state welfare: Labor market and family policies in Sweden. *Feminist Studies,* 18(1):59–73.

NHRC. 2004. *A report on trafficking in women and children in India 2002–2003,* Vol. 1: New Delhi: National Human Rights Commission, UNIFEM, and Institute of Social Sciences.

Niemi-Kiesiläinen, Johanna. 2001 Criminal law or social policy as protection against violence. In *Responsible selves,* eds. Kevät Nousiainen, Åsa Gunnarsson, Karin Lundström, and Johanna Niemi-Kiesiläinen. Aldershot: Ashgate.

Östergren, Petra. 2004. *Sex workers critique of Swedish prostitution policy.* June 2. http://www.petraostergren.com/content/view/44/108/ (Accessed September 17, 2006).

Point of View. 1997. *Of veshyas, vamps, whores and women.* Mumbai: Point of View.

Rikskriminalpolisen. 2004. *Trafficking in human beings for sexual purposes.* Situation Report 6 (KUT/A-492-226/04). Stockholm: National Criminal Investigation Department.

Roy, Saumya. 2005. Chandni barred. *Outlook New Delhi,* June 6.

Seshu, Geeta. 2004. Bar girls seek rights. *Women's Feature Service,* September 6. http://www.boloji.com/wfs2 (accessed June 28, 2005).

Shah, Vidya, Beverly Brar, and Sonam Yangchen Rana. 2002. Layers of silence: Links between women's vulnerability, trafficking and HIV/AIDS in Bangladesh, India and Nepal. Draft paper prepared for the UNRISD project HIV/AIDS and Development, United Nations Research in Social Development,.Geneva.

Shivdas, Meena. 2003. *Resisting stigma and interventions: Situating trafficked Nepali women's struggles for self-respect, safety and security in Mumbai and Nepal.* Unpublished PhD thesis. Institute of Development Studies, University of Sussex, Brighton.

Sjögren, Torgny, and Elisabeth Petterson. 2001. *Sweden: Early effects of changing legislation on Prostitution.* International Abolitionist Federation (IAF) Newsletter, August 2001.

Socialstyrelsen. 2003. *Prostitution in Sweden 2003: Knowledge beliefs and attitudes of key informants.* Stockholm: National Board of Health and Welfare.

Svanström, Yvonne. 2004. Criminalising the john—A Swedish gender model? In *The politics of prostitution,* ed. J. Outoshoorn, 225–244. Cambridge: Cambridge University Press.

Westerstrand, Jenny. 2002. *Prostitution and the cunning patriarchy—Towards a new understanding.* Seminar on the effects of legalisation of prostitution activities, Stockholm, November 5–6.(pp. 47–55).

7 "Women Are Like Boats"
Discourse, Policy, and Collective Action in Sweden and India

Seema Arora-Jonsson

INTRODUCTION

During a visit to a village in Nayagarh district in Orissa, India, the women in the *mahila samiti* (women's group) in the village complained that the men from their village were always going out on visits and training. The women rarely had such opportunities. Kailash, a man from the Nayagarh forest federation, the *Mahasangha*, who had accompanied me to the village, asked them, "Would any of you agree to go to these meetings alone?" "No, not alone but together . . . in a group," said several women.

In a conversation one day later, Kailash held this to be one of the many reasons for women's inferior status or lack of independence. "Women are like boats . . . they always like to go out together . . . when they will be able to go out alone, become educated and do things on their own, they will be independent . . . empowered . . . It will come."

Kailash was referring to the catamarans that went out to fish in the coastal waters of Orissa. These small boats, sometimes no more than a plank, are often at the mercy of the sea. It is the company of other boats that provides security. The women in the *mahila samitis* chose to "go out to sea" together. However, organizing in women's groups, as Kailash pointed out, did not automatically or necessarily lead to personal change in gender and power relations in their household or in their personal lives. Nevertheless, the women in the *mahila samitis* had gotten their strength in numbers and the moral support provided by other women. Yet Kailash spoke about an individual independence that they did not have. And he voiced what was perceived by many, that it was a problem for women or a women's problem, but also that "empowerment would come" in the larger project of modernizing society and greater progress.

A foil to the village in India is a small village in northwestern Sweden. The women were independent and autonomous in the sense that Kailash spoke about as being empowered. They were able to act as individuals and had stronger rights as citizens and women. But when they chose to organize within a women's forum, it seemed all the more difficult. If the women in Nayagarh were indeed as poor, uneducated, victimized, and powerless as discussions with several men and some development reports suggested, they should have had more difficulties in taking up issues of gender and power than the women in Sweden. However, resistance to the existence of the women's forum was expressed strongly by some men in the village association in Sweden. This was despite the fact that the women were not as vocal in taking up questions of power compared to the women in India. Given that, in absolute terms, the women in Sweden were far better off with regard to health care; wealth; facilities like day-care; availability of food; choice to work and to marry; and geographical mobility, how is one to analyse the difference in these villages in India and Sweden?

In this chapter, I explore the possibilities and tensions of organizing as "women" in these two different contexts. It is based on research carried out in villages in Nayagarh district in Orissa, India, and in a village in a sparsely populated area of northern Dalarna, Sweden, where I follow the processes of women's organizing in the two contexts. The ways in which the women organized and the responses to their organizing provide important insights into the spaces the women had to exercise agency. Studying women's organizing in relation to attempts at village development and local resource management in the South and the North helped in understanding the particular in each as well as in understanding and interpreting local experience against a backdrop of discourses on development, local resource management, and women's empowerment that circulate globally.

The arguments by villagers for and against the women's groups in India and Sweden reflected discursive practices in their particular societies about gender equality and, more importantly, about accepted ways of practicing equality. I examine the ways in which notions of autonomy and collectivity are framed in the societal discourse on gender and equality mobilised by men and women in both places. By looking at how these understandings gave meaning to and challenged wider discourses in society, I take the discussion beyond the micropolitics of the villages to identify/comprehend a wider discursive context that was constitutive of and constituted by the women's efforts.

I begin with a brief description of the methods of inquiry and analysis, and look briefly at how gender equality and empowerment have been conceptualised by researchers and in policy in India and in Sweden. I then discuss how empirical material from the villages raises questions on what constitutes empowerment or equality in the two places, and examine the connections that emerge between them. The chapter ends with a discussion of how, in their relationships with the formal organizations in their villages, women were both empowered but also marginalised.

Methods of Inquiry and Analysis

The research in the villages was based on group interviews with women's groups, with individual women and men, with the staff of the women's development programme in Nayagarh, with men in the forest associations, and on participant observation at meetings and other get-togethers (1993, 1998–1999). In addition to this, the major part of the research in Sweden was carried out through a collaborative inquiry (1998–2002) with women in the village where the overriding aim was to decide on the research question and conceptual frame for the collaborative inquiry together (Arora-Jonsson 2005). In the process, the women in the village created a space to organize themselves, and a *kvinnoforum* (a women's forum) came into being.

THE PRACTICES OF GENDER EQUALITY: JÄMSTÄLLDHET (EQUALITY) FOR INDIVIDUALS AND EMPOWERMENT FOR OTHERS

Ideas about gender and equality were given meaning in the process of forming groups, and in the activities of those groups, for both women and men in both village contexts. These ideas shaped the discursive constraints and opportunities the groups faced, and what issues they were able to uphold or challenge.

Gender-Equality/Jämställdhet[1] in Sweden

Male dominance and the different treatment of women and men have become illegitimate in Sweden as a basic social principle. This can be seen in state policies and the wider discourses in society. The issue of gender or the organization of relationships of power has been approached as a question of equality between men and women and the avowed neutrality of the state, the market, and social institutions through which equality is to be achieved (Eduards 1995; Gustafsson 1997; Magnusson 2001; Rönnblom 2002). Sex/gender equality in the late modern Scandinavian context make the positions of a dominant male and subordinate female illegitimate (Søndergaard 2002, 194). Discourses of the "new fatherhood" and gender equality are culturally dominant today, regardless of actual practice (Magnusson 2001, 3).

State policies have been important in framing discourses of gender and equality in Sweden. Policies set up guidelines for political rule and have been shown to have important implications for the ways in which political subjects think about themselves and about their relationships with others (cf. Bacchi and Beasley 2002, 331).[2] Mainstream researchers often describe Sweden as having created a society that is both more egalitarian and more women-friendly than most others. Public policy is intended to achieve "gender neutrality, defined as equal opportunities for women and men in the labour market, the family and political life" (Gustafsson 1997, 42). Independent women's groups, especially in the 1970s, were instrumental in shaping what has been dubbed "state feminism," and the state is seen as the main source of economic and moral support for gender equality through its welfare policies. The public sector is the largest labour market for women. Academics have shown that the infrastructure provided by the state has an important role in forming what they call the *könskontrakt*[3] (Forsberg 1997).

Discrimination is practised in everyday life, but less overtly. Florin, for example, writes that women must always give "right of way" for others and for "more important" issues,—the market, the state finances, religion—that are seen to come in conflict with gender equality (2004). However my point here is not to speak of the discrepancy between the ideal and the practice of gender equality but to show how, by making discrimination illegitimate, these discourses may also be used to create limitations on what one may do.

One strand of feminist argument is that the emphasis on equality or equal worth,has shifted the attention from the real problem, that of discrimination against women (Friberg 1989). The word for gender equality, *jämställdhet*, which gained currency in the 1990s, is considered problematic by several researchers. Rönnblom writes that one reason the term is problematic, for example in official documents or in "the so-called equality plans," is because a word symbolising a vision is used to name what happens to be a problem (2002, 213), and it does not name the group that is disadvantaged (Eduards 1995). To speak of injustice in society by linking power and gender becomes difficult when the official word available is a description of a political ideal and one that emphasizes harmonious interdependence. Thus a space is created within existing frameworks and norms where the rhetoric of equality obfuscates a reality where man is the norm (Rönnblom 2002, 21; Tollin 2000).

Political scientists have argued that the Swedish political order is an expression of a gendered power order, and yet there is an assumption that decision making is a gender-neutral activity (e.g., Dahlerup 1987; Eduards 1997; Gustafsson 1997). This gender-neutral image of the political in society is believed to legitimise the continued subordination of women (Gustafsson 1997, 27). According to Eduards:

There is a public discourse in Sweden about the welfare state's and equality policies' successes that has clear nationalistic undertones: we top the equality charts (*jämställdhetsligan*). These ideas are espoused both by politicians and researchers. The question is in what measure feminist social scientists and historians are allowed to point to the persistent features and fissures in the development. (2002, 122)

Post-colonialist feminist writers in Sweden illustrate how *jämställdhet* has been used as a marker in relation to immigrant populations to distinguish "us" from "them" and has been established as a basic part of the Swedish self-image, in relation to the rest of the world as well as to the immigrant populations (Molina and de los Reyes 2002, 306). Mulinari and Neergard suggest that Swedish welfare state nationalism is based on a "we-pride" against a world outside that is chaotic, filled with conflict, and irrational. They add that the image of the generous and tolerant Swedish identity has been weakened in the past 20 years in the context of the shrinking welfare state and through events like the Palme murder that have acquired symbolic significance (2004, 210). Against this background, they claim *jämställdhet* as the only "successful cultural product" (de los Reyes et al. 2002) that can be used as an ethnic marker against those who are created as "the other." Some aspects of this self-image are re-created in the village discussions presented later in this chapter.

Jämställdhet as a policy focuses on individual women and men (Eduards 2002; Tollin 2000); the space it creates for equal individual endeavour is through institutions that are considered to be gender neutral. At the same time, there is a strong belief that Sweden has achieved a state of being equal or is "on the way to" total equality (Florin and Bergqvist 2004, 6).

Gender and Empowerment in India

The Nayagarh women's encounter with a discourses on "gender" came in the shape of programmes and agendas set for them by a combination of government policies, international aid agencies, and NGOs. Declining demographic indices and discrimination in all walks of life have led to a situation in which "gender" now figures as an "issue"—a problem—as well as a category of analysis (Sundar Rajan 1999, 2–3). Government policies have served to identify women as a special group in much developmental activity. Not infrequently, this has been done in an attempt to win over women voters. Theoretically, legislation and policies for women provide spaces for negotiating rights and privileges according to a constitution in which equality is guaranteed for all men and women. Reservation for women's seats on municipal corporations and councils (*panchayats, zilla parishads*) were guaranteed by the 73rd and 74th amendments to the Constitution. In general, however, researchers show that adopting a "pro-women" stance is largely limited to rhetoric, policy documents, or enactment of a piece of legislation. The legislations have in-built loopholes; the policy documents remain inoperative and unoperationalised (Lingam 2002, 316).

While development language has recently posited women as efficient workers and economic subjects in the new legitimacy accorded to the market (Harriss-White 1999; John 1999, 112), policies and programmes for women still treat women as needy, and the older images of victimhood or incapacity persist. Women's empowerment programmes were introduced by the central state from the mid 1980s, with an emphasis on "awareness raising" and "mobilisation." In several places this led to contradictory situations as women organized themselves against oppressive state organs. "This leads to a peculiar situation of the state sponsoring women's struggles against itself. This is like waking a sleeping giant" (Lingam 2002, 317), demonstrated by the unrest and resulting unionisation among women in several such programmes.[4]

The state is not the only major actor in the context of development. International donor agencies, NGOs, both national and international, are important in shaping policies and development activities. Discussion of women's marginalisation from centres of power is widely held within development work, not least due to the large amount of development literature that has helped to create a space for "women's issues." One outgrowth of the expansion of international feminist networks has been the possibility of feminist influence on where and how various forms of development aid are channelled. Aid agencies in the North often demand a gender perspective or gender component to their programmes in the South. Although the effects vary, they often succeed in treating women as a special category (for better and for worse). Empowerment through self-help groups or support for women's groups has often been interpreted in a simplistic manner and bureaucratised. On the whole, there is an assumption of inequality and of an obvious male dominance that characterises much of the discussion on gender. Formal structures are notable for the absence of women and are not necessarily seen to be representing women as a group.

I now examine how the threads of the preceding arguments turn up in the stories of the two places and contribute to a discussion of what empowerment might mean.

THE POWER TO NAME THE DIFFERENCE

A Presumed Identity

Ideals about equality and the gender neutrality of common spaces were present in the village in Sweden in several ways, in the women's own doubts about organizing separately and in the opposition expressed to it. It became apparent that the women saw themselves as autonomous but they also talked about male dominance in the countryside. They saw such dominance ingrained in much of the *föreningsliv* (associational life of Swedish villages) that was dominated by older men. However, none of the women thought of themselves as being personally disadvantaged simply by being women. On the personal and individual levels, they saw themselves as equals with men. In spite of this (or perhaps because of this), when it came to forming the women's group there was a certain amount of tension. An identity as a member of a women's group was uncomfortable, at least in the beginning, as there already existed other "neutral" committees in the village where formally both men and women could be involved.

The women spoke of being strong women. Having to acknowledge discrimination was also in part to make a victim of oneself. In justifying their group, the women chose consciously to build on their strengths rather than emphasize disadvantages. This did not mean that they did not see disadvantage, but there was a tension, on one hand, in acknowledging power relations, while on the other hand acknowledging discrimination could imply loss of self-worth and power in a system in which everyone was supposed to be equal. Tensions such as these made it difficult at times to articulate a common identity (or rather the identity needed to be constantly reaffirmed), or to make its activities and discussions stable and continuous as they were in Nayagarh. Their need for informality, which I discuss further in this chapter, stemmed partly from this.

In Nayagarh, alternatively, the women's identity as a "women's group" was not in question. There were different justifications offered for why a women's group was needed: differences due to timings, roles, and power to speak. Some women claimed that it was in the *mahila samitis* that they saw themselves as making a difference to the village. They were actually doing something purposively. They were doing more than just going about their daily activities, which they do at the individual or family level and which are often governed by tradition and custom (regulated by the men and for the younger women also by older women). In the groups they were communicating and acting together in order to achieve something. In one of the villages, the women challenged the ways in which the funds were being spent and the decisions made by the forest organization. In another, the women wanted to be a part of the *Mahasangha*, the forest federation, and were confused about the limitation of sending only two women representatives to the village forest committee comprising in total of five members. They felt that as they had acted as a group and got their strength as a group, they needed to speak from within their *mahila samiti* together.

Some of the groups also pointed out that acting together did not mean that issues affecting individual women were not their concern. But when it came to taking action, they did so for something that concerned most of them or when individual women needed the support of the others. They seemed to have more of a sense of identity and could call upon a collectivity. Although they were involved in projects designed by others (government and international aid agencies, NGOs), in several places, the village women began to take over the agenda of the groups. As one of the women's groups coordinators said: "What is the point of saving money and making mixtures[5] when everything else stays the same?" Women from different village groups met occasionally to discuss coming together in a larger federation. They encountered opposition from some other villagers, but they continued to meet in large numbers. The forest federation aimed to integrate the women through the *mahila samitis*, into the forest federation (not without opposition from many men), but when I spoke to the women, many insisted on having their own federation as well: "We can't keep waiting for them to decide when they feel that our issues are important to take on."

The Opposition

Resistance to the groups in the villages in Sweden and in India expressed itself in different ways. In Nayagarh, there was an acceptance that the women needed their own groups, although some of the men dismissed the idea of the women forming their own federation on the grounds of their incapacity to do so, especially "without guidelines" from the men. Here, the concern of the contending male-dominated community organizations was to have access to and control over the women's groups.

In the village in Sweden, in contrast, resistance to the women's forum was justified on the grounds that there was no need for such a group as there were other associations in the village for both men and women. As one of the men in the village association said, "It is a crazy solution to the fact that the village association is not working for the women." The strong reaction from the men might seem strange in light of the fact that the women mainly discussed arranging village festivities and other such activities. The group did not take up the question of male dominance publicly until much later.

The men in the association sought to defuse criticism of the village association by making it out to be the problem of some individual women. Women who did not attend village meetings were considered passive or lacking in self-esteem or generally disgruntled, and the men who dominated the meetings were seen as a matter of one or two strong individuals. Power relations were thus sought to be individualised. For example, one man in the association, countering the suggestion that the women needed their own space because they found no place for themselves in the village association, pointed out that he often stayed at home with the children while his wife attended meetings.

What may be seen as a common element in all these assertions is the fact that only individuals and personal relationships are the reference points—the issue is reduced to a private relationship, so that seeing men and women as a group is made more difficult. By talking about personal relations in which the heterosexual couple relationship is the scene, the gendered relationship is individualised, and its political force neutralised (Tollin 2000, 29). Florin writes that although individual relationships may appear equal, on looking at them in a societal perspective the structures of discrimination become obvious (2004). However, research has also shown how unequal relations can be seen to be reproduced in new forms in the home and between individuals (Magnusson 2001; Søndergaard 2002) and that the love relationship may be the very prototype of unequal relations between men and women (Holmberg 1991). By making discrimination a private question and an individual one, it is acknowledged, but it is placed somewhere else where it cannot be reached. Men's privilege was hidden, though it became apparent later when they felt themselves challenged. A response to this challenge was to stress the role and importance of the formal institutions. At the same time, the rhetoric on gender equality and feminism perhaps also posed a potential threat.

On the other hand, the dominant rhetoric of women as illiterate and victimised was shared by several male activists in Nayagarh. There was an understanding that women are oppressed by the present social system. The literature produced by the forest movement referred to the discrimination and the inferior status of women, and the problem was also discussed at village meetings, especially at youth meetings (often without many women involved). This understanding formed the basis of the work done by NGOs and development workers. In the *mahila samitis*, however, there was often a mixture of awareness of everyday practices and rhetoric that made their limits as women tangibly clear to them, alongside a sense of their own agency, echoed in statements like "what the men can't do, we have done."

The "surprise factor" (Smith and Smith 1983 [1981], 114), or what O'Reilly has dubbed the "click" experience (cited in Mansbridge 1999), of recognising their subordination as a result of an order larger than their particular relationships, was not new for the women in Nayagarh. They had little influence over the committees or state agencies as individual women. They had less to lose and much to gain by speaking from within a women's group.

Being Publicly Different . . . Being Publicly "Women"

The women chose various forms in which to organize. In the case in Sweden, the women found it necessary to work informally since they had little prospect of being able to influence the discussions in the formal structures, and the issues they took up were often considered subordinate to more important questions. It was important for them that they had an informal space in the village to meet and to discuss issues that they felt unable to take up elsewhere. In Nayagarh, on the other hand, it was the formality of the group that made its existence acceptable and possible within the village.

When I speak of the formal and informal, I distinguish them in the sense that the groups in Nayagarh were part of a women's development programme of the forest organization, that the *mahila samitis* (not all) were registered at the district and followed certain formal rules and regulations. They had a president, a secretary, treasurer, they were meant to keep a documentation of their activities, and carried out economic activity together. Importantly, they presented themselves as a women's group to the rest of the village, and were accepted as such. The *mahila samitis* also provided a space sanctioned by the forest organization and the village. The women's programme accorded them a legitimacy. They "drew the women together outside their households into a public space sanctioned by the community and the state. In acquiring even limited visibility as a formal group, the women had non-domestic reasons to meet, to establish linkages and perhaps to build nascent ideas of solidarity" (see Krishna 2004, 33, for this formulation of self-help groups as a legacy of the community development era).

The formality of the *mahila samitis* gave them the opportunity to become a stable entity within the village (for a while) and also to link up with other groups. In some cases this resulted in greater bargaining power for women vis a vis other social groups such as the landlords, violent husbands, or in-laws.

In the village in Sweden, existing power relations were sought to be maintained by asserting the gender neutrality of common spaces. This was reflected in the view that "nobody has stopped the women from attending the village associations." For the women it was difficult to challenge a system that was suffused with notions of equality and welfare for everyone and existed under constant threat from the urban "centre." Speaking of discrimination or gender made you someone who was looking for problems. It was against village harmony. This was reflected in the women's ambivalence about speaking from within or as an all-women's group. It was not as if disadvantages for women were not recognized at all. But the problem was made into one of individual women and not one of an order of gender and power. In this conception, there were other "normal" ways of dealing with such problems, through proper channels, and this was another reason for the need for informality. Thus, while in Nayagarh it was through the formal nature of the group that the women were able to wield greater bargaining power vis a vis other groups(landlords, violent husbands), in Sweden it was the group's informal nature, of not really having "a group" at all nor being a women's "project," that was important. The *kvinnoforum* came into being whenever they met. The informality enabled them to be more inclusive and open up to different women and to take up a range of issues.

Nayagarh was more gender segregated than the village in Sweden. This gender segregation was taken for granted by both men and women. The women in Nayagarh often said, "the men do their work and the women do theirs," although in practice the women could also be seen doing men's work, like patrolling the forests. The importance of sex/gender differences, social and bodily, were enmeshed in why they needed to organize differently. However, this difference was not often recognized as a difference of interests and power; rather, it was positioned as a natural/social role difference that makes it reasonable to support men working with issues of forestry while family planning, tailoring classes, and micro-credit were reserved for women. Even in these women's programmes, it was not the women who decided what they were going to work on—choices were made by outside research or development agents and depended on what was fashionable in development aid just then. Gender segregation and its recognition did not mean that a gender approach with power at its centre was adopted. However, being seen as a group also made it harder to avoid an analysis of difference.

In one village in Nayagarh, some of the changes that the women had been able to effect came about after their confrontation with state authorities. For example, they were able to get a hand pump for their village after they *gheraoed* (surrounded) the Block development officer (BDO) and refused to budge until their demand was looked into. They were openly challenging the bureaucracy and, through collective action, politicising their actions and exercising power. In another such incident, several women lay on a road on a hot summer day and stopped people from passing to force landowners to part with their land for a road to their village. The politics in the village in Sweden did not include space for such action by the women. Perhaps similar actions by women would just be seen as over-dramatic or embarrassing and would have different effects. In Nayagarh, by protesting in this way, the women were demolishing the myth of being victims and beneficiaries as they demanded what they considered was rightfully theirs. They communicated their message in a bodily way, exhibiting bodies that are otherwise meant to be confined to the home. By taking part in the action, they affirmed their own identity. Although these actions initially were started by the *mahila samitis*, other women also joined in, making their identity as women in the process important for the moment.

Similar action in Sweden would not be seen in the same way, as women already were meant to be equal, definitely not victims, even though they were considered to be passive some of the time. The importance of the women's bodies in Nayagarh and the way in which the women made use of them is significant. In Sweden, in an assumed neutrality of male and female, the implications of the body are sought to be denied. Here, it was something far less dramatic—merely meeting as women—that became controversial. The collective brought to light unequal gender relations in Sweden in a way that was already obvious in India. Perhaps that also explains why it appeared more threatening: difference was given a political meaning. This does not imply that power was not an issue in the Swedish village but rather that the space for taking it up was smaller. The women were resisted not for what they said, but for what their collectiveness suggested.

To organize as women in the village in Sweden felt illegitimate not only because of a rhetoric of collaboration and gender harmony within the village that hid unequal power relations (Arora-Jonsson, 2005, 230–250) but also in the wider orders of meanings in policy and institutions: it was a forbidden action, as Eduards (2002) calls it. The difference between the Indian and Swedish contexts in this regard was not so much a difference in *perception* of difference, but in the *response* to it.

"Other Men Are Jealous but Our Men Are Good" Versus "Our Men Are Backward"

Women in the two contexts also differed in their perceptions of men. When I asked the women in the village of Talapatna what made them successful as a group, one of the reasons they cited was: "Our men are good. The men in other villages get jealous when their women get more advanced and try and stop them from acting together."

This contrasted with the views of some women in the forum in Sweden, especially those who had worked and lived in towns. They often spoke of how "old habits die hard," implying a backward-looking view on gender relations among many men in the rural areas. They compared them to the men from the city university working with the forests, who, they believed, did not know about the discrimination in the village.[6] There was a belief that times had changed and the unequal relations that kept recurring were not part of the present, but remains of the past.

The married women in Nayagarh were much more outspoken about expressing conflictual relations with the men in their households or their villages. In Sweden, personal relationships to male partners were rarely the subject matter of group discussions. When they were, they may be said to be characterized as closer to the "love-contract" (Magnusson 2001) where relations were negotiated through "love," making the relationship personal and unique. This is not to say that there are no conflicts in Swedish households or love in the Indian, but more that these images are descriptive of the legitimate ways of talking about male–female relations and especially marital relationships.

These parameters of discussion reflect larger discourses in their societies. Feelings of injustice are always shaped by public discourses (Honneth 2003, 250). Orissa was considered male dominated, and individual men who were different were seen as aberrations and progressive. In Sweden, on the other hand, men in rural areas who exercised power over others were seen as relics from the past. Nevertheless, the exercise of power is rooted very much in the present. References to the past to explain unequal relations make acceptable inequalities that are embedded in and have their own history and complexity in existing relations of power.

DIFFERENCES (IN RESPONSE) BETWEEN THE MEN

Differences in the men's responses were as important as the differences among the women and had a role in shaping women's activism. Women's groups may have distinct sets of social interests, but the deep interdependencies between men and women are equally vital for understanding gender relations.

In Sweden, many of the projects spearheaded by the women could be carried out because of the support of men and women in the village. Both in Sweden and in Orissa there were men who believed that the women needed their own groups. The women in the Swedish village saw a generational difference among the men in the village: it was considered easier to speak to the younger men working with village activities, and it was through younger men, often relatives, that the women sometimes tried to influence association meetings. The opposition expressed by some of these younger (and "good," to use the terminology of the women in Nayagarh) men, however, may have contributed to a sharpening of the sense of discrimination by bringing up the contradictions in the assumption in Sweden that gender equality goes via a generational shift and what Hirdman calls the passive strategy for bringing about gender equality (Holmberg 1991, 48).

In Nayagarh, also, different men had different ways of responding to the women's groups. The men in the leadership of the forest organization and other members, mainly the older generation, spoke of the need to make the women aware, to impart training. Many of the younger generation spoke about needing to try and involve women in the *mahasangha* both for reasons of efficiency and equity, as did the Oxfam officer responsible for the funding of the women's development programme. Men's responses to the women's groups in both contexts depended on the particular situation and the men's involvement in that situation, although a normative order was also being negotiated. For example, in the village in Sweden, it was generally supposed to be good to have women's networks and considered to be important to work with gender equality, yet "gender" was considered dangerous in this case. Women's activism in Orissa was sometimes aided by the men ("our men are good") and at other times, it was a response to violence by men. In their activism, too, they were supported differently by their male relatives than by other men. Forest committee members at the forestry offices often invited me to come and see how well the *mahila samitis* in their villages were working. This does not mean that they necessarily believed in them for the same reasons as the women did, but it does show support for the women's organizing. As the coordinator for the women's programme told me in an interview:

> As it is now, some men are supportive in some places while in others they do not want the women to get together or go for training camps or get-togethers. They feel that the women just go there to eat and get smart and then destroy the household. They are afraid that the women won't listen to the men after having organized. Mahila samitis can be strong if they are supported by the men.

On one hand, by regarding the women as incapable, the men's attitudes limited the women. On the other hand, the experience of discrimination due to poverty and caste gave both men and women in Nayagarh a structural analysis of certain inequalities and the need for collective action to combat some of these problems. The men and women here were, "by and large, spared the kind of individualism that attributes every inequality to personal failures on the part of the less rewarded" (Mansbridge 1999, 300). This may be one reason that several men active in the community forestry movement supported the women's groups. The women active in the other *mahila samitis* did not position themselves against individual men but against what they considered "male behaviour," especially in cases of violence and dowry, because their men or some men could be good. In their view, development was indeed "incomplete without gender," and this included a transformation not only of the women to becoming independent or empowered but also of the jealous men to good.

Men from outside the villages played an important role in both places. The development agents who worked with the men in the communities in these two cases also happened to be mostly men. Development projects and especially participatory approaches have been criticised for reinforcing unequal relationships by prioritising those most vocal (Cooke and Kothari 2001; Krishna 2004) or as taking certain male members as "the community" (Guijt and Shah 1998). This has also been true in these cases in India and in Sweden. In the case of the *mahila samitis*, the women had support in their organizing through programmes introduced from the outside by Oxfam that were implemented through the forest organizations, providing a little extra space for the women, which some of them used to negotiate power relations. Compared to the case in Sweden, in India it was more permissible to challenge the unequal relationships as perceived by the development practitioners, partly because it is more permissible to do so in a "third world" rural society where inequality is a premise. In Nayagarh it was gender or male dominance that became an issue, but in Sweden it was equality and participation.

EMPOWERMENT: THE PERSONAL AND THE COLLECTIVE[7]

Placing the processes of the two groups in relation to each other directs attention to how the personal and collective take shape in ways that are different. According to Kabeer, one facet of empowerment is the ability to choose (Kabeer 2001). In this sense, empowerment may be seen as a somewhat normative idea. The women of Drevdagen, for example, were able to choose (more or less) where they lived, whom to marry, and how many children to have—choices that were not available for many women in Nayagarh. In that respect, the women of Sweden were already empowered. But their space for agency was circumscribed by the dominant (a particular) discourse on equality and modernisation. There are, of course, positive aspects for individual women who can claim advantages and equality within this discursive system, and collective organising can be seen as harming individual women who have found a place for themselves. But taking action on their own terms was what constituted empowerment for the women at the collective and village level.

In Nayagarh, the women's activism did not always lead to a better life for them. On a personal level, once home from meetings, they were still expected to cover their heads and not to speak in the presence of older males in the household. These were the same women who had fought for their cause with local male money-lenders and official authorities. Their confidence in themselves and their success, in certain instances, did lead to changes in household gender relations, but there was not necessarily a direct cause and effect. In a draft report on the community forestry groups (Mitra and Patnaik 1997), the story is narrated of the president of one women's group who was beaten by her husband for taking up the cause of a woman in the village who had been thrown out by her husband. The authors used her case to show that the programme was ineffective in changing the structures of gender domination in the home, thus espousing an idea of empowerment based on the individual. The authors did not look at what the women were saying collectively, such as solving disputes, dealing with violent husbands and nasty mothers-in-law, and working with problems related to dowry.

The attention to individual achievements is a humanist conception of empowerment that leaves unchanged structural conditions and places failure on the individual (Treleaven 1998, 53). "Third world feminists," among others, have criticised a focus on "singular women's consciousness." Referring to Sommer, Mohanty writes that the strategy is to speak from within a collective "to get beyond the gap between public and private spheres and beyond the often helpless solitude that has plagued Western women even more than men since the rise of capitalism" (2003, 82).

In an ideal world, there would be more direct correlation between the personal and collective agency that leads to empowerment. However, discrimination takes many different forms, though it may be systematic. In the words of Spelman, "we need to be at least as generous in imagining what women's liberation will be like " (2001, 87) in the multiple spaces in which women may choose to act individually but also collectively.

Creating Alternative Spaces

Women, both in Orissa and Sweden, shared several common spaces. In Orissa, these were the village wells and ponds, fields, and fairs, and in Sweden they were school meetings, village festivities, and other socializing. It was often these prior networks that they built upon in forming the groups. However, those spaces also had the potential of reinforcing subordinate relationships where power relations between men and women and among women may be reproduced. The micro-credit group in one village in Nayagarh, for example, was built up with the help of an older man from the forest organization and on prior networks in which he played an important role. It also deferred to existing social relations in the village.

In the groups that were active in Nayagarh, the coordinator of the programme and the field workers helped toward creating a space within the official programme that responded to what the women thought was important. It was the creation of the space that enabled them to come together and develop their collectivity and go on to take on other activities. In the village in Sweden, it was the lack of any one clearly defined activity that also made the space different and specifically the women's. The women's plans in the groups were not very different from what they may have done otherwise. It was instead the structure of the political space that they created that made it different.

The groups in both countries were inclusive in new ways. Although the *mahila samitis* were formed more or less along caste lines, in their actions— in the case of the road protest, for example—women from different castes joined together. Other women's groups who had not taken part in the collective incidents also related stories about the action as examples of what women could do. Similarly, the fact that all kinds of women, who might not have met otherwise, got together in the *kvinnoforum* made it a different space. In both places, women did not erase differences but met over them, creating the potential of changing existing relationships between the women, and their relationships to their villages.

Politicising that Difference

The very naming of difference became political. Meeting together led to identifying their differences, and for several women the basis of this difference lay in power relations with men. The women in India had to tread a fine line between the permissible and the nonpermissible, making use of different strategies and opportunities at different times to fulfil their aims. The successful groups always went to great lengths to show that their work had been successful thanks to the cooperation of the men. Kabeer refers to such situations as private forms of empowerment, which leave intact the public image but nevertheless increase the women's backstage influence (2001, 37). Meanwhile, the ambivalence of the women in Sweden to openly challenge the system may be understood as that of "tempered radicals" (Meyerson and Scully 1995) working from the margins of the system. They may be called "radicals" because they challenge the status quo—in this case through their organizing as women—as people who do not fit in perfectly, but at the same time who seek moderation.

Empowerment may be seen as a process that brings about social change (e.g., Kabeer, 2001, 28). But what does this say about transitory processes that are collective and where change may be difficult to measure? The *kvinnoforum* did not continue indefinitely. Can we speak of the women being empowered (temporarily?), through being able to mobilise resources, having a sense of agency and achieving a sense of identity, and a base from which to act? For some women, what they felt about gender and power relations became better articulated. It also became legitimate to talk about them, which in itself was empowering (cf. Eduards 2002, 129).

The women in Sweden and Orissa were being proactive. The women's initial objections about the top-down running of the village association in Sweden did not arouse much reaction within the village. But when the women organized themselves, when they were proactive, tensions began to arise. They were transforming their demands, wishes ,and dreams into self-organized activity (cf. Eduards 1997, 21). The women were exercising power generatively by choosing to form a *kvinnoforum*, and thereby transformed not only themselves but also the identities of the men: by forming the group they had defined the men in the village association as "men," as a group and not as individuals. Similarly, by wanting to form their own groups and federation, the women in Orissa were assuming power by "simultaneously controlling access and defining" (Frye 1983, 107).

A Faith in Progress

Empowerment in the context of India is linked closely to the idea of development. And although development has been debated at length with its many dimensions, economic development has been a dominant aspect. Income generation programmes and micro–credit schemes such as the ones started in Orissa are important in this respect, and they are meant to lead to some form of empowerment for the women. Yet, without linking them to other kinds of activities, they do little to change unequal gender power relations (Endeley 2001) and, while important, are not always sufficient. Reaching equality through women's involvement in the labour market has also been a cornerstone of gender equality measures in Sweden (Hobson 2000). But even here the importance given to the economic was limiting for the women in the rural areas (Arora-Jonsson 2005).

In India, one idea of development was that it was leading somewhere. As I cite Kailash at the beginning of the chapter, development and empowerment were something "that would come." Implicit in the idea of development is also the notion that it is meant to lead to a modern, equitable society. The referent for the meaning of development and progress is the West. Being modern and developed meant that women would behave in a certain way: be independent, dare to go out alone. Also implicit is the role of aid, trade, and international organizations. How gender is conceptualised is also a result of broader interactions and "carr[ies] the impress of forces that make a global society" (Connell 2002, 90). These implications were seen clearly in Orissa, where the women and men related to the "global order" in tangible ways as NGOs, donors, and other outsiders were part of trying to change their lives. They are more diffuse in the case in Sweden. However, the presence of the men and women in the South was palpable, as for example, when the women defined themselves in relation to my discussions about the women in Orissa.

Much after the main research process, I attended one more meeting with the women in the Swedish village. It was a changed group; some of the women who had been active had moved out of the village and some women, new to the village, also came for the meeting. I spoke about my thoughts on the organizing of the women's forum and of the *mahila samitis* in India.

A woman new to the village responded, "I have heard that in India women have become stronger . . . have developed quite a lot, ever since India has become modern. Perhaps that is why they have been able to do these things together."

Earlier, when I had spoken to another woman about the women's groups in Orissa, she was somewhat offended by the association. "But we are different," she told me. "We are working women." Baaz (2002, 143) comments that ". . . third world woman has functioned as the oppressed backward other in relation to which a certain image of a liberated educated female western Self has been constituted." In Sweden, the image of immigrant women as traditional, passive, and victimized has been contrasted with the image of Swedish women as modern, active, and equal (Brune 2002). Eduards (2002, 124) writes that the Swedish debate on equality is characterised by an understanding that it is better in Sweden than in other countries.

The image of the "liberated, educated female western self" (Baaz 2002:, 43) is also a part of the development discourse in India. There is an assumption that women's empowerment results in a modern, independent woman. At the same time, there are norms in each societal context that decree how women dress, the spaces they may inhabit, and what they may or may not do. The dissonance among these norms may make for a situation that is all the more constrictive but, at other times, it may provide openings.

Relating to the West is not limited to images but is also basic to ideas about gender and women's movements. Ferree and Subramaniam (1999, 18) write: "Allowing local women the space to develop their own forms of feminism is a challenge that the international women's movement has not always met in practice." Allowing for a space within a movement implies that there must be a given order in which a place has to be made. This relation is also present in the literature on gender and feminism emanating in the North and South. Chaudhari (2004, xiv–xv) writes:

> . . . . while, for western feminists whether or not to engage with non-western feminism is an option they may choose to exercise, no such clear choice is available to non-western feminists or anti-feminists. For us our very entry into modernity has been mediated through colonialism, as was the entire package of ideas and institutions such as nationalism or democracy, free market or socialism, Marxism or feminism. Any question of feminism therefore, had to confront the question of western feminism as well.

Thus, relating to the debate on feminism from the west is unavoidable. In many ways the roots of feminism lie in the same modernist ideas of emancipation and justice and power/knowledge relations that it criticises (Brandth 2002).

Taking account of these traditions does not invalidate the use of feminist thinking. It *locates* its use and insists on its partiality and accountability (cf.

Haraway 1991, 111). It directs attention instead to how uses and meanings are connected across specific places and to the ways in which hierarchies are formed between them. So, in a very abstract or obtuse way, while in one context a discourse of modernization and progress opened up a space for women in the "developing" world, that space was closed off in the "developed" world.

BOTH EMPOWERED AND MARGINALIZED

While shades of a strong normative notion about development and equality or empowerment could be detected in both the Swedish and Indian villages, there was in practice no obvious line of development. In both places, in their relations with formal spheres of the village associations and forest organizations, the women were both empowered and marginalized (Cooper 1995). The notion of equality did provide individual women with a relative power in village politics in the village in Sweden; some women took up questions of interest to them in the village association, and a woman was made its chairperson with the support of some of the men. Women's inclusion in meetings and conferences gave them confidence, and they often discovered that they were not alone in the issues they wanted to take up.

The women in Orissa were able to come together in a network as a result of contact with the forest organizations. The programme also provided them with the legitimacy to meet and carry out activities in the village, which may have been difficult otherwise. In a sense, the committees and organizations were "new" organizations in Orissa and had the potential of reworking or creating more equal relationships. Women claimed that they felt less restrained by social norms to talk and express themselves at meetings that were organized in villages other than their own and which were not dominated by men from their own families and villages.

But although these instances of acting collectively provided openings, there were also limits. In the Swedish village, a change in the leadership of the village association and the involvement of more women did not automatically imply a change in routines or procedures, or in who decided on village affairs. Women as individuals found a place sometimes, but as a group they had more difficulties in expressing themselves vis a vis formal arenas. In Orissa, the women's groups became more controversial the more independent they became, and the more they started taking up questions outside of the limits of the programme. Their desire to have a women's federation was considered unnecessary and became threatening when they proceeded to throw off their "victimhood."

In both places, the women had claimed that they needed a separate space because they were "women." By placing themselves outside of the dominant gender order in this way, women were making clear its biases but also were seen to be actively challenging these. In both places, the rhetoric of democracy and equality allowed them a space for their own claims within village politics. In many ways it was their contact with the formal associations that provided the momentum for them to start off on their own, but it was also in their relations to these organizations that the limits of their actions became clear. Nevertheless, an action has no end and, in ways that rippled through, the women had rocked the boats.

NOTES

1. All translations from Swedish have been done by the author.
2. There are, of course, differences in the implications and effects of policy. In India, for example, policies do not have the same effects in implementation as in Sweden. But then it differs from policy to policy in each country as well as in the specific context for which it is meant.
3. The term *könskontrakt, sex/gender contract* was first used in the Swedish context by Hirdman, who built on Carole Pateman's theory of sexual contract.
4. The support for empowerment programmes in India, on the other hand, may be understood if the state is viewed as a focus of power but also "as a set of arenas; a by-product of political struggles whose coherence is as much established in discourse as in shifting and temporary connections" (Pringle and Watson 1990, 229).
5. Snacks.
6. But these men did not only know, but were part of making the women's critique irrelevant by referring to it as personal and village politics.
7. With some exceptions, empowerment is not a concept used in terms of gender relations or in discussions of equality for women in Sweden. The research literature shows that the concept has been used primarily in research with handicapped people, in the context of immigrant women, in some cases in *byggforskning* (building research) mainly in the case of immigrant settlements and in business management literature.

REFERENCES

Arora-Jonsson, Seema. 2005. *Unsettling the order: Gendered subjects and grassroot activism in two forest communities.* Doctoral thesis, Swedish University of Agricultural Sciences, Uppsala.

Baaz, Maria Eriksson. 2002. *The White wo/man's burden in the age of partnership: A postcolonial reading of identity in development aid.* Doctoral thesis, Department of Peace and Development Research, Göteborg University, Göteborg.

Bacchi, Carol Lee, and Chris Beasley. 2002. Citizen bodies: Is embodied citizenship a contradiction in terms? *Critical Social Policy* 22:324–52.

Brandth, Berit. 2002. On the relationship between feminism and farm women. *Agriculture and Human Values* 19(2):107–17.

Brune, Ylva. 2002. "Invandrare" i mediearkivets typgalleri [Immigrants typecasted in the medafiles]. In *Maktens (o)lika förklädnader: Kön, klass och etnicitet i det postkoloniala Sverige* [*Power's different disguises: Sex/gender, class and ethnicity in postcolonial Sweden*], eds. Paulina de los Reyes, Irene Molina, and Diana Mulinari, 150–181. Stockholm: Atlas.

Chaudhari, Maitrayee. 2004. Introduction. In *Feminism in India*, ed. Maitrayee Chaudhari, xi–xlv. New Delhi: Kali for Women & Women Unlimited.

Connell, Robert W. 2002. The globalization of gender relations and the struggle for gender democracy. In *Geschlechterforschung als Kritik*, eds. Eva Breitenbach, Ilsa Bürmann, Katharina Liebsch, Cornelia Mansfeld, and Chritian Micus-Loos, 87–98. Bielefeld: Kleine Verlag.

Cooke, Bill, and Uma Kothari. 2001. The case for participation as tyranny. In *Participation: The new tyranny?*, eds. Bill and Uma Kothari Cooke. London: Zed Books.

Cooper, Davina. 1995. *Power in struggle feminism, sexuality and the state*. Buckingham: Open University Press.

Dahlerup, Drude. 1987. Confusing concepts—confusing reality: A theoretical discussion of the patriarchal state. In *Women and the state: The shifting boundaries of public and private*, ed. Anne Showstack Sasson, 93–127. London: Routledge.

de los Reyes, Paulina, Irene Molina, and Diana Mulinari (eds.). 2002. *Maktens (o)lika förklädnader: Kön, klass och etnicitet i det postkoloniala Sverige*. Stockholm: Bokförlaget Atlas.

Eduards, Maud. 1995. En allvarsam lek med ord [A serious play with words]. In *SOU 1995:110 Viljan att veta och viljan att förstå: Kön, makt och den kvinnovetenskapliga utmaningen i högre utbildning* [Swedish Government's official reports 1995:110 The will to know and the will to understand: Gender, power and the challenge of women's studies in higher education]. Stockholm: Utbildningsdepartementet.

Eduards, Maud. 1997. Interpreting women's organizing. In *Towards a new democratic order? Women's organizing in Sweden in the 1990s*, ed. Gunnel Gustafsson, 11–22. Stockholm: Publica.

Eduards, Maud. 2002. *Förbjuden Handling: Om kvinnors organisering och feministisk teori* [Forbidden action: On women's organizing and feminist theory]. Malmö: Liber.

Endeley, Joyce B. 2001. Conceptualising women's empowerment in societies in Cameroon: How does money fit in? *Gender and Development* 9:34–41.

Ferree, Myra Marx, and Mangala Subramaniam. 1999. The international women's movement at century's end. Paper presented at ESS, March 5, 1999. Prepared for *Gender stratification*, ed. Dana Vannoy. Roxbury Press.

Florin, Christina. 2004. "Väjningsplikten": Samtidens könsrelationer i ett framtidsperspektiv ["Right of way": Present gender relations in the perspective of the future]. In *Framtiden i samtiden: Könsrelationer i förändring i Sverige och omvärlden* [The future in the present: Gender relations in transformation in Sweden and abroad], eds. Christina Florin and Christina Bergqvist, 5–43. Stockholm: Institutet för framtidsstudier [Institute of Future Studies].

Florin, Christina, and Christina Bergqvist (eds.). 2004. *Framtiden i samtiden: Könsrelationer i förändring i Sverige och omvärlden* [The future in the present: Gender relations in transformation in Sweden and abroad]. Stockholm: Institutet för Framtidsstudier [Institute of Future Studies].

Forsberg, Gunnel. 1997. Rulltrapperregioner och social infrastruktur [Escalator regions and social infrastructure]. In *Om makt och kön: i spåren av offentliga organisationers omvandlig: rapport till Utredningen om fördelningen av ekonomisk makt och ekonomiska* [On power and gender: In the wake of the transformation of public organizations: report for the inquiry on the distribution of economic power and economic resources between women and men], ed. Elisabeth Sundin, 31–68. Stockholm: Fritzes offentliga publikationer.

Friberg, Tora. 1989. Kvinnor och Regional Utveckling. In *Kvinnor på landsbygden*, ed. Lars Olof Persson, 7–17. Expertgrupp för Forskning om regional utveckling (ERU).

Frye, Marilyn. 1983. *The politics of reality: Essays in feminist theory*. New York: The Crossing Press.

Guijt, Irene, and Meera Kaul Shah (eds.). 1998. *The myth of community: Gender issues in participatory development.* London: Intermediate Technology Publications.

Gustafsson, Gunnel (ed.). 1997. *Towards a new democratic order? Women's organizing in Sweden in the 1990s.* Stockholm: Publica.

Haraway, Donna J. 1991. Reading Buchi Emecheta: Contests for "women's experience" in women's studies. In *Simians, cyborgs, and women: The reinvention of nature,* 104–109. New York: Routledge.

Harriss-White, Barbara. 1999. Gender-cleansing: The paradox of development and deteriorating female life chances in Tamil Nadu. In *Signposts,* ed. Rajeswari Sundar Rajan, 124–154. New Delhi: Kali for Women.

Hobson, Barbara. 2000. *Gender and citizenship in transition.* New York: Routledge.

Holmberg, Carin. 1991. Om makt i parrelationer. *Varför feminism i ett jämställt samhälle? Kvinnovetenskapligt forums skriftserie* [*Why feminism in a gender equal society? Center for women's studies series, Gothenburg*]. Göteborg 7:39–62.

Honneth, Axel. 2003. The point of recognition: A rejoinder to a rejoinder. In *Redistribution or recognition? A political-philosophical exchange,* by Nancy Fraser and Alex Honneth. London: Verso.

John, Mary E. 1999. Gender, development and the women's movement: Problems for a history of the present. In *Signposts,* ed. Rajeswari Sundar Rajan, 100–124. New Delhi: Kali for Women.

Kabeer, Naila. 2001. Resources, agency, achievements: Reflections on the measurement of women's empowerment. In *Discussing women's empowerment —Theory and practice,* 17–57. Stockholm: Sida.

Krishna, Sumi. 2004. A "genderscape" of community rights in natural resource management. In *Livelihoods and gender: Equity in community resource management,* ed. Sumi Krishna, 17–63. Thousand Oaks, CA: Sage Publications.

Lingam, Lakshmi. 2002. Taking stock: Women's movement and the state. In *Social movements and the state,* ed. Ghanshyam Shah, 310–34. Thousand Oaks, CA: Sage Publications.

Magnusson, Eva. 2001. Politics, psychology, and gender in heterosexual couples: Welfare states as laboratories for the future? In *109th APA Convention. Symposium: All quiet on the home front? The discursive production of quiescence in domestic life,* San Francisco.

Mansbridge, Jane J. 1999. "You're too independent": How gender, race and class make many feminisms. In *The cultural territories of race: Black and white boundaries,* ed. Michèle Lamont, 291–317. Chicago: University of Chicago Press.

Meyerson, Debra E., and Maureen E. Scully. 1995. Tempered radicalism and the politics of ambivalence and change. *Organization Science* 6:585–600.

Mitra, Amit, and Sanjoy Patnaik. 1997. Community forest management in Orissa and the role of Oxfam: A review Draft report for discussion and comments, New Delhi.

Mohanty, Chandra Talpade. 2003. *Feminism without borders: Decolonizing theory, Practicing solidarity.* New Delhi: Zubaan (an associate of Kali for Women).

Molina, Irene, and Paulina de los Reyes. 2002. Kalla mörkret natt! Kön, klass och ras/etnicitet i det postkoloniala Sverige [Calling darkness night! Gender, class and race/ethnicity in poscolonial Sweden]. In *Maktens (o)lika förklädnader: Kön, klass och etnicitet i det postkoloniala Sverige* [*Power's different disguises: Gender, class and ethnicity in postcolonial Sweden*], eds. Paulina de los Reyes, Irene Molina, and Diana Mulinari, 295–317. Stockholm: Atlas.

Mulinari, Diana, and Anders Neergard. 2004. Syster, du är ju annorlunda: Migration, institutionell förändring och kön [Sister you are after all different: Migration, institutional change and gender]. In *Framtiden i samtiden: Könsrelationer i förändring i Sverige och omvärlden* [The future in the present: Gender relations in transformation in Sweden and abroad], eds. Christina Florin and Christina Bergqvist, 204–231. Stockholm: Institutet för Framtidsstudier.

Pringle, Rosemary, and Sophie Watson. 1990. Fathers, brothers, mates: The fraternal state in Australia? In *Playing the state: Australian feminist interventions*, ed. Sophie Watson. London/New York: Verso.

Rönnblom, Malin. 2002. *Ett eget rum? kvinnors organisering möter etablerad politik [A room of one's own? Women's organizing meets established politics]*. Doctoral thesis, Statsvetenskapliga institutionen, Umeå Universitet, Umeå.

Smith, Barbara, and Beverley Smith. 1983 (1981). Across the kitchen table: A sister-to-sister dialogue. In *This bridge called my back: Writings by radical women of color*, eds. Cherríe Moraga and Gloria Anzadua, 113–127. New York: Kitchen Table: Women of Color Press.

Spelman, Elizabeth V. 2001. Gender and race: The ampersand problem in feminist thought. In *Feminism and race*, ed. Kumkum Bhavnani, 74–88. Oxford: Oxford University Press.

Sundar Rajan, Rajeswari (Ed.). 1999. *Signposts: Gender issues in post-independence India*. New Delhi: Kali for Women.

Søndergaard, Dorte Marie. 2002. Poststructuralist approaches to empirical analysis. *Qualitative Studies in Education* 15:187–204.

Tollin, Katharina. 2000. Det måste finnas män med för att det skall bli jämställt: En utvärdering av Mainstreamingprojektet inom Arbetsmarknadsverket i Västerbotten [There have to be men for it to be gender equal: An evaluation of the Mainstreaming project within Labor market department in Västerbotten]. Statsvetenskapliga institutionen, Umeå universitet, Umeå.

Treleaven, Lesley. 1998. *Unsettling tensions: Gender, power and a new university*. Sydney: Sydney University of Technology.

8 Quotas and Interest Representation
South Africa and Sweden in Comparative Perspective[1]

Shireen Hassim

INTRODUCTION

In the past ten years, there has been a remarkable refocusing of feminist attention on the formal political spheres of state and political parties in a wide range of countries. A global movement demanding women's increased access to political power through the use of gender quotas has emerged, with surprisingly effective consequences. Over fifty countries have adopted some form of quota for women in national parliaments (Dahlerup and Frie-denvall 2005). The rapid adoption of gender quotas across the globe has overturned the conventional association of high levels of representation of women with high levels of national wealth and political modernisation (Inglehart and Norris 2003). Rwanda, South Africa, Costa Rica, Argentina, and Uganda now are all among the countries with high levels of women's representation.

"Quota fever" has spread through women's movements across the globe, in part because of the perceived association between women's increased representation and the pursuit of gender-equitable public policies. The assumption of a "virtuous political circle," in which women's participation is rewarded with shifts in the allocation of public resources to address women's needs, is based on the experiences of Scandinavian countries, where high levels of women's representation are strongly correlated with relatively high levels of gender equality. These countries' historical dominance on the representation leaderboard is matched by their performance on the Gender and Development Index of the United Nations, on which Norway, Iceland, and Sweden occupy the top positions for 2003.[2] It has been argued that the long historical process of increasing women's representation in Scandinavian countries—the incremental or gradualist track—is no longer an appropriate model (Dahlerup and Friedenvall 2005) because "women's movements are unwilling to wait" as long as sixty years to achieve equal representation (Dahlerup and Friedenvall 2005, 27).

Early quota debates were based on an (incorrect) assumption regarding the Nordic model, in which quotas were seen as a mechanism which fast-tracked women into power. It is now recognised that women's representation in many Scandinavian parliaments was achieved through a more complex politics of economic and educational change, the nature of political parties, and transformations in the roles of the state. The assumption about the extent to which representation and policy outcomes are positively correlated in a virtuous circle therefore bears closer investigation. The fast-tracking approach opens up important new discussions about the kinds of organization and mobilization necessary for feminist engagement with formal political institutions.

This chapter addresses these questions by comparing an archetypal "incremental" approach to integrating women in the political system (Sweden) with an archetypal "fast-track" approach (South Africa). It explores the conditions under which quotas are likely to produce the equality outcomes desired by feminist activists, and hence the costs and benefits of a "fast-track" approach to political representation. The chapter compares the ways in which South Africa and Sweden have incorporated women into political institutions and the relationship between parties, the state, and women's movements in developing strategies for women's equality in each country.

The chapter begins from the assumption that increasing the representation of women is a democratic good in itself. As Anne Phillips (1995) has pointed out, the notable absence of women in legislatures exposes a fundamental weakness in democracies and constitutes a political problem for democrats committed to substantive and not merely procedural democracy. She suggests that without representation in legislatures, it would follow that women citizens have a diminished ability to hold governments accountable. "Normal" processes of electoral competition cannot be seen as fair if they persistently produce the underrepresentation of the same socially subordinate groups. I am therefore *not* arguing that women cannot make group-based electoral claims, that special rules for disadvantaged groups are unfair, or that liberal democracies should be left intact. Rather, I argue that the *form* and *process* of women's democratic inclusion need closer attention. *How* women are included can have effects on their ability to aggregate as a political power bloc, and on the kinds of political and policy outcomes that are possible through increased representation. I also argue that restricting representation demands to quota mechanisms can result in representation being disembedded from processes of constituency formation. This impacts significantly on feminist ambitions to shift the nature of gender power relations, as once women are in parliament their legislative and policy interventions will depend on the extent to which they are able to draw on constituencies and alliances. The "fast-track" to representation is unlikely to school feminists in these strategies if it is delinked from processes of collective mobilization, on one hand, and intensive debate about the meanings of equality and the desirable outcomes of policy for different groups of women on the other.

UNDERSTANDING THE ROLE OF QUOTAS

Nancy Fraser has argued that gender is a "bivalent mode of collectivity," having the face of cultural devaluation as well as being economically rooted (Fraser 1997, 20). Women's struggles for justice thus encompass both struggles for recognition as well as struggles for redistribution. Although both forms of struggle co-exist and are arguably interdependent (Young 2002), they may nevertheless lead to a strategic tension in modes of mobilisation. Recognition entails the constitution of women as a group, while redistributive struggles demand the deconstruction of women as a group and the articulation of poor and working class women's claims in alliance with other social forces. Seeing representation through the recognition-redistribution lens offers new ways to think about the possibilities and limits of strategies for gender representation and equality. Quotas are a means of achieving recognition; indeed, they are best understood as a form of symbolic politics, as there is no predictable relationship between the greater number of women in decision making and feminist outcomes. Rather, quotas have symbolic effects on political elites that may cause changes in the political culture of a society (Phillips 1995). Quotas, and representational demands more broadly, are struggles for political voice and inclusion, but they are means to an end rather than ends in themselves. Although the strategic approach of many women's movements has been to delink the question of increasing women's presence in parliaments from the questions of whose interests they represent and the content of their politics, a feminist approach to representation must necessarily focus on the relationship between means and ends. The bivalent nature of women's justice claims suggests that we need to explore the interrelationship between struggles for recognition and struggles for redistribution.

Recognition through quotas is a deceptively easy strategy and may have the unintentional effect of validating one form of mobilisation (for the recognition of women's group-based historical disadvantage) at the expense of mobilization in support of redistributive policies. Although it is generally accepted in feminist literature that a combination of factors is responsible for women's increased access to political office—the nature of the political system, the organization of political competition, the nature of civil society and especially of the feminist lobby within it, and the nature and power of the state[3]—all too often, actual political strategies are collapsed into a demand for a quota. This is not surprising; it is without doubt more difficult to re-shape the nature of the political system except, as the South African case demonstrates, during periods of major transition. Quotas are a fast-track mechanism to cut through more intractable institutional blockages, to at least get "a foot in the door" of the political system. Quotas are also politically cheap (and therefore politically sale-able) in political systems where there is a single dominant party; extending a quota to women does mean that some men will not get onto party lists, but with sufficient power a dominant party can in any case redirect men to other important positions in the state and in parastatal organizations. Electoral systems play a key role in determining the nature of the relationship between elected representatives, political parties, and constituencies. Unsurprisingly, the proportional representation (PR) system has been identified as the most conducive for advancing women's representation (Reynolds 1997; Meintjes and Simons 2002) and is now standard demand in association with quotas.

However, the PR system privileges power brokerage within political parties over constituency formation and representation and may therefore have a different impact on redistributive demands. The ability of women representatives to mobilise within their parties and their willingness to challenge party hierarchies are important determinants of the extent to which women will be effectively represented in a PR system. Consequently, quota demands that are pursued independently of building constituencies and alliances are unlikely to produce effective representation even though they may have short-term strategic advantages.

For strategic reasons, debates about quotas have now become delinked from debates about the desired outcomes of policy or evaluations of the effects of quotas. Nevertheless, there is an assumption that greater representation will eventually promote greater equality. The extent to which this link between presence and influence is justified needs to be interrogated from the perspective of processes of constituency composition and mobilization, as well as the notions of equality that are advanced by women's organizations inside and outside the state.

SWEDISH FEMINISM, POLITICAL PARTIES, AND THE STATE

Transformations in gender relations in Sweden are the outcome of changes in the labour market, secularisation of society, improvements in access to education, and struggles within the Swedish Social Democratic Party from the middle of the nineteenth century. Among the factors that shaped a relatively smooth process of democratisation was the homogeneity of its population and culture, which resulted in a relatively low level of social inequalities (Eduards 1991). At the beginning of the twentieth century, Sweden was a poor rural country with extensive migration (mainly to North America) and sharp distinctions in gender roles. Rapid growth and industrialisation between the late nineteenth and early twentieth centuries proletarianised both women and men, with women fairly rapidly carving out spaces within the labour market. Typically, these spaces were gendered, with women occupying lower paid jobs associated with "feminine" roles—such as domestic service, seamstresses, shop assistants, and teachers (Hirdman 1987, 14).

For middle-class women, employment prospects were linked to marriage: employment was for single women (who might also have been mothers), and marriage very often resulted in women's withdrawal from the labour market (as well as subordination to the husband and the loss of legal competence). There was a distinct incompatibility between women's productive and reproductive roles. Various legal measures were introduced between 1900 and 1912 to "protect" mothers—such as (unpaid) mandatory maternity leave. Until 1938, women in middle-class professions such as nursing and teaching were likely to be fired upon marriage or pregnancy. Maternity leave presumed the existence of a male breadwinner, and reinforced rather than resolved the tension between motherhood and work, as having children meant the loss of income. For working-class women, the situation was somewhat different, as it was always assumed that women would combine paid work with caring. The tension between the ideal notion of gender roles and the realities of women's lives resulted in social and political conflicts. As Hirdman notes, the farther a family was from the bourgeois image (man as breadwinner, woman as mother) the more "home" became a place of conflict (Hirdman 1987, 18). Many working-class men and trade unions were opposed to women's presence in the labour force, arguing both that women should be in the home and that women workers depressed wages. Women workers were weakly unionized until after the turn of the century and until 1918 did not have political rights.

Although women and men were unequal, by the twentieth century women's social and political rights were accorded on an individual basis rather than through the family. The 1921 Marriage Code established the equality of women and men in relation to legal and economic affairs within the family. Although there was opposition to mothers working, on the grounds that they were morally responsible for children's well-being, single women were an accepted part of the labour force and, as workers, were assumed to gain legitimacy and fulfilment through their work. Despite the patriarchal features of family and the labour market described previously, neither the political culture nor relations between women and men were based on deep levels of coercion. Rather, as Florin and Nilsson argue, there was a long tradition of political decision making based on consensus and compromise. This culture shaped the women's movements strategies of resolving gender-based conflicts through drawing on notions of solidarity. From the beginning of the twentieth century, Swedish women had an "independent civic relationship" with the state (Florin and Nilsson 1999, 22). It was, moreover, a strong state—the state had enormous legitimacy, and there were few competing institutions either to block state attempts to shape equality or to which social groups might direct their claims. As Eduards (1991, 167) puts it, "faith in the benevolence, capability and responsibility of the state is an old tradition in Sweden." This shaped the nature of Swedish feminism: women "preferred to aim their wishes beyond 'men' towards a kind of abstract justice: the state" (Hirdman 1987, 23). The result was that a politics of institutionalized feminism emerged in which women's activism was sited in parliament, political parties, bureaucracies, and the unions (Hobson and Lindholm 1997).

In the early part of the century, women mobilised for the right to vote, which was eventually granted in 1919–1920, the last of the Nordic countries to extend citizenship to women. Mobilization for women's suffrage took place within all political parties, laying the basis for developing an important collective movement of women. There were competing feminist approaches to the question of what ought to be the basis for women's liberation. Early attempts to deal with women's position were shaped by new interpretations of maternalism that recognized women's interests as mothers as one among many identities of women—as workers and citizens, for example. Socialist feminists, on the other hand, sought to extend the notion of worker solidarity to gender solidarity. Led by the feminist Alva Myrdal, they focused on women's labour market participation as the basis for emancipation.

The emphasis on women's labour market participation as the basis for rights, rather than on women's difference (that is maternalism per se) reflected the universalist assumptions in Swedish political attitudes. By the 1930s there was a steep decline in the birthrate, a factor that might have resulted in women being encouraged to withdraw from the labour market and have more children. However, the influence of feminists such as Alva Myrdal stimulated attempts by the Social Democratic government to make it possible for women to work as well as bear and maintain children.

Despite the universalist assumptions of political and economic inclusion, women's public participation was deeply gendered. The ideological master frame of Swedish democracy, "the People's Home," was projected as a universal frame that included women but without specifying the particular historical disadvantages and identities that women shared as a group (Hobson 2003, 68). These submerged gender identities and roles nevertheless shaped the ways in which women were incorporated into "the People's Home," as the objects of pronatalist government policies and as administrators of the various programmes that were designed to distribute resources to Swedish homes such as children's allowances, housing allowances, etc. Women were, in effect, the link between family and state. By the 1940s and 1950s, Sweden's economic strength allowed the state to extend these social reforms more broadly into old-age pensions, health insurance, and so on. These policies, although premised on a notion of gender divisions of labour, nevertheless began to reshape the social landscape. Huge areas of family life were opened to bureaucratic intervention. Mothers were subjected to new forms of social controls but also found new opportunities for employment in the expanded state, in the day-care centres and schools, as well as in the labour market more broadly. The nuclear family was displaced, and family forms became more diverse as more women became economically independent,; society became more secular, and the divorce rate grew (Florin and Nilsson 1999, 27). From the 1930s, the number of women's organizations increased with a concomitant rise in the extent to which women asserted their collective identities across party and class lines (Hobson and Lindholm 1997).

By the 1960s, in the context of economic expansion and a growth in job opportunities for women, as well as the rise of an international feminist movement, there was a resurgence of feminism. Feminists criticized the gender inequalities in the labour market (women were paid less than men, sexual discrimination was rife, and married women were jointly taxed), as well as the shortage of day-care centres and the double standards in sexual norms.

Joyce Gelb's notion of "feminism without feminists," while accurate in terms of revealing the lack of an autonomous feminist movement, elides the very real and growing presence of feminists within all political parties. Feminist struggles within the Social Democratic Party for *jämställdhet* (gender equality) were greatly facilitated by the enormous need for women's labour in the context of a series of labour market crises. Within the party, these concerns gave rise to new discourses of equality, with feminists arguing for freedom of choice and the creation of the conditions for women to participate fully in all aspects of public life. By the 1970s, the notion of *jämställdhet*, recognizing women's specific disadvantage, began to be used in preference to the term *jämlikhet* which denoted a more universalist and gender neutral notion of equality (Hirdman 1987). Hobson argues that this shift "reflected the power and agency of feminists to represent themselves as a women's constituency to articulate a politics of recognition" (Hobson 2003, 73). By the 1972 congress, feminists had succeeded in putting equal rights for women—particularly the right to work—on the congress agenda and had won the support of the party chairman and Prime Minister Olof Palme. The congress approved a massive five-year plan for creating new openings in day-care and after-school recreation centres and new positions for paid "day mothers." By the 1978 congress, women delegates constituted the largest proportion ever—117 out of 350—roughly proportional to the number of women members of the party (Sundberg 1995). These feminist successes reflected the importance of party unity to the Social Democratic party leadership, who were keen to respond to feminist demands rather than precipitate a rift that might lead to the formation of an independent feminist movement (Christensen 1999, 75).

These trends in the Social Democratic Party must be set against an important external factor. In 1976 the Social Democrats were voted out of power. The Centre/Liberal government was not against women's equality—indeed, Liberal women were well organized within the party. Outside parliament, women were mobilised in non-partisan organizations such as the Fredrika Bremer Association, which actively campaigned for more women in politics. After the 1979 election, women from all the parliamentary parties agreed to campaign for greater representation of women in politics (Eduards 1991). They joined forces with the Communists and the Social Democratic Party in promoting the idea of a quota, against enormous resistance on the grounds that quotas were an infringement of democracy itself.

Electoral competition itself facilitated demands for women's increased representation. All the political parties had, by the 1980s, adopted supportive positions on gender equality. In the Social Democratic Party, the women's section was always more radical on gender equality matters than the men. They were prepared to challenge party leaderships where they felt their interests diverged and formulated demands independently, which frequently created tensions. For instance, in the mid-1950s women opposed the party's defence policy to develop nuclear weapons. Despite enormous opposition to the notion that women should formulate a position on nuclear weapons independently of male leadership (as well as media vilification of women), the Women's Association of the party steadfastly refused to support nuclear weapons while reiterating its loyalty to the party (Karlsson 1996). Women eventually did persuade the party to drop its support for nuclear weapons, although not without threatening to form a separate Women's Party. Through the 1970s and 1980s, it became more common for women from different parties to act together in parliament, as virtually all the party leaderships were more conservative on equality issues than their women's structures. Differences between party leaderships and women's organizations became more marked as women became more militant and established a strong sense of women as a political constituency that could affect electoral outcomes.

There was considerable resistance to quotas per se in the Swedish political system, even though all parties agree to the principle of increasing women's representation. This rhetoric of equality was confronted head-on in the 1990s, when for the first time since winning the vote, women's representation in the *Riksdag* declined from 37.5 percent to 33.5 percent (Eduards 1992, 86). The progressive parties that already had high numbers of women representatives on their lists—the Social Democrats, the Greens, and the Left party—all lost ground in this election. Reaction to this drop in women's representation spanned all political parties. In the winning coalition of Conservative, Liberal, Centre, and Christian Democratic parties, women demanded important posts in parliamentary standing committees.[4] Outside parliament, women began to meet in "closed and secret circles . . . organizing a web of networks, probably numbering in the hundreds, across the country" (Eduards 1992, 86). Feminists were concerned about the impact of the decline in women's representation on the equality gains already made. Agneta Stark (1995) points out that during the early 1990s there was an economic decline and rising unemployment (from 2–3 percent to 8 percent), a fiscal crisis, and cuts in welfare benefits. There were definite fears of further cuts in health care, education, and care of the young and the elderly (Stark 1995, 226). These concerns catalysed the network that came to be known as the Support Stockings, who campaigned for "a whole salary and half the power." Intense mobilization for gender-balanced party lists by the Support Stockings in advance of the 1994 elections had a direct effect on the Social Democratic Party, which in 1993 adopted the principle of "every other seat for a woman"—in effect a policy of gender parity— and institutionalised this requirement in the party statutes in 1997. This principle emerged, as this brief discussion highlights, out of a broader process of mobilization of women, a long history of feminist activism and policy formulation within the Social Democratic Party, a broad consensus in society and among political parties on the importance of gender equality, and alternation in government. It is grounded, furthermore, in the existence of a strong and legitimate state in which there are no competing bases of political power. The gradualist approach may have taken a long time, but it put in place both a strong bloc of feminists within the political party who, over time, "transformed women's issues into party issues" (Sainsbury 1993, 279) as well as a process of establishing the desired content of social policy that included women's participation.

REPRESENTATIONAL CLAIMS IN SOUTH AFRICAN FEMINIST DEBATES

As the foregoing discussion highlights, quotas were only adopted as a strategy in Sweden after a considerable period of engagement with the state. In South Africa, debates on quotas began in the context of transition from apartheid to democracy, but were rooted in a long struggle within the ANC for women to have access to positions of power within the movement. Women only gained full formal membership of the ANC in 1943, thirty-one years after the organization was formed. Throughout the ANC's thirty-year period of exile, the women's structure sought to gain a stronger presence in the organization's decision-making bodies and to develop the relative autonomy to define strategies for mobilization of women. In the process, feminists within the ANC made considerable progress both in democratising the internal workings of the exiled movement and in making gender equality a core value in its political framework. Similar processes of organizational struggle with anti-apartheid movements inside the country also succeeded, by the late 1980s, in inscribing the idea of women's emancipation into their democratic frameworks. Unlike the Swedish Democratic Party, however, these processes did not occur simultaneously with the ANC being in government. This is an important distinction, because it separated constituency formation from representation and left the content of social policy to be dealt with at a future date.

When the process of negotiating a future democratic state began in 1991, the dangers of relying too much on party would became apparent to women in the ANC. The first negotiating teams of all political parties, including the ANC, were all male. The Women's League adopted the view that quotas would be the most effective means to break the blockage on women's access to power within the party. In July 1991, at the first congress of the ANC since its unbanning, the ANC debated a new constitution for the party. The

Women's League called for a quota of seats, but the proposal failed to find sufficient support. However, an electoral quota was accepted in advance of the 1994 elections, and in advance of the 2009 elections, the ANC has committed to parity in gender representation on its party lists.

The quota stance was not shared by feminists in the ANC's alliance partner, the Congress of South African Trade Unions (COSATU). Within COSATU, women's demands for affirmative action mechanisms for increasing the number of women in leadership positions were consistently countered by the overwhelmingly male leadership and by male delegates to national congresses. Opposition was based on a number of reasons, including "that the quota is insulting to women, as it assumes they need special treatment [and] that women's empowerment should start at the factory floor" (Orr et al. 1997, 26). Rather, the union leadership committed COSATU to actively building women's leadership without the use of quotas. The COSATU debate is interesting in this context because it offers a view of women's representation that is located within a progressive political framework and is shaped within a context of a strong emphasis on democratic accountability. In this view, representatives elected through quotas are less likely to act on the basis of mandates from the people and are more likely to seek favour with political elites. Quotas were viewed as mechanisms that would be open to manipulation by party elites and that might act as barriers to direct accountability of party leaders to members. However, women activists within the federation argued that the culture of participation was limited by patriarchal norms that thrived within the male-dominated movement. In fact, COSATU unwittingly adopted a double standard, opposing quotas for women within its union structures while supporting affirmative action in the workplace.

The ANC was the only party to use a quota (one third of all candidates, with women appearing in every third position) for all three democratic elections. The dramatic increase in the representation of women (from a handful of women in apartheid parliaments, to 30 percent in the 1999 elections) was largely due to the ANC's overwhelming majority, although there has been diffusion in the political system. The ANC in effect upped the moral ante, making attention to the representation of women a marker of democratic commitment. Research conducted by the Commission on Gender Equality (CGE) prior to the 1999 election showed that all parties had identified women as "voting populations" (Seedat and Kimani 1999, 40). Even the most vociferous opponent of quotas for women, the Democratic Party, found that in 1999 40 percent of its branch chairpersons and 33 percent of its local councillors were women (CGE/PWG 1999, 102), although only 18 percent of its MPs were women. Despite its principled opposition to quotas (DP MP Sandra Botha says women should be at home looking after children, and that she is only in parliament because her children are adults), the party constantly reiterates its commitment to increased gender representation.

It is important to note that quotas were understood by women activists to be part of a much broader strategy of advancing equality. The demand for quotas received support among feminists because it was seen as an instrument to facilitate women's access to decision making and to create a political space to articulate a transformatory ideal of citizenship. Representation was conceived as part of a broader agenda of redistribution of social and economic power. It is also important to note that the collective mobilization of women in South Africa took place in the context of nationalism. Common gender identities were built on the basis of a struggle for non-racialism, and although the class concerns of working-class women were incorporated into the Women's Charter for Effective Equality, adopted by the Women's National Coalition in 1994, union-based women's structures took a secondary role politically. In Sweden, by contrast, the main forces behind mobilization appear to be women's participation in paid work and access to education. The connection to the labour market and educational institutions ended women's "social isolation and [created] a social homogeneity consistent with a common identity" (Christensen and Raum 1999).

REPRESENTATION AND LEGISLATIVE CHANGE IN SOUTH AFRICA

The immediate challenges facing newly elected women MPs in 1994 were to understand how parliament itself worked and to address the culture and working conditions in parliament so that their participation would be facilitated. Historically predominantly male, parliamentary sitting times did not accommodate the needs of MPs with children. There were only a few toilets for women. The Westminster culture of debate was adversarial in style, and many women felt intimidated and unwilling to enter into parliamentary debate. Ideological differences between women also emerged very quickly as the "critical mass" of women came to grips with the real differences in legislative and policy priorities between political parties. The establishment of a multiparty women's caucus (the Parliamentary Women's Group) failed to provide either a support structure or a lobbying point for women MPs. The ANC Women's Caucus, with a long history of gender activism, acted as the key pressure point within Parliament, even within the multiparty Joint Monitoring Committee on the Improvement of the Quality of Life and Status of Women (JMC). The most notable example of the tension this engendered was the process surrounding the introduction of employment equity legislation. ANC women MPs worked extremely hard to ensure that women were recognised as a disadvantaged group in the new laws. However, Democratic Party women MPs voted against the legislation because the party as a whole was opposed to the imposition of strong labour market regulation.

The JMC, under the chair of experienced gender activist Pregs Govender,[5] established in part as a consequence of the new government's signing of the United Nations Convention on the Elimination of All Forms of Discrimination Against Women (CEDAW), provided an important institutional forum within which to identify a set of legislative priorities and begin to lobby for policy changes. Working closely with civil society through a series of public hearings and expert submissions, the committee arrived at an independent assessment of the nature and scale of the HIV/AIDS crisis and called on parliament to make eradicating the disease and dealing with its effects the "number one priority." Despite ANC and presidential pressures, ANC members of this committee, led by Govender, stood firm on the need for anti-retrovirals. The committee was also the only parliamentary committee to openly oppose the arms deal. At the opening of parliament in 2003, Govender joined the Treatment Action Campaign outside parliament rather than take her seat in the house. Addressing Mbeki directly, she said, "It is time my President to say no to so much unnecessary death, to so much grief, to so many wars." This is an important indication of the willingness of a few MPs to challenge the party in the face of contestations between different interests. It is not insignificant, however, that Govender resigned from parliament at the end of the 2002 session. Individual feminists were not supported by a strong women's structure within the ANC. The ANC Women's League has preferred to work (at least openly) within the ambit of existing party policy rather than to challenge the party leadership or embarrass the leadership in public debate.

Despite the formal commitments to gender equality by the ANC, in the first years of the new Parliament, gender equality was not prioritized as an area for legislative attention. Nevertheless, some gains were made. The "gender equality bills," which were stalled in the South African Law Commission (the legislative drafting agency) until almost the last sitting of the first parliament, were only placed on the parliamentary calendar after high-level lobbying by the ANC Women's Caucus with the support of progressive men MPs, including, by some accounts, President Mbeki. The legislation then had to be "fast-tracked" through the National Assembly so that the first Parliament would be seen to be concerned with gender equality as a substantive issue. The key advocates for the legislation were women MPs who would in all likelihood have been on the ANC list regardless of the quota, and male MPs who had a commitment to gender equality. In the case of the Termination of Pregnancy Act, the proposed legislation was consistent with the ANC's health policy, which included reproductive rights. This pressure had been exerted within the ANC before quotas were introduced, which suggests that key interventions related to processes of democratisation within the party, supported by constitutional commitments, rather than a politics of presence.

The first five years of South African democracy (1994–1999) was a period dominated by the need to elaborate the rules, procedures, and norms of the new institutions, policies, and laws. Three key pieces of legislation sponsored during this period by the Joint Committee on Women, a special portfolio committee responsible for legislative oversight with regard to gender equality, were the Domestic Violence Bill, the Maintenance Bill, and the Recognition of Customary Marriages Bill. The Domestic Violence Act of 1998 provides protection against abuse for people who are in domestic relationships, regardless of the specific nature of the relationship (i.e., whether marital, homosexual, or family). It is a highly significant piece of legislation in that it entails the recognition that the "private" sphere of the family is not inviolate from the democratic norms established by the constitution, and that women are entitled to state protection of their rights even in the private sphere. The Maintenance Act of 1998 substantially improves the position of mothers dependent on maintenance from former partners. The Recognition of Customary Marriages Act of 1998 abolished the minority status of women married under customary law and legalized customary marriages. Other legislation not directly aimed at improving women's condition, such as the Employment Equity Act, also included women among its target groups for redress of apartheid-era inequalities. In addition, a number of policy programmes were introduced, such as free health care for pregnant women and children. During this period, there were also significant gains in embedding gender equality concerns in the broad frameworks of social policy (Gouws 2005; Hassim 2003).

A number of areas of legislative discrimination against women remain intact, and there are other areas in which legislation is needed to enable the freedom of women. While discussion of these is beyond the scope of this chapter, interrogating the assumption of a virtuous circle of representation requires an examination of the strategic routes through which legislative gains were achieved and the conceptual underpinnings of key policies.

CONCEPTUALISING GENDER EQUALITY IN KEY LEGISLATION

The different organizational bases of women's collective mobilization and women's different relationships to the labour market have shaped the ways in which gender equality has been pursued in Sweden and in South Africa. Although both South Africa and Sweden can be characterized as countries with relatively weak autonomous feminist movements, the relationships between women and political parties have different historical and political roots that have produced important differences in outcomes. In the following discussion of the ways in which care work has been understood in South Africa, I seek to underscore my argument that delinking representation from feminist debates about equality can limit the effect of increased representation on policy outcomes.

In Sweden, women's integration into the institutions of democracy was incremental and located within economic transformations—particularly the massive increase in women's participation in the labour force between the 1950s and the 1990s—that gave women new levers for advancing political claims. The central problem that higher labour force participation rates posed was how care work, traditionally conducted within a nuclear household with a male breadwinner, would be organized in dual-earner families.

By contrast, South African women's political claims for inclusion were facilitated by the particular context of the transition to democracy, which broadly legitimated the notion of "fast-tracking." The integration of gender (and women) into democratic institutions was part of an overall (nationalist) political struggle, rather than primarily as a result of changes in women's position in the labour market. Although working-class women were unionized fairly early in the twentieth century, they constituted a small proportion of the urbanised working class. The policies of migrant labour and influx control prevented women from becoming fully settled as permanent urban dwellers. Those women who did live in cities worked primarily as isolated domestic workers. Neither black men nor black women had political rights until 1994, and claims-making on the illegitimate apartheid regime was limited, mainly centring on demands for political rights and later the installation of majoritarian democracy.[6] The discursive frame within which these claims were made was that of nationalism, and throughout the twentieth century organized women engaged in struggles for recognition as full members and then equal decision makers within national liberation movements.

These different bases of mobilization in South Africa and Sweden led to differences in strategy and differences in the ways in which equality outcomes were conceptualised. In Sweden, feminists argued that the distribution of paid and unpaid work was the key to how equal gender roles could be. This was coupled with the question of women's access to paid work, as labour force participation was seen to create the basis for gender solidarity. This produced a particular kind of feminist politics centred on state, as the key question became "what kinds of support are needed from the state to make full labour force participation possible for women?" Thus, a key plank of feminist intervention through the state was to enable the shift of care work from the family to the public sector.

In South Africa and in other developing country contexts, the conceptualization of equality primarily in terms of labour market participation and autonomy from family responsibilities is flawed. The issue of access to labour markets is different in the context of joblessness (estimated in South Africa to be as high as 30 to 40 percent). The lack of access to paid employment is a problem not only for women but for the poor as a whole. The caring needs of middle-class women have not resulted in demands for publicly funded systems of family support, unlike the Swedish case, because of the availability of cheap childcare and domestic work perfomed by black women. In Sweden, the demand for public childcare was always greater than the supply (Bergqvist and Nyberg 2002, 288), whereas in South Africa supply has outstripped demand.

The gains made by gender advocates in South Africa are confined mainly to areas where women have clear and definable gender needs that do not impinge on (or that impinge positively on) men's needs and interests (for example, maternal health), while areas in which attention to women's gender needs might challenge the power of some groups of men (for example, land rights) have been slower to change, or have not changed. As in many welfare states, women's gains have been advanced on the basis of a maternalist politics, often invoking the need to address "family failures" and children's needs, rather than directly empowering women. Thus, for example, free health care for women has been supported because maternal health is seen to be crucial (in an ironic twist, HIV-positive pregnant women get antiretroviral drugs in doses large enough to protect the newborn baby but too small to be effective for the mother). Similarly, the Maintenance Act, which empowers the state to hold defaulting parents (mainly fathers) accountable for debts, has won support in government not least because it entrenches the notion of privatised responsibility for children. Discourses of violence against women can also easily fall back on notions of women's vulnerability and on the idea that the role of the state is to "protect" women and children when families fail.

Yet, despite these problematic assumptions underlying policy, the legislation has been claimed by women's organizations as a significant example of the benefits of increased representation. Maternalist politics can indeed be the basis on which to "forge a new, more inclusivist definition of 'the political'" (Boris 1993, 214), and there is a consistency in the group-based difference strategy of quotas and the strategy of addressing women's group-based needs.

In Sweden, in the first half of the twentieth century maternalism still held considerable sway. The need for women's labour did not initially mean that childcare would be collectivized; rather, the organization of caring was still women's responsibility, and families played a considerable role in sharing the burden. Nevertheless, bolstered by feminist lobbies, the recognition of care work did eventually lead to the introduction of state-sponsored or subsidized crèches and old people's homes, and for extensive maternity leave privileges. It was the growing political involvement of women and the articulation of interests based on identities other than motherhood that shifted the state's approach to caring. Feminists did not merely seek to *combine* their dual roles as earners and carers, but to *question* gender roles (Hirdman 1987). Activism within the trade union and the political party (and the association between a socialist trade union movement and a social democratic party) made the shift to an egalitarian norm of family and work possible. In other words, care work, when interpreted within a progressive ideology of equality, can lead to substantive shifts in gender relations. On the other hand, when these policies are promoted in the context of scarce resources and in the absence of a clear feminist commitment to equalising gender responsibilities, they lead to residual welfare programmes that do not shift ideologies of privatised and gendered caring.

In South Africa, for example, the emphasis on the *cultural value* of caring in social welfare policy is not accompanied by a recognition of the *work* of caring. Importantly, care work is not linked to women's access to the public sphere of political participation or to women's access to labour markets. It has been estimated that urban women spend 207 mean minutes per day on care work (household maintenance, care of persons, and community service) compared to the 81 minutes spent by men (D. Budlender 2004, 15). Women's caring burdens have also dramatically increased as the HIV/AIDS infection rates have assumed pandemic proportions. Although a feminist language of rights and entitlements has been included in many legislative frameworks, the key welfare policy document (the White Paper on Social Welfare) is couched within a more traditionalist discourse that understands women's caring roles in terms of their responsibilities to families and communities and not in terms of their class interests as working women. Indeed, caring is conceptualized as a problem arising out of apartheid-based familial breakdown rather than needing resolution in order that women may exercise their rights to full economic and political citizenship. The particular (and greater) responsibility of the state in meeting social security needs through the redistribution of public resources is diluted by the emphasis on tapping into communitarian values. This limits the effectiveness of the state in addressing women's caring burdens as well as the impact of social policy expenditures on relations of power between women and men. The caring model, while ostensibly valuing collective social responsibility, does not value the importance of women's autonomy from the expectations of family and community. Collective social responsibility is in effect privatized (by shifting it onto communities, and therefore women) rather than made a responsibility of the state, and the opportunity to create the conditions for women to exercise their agency in a variety of social and economic arenas is lost.

THE COMMUNAL LAND RIGHTS BILL

The real test of whether the virtuous model of representation works lies in whether women's organizations are successful in gaining legislative changes that directly challenge entrenched patriarchal interests. To what extent would a critical mass of women MPs be able to shape legislative outcomes in the face of a concerted opposition? The contestations over the Communal Land Rights Bill are an instructive case study in this regard, for a number of reasons. During the constitution-making period, the principle of gender equality was opposed by some traditional leaders, setting the stage for a protracted conflict. The constitution itself validated both equality and cultural autonomy, while placing equality as the "trump" criterion in cases where both came into conflict. In the proposed new land legislation in 2003, concerns about gender equality once again came up squarely against those of traditional leaders. At issue in this particular contest was the extent of traditional leaders' formal authority over land allocation in rural areas. The

Communal Land Rights Bill was set to become the biggest test of the extent to which a constituency of (rural) women could successfully defend their policy claims against other powerful interests.

Since 1994, traditional leaders have consistently opposed democratic limitations on their authority over land use in rural areas. In the run-up to the 1999 elections, their opposition was strong enough that the ANC feared an electoral backlash, particularly in KwaZulu Natal, and proposed legislation was shelved. After the 1999 elections, the new (woman) Minister of Land Affairs, Thoko Didiza, announced that a land rights bill would be introduced in April 2001. Subsequently, lengthy and factious debates emerged within the ANC, and between the ANC and land NGOs. The bill recognized "communities" as juridical persons and proposed to transfer state land to communities. ANC MP Lydia Kompe-Ngwenya, a veteran women's and land rights activist, rejected this proposal, arguing that the land rights of individual users and occupiers needed to be recognised and protected in law, in accordance with the Freedom Charter. Her party colleague and leader of the Congress of Traditional Leaders of South Africa Nkosi (Chief) Patekile Holomisa, on the other hand, argued that the legal title to communal land should be bestowed on the traditional authority. For the traditional leaders, the bill did not go far enough in securing traditional authority, as "communities" would now have rights. For women, the emphasis on communities reinstated the power of traditional leaders as they became the officially recognized representatives of community interests.

Traditional leaders vociferously opposed subsequent drafts of the bill, particularly the proposed creation of land administration structures which would comprise community representatives as well as traditional leaders. Communities would be given discretion as to whether the land would be held by communal title or subdivided and registered in the names of individuals. Once again, traditional leaders threatened electoral retaliation and political violence, particularly in KwaZulu Natal. In October 2003, six months ahead of the third national elections, a final draft of the bill was published, this time containing last-minute alterations which provided that traditional councils, set up in line with the Traditional Leadership and Governance Framework Bill, would have powers of land administration, allocation, and ownership in communal areas. Cabinet endorsed the bill and announced that it wanted the bill enacted before the 2004 elections, leaving less than a month for the bill to pass through the appropriate parliamentary processes.

The issue of women's rights remained unresolved. The Traditional Leadership and Governance Framework Bill provided for 30 percent representation of women in traditional councils. It also provides that while 40 percent of the members of the council were to be elected, the remaining 60 percent "must comprise traditional leaders and members of the traditional community selected by the principal traditional leaders concerned in terms of custom" (Traditional Leadership and Governance Framework Bill (3)(2) (b)). The bill also gave the Minister of Agriculture and Land Affairs discretionary powers to determine the nature and content of land rights. This was in part a response to women's organizations' concerns that gender equality issues might not be automatically taken into account, or might be overridden by the traditional councils. In these cases, the Minister would be able to confer rights to ownership or occupation on women. These changes were far from satisfactory for traditional leaders, who saw them as further eroding their authorities. Despite the concessions to women's representation in the amendments to the bill, reactions from women' organizations and land NGOs were equally vociferous, albeit without the threats of violence.[7] The key objections related to the failure of the bill to protect the rights of rural women, the undemocratic nature of the traditional councils, and the entrenchment of the control of chiefs over key aspects of women's lives. Under customary law, as well as under apartheid law, women's rights in land were derivative and temporary. Women could not own land or occupy property in their own right but were dependent on male spouses or customary partners. They lost these rights upon the death of the male spouse, in part also as a result of the principle of male primogeniture, which required that property be passed to the nearest male relative. This principle was upheld as recently as 2000 by the Supreme Court of Appeal (G. Budlender 2003). While earlier versions of the bill had explicitly provided for the right to gender equality in respect of ownership, allocation, use of, or access to land, this provision disappeared from the final version of the bill. There was no longer any provision clearly banning discriminatory practices.

This rather truncated narrative of the debates around the Communal Land Rights Bill raises crucial questions about the power of women's organizations and women's representatives in parliament to successfully defend women's rights. Rural women have never been strongly organized in South Africa. In many instances, rural NGOs with dedicated feminist activists (such as AFRA and TRAC) spoke on behalf of rural women and attempted to give profile to their specific concerns. However, there has been little independent organization of women, and in policy terms there was certainly no strong organizational base or political resources to draw on. Local rural women's groups lacked connection to urban-based policy debates. As Claasens and Ngubane (2003, 3) point out:

> there are vibrant groups of rural women, keen and committed to supporting one another and organizing around these issues. However there are currently no resources available to enable rural women to come together in a regular basis to take these matters forward . . . nor . . . are there provincial or national rural women's organizations that can support and co-ordinate the process of organizing rural women.

In this vacuum, it was research NGOs and land rights organizations that attempted to provide some link between local women's groups and the policy makers, not elected women politicians. This link was both enabling and problematic. It made it possible for rural women's concerns to be heard by the legislators in the absence of parliamentary hearings in rural areas. The Commission on Gender Equality played a leading role in highlighting rural women's interests and concerns, testament to the more effective advocacy role it has adopted since 2002. However, the alliance with and representation by urban-based land rights NGOs also had drawbacks. Some of these NGOs were labelled by ANC MPs as "ultra-left" critics, and while they had a strong voice it was not always an influential or feminist voice.

By contrast, ANC women MPs did not appear to recognize the significance of the bill until relatively late in the process. No objections were raised to the bill in Cabinet and, of course, it was sponsored by a woman Minister. However, when approached by the Commission on Gender Equality, CGE, and women's rights NGOs, MPs did signal their concerns about the bill. Naledi Pandor, chairperson of the National Council of Provinces, worked with other women MPs and women activists to facilitate debate about the bill. The JMC made a submission to the portfolio committee on Land and Agricultural Affairs laying out their objections to the bill—a rare occurrence of one portfolio committee opposing another. The ANC Women's Caucus also voiced their objection to the bill. However, when it came to voting on the bill in parliament, there were no official abstentions among ANC women MPs. The bill passed unanimously through the portfolio committee, parliament, and cabinet. Several explanations have been offered for this degree of public support despite the private reservations of ANC women MPs. The first is that there was little strategising in relation to the bill early on in the process. Second, some have argued that women MPs had instructions "from above" not to oppose the bill. The finalisation of the bill and its appearance before the National Assembly occurred in the midst of party electoral lists being drawn up, and some activists have suggested that women MPs feared that they might be left off or pushed low down on the lists. One ANC MP argued that "it didn't appear to be an opportune time to take on the party." Ironically, some of the very factors that had assisted women activists with regard to the Termination of Pregnancy Act—the role of senior members of the cabinet and the portfolio committees and the "party line" of the ANC— now appeared to have worked against them. This has led one prominent feminist activist to question "whether there is a strong anchor for gender activism in parliament any more. . . . Especially at election time the party is what matters."[8]

CONCLUSIONS

The model of a virtuous circle of representation offers a helpful way to conceptualise the relationship between activism around gender equality at different sites in the state and civil society. However, comparing Swedish and South African experiences suggests that the ways in which representation is achieved make a crucial difference to its outcomes. In both South Africa and Sweden, a high degree of representation of women in government was achieved through feminist mobilization within the ANC and the Social Democratic Party, respectively. However, in Sweden women created a constituency both within the party as well as outside it, through associations with feminists in other parties and in the trade union movement, and were able to use this notion of a constituency at key moments of conflict with the party leadership. In South Africa, the idea of a women's constituency was relatively poorly developed, being directed toward the ends of national liberation rather than women's emancipation in the first instance. Although there has been a vibrant movement of women inside and outside the ANC, this movement has only rarely been mobilised to confront party leadership in the context of fights over policy directions. This suggests that constituency formation is as yet weak, and certainly is not evident as an electoral threat. Although Swedish feminists did not engage in massive collective mobilization, they did build effective allies with women organised in other movements and achieved a high level of influence within the party as a result. Both the Swedish and South African cases demonstrate the importance of the support of a strong political party for women's interests. However, the nature of the political party and the external context in which the party is seeking—or maintaining—electoral strength also matters. In Sweden, the Social Democrats were in alliance with strong socialist unions, and women were making equality claims in the context of an expanding welfare state, rising levels of women's education and high levels of labour force participation and worker organisation. In South Africa, by contrast, levels of women's organisation in the labour movement are low, the labour movement is itself experiencing a crisis of representation in the face of shifts in the nature of the economy, and fiscal constraints in a context of high levels of poverty are leading to intense competition for scarce public resources.

A second key lesson from this comparison is that representation is most effective when there are strong forms of political participation and a clear vision of what kinds of gender equality are desirable. If initiatives are not tied to the articulation of the desirable content of gender equality, they are likely to be evacuated of their progressive content. However, even if equality is given progressive meaning in the legislation and policies sponsored by women MPs, such sponsorship may not stand up against intense mobilization of competing groups in society. In the case of the Communal Land Rights Act, the party was subjected to conflicting pressures from a constituency that was hostile to women's interests and which posed a perceived electoral threat. Women's vote, on the other hand, was relatively poorly mobilized and in any case the party could rest on its track record of being the key promoter of gender equality. While women MPs might see themselves as organically linked to women's organizations in civil society, they placed considerable emphasis on intra-party debates and were aware of their need to survive within the party. Without an electoral constituency to back them up, the reality was that women activists remained hostage to the good will and support of the party leadership. Without the pressure from outside, and without a strong articulation of the interests of different constituencies of women, the virtuous circle model is reduced to its thinnest form—that is, increased representation of women as a group without any concurrent representation of the policy interests of disadvantaged women. The use of quotas as the key breakthrough strategy can therefore lead to a thin version of recognition, in which elite women's access to the formal political system is reinforced while not (as yet) translating clearly into policies that address the needs of poor women.

A key difference between Sweden and South Africa seems to lie in the extent to which *feminists*, and particularly socialist feminists, were able to use their access to the Social Democrats to advance equality strategies. In South Africa, feminism as an ideology has been relatively marginal to the ANC, *even though* gender equality has become a key party platform. Gender equality was ideologically incorporated but in a language and form that resides within a progressive nationalist framework. The reasons for this are complicated, and have their roots in part in the tense relationship between feminism and the nationalist movement and in part in the elite biases of the democratic model adopted during the transition. Key actors within the state as well as in the women's movement remained suspicious of the intentions of middle-class (mostly white) feminists. Where feminists did have technical expertise that could not easily be bypassed (for example, feminist lawyers) or where women's advocacy groups were politically well connected, state openness to women facilitated progressive outcomes. Within the constraints of the terms of reference set by bureaucrats,[9] feminists were able to make long-term gains in embedding gender equality in overarching policy frameworks and ensuring that in many cases the details of legislation, such as the Employment Equity Act and the local government policy framework, specified gender equality as a criterion. Where these positive conditions were lacking, as in the case of rural women, policy and legislative frameworks were less firmly favourable for poor women.

Despite these fundamental differences, there are a number of striking similarities between South African and Swedish women's paths to political office. As in Sweden, women in South Africa achieved a breakthrough in political representation on the basis of a combination of an enabling electoral system and a dominant political party predisposed to gender equality. In both countries, candidate quotas were adopted by left political parties after considerable participation by women in the political process. In South Africa and in Sweden, women's integration into the political party was the crucial lever in terms of increasing women's representation in the political system as a whole. However, in both cases, women's claims within the party were strengthened by the existence of a non-partisan women's organization exerting pressure from civil society. The trajectory of quota demands differs in that, in Sweden, both the Greens and the Left Party introduced party quotas before electoral quotas, whereas in South Africa the ANC has not yet adopted party quotas. However, in both cases, women in the political parties moved toward full parity demands for electoral lists. It can therefore be argued that South Africa and Sweden are examples of an elite route to women's political integration. Their experiences challenge the assumption of many feminists that the women's movement is only effective when it is completely autonomous from male-dominated political organizations. Yet this comparison highlights very clearly that importing a model of representation which borrows the *form* of representation without adequately operationalising the political and institutional processes that underpin that form, can limit the effectiveness of the representational model.

NOTES

1. This comparison between South Africa and Sweden is clearly done by a South African rather than a Swedish specialist, and the chapter should be read in this context. I have had to rely on Swedish material published in English, which has imposed further limitations on my reading of the complex processes of political change in that country.
2. The association between high positions on the parliamentary rankings and GDI is not tight: the United States, for example, ranks seventh on the 2003 GDI (having slipped from fifth in 2001) but 59th on the parliamentary ranking.
3. For a more extended discussion of these factors, see Goetz and Hassim (2003).
4. As a result, the first woman Minister of Foreign Affairs, Margareta af Ugglas (a Conservative MP), was appointed.
5. Govender was the Project Manager of the Women's National Coalition and a leading union and women's organizer.
6. This is not meant to suggest that the colonial, and later the apartheid state, ignored black women. On the contrary, black women's mobility, economic prospects, and private relationships were subjected to various repressive measures and forms of surveillance.
7. The Landless People's Movement warned that it would encourage voters to boycott the 1994 elections if land redistribution processes were not speeded up.
8. Confidential interview, Cape Town legal lobbyist, April 2003.
9. An example of this is the ways in which the members of the Lund Committee of Inquiry, among whom were a number of prominent feminists, were restricted by a very narrow budgetary allocation for child support grants (Hassim 2003).

REFERENCES

Bergqvist, Christina, and Anita Nyberg. 2002. Welfare state restructuring and childcare in Sweden In *Childcare policy at the crossroads: Gender and welfare state restructuring*, eds. Sonya Michel and Rianne Mahon. New York: Routledge.
Boris, Hielen. 1993. The power of motherhood: Black and white activist women redefine the "political." In *Mothers of a new world*, eds. Seth Koven and Sonya Michel. New York: Routledge.

Budlender, Debbie. 2004. Women and poverty. Paper prepared for the Gender-stats Project, Women'snet, www.womensnet.org.za/genderstats/poverty.shtml (Accessed May 27, 2005).

Budlender, Geoff. 2003. *Expert opinion on the Communal Land Rights Bill*, prepared for the Commission on Gender Equality, Johannesburg.

Christensen, Ann Dorte. 1999. Women in the political parties. In *Equal democracies? Gender and politics in the Nordic countries*, eds. Christina Bergqvist, Jaana Kuusipalo, and Augur Styrkasdóttir. Oslo: Scandinavian University Press.

Christensen, Ann Dorte, and Nina C. Raum. 1999. Models of political mobilisation. In *Equal democracies? Gender and politics the in Nordic Countries*, eds. Christina Bergqvist, Jaana Kuusipalo, and Augur Styrkasdóttir, 17–27. Oslo: Scandinavian University Press.

Claasens, Aninka, and Sizani Ngubane. 2003. Rural women, land rights and the Communal Land Rights Bill. Draft paper presented at the Women's Legal Centre Advancing Women's Rights Conference, Cape Town, October 2003.

Commission for Gender Equality (CGE) and Parliamentary Women's Group (PWG) 1999. *Redefining politics: South African women and democracy*. Braamfontein: Commission on Gender Equality and Parliamentary Women's Group.

Dahlerup, Drude, and Lenita Freidenvall. 2005. Quotas as a "fast track" to equal representation for women: Why Scandinavia is no longer the model. *International Feminist Journal of Politics* 7(1):26–48, March.

Eduards, Maud. 1991. Towards a third way: Women's politics and welfare policies in Sweden. *Social Research* 58(3), 677–705.

Eduards, Maud. 1992. Against the rules of the game: On the importance of women's collective actions. In *Rethinking change: current Swedish feminist research*, eds., Maud L. Eduards, I. Elgguivst-Saltzman, E. Lundgren, C. Sjoblad, E. Sundin, and U. Wikander, 83–104. Uppsala: Swedish Science Press.

Florin, Christina, and Bengt Nilsson, 1999. Something in the nature of a bloodless revolution . . . How gender relations became gender equality policy in Sweden in the nineteen sixties and seventies. In *State policy and gender systems in the two German states and Sweden 1945–1989*, ed. R. Torstendahl, vol. 22:11–78. Uppsala: Opuscula Historica Upsaliensis.

Fraser, Nancy. 1997. *Justice interruptus: Critical reflections on the "postsocialist" condition*. New York: Routledge.

Goetz, Anne Marie, and Shireen Hassim. 2003. Women in power in Uganda and South Africa. In *No shortcuts to power: African women in politics and policy-making*, eds. Anne Marie Goetz and Shireen Hassim, 1–28. London: Zed Books.

Gouws, Amanda (ed.). 2005. *Unthinking citizenship: Feminist debates in contemporary South Africa*. Aldershot: Ashgate Press.

Hassim, Shireen, 2003. The gender pact and democratic consolidation: Institutionalising gender equality in the South African state. *Feminist Studies*. 29(3):505–528.

Hirdman, Yvonne. 1987. *The Swedish welfare state and the gender system: Theoretical and empirical sketch*. The study of power and democracy in Sweden. English series: Report No. 9, Uppsala.

Hobson, Barbara. 2003. Recognition struggles in universalistic and gender distinctive frames: Sweden and Ireland. In *Recognition struggles and social movements*, ed. Barbara Hobson. Cambridge: Cambridge University Press.

Hobson, Barbara, and Marika Lindholm. 1997. Collective identities, women's power resources and the making of welfare states. *Theory and Society* 26(4):475–508.

Inglehart, Ronald, and Pippa Norris. 2003. *Rising tide*. Cambridge: Cambridge University Press.

Karlsson, Gunnel. 1996. *From brotherhood to sisterhood. The Swedish Social Democrat Women's Federation's struggle for power in the Social Democrat Party*. Short English summary of the thesis. Lund: Lunds Universitet.

Meintjes, Sheila, and Mary Simons. 2002. Why electoral systems matter to women. In *One woman, one vote: The gender politics of South African elections*, eds. Glenda Fick, Sheila Meintjes, and Mary Simons, 1–10. Johannesburg: Electoral Institute of Southern Africa.

Orr, Liesl, Jeremy Daphne, and Claire Horton. 1997. COSATU Congress: Did women reject the quota? *Agenda* 35:3–10.

Phillips, Anne. 1995. *The politics of presence*. Oxford: Oxford University Press.

Reynolds, Andy. 1997. *Women in African legislatures and executives: The slow climb to power*. Johannesburg: Electoral Institute of Southern Africa.

Sainsbury, Diane. 1993. The politics of increased women's representation: The Swedish case. In *Gender and party politics*, eds. Joni Lovenduski and Pippa Norris, 263–290. London: Sage.

Seedat, Fatima, and Lillian Kimani. 1999. Gender profile of parties. In *Redefining politics: South African women and democracy*, ed. CGE/PWG, 133–145. Braamfontein: Commission on Gender Equality and Parliamentary Women's Group.

Stark, Agneta, 1995. Combating the backlash: How Swedish women won the war. In *Who's afraid of feminism: Seeing through the backlash*, eds. Ann Oakley and Juliet Mitchell, 224–244. London: Penguin Books.

Sundberg, Jan. 1995. Organisational structures of parties, candidate selection and campaigning. In *The Finnish voter*, eds. Sami Borg and Risto Sankiaho. Helsinki: The Finnish Political Science Association,.

Young, Iris Marion. 2002. *Inclusion and democracy*. Cambridge: Cambridge University Press.

9 What's in That Little Book?

Gender Statistics and the Nordic Road Map Toward Evidence-Based Policies in Africa

Bola Akanji

INTRODUCTION

The availability of social and economic data allows for the use of statistics as a tool for research and analysis, providing empirical evidence for observed patterns of behaviour of development variables. Data allows further systematic integration of important variables into development models for the purpose of planning, policy analysis, or policy advocacy. In the quest for gender equality, the need for statistics that are disaggregated by sex and reflect gender concerns, produced by states' statistical agencies, has been recognized in recent global declarations, including the Beijing Platform For Action 1995 and The Millennium Declaration 2000. The relevant clauses of these resolutions state implicitly that profiling the situations of women and men within the same environment and circumstances is the most powerful form of advocacy, bringing existing gender gaps that require strategic policy action into close focus. Indicators generated from gender-sensitive statistics also allow the analysis of causality between observed gender differentials and other important development variables, such as growth, income, employment, and poverty, as well as the assessment of impacts of development policies on women and men. They therefore pave the way for the justification of woman-friendly policies or affirmative action toward gender equality. They also create a framework for monitoring progress in gender equality and gender mainstreaming. Finally, from a contemporary development perspective, they provide a framework within fiscal policy analysis for the rationalization of gender-responsive budgets by generating sex-differentiated costs and benefits of development programmes, sex-differentiated performance budgeting tools, and sex-differentiated revenue and tax incidence analysis (UNIFEM 2003).

The concept *gender statistics* implies that statistics on individuals are collected, compiled, and analysed by sex and presented with sex as a primary and universal classification while also reflecting gender equality concerns. To be effective, gender statistics cannot be produced and improved in isolation. The work must be integrated into the development context of the entire national statistical system. A gender perspective must be included not only in improvements of content, but also in methods, classifications, and measurements from various statistical sources.

Today, no country has accomplished this goal. Although official statistics to a large extent are collected by sex, sex is not always used as a primary and universal classification throughout the analysed and presented data. Further, even if statistics are presented disaggregated by sex, this does not necessary imply that the information is relevant to the gender concerns to be analysed.

In spite of global resolutions, which have been ratified by most countries, very few countries generate and use gender statistics systematically in their national databases. Worldwide, gender statistics have mostly been generated and used by academics and researchers for specific purposes, for instance in the evaluation of particular programmes for their gender effects or in validating gender theories, and these are rarely economy-wide. The Nordic countries, including Sweden and Norway, stand out among those countries that collect statistics disaggregated by sex in a systematic way and for most variables in the national statistics profiles. The experiences of these two countries, therefore, need to be assessed with a view to providing lessons of experience for developing countries.

The main objective of this chapter is to investigate the historical and political context of the development and use of gender statistics as a state policy in Sweden and Norway, and to identify the main policy drivers with a focus on the arguments and counter-rguments that shaped the adoption of concepts, methods, and applications of gender statistics. The chapter looks at the development of methodologies for data collection and analysis and whether they can help to create a workable framework for other aspiring nations. The chapter also looks at how far using gender statistics has accelerated the enactment of specific gender-friendly policies or whether these evolved as a result of state welfare policies. Lastly, as a showcase for lessons of experience, the chapter looks at how African countries fare in terms of progress in the generation and use of gender statistics and asks whether there are lessons that the Nordic countries can learn from Africa.

A CONCEPTUAL FRAMEWORK: WELFARISM OR FEMINISM?

It would appear that progress in gender equality is greatest in countries that have institutionalised the use of gender statistics, like the OECD countries and especially the Nordic Social Democratic welfare states. It can therefore be hypothesised that gender statistics have sharpened the tools of advocacy around gender equality and led to a positive impact on family life and the overall quality of life of citizens. It is helpful to look at the conformity of some development indicators to this hypothesis. According to Table 9.1, there is higher correlation of the key gender development

Table 9.1 Macroeconomic Growth, Human Development, and Gender Indicators for Selected Countries (1998–2003)

	Human Development Indicator			Gender Development Indicator			Macroeconomic Growth (GDP per Capita)$/Year		
	1995	2002	Percent Change	1995	2002	Percent Change	1995	2002	Percent Change
Norway	0.935	0.956	2.25	0.932	0.955	2.47	30,356	36,660	20.76
USA	0.926	0.939	1.40	0.927	0.936	0.97	36,849	35,750	-2.98
Germany	0.911	0.925	1.54	0.905	0.921	1.76	29,476	27,100	-8.06
Brazil	0.739	0.775	4.87	0.736	0.768	4.34	9,463	7,770	-17.89
Thailand	0.745	0.768	3.09	0.741	0.766	3.37	5,457	7,010	28.45
Ghana	0.532	0.568	6.77	0.552	0.564	2.17	1,980	2,130	7.58
Nigeria	0.430	0.466	8.37	0.425	0.458	7.76	1,118	860	-23.07
Sudan	0.465	0.505	8.60	0.453	0.485	7.06	2,139	1,820	-14.91
Botswana	0.666	0.589	-11.56	0.584	0.581	-0.51	8,550	8,170	-4.44

Source: Akanji 2004.

variable the Gender Development Index (GDI) with other development indicators, such as the human development index (HDI) as well as GDP per capita, in the OECD countries than in the less developed countries. This would imply that gender equality has become an integral part of macro-economic planning rather than a disparate ideological issue, as it tends to be viewed in less developed economies. In less developed countries where basic data generation often constitutes a problem and gender statistics availability is low or nil, the percentage change in the GDI between 1995 and 2002 is unrelated to percentage change in GDP per capita, although it appears to move more systematically with HDI. It is, however, question-able to what extent these universal indicators are sufficient for this kind of comparison.

This chapter explores the logic of the preceding illustration by assess-ing the ways in which gender statistics have been developed and used to contribute to the progress of gender equality in Sweden and Norway. It has been claimed that the measures of gender equality achieved in the Nordic states have resulted from the evolution of the Scandinavian model of the welfare state and as a natural progression in human quality of life and less as a result of gender advocacy. However, feminist have also critiqued the social democratic welfare state, pointing out that social policies extended to women bypassed issues of unpaid labour and the interplay between the divi-sion of work in the home and in the labour market (Esping-Anderson 1990). The gender equality-friendly policies of the 1980s have not led to equal participation in family life and work as the experts had imagined (Haas and Hwang 2000) but rather the accentuating of women's breadwinner roles without relieving their motherhood roles (Sainsbury 1996).

Sainsbury (1999) has pointed out that although the Nordic countries are often seen as representing a single model, when it comes to gender rela-tions there are important differences. She identifies differing "gender roles regimes" across the Nordic countries based on the extent to which men and women's entitlements are based on earning and caring. She finds that in Sweden the regime is based on a notion of the individual earner-carer lead-ing to a citizen-based rather than family-based structure of social provision, while in Norway the predominance of the separate gender roles for women and men has remained stronger, leading, for example, to a much greater recognition and willingness to evaluate women's unpaid work.

It has also been noted that the welfare state has the potential to liberate but also to reproduce gendered power relations in a new form (Portocarero 1990; Nyberg 1998). Wage inequalities (Statistics Sweden 1989) and other forms of inequality in and outside the workplace, including unemployment (Gonäs 1990), occupational segregation (Winqvist 2004), and gaps in occu-pational mobility (Portocarero 1987), have persisted in spite of high female labour force participation and many earnings-related benefits. These are some of the arguments that must not be ignored when discussing the much-admired achievements in gender equality in the Nordic countries.

Whatever the importance of the availability of gendered profiles for shaping policies and changing gender relations in the Nordic countries, the processes involved provide great lessons for Africa, where the availability of gender statistics is, at best, at a rudimentary stage and application is still limited. However, some recent African initiatives in the generation and use of gender statistics are noteworthy. Efforts are, for example, geared toward the integration of gender variables into National Accounts as well as creating an integral model for monitoring of progress in gender equality via the African Gender and Development Index (AGDI). If these African initiatives, which are being pioneered by the Economic Commission for Africa, succeed and truly gain ground across the continent, it would validate the concerns that have been raised about the validity of universal indicators like the GDI and GEM as adequate measures of gender equality for all countries. It would also substantiate the notion that different regions of the world can develop and use gender statistics based on their own demand-driven agenda and that indicators for monitoring gender inequality must evolve contextually and not universally.

DEVELOPMENT AND ORGANIZATION OF GENDER STATISTICS IN SWEDEN AND NORWAY

The Historical Context of Gender Statistics in Sweden

The development of gender statistics in Sweden has followed two parallel paths over the past decades: one might be called the official path, involving laws and international guidelines; the other, and perhaps the most interesting, follows the unofficial path, involving individual and group advocacy for evidence-based policymaking.

Officially, the first steps toward working on gender statistics by the National Statistical Office in Sweden were made in 1983, leading to the formation of a Gender Statistics Unit (GSU) the same year. The work of the unit was influenced by the Third World Conference on Women in Nairobi in 1985 and strengthened with the call for improved gender statistics in Beijing Platform for Action in 1995. Other policy drivers have included the European Union's Community Framework Strategy on Gender Equality of 2000, where gender statistics are required for development of comparable information on the situations of women and men in different policy areas, and to develop indicators evaluating the effectiveness of gender equality policies (Hedman 2004).

The formal basis for gender statistics work was finally provided in 1994, more than a decade after the formation of the GSU, when the new National Plan of Action for Gender Equality stipulated that gender statistics should be part of Sweden's Official Statistics. A new paragraph stipulated that "Official statistics related to individuals should be disaggregated by sex, unless there are special reasons not to do so" (Article 14, Ordinance of

Official Statistics). Furthermore, Statistics Sweden was required to give a yearly report to the government on remaining deficiencies in official statistics concerning gender disaggregation, thereby taking steps toward fulfilling the Beijing recommendations (Statistics Sweden 2004b) In summary, the objectives of gender statistics and indicators, as expressed by Statistics Sweden and backed by law, are to raise consciousness, inspire measures for change, provide an unbiased basis for policy action, and monitor and evaluate gendered impacts of policies and measures.

The events that shaped the establishment of the GSU and related activities, however, predated any laws or international calls for action. The awareness of the need for gender statistics was raised through the demand by users of statistics, that is, researchers and individuals who came from both government and non-governmental organizations and were dealing with gender issues in society (Hedman 2004). The history of the Unit is therefore not unrelated to the long history of women's empowerment struggles and legislation in the Nordic countries as well as the human-centred policies of the Social Democratic Welfare States.

The history of policies concerning gender equality in Sweden is replete with legislation and policy enactments dating back over 150 years: equal inheritance rights for women and men (1845); maternity insurance benefits (1931); equal basis for pension for women and men (1935); equal pay for equal work for state employees (1947); paid maternity leave for women (1955); promotion of equal opportunity in schools curriculum (1970); and separate income tax assessment for husband and wife (1971), to name a few (Statistics Sweden, Women and Men in Sweden 2004). Thus a sustained culture of gender-equitable policymaking and public consciousness led to the widespread use of and demand for gender statistics by policy analysis and academics, spurring related action within Statistics Sweden.

The development of gender statistics was the result of public responsiveness and unbiased self-assessment by the statisticians of the Bureau, fuelled by strong networking among women in and outside government. According to Pehr Sundström, the Head of the GSU, it was the women within the organization who pushed for greater attention to gender. Had it not been for the presence of a large number of women within the establishment, many in top positions, events could have unfolded differently. The importance of this fact combined with effective networking is corroborated by Birgitta Hedman et al. (2004), who implies that the "production of gender statistics must be visible and formally organized with strong commitment and active support from the highest management level" (p. 47). Hedman, the first head of the officially recognised GSU at Statistics Sweden in 1983, said:

> We saw that there were some differences between what we might call the 'norm' and the 'deviator' in the statistics, depending (on) if it was about family and reproduction where women were the 'norm' or whether it was about the labour force (where) men were the 'norm'. This was

very clear and became the first push for attention to gender issues in-side Statistics Sweden . . . It was women who pushed of course. These were women within the department although they were in contact with women in politics and women in research (academics). The demand for gender statistics was coming from women in research but for us at the time it wasn't so clear.

(Interview with Pehr Sundström[1])

Institutional Structures for Gender Statistics

Sweden stands out as the only Nordic country that regularly produces and publishes gender statistics. In the other Nordic countries, although sex-disaggregated data is generated annually, the levels of analysis and presentation have not been institutionalised. Most of the countries either have an established gender statistics unit or permanent staff for gender-related statistics. However some, including Norway, still have no specific unit for gender statistics. Generation of gender statistics is done ad hoc, according to public demand or in connection with specific projects and subject to funding support.

Statistics Sweden has a permanent GSU with a staff of two persons. In addition, the Unit can, under commission, carry out special compilation and analysis of gender statistics for various groups of users. Gender statistics work is provided for within the main budget of the Statistics Sweden office. The official statistical system is organized by statistical fields, and each field/office is responsible for collection, compilation, analysis, and presentation of data from its field, for instance, labour force data, education data, and so on. All subject matter statisticians are responsible for the integration of a gender perspective into the development of their field. In addition to specific tasks, the GSU has a coordinating role in mainstreaming gender statistics in the whole statistical system. To fulfil this task, the unit gives support to and collaborates with colleagues in all other field offices covering a wide range of issues, all relevant to gender.

> In the unit we looked at ourselves as statisticians and considered what we could do to look at the situation of women and men in Sweden and that created a lot of questions. We started to form focus groups to discuss what we thought were the major gender issues in Sweden at the time. We also had meetings with journalists, researchers and people active in gender issues. Out of these discussions and meetings came the first Women and Men in Sweden publication in 1984 which was not only about disaggregating statistics by sex but also about identifying important issues to highlight through statistics.

(Interview with Pehr Sundström by Edda Magnus, October 2004)

Table 9.2 A Time-line for the Evolution of Gender Statistics Use in Sweden

Period	Landmark Event	Action in Statistics Sweden
1749	Establishment of Statistics Sweden	—
1979	National Plan for Gender Equality	—
End of 1970s	Awareness of a norm in statistics based on societal stereotypes	Took a more critical look at what the data reflects First report on deficiencies in statistics and suggestions to improve its gender-responsiveness
1980	Equal Opportunity Law	
1983		The GSU was created to strengthen capacity to respond to users' needs
1984	First published statistical booklet *Women and Men in Sweden*	First in a series of three and later two yearly published booklet. Statistics Sweden's best-seller
1984	First Public Exhibition of Gender Statistics at Public Fair "Women Can"	Far reaching impact of exhibition 100,000 copies of *Women and Men in Sweden* sold
1985	Third World Conference on Women, Nairobi—Recognition of the need for gender statistics	Presented the first English version of *Women and Men in Sweden* at the NGO Forum in Nairobi
1986	Follow-up actions on Nairobi Forward-Looking Strategies	Publish *The World of Women and Men Equal Opportunity in Sweden*, a more in-depth analysis of the situation, aimed at a broader audience
1994		National Plan of Action on Gender Equality and Ordinance of Official Statistics (Article 14) stipulate the need for sex-disaggregated statistics
1995	Beijing Platform for Action strengthen the need for gender statistics	Strategic Objective H.3 focuses on the "Generation and Dissemination of Gender-disaggregated data and information for planning and evaluation"
1996	Statistics Sweden publish the Methodology Manual *Engendering Statistics: A Tool for Change*	Institutionalizing the framework used for training within and outside Sweden. The Africa project "Improving Gender Statistics in East, central and Southern Africa through regional cooperation 1993–1996" ends
2004	Statistics Sweden publishes a manual *Statistics by Sex. A Necessary Tool for Gender Analysis*	This report in a series of Current Best Methods (CBM) is part of Statistics Sweden's role as coordinator of the official statistical system

Source: Interview with Pehr Sundström, 2004.

Partnership is an essential tool for mainstreaming gender issues within national and international networks and for commanding the necessary government and management cooperation and commitment. In Sweden, the GSU works in partnership with the Ministry of Industry, which has a coordinating role on gender equality policy in Sweden. There are also essential partnerships with users who are journalists, the business community, academics, women activists, and government and nongovernmental change agents. The identification of relevant data is always based on consultation with a wide variety of users. However, there is more limited use in terms of adapting the gendered variables for policymaking. This limitation has fuelled the questioning of the extent to which feminism has influenced social welfare policies in the country.

Norway has no GSU. Gender statistics are not part of the basic budget, nor are they prioritised. The need is met as the demand emanates and as funding permits, and most of the work on gender statistics has been funded from external sources, making it less sustainable. There is no routine system of registering request for gender statistics. The Ministry of Children and Family is the most important partner, while the Ministry of Labour and Employment is the most important user of the gender statistics output. Academics in Norway have, however, extensively used available gender statistics, especially in relation to gender equality and family values, and in promoting family-friendly policies. They have also been used in attempts to integrate gender at the heart of policy, such as in valuing time use in order to create a household production matrix in social accounting procedures (Aslaken et al., 1995, 1996).

In response to official guidelines, both nationally and internationally, but also clearly fuelled by effective demands from users and gender advocacy from within the organization, the GSU of Statistics Sweden has an impressive output. The booklet *Women and Men in Sweden: Facts and Figures* gives an overview of the situation of women and men and is published every other year in addition to other gender-sensitive statistical reports and publications. Further, there are regular improvements being made based on an in-built evaluation system, resulting in an annual publication looking at gender-disaggregated statistics. The GSU provides training to other government agencies, schools, and NGOs to promote gender equality in Sweden in addition to assisting other countries to develop gender statistics units and to train staff in the development and presentation of gender statistics. Because Statistics Sweden gets specific requests, which differ from time to time, the office has a system of responding to the evolution of new thinking among the general public on what is believed to promote gender equality. International cooperation is extensive, through the European Union initiatives, changing UN initiatives, and Nordic initiatives through the Nordic Institute for Women Studies and Gender Research (NIKK).

THE CONCEPTS OF THE LITTLE BOOK

Data Identification and Coverage

According to Hedman (2004,) the type, coverage, and use of gender statistics in Sweden has changed over the years, following closely the global shifts in understanding of the issue of gender. Twenty years ago, with needs dictated by women's organizations and women advocates who found that data had become crucial to their ability to press for change, the focus was on gathering information on the situation of women, and this was specifically related to health and education, the most practical areas of concern for women given their traditional roles. The more recent understanding of gender has shifted the focus to a more holistic perspective. In the sense that the coverage of data has emerged mostly from cooperation with users, the availability of gender statistics has tended to reflect areas where research, advocacy, and policy attention are focused. These are the areas of population, health, education, political participation, and labour force participation, including time use. Other areas are income, taxation, transfer payments, child care and elderly care, violence, and crime (Hedman et al., 1996; SIDA 1998). Today, more attention is paid to cooperation between users and producers and this determines the variety of data and helps with the identification of topics to be addressed by data and the type of analysis required.

Data collection and analysis follows the logic of users' identification of problem areas and policy concerns, followed by discussions with the data producers to identify statistics needed to showcase the concern. Different hypotheses are then raised as to the causality between the problem and other factors, and finally different types and levels of statistics are identified, collected, and analysed to test the hypotheses, which can then validate the need for specific intervening gender policies. A schematic model for user–producer cooperation and identification of needed statistics has been developed by Statistics Sweden (Hedman et al. 1996). Table 9.3 simulates this conceptual model.

ANALYSIS OF THE LITTLE BOOK IN SWEDEN: PROFILES AND TRENDS (1970–2003)

The reporting of gender statistics in Sweden has resulted in the production of the Little Book on the position and situation of women and men in Sweden every two years since 1984. The presentation in tables and graphs has served to meet the demand for an equality status report for policymaking and has been important for research and especially for advocacy.

Some of the profiles with sufficiently long time series in the book have been analysed here, to test the hypotheses that the existence of gender policies based on statistics is a necessary but insufficient condition to fundamentally

Table 9.3 The Conceptual Framework for Identifying Relevant Gender Statistics

Issue	Problem (One Example)	Causes (Some Examples)	Statistics Needed by Sex (Some Examples)
Economic life of women and men	Occupational segregation in the labour force with women in lower status occupations than men	Gender segregation in education	a. Population 15 years and over by level of education and age b. Population with tertiary education by field of study and age c. Population economically active by level of educational and occupation
		2. Women's reproductive role	a. Employed population on maternity leave b. Economically active/not economically active population by marital status and number of children

Source: Adapted from Hedman et al. (1996)

change gender relations or create gender equality in the home and workplace. The measure of gender equality used is the gender disparity index, which is the parity ratio of the female and male situation for a particular variable. A ratio of 1.0 indicates perfect parity or equality of status, which is the ideal. For a sign-positive indicator, a value less than 1.0 indicates a superior male position or a disparity against women. while a value above 1.0 indicates a superior female position or a disparity against men. The reverse applies to sign-negative indicators.[2]

The key findings (Figures 9.1–9.7) show that gender relations appear to have changed over time with respect to most of the variables. In the area of private pension claims, which are a function of greater participation in paid work, the disparity index rose from 0.33 in 1984 to 1.40 in 2002. For the number of days of parental allowance claims, the disparity index dropped from 19.0 in 1980 to 4.88 in 2003, indicating that more men are taking days off for parental duties. In the area of occupational segregation, there was only a slight drop in the disparity index from 10.11 in 1997 to 6.14 in 2003 for female participation in social sector work, implying that gender-stereotypical norms may still be at play in determining the entry of women and men into specific sectors of the economy. For nontraditional occupations, like finance and agriculture and fishing, the disparity index, although much lower than in female-designated jobs (social and education sectors), has actually changed little over the period 1997 to 2003. Occupational

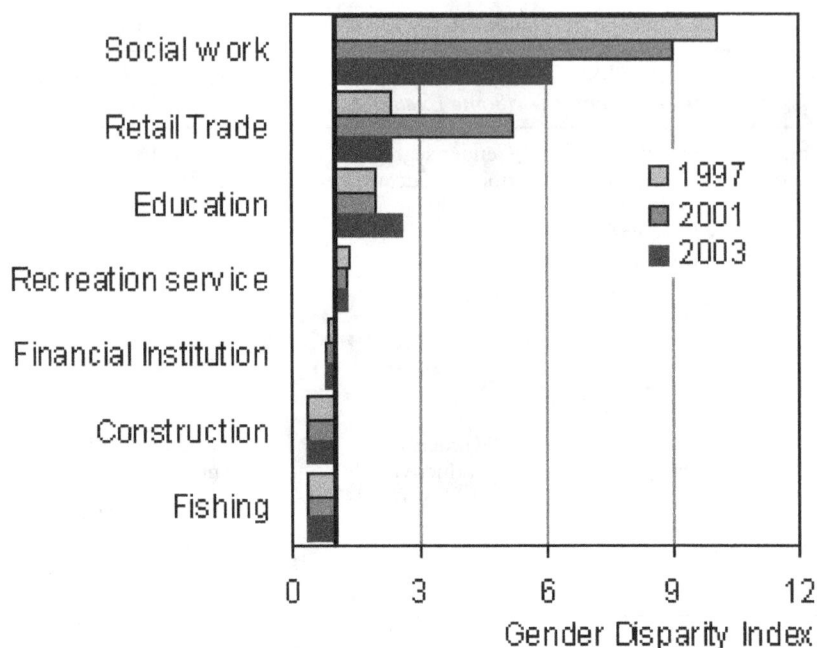

Figure 9.1

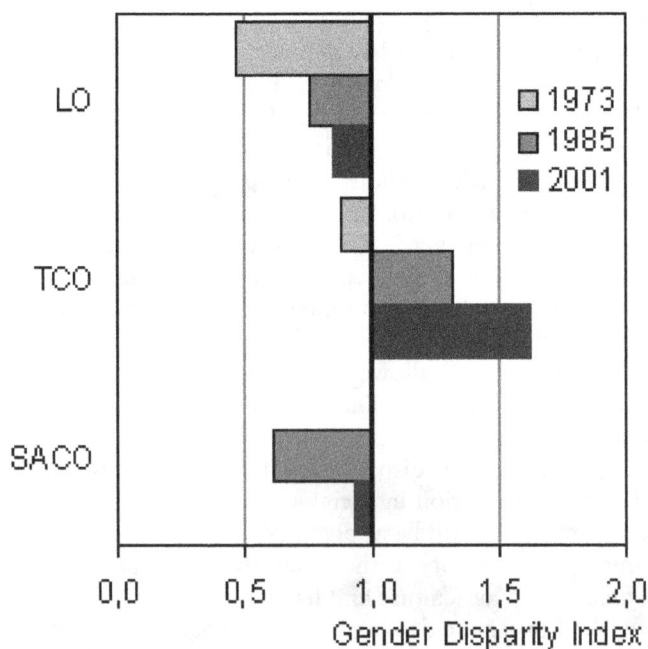

Figure 9.2

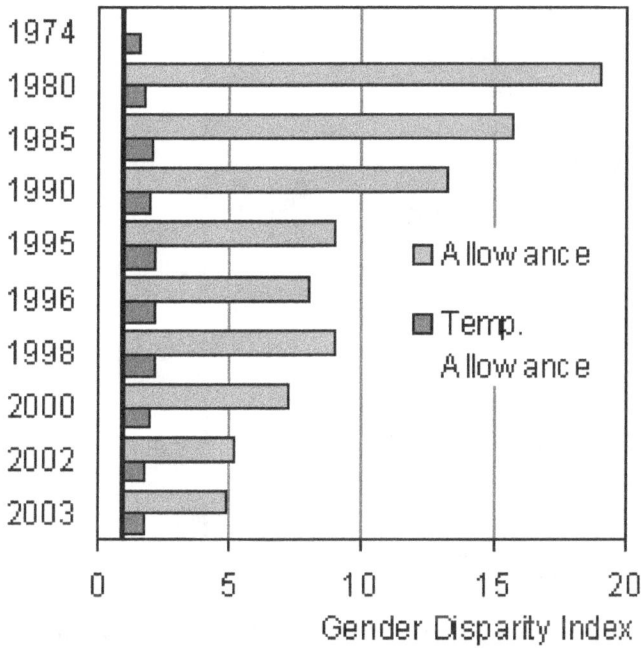

Figure 9.3

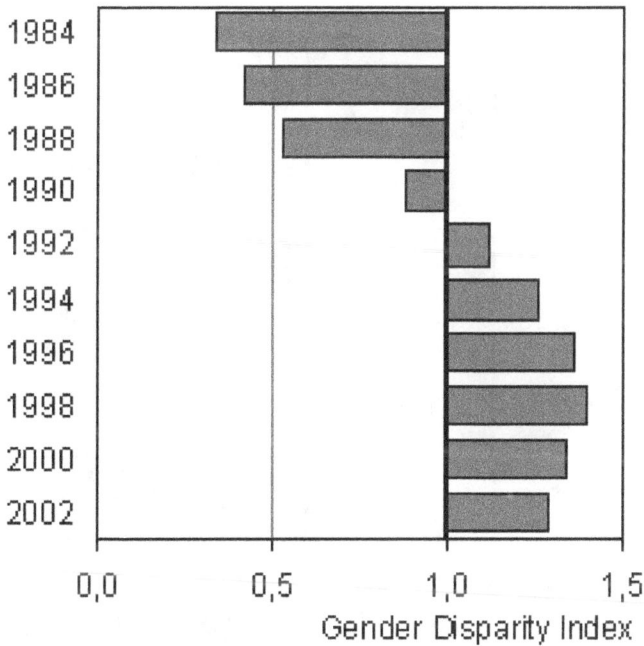

Figure 9.4

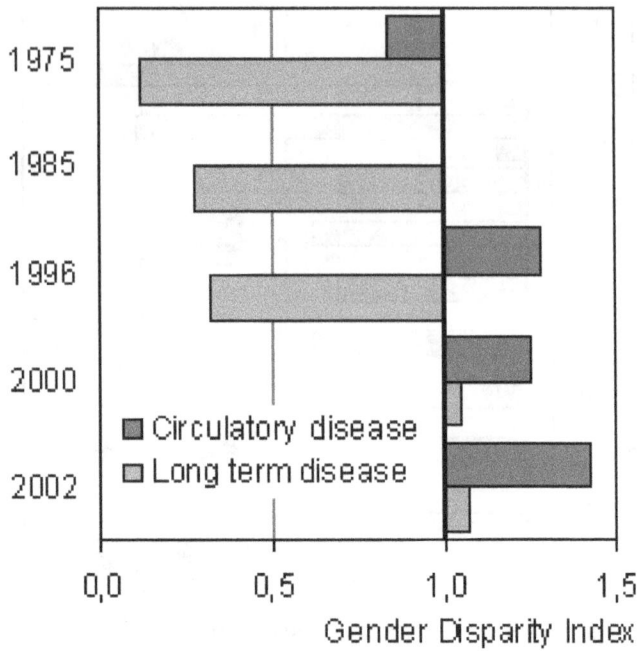

Figure 9.5

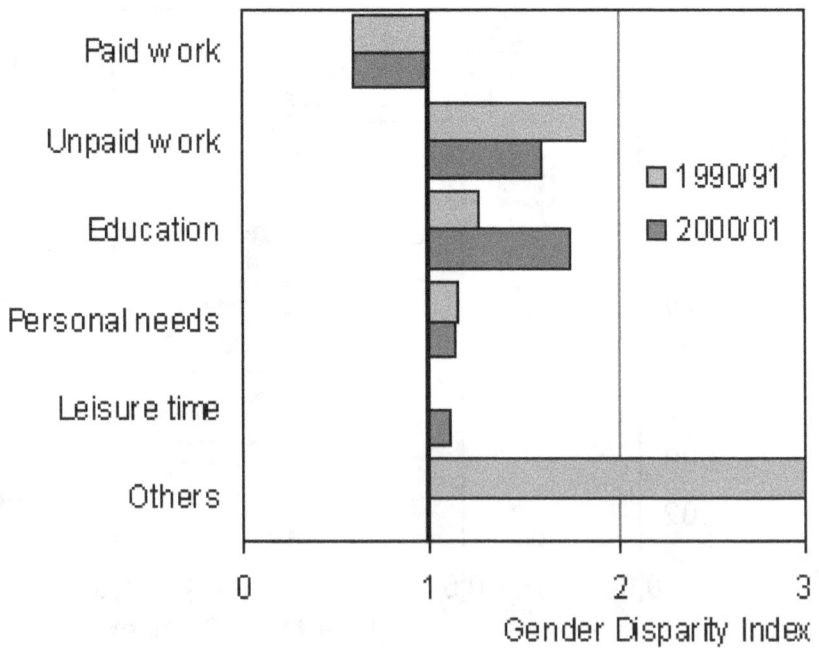

Figure 9.6

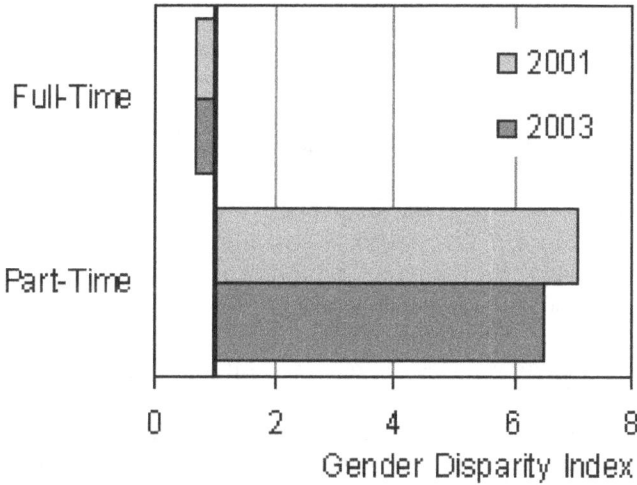

Figure 9.7

segregation still exists in spite of increased participation in paid work. The last of the sign-positive variables studied is the membership of trade unions by men and women. The existing low parity of 0.65 in 1973 rose to 1.08 by 2001, implying that the entry of women into the labour force is gradually being accompanied by a shift in their relegated position in the decision-making structures in the workplace. The superior female position in 2003 is in tandem with the huge shifts in political participation of women in Sweden.

Of the sign-negative variables, findings show that "time loss due to long-term illnesses," which in the past reflected high gender disparities, with higher susceptibility among men, now shows a shift in pattern with a strong bias against women. The variable for most part is proxied by incidence of heart conditions (two variables). The variables' disparity indices moved from 0.83 and 0.11 in 1975 to a higher than unitary index of 1.42 and 1.06 in 2002, perhaps demonstrating the stress implied by the "mother-carer model." They also show that there is greater disparity in the distribution of part-time work than in the distribution of full-time work among parents with young children, and although there is still disparity in the distribution of paid and unpaid work, this disparity appears to have lessened between 1990 and 2000.

These findings suggest that the availability of gender statistics has allowed for gender policies that have changed negative gender relations in certain spheres of life, although not always at the same rate. While ground has been gained in most areas, negative effects have been reinforced in some. There are still underlying causes of gender inequality that gender statistics profiling has not addressed.

ANALYSIS OF THE LITTLE BOOK IN NORWAY: THE GENDER EQUALITY INDEX

A Gender Equality Index (GEI) is generated annually in Norway. The variables that reflect the greatest gender concerns in the country are incorporated to compile a single index that is comparable to the UNDP gender-related development index (GDI) and the gender empowerment measure (GEM). This makes international comparison possible as well as allowing internal comparison across often-diverse regions, which have different concerns motivating gender-equality interventions. Although there is widespread variety of opinion as to whether any such indices adequately reflect the variety of crosscutting issues, there is general agreement on their broader implications.

Variables used include the percentage of pre-school children registered in the municipally funded day-care centres, the female percentage of municipal council members, educational level, and labour force participation. A demographic variable is also included, reflecting the fact that municipalities with few opportunities for education and a non-diversified (male-dominated) industry structure usually experience out-migration of young women. A low percentage of women therefore indicates that the basis for gender equality in the municipality is weak.

This initiative of a Norway-specific GEI is not seen as a Statistics Norway standard measure but rather as an experiment that could lead to such standards. The greatest utility of the findings is that they provide a mapping of regional patterns of gender equality in Norway—a sort of League Table. Tentative though it is, it reflects a clear regional pattern in the gender orientation of different parts of the country. For instance, the fact that women in the north of the country are more active in the labour market and in municipal politics compared to the south is reflected in a higher value given for gender equality (Kjeldstad and Kristiansen 2001).[3]

ENGENDERING STATISTICS IN AFRICA

First, it is important to document the fact that the availability of gender statistics in African countries is much below what exists in the Nordic countries. It must be surmised that this is because, despite global conferences and resolutions on women's empowerment and gender equality, the governance process on the continent does not give room for any form of equity-based policies. Equal Opportunity clauses have not been an issue, except in countries like South Africa and United Republic of Tanzania, where other forms of liberation struggles created entry points for gender-equity struggles. Patriarchy continues to be a strong force in the cultural and political scenario of most African countries. Contemporary policies have been formulated largely based on the World Bank Consensus, due to the debt crisis. This has given little or no room for feminist access to the policy arena, thus limiting the demand for gender statistics for policy formulation.

The concern regarding gender statistics in African countries is fuelled by the relative difficulties in obtaining data due to the nature of production processes. The informal sector and agrarian processes dominate production. Low literacy rates combined with informality have meant that entrepreneurs cannot document records of inputs and outputs. Lack of appropriate institutions to regulate standards, as well as the lack of effectiveness of worker's unions in promoting collective modes of production, has reduced the demand for information and data on work-related conditions, both for men and women. Gender advocacy to promote the visibility of women's roles in subsidising the market economy has been hampered by this lack of data. Because of the lack of gender statistics, the evolution of gender equality policies in the workplace has not enjoyed fundamental support. Rather, most policies have relied on the political will of governments, gender activism in the NGO sector, and legislation around affirmative action. As a consequence, gender advocacy has been met at best with tokenism mainly organized around the National Women's Machineries in each country and the region. Gender equality-friendly policies in Africa do not predate the International Summits on women, unlike in the Nordic states. Whatever limited gender-aware policies exist have been due to the recent wave of global women's development programmes based on CEDAW and the African Charter on Human Rights.

In the area of statistics, databases of international partners/agencies remain some of the most commonly used sources of gender statistics in Africa. However, global indices like the GDI/GEM that have been developed based on these have been highly criticised for their inability to capture the complex configuration of African social and economic processes and for representing structural issues through the eyes of developed country experts. That is why the efforts of regional organizations like the FAO and more recently the ECA became important in promoting a home-grown impetus for change. The ratification of global conventions has proved to be a necessary but insufficient mechanism to bring genuine progress on gender equality in the continent, without the evolution of national and regional initiatives. Regional initiatives may be more effective in promoting the availability of gender statistics than the existing global resolutions. We will now look at examples of such initiatives.

Engendering Agricultural Data in Africa: The FAO Initiative

FAO's effort to engender the agricultural data-gathering mechanisms is instructive and represents one of the earliest attempts to promote the agenda for gender statistics on the continent. The focus emanated from the agency's development of socioeconomic indicators as part of the preparation of a programme of work on social statistics in food and agriculture. In the Africa

Region, the need for gender-specific agricultural data was formally recognised in 1999 (Keita and Tempelman 2004).

The rationale for this pioneer effort to focus on gender in agriculture is that in the past, policies in agricultural development have aimed at product growth while overlooking labour as a major factor. The importance of human resources as well as the social and welfare aspects of development has been ignored. Thus, with focus on physical outputs, the data collection process has been limited to a few variables concerning the human resources involved. In the past, rural development depended much on the public sector, but with recent emphasis on the role of the private sector and NGOs and calls for decentralisation and participation, governments will require solid and broad statistical information on all participants in agricultural processes in order to create an enabling environment for all stakeholders in development (Keita and Tempelman 2004).

A survey of activities in National Agricultural Statistics Bureau in several countries revealed that there were differences in priorities of the national statistical offices that influenced the degree of gender integration. For instance, the assessment showed that data collection and presentation by sex was not a priority of the Central Bureau of Statistics of Namibia, given the lack of clear demand by users. In Senegal, sex was reflected in the fundamental objectives of the National Agricultural Census, thus ensuring a mainstream approach by presenting all tables with information on women and men. In Mozambique, although one of the specific objectives of the Census was to collect sex-disaggregated data, the lack of demand for such data and limited guidelines and understanding of the concept of gender led to a limited outcome of the exercise. In Nigeria, the National Demographic Household Survey has presented most of its statistics both on spatial (rural–urban) or gender contexts in the past decade or more. The National Bureau of Statistics also has a lot of its household data designed and collected by sex. However, only limited sections (mostly demographics and education) are analysed and presented by sex "due to low demand for such disaggregation," according to the Director General of the Bureau. In agriculture, although it has been possible to disaggregate land ownership and land use patterns by sex, it has not been possible to analyse output and income data by sex. The new Core Welfare Indicator Questionnaire (CWIQ), which is expected to provide basic statistics for poverty assessment (as from 2005), will be administered on a household rather than an individual basis. While this will allow analysis based on the gender of household head, intra-household gender relations which are very critical to poverty analysis will have been left out. What has not been done is to bring all these pockets of gender statistics together into a central database where gender analysis can be carried out in a consistent and comprehensive manner and for most important aspects in relevant policies, like income, assets ownership, access to social infrastructure, access to markets and to new opportunities in expanded agricultural markets, trade, and services. This scenario represents the situation in the majority of African countries with respect to a sector as important as agriculture in the region's economy.

FAO's work does not cover all the aspects that require sex distinction in the area of agriculture, such as ownership of resources and access to technology, markets, and capital. Most of these areas of concern are being addressed through individual or organizational research efforts and scattered in grey literature. Thus, access to systematic data on agriculture hardly goes beyond what is made available through FAO and a few National Statistical Agencies.

Gender Statistics as a Peer Review Mechanism: The ECA-ACGD's African Gender Development Index

There is a vast potential for genuine progress in gender equality in the current initiatives of the ECA. One initiative is application of time-use data for the valuation of non-market work and for modelling the effects of policies on the household economy and vice versa. Another is the development of an African Gender Development Index as a monitoring instrument for gender equality goals, the most recent project at the ACGD.

This index will be an important tool for informing regional and global work on the situation and status of African women and, more importantly, will be a monitoring mechanism for gender equality within the region. It is a composite index, similar to the Norwegian one, composed of two parts: a Gender Status Index (GSI), which compares the situations of women and men (similar to the concept of "The little book"), and the African Women's Progress Scoreboard (AWPS), which measures the political will of African governments to implement ratified conventions. A third objective of the index is to democratize statistics and qualitative monitoring tools. The GSI will rely on the availability of gender statistics in most sectors of the economy, classified into three blocks—social power "capabilities," economic power "opportunities," and political power "agency." The AWPS also includes a fourth block—women's rights. The creation and use of these indicators in a systemic way poses a major challenge, as all African governments are expected to adopt them and make the statistics available.

A review of the status of data availability on the continent has been undertaken. The results show that many countries' statistical bureaus carry out annual surveys with sex-disaggregated modules (Sinha 2002), but because the demand for their use has been limited, a lot of these lie as raw data in the archives of the agencies unless requested for specific purposes, usually by academics, some gender policy analysts, and some NGOs who wish to profile impacts of programmes on women and men, and more recently for the analysis of fiscal policies toward gender-responsive budgeting.

Lack of data remains one of the greatest challenges of this project. Its success depends on the willingness of individual countries or even subregional groups to prioritise the production and use of gender statistics beyond what is currently available. The fact that demand is critical in generating supply is clearly played out in pilot studies for the development of the AGDI, which revealed that a lot of data lie unutilised and will not be unearthed until the demand for them exists. The studies have also helped to identify the missing data, which will be the targeted focus of supplementary action.

Although the AGDI currently identifies and uses a limited set of indicators, it will provide a good start for the systematic use of what is available, hopefully leading toward gradual improvement. The ECA will be instrumental in the fundamental integration of gender in the development process, if supported and adopted across the continent. Indeed, the intrinsic philosophy of the project also needs international recognition and support. Gender equality advocates in the Nordic countries may also benefit from the fundamental objective and conceptual framework of the project, aimed at monitoring genuine progress in gender equality, beyond social welfarism.

PROSPECTS FOR EVIDENCE-BASED POLICYMAKING IN AFRICA

The demand for greater visibility of women in national economic data is increasing in many parts of sub-Saharan Africa. This is because of the failure of global macroeconomic policies and their dominant paradigms driving the engine of national development efforts to address poverty on the continent in a sustainable way. Many have pointed to the failure of Structural Adjustment Policies (SAPs) and Poverty Reduction Strategies (PRSPs) to grapple with the fundamental nature of development processes in Africa which are hinged very extensively on the female-dominated areas of small-scale agrarian systems, informal sector production, and the underlying intra-household power relations that inform these. The need to analyse the gender dimensions of poverty therefore becomes increasingly important.

In order to address this new development paradigm, feminist discourse emphasises the analysis of the impacts of macro policies on women and men. This would entail the integration of gender modules into existing and evolving tools of macro-policy analysis. Empirical evidence will support greater accountability of governments to women and will produce evidence-based advocacy tools that promote gender-responsive programming. African scholars will also increasingly demand more systematic gender statistics. The ability of national governments to respond to this demand will depend on both the political will to achieve gender equality and the resource capacity to effect the necessary transformation within national statistical agencies. The support of the donor community, especially of those who focus on gender and women's empowerment, will be critical to the achievement of this goal.

It is instructive that the crux of efforts for the generation and use gender statistics in Africa is the fundamental shift in the understanding of dominant development paradigms that reinforce gender inequality. Unlike in the Nordic countries, where the quest for gender equality has come in the wake of rapid economic development, the quest for national economic growth via the reduction of inequalities is integral to the African initiatives to collect gender statistics, simultaneous with the quest for gender equality from its right-based and accountability perspectives. African countries may therefore achieve gender equality in more transformative ways than has occurred in the Nordic countries.

LESSONS AND CONCLUSIONS

This assessment of strategies and developments in the area of gender statistics and evidence-based gender equality policy in the Nordic countries and in Africa has shown that gender-biased relationships in market and non-market production exist and persist in the North just like the South, in spite of significant economic development. It has, however, suggested that a systematic process of evidence-based policymaking can make moderate but consistent changes.

The availability of gender statistics is a function of demand both in the North and in the South, which in turn is generated by awareness of its utility. The development of the institutional mechanism for gender statistics through the GSU of Statistics Sweden also reflects the positive effect of networking on the process of change. Women's groups in Sweden, both internal and external to the process, were united in their vision, channelled their data demands systematically to the relevant institution, and cooperatively built alliances to ensure the successful establishment of the unit. It is therefore clear that African countries will only utilize gender statistics effectively if a culture of evidence-based policy is allowed to thrive in an open environment of participatory governance. However, the availability of gender statistics is not a sufficient condition for achieving gender equality; rather, sensitivity to its intrinsic value must be generated through its positive utilisation in transforming policies, as has been the case in Sweden and Norway.

It is important to note that no single gender policy intervention can be used as a "catchall." Gender equality-friendly policies must evolve from the analysis of different contexts, positions, and situations of men and women. This chapter has pointed to the inability of global indices like the GDI to capture African social and economic processes and has called for a greater emphasis on regional perspectives. The use of the Norwegian index in mapping gender responsiveness bears witness to the regional variation in gender sensitivity of policies. Similar variations also exist in Africa, based for example on the spatial location of women and men (rural–urban), religious divides, and domains of occupation (formal and informal). The African Gender Development Index project bears similarity to the Norwegian experiment as a monitoring tool, and therefore each can learn from the other.

Dependence on external funding for the development of institutional mechanisms for gender statistics has proved to be an inhibitor to sustainable change in some Nordic countries, while Sweden's reliance on its own internal resources has proved to be an enabler and a factor in its sustainability. In the same vein, the ECA initiative will be replicable and sustainable only if national governments have the political will to fund this important process of change. Yet another resolution for national governments to develop gender statistics, however, is unlikely to prove sufficient. Rather, African countries need to be convinced of the need to make more efficient policies through evidence provided by gender status indicators.

NOTES

1. Interviewed by Edda Magnus, Autumn 2004.
2. Examples of sign-positive indicators include the proportion of persons in paid employment, proportion of time spent on educational preoccupation, proportion of men taking parental allowance, proportion of women in nontraditional sectors of work, and so on. A rise in the value over time is indicative of positively changing gender relations. Sign-negative indicators include the proportion of persons losing working hours to stress-related illnesses, the proportion of time spent on unpaid work, and the proportion of women in stereotyped sectors such as social work, and so on. A declining profile over time implies positively changing gender relations and an increasing attainment of gender equality.
3. For information, see the website of Statistics Norway: http://www.ssb.no/likekom_en/

REFERENCES

Akanji, Bola. 2004. *Gender issues in social and economic policy development of Africa: Some theoretical underpinnings.* Paper presented at the seventh African Regional Conference on Women (Beijing + 10), ECA Addis Ababa, Ethiopia, October 2004.

Aslaksen, I., Fargerli T., and Gravningsmyhr H.A. 1995. Measuring Household Production in an input-Output Framework: The Norwegian Experience. *Statistical Journal of the United Nations ECE* 12(2):111–131.

Aslaksen I., Fagerli T., and Gravningsmyhr H.A. 1996. An Estimation of Time and Commodity Intensity in Unpaid Household Production in Norway. *Feminist Economics* 2(3):81–91.

Esping-Anderson, Gösta. 1990. *Three worlds of welfare capitalism.* Princeton, NJ: Princeton University Press.

Gonäs, Lena. 1990. *"Permanent temporariness": Women's fate after plant closures in work life research.* Stockholm: Information from Arbetslivscentrum.

Haas, Linda, and Philip Hwang. 2000. Programs and policies promoting women's economic equality and men's sharing of child care in Sweden. In *Organizational change and gender equality: International perspectives on fathers and mothers at the workplace,* eds. L. Haas, P. Hwang, and G. Russell, 133–161. Thousand Oaks, CA: Sage.

Hedman, Birgitta. 2004. *Engendering statistics—20 years of development.* Paper presented at the 25th CEIES Seminar, Gender Statistics: Extent, Causes and Consequences, Stockholm, June 21–22.

Hedman, Birgitta, Fransesca Perucci, and Pehr Sundström. 1996. *Engendering statistics: A tool for change.* Statistics Sweden, Stockholm.

Keita, Naman, and Diana Tempelman. 2004. *Gender disaggregated agricultural statistics.* Paper presented to the third International Agricultural Statistics Conference, "Measuring Sustainable Agricultural Indicators," Quintana Roo, Mexico, November 2–4.

Kjeldstad, Randi, and Jan Erik Kristiansen. 2001. Constructing a regional gender equality index: Reflections on a first experience with Norwegian data. *Statistical Journal of the United Nations ECF* 18(2001):41–49.

Nyberg, Anita. 1998. *Women, men and incomes: Gender equality and economic independence.* Swedish committee on the distribution of economic power and economic resources between women and men, Kvinnomaktutredningen. Stockholm: SOU 1997:87.

Portocarero, Lucienne. 1987. *Social mobility in industrial societies: Women in France and Sweden.* Stockholm: Almqvist and Wiksell International.

Portocarero, Lucienne. 1990. *About gender, statistics and sociology.* Stockholm: The Swedish Institute for Social Research, Stockholm University.

Sainsbury, Diane. 1996. *Gendering welfare states.* London: Sage.

Sainsbury, Diane. 1999. *Gender and welfare state regimes.* Oxford: Oxford University Press.

Swedish International Development Agency (SIDA). 1998. *A brief representation of Swedish work and policies on gender equality.* Stockholm: SIDA.

Sinha, Anushree. 2002. *An inventory of existing like use data and capacity to collect and use time-use data for engendering national planning industries in Africa.* Addis Ababa: ACGD, United Nations Economic Commission for Africa.

Statistics Sweden. 1985. *Women and Men in Sweden. Facts and figures.* Stockholm: Statistics Sweden.

Statistics Sweden. 1989. *Arbetskraftsbarometer.* Stockholm: Statistics Sweden.

Statistics Sweden. 1990. *Women and Men in Sweden. Facts and figures.* Stockholm: Statistics Sweden.

Statistics Sweden. 1998. *Women and Men in Sweden. Facts and figures.* Stockholm: Statistics Sweden.

Statistics Sweden. 2000. *Women and Men in Sweden. Facts and figures.* Stockholm: Statistics Sweden.

Statistics Sweden. 2004a. *Women and Men in Sweden. Facts and figures.* Stockholm: Statistics Sweden.

Statistics Sweden. 2004b. *Statistics disaggregated by sex. Report on assignment from the 2003 appropriations directions.* Orebro: Statistics Sweden.

United Nations Development Programme. 1995. Human Development Report, 1995. New York: Oxford University Press.

United Nations Development Programme. 1998. Human Development Report, 1998. New York: Oxford University Press.

United Nations Development Programme. 2002. Human Development Report, 2002. New York: Oxford University Press.

United Nations Development Programme. 2004. Human Development Report, 2004. New York: Palgrave Macmillan.

UNIFEM. 2002. *Gender Budget Initiatives: strategies, concepts and experiences.* Papers from a high level international conference "Towards Gender Responsive Budgeting." Brussels, October 16–18, 2001. http://www.bridge.ids.ac.uk/gender_budgets _cd/Budgets%20CD%20subsection%204.1/4.1c%20Gender%20budget%20initiatives%20UNIFEM%20link%20for%204.4f.pdf (accessed October 31, 2007).

Winqvist, Karin. 2004. *The Life of Men and Women in Europe.* Paper presented at 25th CEIES Seminar, Gender statistics: Occupational segregation: extent, causes and consequences. Stockholm, June 21–22, 2004. http://epp.eurostat.ec.europa. eu/cache/ITY_PUBLIC/KS-PB-04-001/EN/KS-PB-04-001-EN.PDF (accessed October 31, 2007).

10 Institutionalising Equality
Putting Gender Issues at the Centre in Mexico and Sweden

Francisco Cos-Montiel

INTRODUCTION

As 2005 marked the thirtieth anniversary of the inauguration of the UN Decade for Women, it seems appropriate and worthwhile to reflect on the last three decades of global policies aimed at addressing the disadvantages that women experience across all spheres of life. While inequality itself has persisted (Jackson and Pearson 1998), the kinds of thinking that have driven policy discourse have changed—from a fairly narrow economic approach (Boserup 1970) to a much broader and more ambitious strategy of *gender mainstreaming*: "situating gender issues at the centre of policy decisions, institutional structures and resource allocation" (United Nations 1995). Gender mainstreaming can be defined in a number of ways, all of which are contested in one way or another. Nevertheless, the most common usage in Sweden is as a long-term strategy or systematic institutional approach for promoting/producing gender equality as a policy outcome (SIDA 1996, 1, cited in Woodford-Berger 2004). Nevertheless, although some advances have been made, particularly in terms of increasing awareness (Jahan 1995; Molyneux 2004), gender mainstreaming has led to different processes and outcomes (Standing 2004; Mukhopadhyay 2004). This chapter looks at the effectiveness of gender mainstreaming strategies in Mexico and Sweden between 1995 and 2005, to glean the lessons they have to teach each other and the world. While this chapter examines the strategy of gender mainstreaming, it also explores issues of institutionalisation of gender, that is, to what extent gender equality has become a regular and continuous part of Swedish and Mexican institutions, maintained by social norms, having a major significance in the social structure. It offers new insights in answering the following questions: Have gender issues, in fact, been placed centre stage in the policy arena? Has an active concern for gender equality been woven into all areas of policy discourse? What are the institutional arrangements—including cultural norms—that can foster gender mainstreaming as a strategy that furthers the struggle for equality? What Swedish lessons can be integrated into the variety of contexts of the developing world? To what extent can Sweden learn the valuable lessons offered by the experience of

Mexico, and how can they be integrated into future programmes and projects within the Swedish International Development Cooperation?

The chapter begins by reviewing gender mainstreaming origins and current challenges. It then analyses the strategies used to mainstream gender in Mexico—the achievements and the challenges—with a greater focus on the role of gender machineries. Thirdly, it examines the Swedish experience in mainstreaming gender concerns and the institutional arrangements which contributed to this process. The final section of the chapter suggests ways of boosting the effectiveness of gender mainstreaming in the developing world. Greater focus on institutional development, leadership, and accountability is needed in order to strengthen the capacity of institutions to put gender issues at the core of countries' development processes. It is argued that gender has been institutionalised in Sweden, whereas attempts to do so in Mexico have taken another path and yielded different outcomes.

THE EMERGENCE OF "GENDER MAINSTREAMING"

The first UN World Conference for women in 1975 ushered in a period when the integration of women into development policy through their participation in income-generating activities was seen as a key strategy for achieving equality. The early years of these efforts were characterised by the creation of women's ministries and bureaus in national governments, Women in Development desks, and "focal points" in international agencies. Looking back on this strategy, Levy (1992, 135) notes its limitations: the women's sector is a "weak sector . . . characterised by a lack of any real political influence, and is therefore underfunded and understaffed, both in numbers and qualifications. A key factor underlying these characteristics is the conceptualisation of both the problems and strategies of this sector in terms of women, not gender."

If women's affairs had been marginalised from mainstream development or compartmentalised into women's projects, ministries, or policies, then it was necessary to incorporate gender as a crosscutting issue along all policy lines. Gender mainstreaming—"situating gender issues at the centre of policy decisions, institutional structures and resource allocation"—was given a high level of prominence in the Beijing Platform of Action (United Nations 1995).

However, as Kabeer (2004, 4) warns, "There is no single correct way of 'doing gender.'" Beall (1998) observes that there is considerable confusion about what a policy of mainstreaming means in practice. The agenda for influencing the mainstream includes altering public policies, improving implementation and delivery of policies through clear programmes for change in administrative systems, and directly benefitting women through "targeted actions and programmes." This is an ambitious agenda, at the core of which is the effort to advocate for change, through training, institutional mechanisms for making gender a more explicit criterion for development programming and effectiveness, and developing "tools" that can help organizations think more deeply and beyond the earlier "add women and stir" approach (Subrahmanian 2004).

One challenge in implementing gender mainstreaming strategies has been translating the concept into operational and manageable actions. Kanji (2003) argues that much work has been carried out on the technical and operational side, particularly in training, analytical and planning tools and guidelines. These have become increasingly complex, moving from the gender-roles analysis that characterised early efforts, to institutional analyses that are the hallmark of later ones.[1] According to Kanji (2003), one of the most comprehensive methodological tools for institutionalising gender is Levy's (1996) "web of institutionalisation." Levy outlines the conditions under which gender can be institutionalised, represented by thirteen elements of the web, with each element representing a site of power. However, it is extremely difficult to find positive examples of such comprehensive processes in any one country or location; the reality is much more fragmented and ad hoc (Kanji 2003).

The idea of *institutionalisation*, a term often used interchangeably with mainstreaming, is a useful one because it draws attention to the organizational nature of the challenge. Abercrombie et al. (1988, 124) describe as institutionalised "social practices that are regularly and continuously repeated, are sanctioned and maintained by social norms, and have a major significance in the social structure." The term *institutionalisation* thus connotes long-term, sustained change, which recognises that regular practices of organisations inevitably reflect a particular set of interests, and may be resistant to change. Studies on mainstreaming commonly focus on policy and programme levels, to the neglect of organisational change, particularly organisational norms and culture.

This chapter attempts to analyse gender mainstreaming efforts in two very different contexts: Mexico, where the outcomes have been poor, and Sweden, where the process has been relatively successful. It takes an institutional perspective based on the premise that closer attention to the institutional rules in specific cultural environments and how these rules interfere, acknowledge, or foster gender inequality can provide a helpful framework for understanding the challenge of gender mainstreaming. It takes a "sociological" approach to institutions rather than the rational-choice one which appears to dominate development discourse. Rational-choice approaches posit that the relevant institutional actors have a fixed set of preferences or tastes, behave entirely instrumentally so as to maximise the attainment of these preferences, and do so in a highly strategic manner that presumes extensive calculation (Hall and Taylor 1996). However, today more than ever before, ample evidence proves that gender inequality hinders development (World Bank 2001). It would not require very extensive calculation to make the case for taking immediate action to pursue gender equality.

The fact that such action has not been forthcoming seems to challenge the rational-choice view of public institutions (Goetz 1992, 2004).

Sociological institutionalists argue that organizations often adopt a new institutional practice, not because it advances the means–ends efficiency of the organization, but because it enhances the social legitimacy of the organization or its participants (Meyer and Rowan 1977; Meyer and Scott 1983; DiMaggio and Powell 1991). In other words, organizations embrace specific institutional forms or practices because the latter are widely valued within a broader cultural environment. In some cases, these practices may actually be dysfunctional with regard to achieving the organization's formal goals. Such an approach seems to fit better with the objective of understanding why gender mainstreaming strategies and eventually the institutionalisation of gender seems to work better in certain contexts than in others (Woodford-Berger 2004).

Institutions are therefore defined in this chapter to include not just formal rules, procedures, or norms, but the symbol systems, cognitive scripts, and moral templates that provide the "frames of meaning" that guide human action. Such a definition breaks down the conceptual divide between "institutions" and "culture." The two bleed into each other so that "culture" is itself an aspect of "institutions." It is the hypothesis of the chapter that the promotion of gender equality requires certain institutional-cultural soil in which to grow. This suggests that gender advocates—particularly those working within governments—have to move away from blueprint approaches to approaches that take account of the nature of the institutions they are working with. Much has been done on the technical and methodological side, but less has been done to deconstruct institutions in practice. Furthermore, while it has been recognised that the achievements of gender equality imply cultural change, culture is embedded in institutional norms and practices which, regardless of how equality goals may appear in formal documents, determine actual outcomes. Therefore, strategies beyond "formal" institutional arenas might offer better places in which to tackle inequality.

GENDER MAINSTREAMING IN MEXICO

The Culture of Politics

Mexico's contemporary culture reflects its tumultuous history, including the Spanish conquest of an indigenous civilisation at the peak of its development. Despite important turning points, such as independence in 1821 and the first social revolution of the twentieth century, which established social ideals that permeated ideology and policy for the next decades, Mexico continues to struggle with a myriad of challenges. Racism, gender inequality, a very rigid class system, corruption, discrimination, and an authoritarian and violent political system inevitably affect, in one way or another, all Mexicans

(Monsiváis 1997). Although it is evident that the indigenous population faces the harshest living conditions in Mexico, the truth is that a very complex set of overlapping inequalities affect all sections of society.

Nobel laureate philosopher Octavio Paz tried to explain these features in *The Labyrinth of Solitude* (1954). He describes how colonial rule had torn asunder the original sense of self-esteem and belonging enjoyed by Mexican men and women. Whether indigenous, white or *mestizo*, Mexicans of the post-colonial era, according to Paz, share an unfortunate legacy of discomfort with themselves and an inability to create solidarity with their fellow Mexicans. This alienation from others and themselves has in fact allowed colonialism to perpetuate itself through a hierarchy of the white-skinned over the dark-skinned, men over women, rich over poor.

Whatever one thinks of the accuracy of Paz's story, it illustrates how some of the characteristics, beliefs, and expectations of Mexicans are embedded in their institutions, which in turn reinforce these beliefs. Thus, the state and other institutions, despite claims of fairness, in reality are pervaded by unfair rules, norms, and practices. How do these norms, rules, and practices of Mexican institutions operate in relation to policies that aim to achieve gender equality?

The Emergence of Gender Mainstreaming in Mexico

The First UN Conference on Women was held in Mexico City in 1975 and generated a great deal of excitement in the small feminist movement that existed then. Some progressive legislation was passed at the time; for example, married women were no longer required to possess a written permit to enter the labour market. However, women's issues were located institutionally primarily in the newly established Population Council for Mexico, and women were drawn into official policy through population programmes aimed at reducing fertility rates and maternal mortality. Later, a Women in Solidarity Programme was set up as part of the safety-net strategy to compensate for the effects of structural adjustment in the country. This provided grants for income-generating projects for women but did little to transform gender roles and relations. It was only with the signing of the Platform of Action at the Fourth UN Conference on Women in 1995, a time when the more progressive President Zedillo had succeeded the discredited Salinas, that the government committed itself to a mainstreaming agenda (Secretaría de Gobernación 1996). A National Programme for Women (PRONAM) was launched in 1996 which eventually transformed into the National Commission for Women (CONMUJER) in 1998. Additionally, to mirror the role that women's NGOs had played during the Beijing Conference, two non-governmental bodies were created to support PRONAM's work: an Advisory Board and a Social Audit. Leading feminists and experts in gender equality participated in these. The Social Audit comprised a group of women, representing civil society, who were to evaluate the gender machinery's performance. The Advisory Board, also made up of renowned female experts, was to advise on policy issues.

After the creation of PRONAM, several states established their own organizations for the advancement of women, with the notable exception of the state of Guerrero, which had already established a Women's Secretariat back in 1987. However, CONMUJER was handicapped in fulfilling its mandate to mainstream gender within government policy by its limited economic resources. In addition, its location within the Secretariat of the Interior gave it very little power to bring about substantial reforms (CONMUJER 2000). Institutional location is key in the very hierarchical Mexican political system. The closer an issue gets to the President's office, the more support it will get from peers.

However, PRONAM and CONMUJER were more a response to international commitments than to women's demands. Between 1996 and 2000, women's organizations struggled to transform the relatively powerless CONMUJER into the National Institute for Women. The idea was to create a body similar to the Spanish Women's Institute, which had positive impacts on women's policies, and the creation of INMUJERES was adopted as a campaign commitment by the three contesting parties in the 2000 Presidential elections.

In July 2000, Vicente Fox won the presidential elections, ending seventy-five years of rule under the Institutional Revolutionary Party (PRI). The PRI had become highly unpopular by this period, as it was identified with rampant corruption through political clientelism. However, despite its authoritarianism, it was relatively open to gender equality issues. By contrast, Fox's party was right-wing and had a long tradition of opposing gender equality issues, particularly abortion. However, the constituency that put him in power represented a myriad of political affiliations who saw in him a real opportunity to defeat the PRI. For that reason, feminist advocates thought that gender equality issues would not be at risk under the Fox administration. This appeared to be the case at the beginning of his term: in December 2000, CONMUJER was transformed into the National Institute for Women (INMUJERES), an independent body with legal and financial autonomy and an annual budget of US$30 million, ten times larger than the budget of the former CONMUJER (Diario Oficial de la Federación 2001).

Achievements through Gender Mainstreaming

The setting up of a national machinery for gender mainstreaming has seen progress on a number of fronts. First of all, awareness-raising in the policy domain has been a significant achievement. Today, it is possible to say that gender issues have gained a firm place in official discourse. Expertise on gender issues has grown with the development of different methodologies for research and data collection, procedures and tools for planning, and various in-house training methodologies (INMUJERES 2002). Discriminatory practices regarded as belonging in the private domain, such as domestic violence, have been actively brought into the public domain: in 1999, CON-MUJER launched a national programme against violence which opened shelters across the country.

Gender budget initiatives have emerged in many states, the result of collaboration among various civil society networks. As a result of continuous mobilisation by NGOs who have focused their attention on the Chamber of Deputies, which approves the national budget, the Equity and Gender Commission of the Chamber earmarked approximately 1.3 billion US dollars in 2003 and 2004 (circa 0.80 percent total budget) toward programmes that promote gender equality (Hofbauer 2002).

However, most of these achievements were either NGO initiatives or initiated during the CONMUJER phase. What is widely agreed is that the picture since the subsequent incarnation of the national machinery as INMUJERES has been very unpromising (Poniatowska 2004; González 2003; Cos-Montiel 2003). This is despite the fact that all the right pieces for a major thrust on gender equality seemed to be in place: a brand new machinery with huge economic resources, politically situated at the core of decision-making processes, at a unique political moment in which Mexico experienced a transition similar to that of Chile (Waylen 1997; Molina 1997) or South Africa (Hassim 2000), and widespread consensus among women's organizations to grant the newly created institute political support, regardless of ideological differences. In the following sections we try to understand why this has been case.

The Special Challenge of Gender Mainstreaming

The gender mainstreaming project faces a particular challenge in operationalising its cross-cutting mandate in highly centralised and vertical administrative structures such as characterise Mexico. In contrast to development sectors such as education, health, or even environment—which have in any case had more experience and built up more expertise in their areas of competence, achieved greater legitimacy in the political agenda, and command larger budgets—the gender machinery faces many challenges. It is a relatively new institutional structure, with little experience, but it is being asked to deliver on goals that are not its responsibility alone but have to be addressed by other ministries. While this has had the advantage of promoting a multisectoral analysis of gender, the coordination of policy planning and implementation is an extremely complicated process for which are required both political and technical competencies (Beall 1998). Essentially, therefore, a new and inexperienced department is being asked to deliver on a politically controversial agenda through forms of practice that go against the organizational routine and ways of working.

Given the politically controversial nature of many issues relating to gender, particularly in a strongly Catholic country, it is under considerable political pressures from different stakeholders to include or to exclude certain issues from the agenda. Reproductive rights and abortion are one example of these issues. Abortion-related deaths are the fifth most important cause of mortality among women in reproductive age, suggesting both that it is widely practised, regardless of its legal status, and that it is practised under unsafe conditions. Despite the fact that Mexico has signed the most advanced international treaties, such as CEDAW's optional protocol (Lamas 2005), the leadership of INMUJERES is openly against abortion and has systematically excluded this issue from policy debates.

The Question of Leadership

Mexican women are not present in large numbers across the political domain or within the policy-making bodies. Only one out of 32 governors is a woman. At the federal level, there is only one female minister among 17 men (INMUJERES 2001). While 23 percent of members of the national parliament are women, only 3.7 percent of municipal councillors are female (Sistema Nacional de Información Municipal 2003). Mexico has various examples of strong female leadership, but few take feminist causes into their agenda. In the absence of a widespread tradition of female leadership, the personality and performance of individual women takes on disproportionate importance.

Various observers suggest that the weakness of INMUJERES in delivering on its mandate reflects the weakness of its leadership, in particular its first director. In one of the leading newspapers of Mexico, Poniatowska (2004) wrote a scathing exposé in documenting in detail the director's inexperience, her incompetence, and her dishonesty, particularly concerning the awarding of contracts along patronage lines. The first director had had no prior experience in public office and had been selected for her close personal and political identification with Fox and his party. Under her, the gender machinery responded to the needs and interests of the conservative party and powerful stakeholders, such as the church and prolife groups.

However, an institutional analysis would need to go beyond the failings of an individual and ask how that individual came to exercise such an influence over her organization's outcomes. It would point out that recruitment outcomes, particularly into leadership roles, are themselves the products of the way in which rules, priorities, and politics play out in relation to gender within the government. Gender machineries, no matter how much they advocate justice, are not immune to a country's institutional and cultural rules. In the context of the institutional culture of Mexico, where mechanisms for participation and accountability are extremely weak, individuals in leading positions can exercise an inordinate influence.

Beyond individuals, there is the question of the wider institutional culture. According to Murison (2001), managerial styles that create a secure environment for teamwork, feedback, and knowledge networking are extremely important for innovation and creativity on the part of officials. Leaders who understand that part of their task is to develop talents in strategic communication contribute to an institutional culture that enables gender-mainstreaming efforts. However, this type of leadership has proven difficult to transplant into the hierarchical, frequently authoritarian, structure of public management in Mexico (Lamas 1997).

This institutional soil seems to clash with many of the ideals of gender mainstreaming where concepts such as justice, empowerment, and deconstruction of hierarchical rules are advocated. Therefore, inside organizations a contradiction soon emerges between the new ways of doing things, such as teamwork and horizontal communication, and the previous vertical and centralised organizational culture. In many cases, the staff are asked to change their values while the organizations' values remain unchanged.

The general literature on organizational change warns that the shift to a more democratic management style has to be managed over a gradual and long-term process. Therefore, change management plays a crucial role on desirable outcomes, such as an empowered organization capable of managing the technical and political aspects of gender mainstreaming. All empowerment processes require—at least in the short term—a zero-sum process in which players lose or win power (Kabeer 1994). This is not free of anguish, resistance, and thus conflict. Every empowerment process thus faces the possibility that it might degenerate into a disempowerment process. This seems to have happened with INMUJERES, where the leadership triggered a "vicious circle of disempowerment" among its staff (Cos-Montiel 2003). Leadership was exercised through a formal and hierarchical authority. This has not only had a negative impact within the organization; it has also had a negative impact on policies. If the people in charge of "doing gender" within the government do not feel any power to do their job, they are unlikely to be able to influence their more reluctant partners in other departments. Therefore, it seems that in Mexico, institutionalisation has not occurred: gender equality considerations are far from becoming social practices that are regularly and continuously repeated (Cos-Montiel 2003). It is noteworthy that Mexico's UNDP GEM ranking fell from 35 to 42 during this period.

The Human Dimension of National Machineries

The question of management styles also intersects with the development of staff capacity to determine outcomes. For over two decades, women's/ gender machineries have been characterised as particularly weak, with poorly trained staff, small budgets, and little bargaining power (Levy 1992; Razavi and Miller 1995; Subrahmanian 2004; Goetz 1992, 1997). In other words, they have not had the economic and political resources to effectively influence national policy. If an organization's best asset is its staff, the staff must develop the necessary competencies, both technical and political, to carry out their jobs and contribute to the organisation's goals. Involvement in gender mainstreaming is essentially a political project. This means that staff must not only have the necessary technical knowledge but also the capacity for negotiation and communication. Without these skills, the technical tools and frameworks are blunt instruments (Beall 1998; Beall and Todes 2004).

Before INMUJERES was set up, the incoming political party under President Fox carried out an evaluation of the staff of the existing machinery of CONMUJER. About half of the staff were dismissed on a variety of grounds, including competence and ideological views. Therefore, the reinvention of the national machinery as INMUJERES entailed finding replacement staff as well as expanding the institution from 60 to 180 staff in less than six months. The leadership had almost no experience of managing bureaucracies, clear job descriptions were not written up, and there was considerable uncertainty about what kind of skills and competencies were needed. This lack of clarity allowed the recruitment process to be governed by arbitrary and politicised criteria. Some of the staff had at least knowledge of sectoral policies, if not from a gender perspective, but others were selected on the basis of their support for the ruling party (González 2003). Over the next years, even those staff who had necessary skills but were regarded as too liberal were dismissed and replaced by political appointments. This has resulted in a very high turnover rate. Of the original staff that was hired in 2001, only 20 percent remained in place by 2005. Most positions had been replaced two or three times, creating very little internal capacity and institutional memory.

While this practice of politically motivated appointments is not unknown in the context of Mexico, the extent to which this happened with INMUJER was considered exceptionally blatant. This partly reflected the inexperience of the leadership, but it also reflected issues of accountability to which we turn next.

Accountability

All the challenges identified in relation to INMUJERES's performance are intimately linked with one of the main tensions in public policy and management: that of accountability. Achieving greater accountability is inherently problematic for all institutions and in most policy arenas. It is particularly problematic within authoritarian political cultures like Mexico. There are also additional problems regarding accountability in relation to INMUJERES. This relates to the fact that there are two meanings of accountability: technical accountability, which is generally upward, and downward accountability, which relates to the democratic process and entails the accountability of public officials to citizens and civil society. In the case of INMUJERES, this would imply accountability to civil society groups concerned with gender issues, and ultimately to Mexican women themselves.

The setting up of the Advisory and Social Auditing Body with representatives from NGOs, political parties, and women's organizations is, on the face of it, a means of improving downward accountability. But the NGOs represented were in fact selected by the political leaders from different parties on party political grounds rather than to represent women's interests, except in a very narrow sense. It was mainly urban-based and middle-class NGOs who had connections with party leadership who became members while grassroots organizations were largely excluded. Since the leadership of INMUJERES is effectively a patronage network brought in to run the organization, upward accountability is strong, as is accountability to the interests of political supporters.

The accountability structure is also very centrally based. There is little scope for decentralised exercise of accountability and grassroots participation. Poor, rural Mexican women have little voice in the policy process in a much wider sense than only with respect to INMUJERES. Most of them are not aware that they have the right to demand accountability. They need greater awareness of their rights as well as training to make these demands. Gender mainstreaming should not only concentrate on policies and programmes as given but also on building grassroots capacity for accountability.

A Positive Case Study of Top-Down Leadership

However, though the National Machinery has faced many challenges, Mexico is a federated state, and local gender machineries in each state have opportunities for following their own course. And, although many still face formidable constraints, there is one shining success: the Southern state of Oaxaca. The Oaxacan case study tells us that in an authoritarian culture, top-down leadership can sometimes be very effective and may be necessary to kick-start a process of change.

The Southern state of Oaxaca has some of the worst welfare indicators in Mexico, with indigenous communities faring even more poorly (Cunningham and Cos-Montiel 2002). Oaxacans face harsh living conditions, with women being disadvantaged in some spheres and men in others. Women, particularly indigenous women, are largely monolingual (speaking only their indigenous language), have exceptionally low levels of education, and are commonly confined to their villages; they have little experience of the mestizo world. Men face some of the highest rates of violent death and HIV/AIDS in Mexico. In a context where machismo, old political practices, and a rather authoritarian regime coexist, addressing women's needs seems a painstakingly slow process. Despite this, the local gender machinery, the Institute for Oaxacan Women (IOW), is now—by far—the most successful example of how a gender mainstreaming policy can be integrated successfully. What processes were adopted by the IOW between 2000 and 2004 that enabled them to mainstream gender concerns in a rather adverse setting?

First, instead of replicating a blueprint approach, the Institute for Oaxacan Women (IOW) has developed a local strategy that has enabled them to bring gender issues into public policy. Second, the director's very strong leadership has allowed her to forge powerful political alliances that have supported the process, and has developed incentives among civil servants within the local ministries, which in turn has created very strong ownership.

Drawing on the experience of a long political career, the IOW's director understood that before deploying the mainstreaming strategy, she had to build the institution's capacity at all levels of the organization, including the top. All staff members, herself included, underwent an extensive training process to familiarise themselves with basic gender and development concepts and debates. From the beginning, they were convinced that in order to influence public policy beyond traditional women's issues such as violence or reproductive rights, they had to be familiar with the domain of policy-making processes. So their training went beyond gender issues and included the nuts and bolts of public policy as well as the development of important managerial tools.

With institutional capacity in place, the IOW launched an ambitious gender training programme for government officials who were not particularly known for having a gender-sensitive approach to policymaking. Particularly reluctant were the staff at the Ministry of Finance, who did not want to be taken from their familiar conceptual territory of growth, welfare, poverty, and efficiency and into the nebulous territory of power and social injustice. However, a clever use of sound evidence on how addressing gender issues could help the governor achieve his goal of poverty reduction proved to be vital in gaining his support. Although he was not particularly aware of gender issues, the arguments used proved sufficient to convince him of the importance of integrating gender into his administration.

The fact that Oaxaca, traditionally seen as one of Mexico's least developed states, was integrating gender concerns drew interest from important stakeholders and showed a progressive side to donors, multilateral organizations, and the federal government, which eventually established Oaxaca as the gender-mainstreaming benchmark for the other thirty-one states. In a still very authoritarian society, and with strong support from the top, the otherwise reluctant civil servants had no option but to show an interest in gender issues. Thus, the IOW selected key high-ranking officials, who went through a year-long intensive gender-training course. The instructors were not only gender advocates but also highly experienced senior staff from other institutions who shared a common language with Oaxaca's civil servants. With the help of consultants who used a language permeated by economic logic, gender advocates finally spoke the same language as policy makers. The training approach was particularly empowering for the senior civil servants. Instead of using the usual argument that blames civil servants for "doing things wrong because they don't integrate a gender perspective," the IOW switched to a more inviting perspective that saw civil servants as trained and experienced people "who had the knowledge of the nuts and bolts of the intricate governmental bureaucracy" but who need a gender perspective to improve some desirable outcomes. And indeed, they needed it for at least two reasons. First, by integrating a gender perspective, they could improve their policy outcomes, and, second, they could gain politically by it. Officials suddenly gained access to privileges: they had regular meetings with the governor and international officials and started to enjoy an importance that they were proud of. Middle management in particular thus had an incentive to integrate a gender perspective into their work.[2]

GENDER MAINSTREAMING IN SWEDEN

For many gender advocates around the world, Sweden is a model, in terms of both its levels of social provision and its degree of gender equality (United Nations Development Programme 2004).[3] How has Sweden managed to do it? Although it adopted gender mainstreaming as a strategy for achieving equality following the 1995 Beijing Conference, in fact, policies to promote gender equality go back a long way. Although it is commonly appreciated that virtually all Swedish women are in the labour force and that public-sector day-care provisions are better than in most Western countries, how this has been achieved is less well known (Lewis and Åström 1992).

Although feminist advocates have been supported by relatively widespread societal pressure and intense lobbying efforts and in turn have played a role in determining the timing and in providing a justification for the dramatic nature of the changes, the policies owed as much to a governmental commitment to improving the position of women (Lewis and Åström 1992).

There appear to be certain distinctive institutional and cultural factors that have played a part in advancing gender mainstreaming in Sweden. First, there seems to be little overt resistance to social justice issues. On the contrary, there seems to be a consensus about the importance of justice at all levels as a Swedish democratic value (Woodford-Berger 2004). This is in marked contrast to Mexico, whose long-standing inequalities have been ignored by successive governments.

Second, the national public administration has had a rather unusual organizational structure, which seems to reflect the specific structure of the pre-democratic Swedish state—centralised, but not closed; bureaucratic and professional, but not especially authoritarian; differentiated, but not without central coordination of policy (Rothstein 1990). Since the end of the nineteenth century, the ministries have been quite small and have dealt mostly with policy issues. The responsibility for actually implementing public policy rested with semi-autonomous national boards and agencies. These government organizations were not under the direct command of any minister, but rather implemented policy under their own legal responsibility. This meant that top civil servants enjoyed a considerable amount of discretion and could take initiatives of their own.

Third, policy "trickles down" and translates into outcomes in a relatively efficient way. This feature seems to be particularly true at the local level. The explanation for this seems to lie in the origins of corporatism, as corporatist institutions were first established at the local level in Sweden, not at the centre (Rothstein 1991).

And finally, Sweden is ethnically, religiously, and politically rather a homogeneous society where political consensus seems widespread. It is not subject to the tensions of a colonial history nor the degree of internal divisions that characterise Mexico. It is against this enabling background that we can understand some of the successes that gender-equality policies have enjoyed in Sweden. We turn next to a more specific account of this.

Gender Mainstreaming as Historical Process

In Mexico, the national machinery for gender equality faced difficulties as a relatively new institution being asked to implement an ambitious and politically controversial set of goals, which required ways of working that went against the established institutional culture. The picture in Sweden is very different. Although attention to gender mainstreaming is also relatively recent in Sweden, co-inciding with the run up to Beijing, it has been given a high priority on the political agenda (Ministry for Industry, Employment and Communications [MIEC] 2001a) as a way to bring about a more coherent approach to the project of gender equality.

The gender equality process in Sweden has also historically been a response to feminist activism and its engagement with both the state and the female electorate over an extended period of time. It has been an internally driven process—in contrast to Mexico, where it was adopted in response to the international agenda. It has consequently been less subject to political pressures from above or contradictory external pressures. Moreover, it lends itself to being institutionalised as an integral part of the Swedish way of life: "There is a general political consensus in Sweden on the principles of gender equality" (Government of Sweden 2005, 7). It is not a particularly divisive issue for competing political parties. On the contrary, it seems it would be rather unpopular to exclude gender issues from one of the political parties' electoral platform priorities.

Present-day gender equality policy in Sweden reflects the combination of research with politics and a firm belief in and commitment to the realisation of gender equality and the achievement of political goals through legislation, top-down directives, and the adoption of gender mainstreaming as the government's official strategy (Woodford-Berger 2004). It is a set of objectives that have an organic place within the political culture and process of Sweden. As Rabo (1997) points out, gender-quality policy provides a way for the Swedish state, the social democratic government, and its historical legacy to safeguard a comprehensive welfare system, to organize, direct, and control the pursuit of gender equality in Sweden.

Leadership and Staff Development

In the Mexican case study, a great deal of attention was paid to the quality of individual leadership. This is because, in the absence of women's representation in the different levels of political and policy decisionmaking, and with the lack of democratic accountability to the population at large, the people who lead the gender machinery take on an inordinate significance.

The Swedish case offers a very different picture. First of all, women are present in larger numbers across the political domain as well as within the policymaking bodies. Consequently, questions of leadership are bound up with the quality of this representation. In political terms, of the 349 members of parliament, 45.3 percent are women (Statistics Sweden 2004). In 2004 there were eleven male ministers and eleven female ministers in the government. Ten women (out of a total of twenty-six) were state secretaries, the rank immediately below cabinet minister. Conditions in the municipalities and county councils are similar to those in parliament. Well over 40 percent of municipal councillors are women. Representation on the county councils, the responsibilities of which include health and medical services, is even higher (Government of Sweden 2005).

Nevertheless, it remains the case that women tend to be allotted fewer influential appointments and do work that is not in the public eye. Moreover, immigrant and minority women are not well represented. Despite Swedish women's relatively strong position in directly elected bodies, men still dominate nearly all policymaking bodies. This holds true for senior positions in employer and employee organizations as well as in political and other associations. In senior management positions in the private sector, the percentage of women is even lower.

These weaknesses appear to be compensated through the efforts given to ensuring the quality of the policy process. At present, the Ministry of Democracy, Metropolitan Affairs, Integration and Gender Equality is responsible for the coordination of gender equality affairs, assisted by the Division for Gender Equality at the Government Offices. The Division for Gender Equality was established at the central government level in the early 1980s. The division supports and initiates efforts to promote equality at the national and regional levels by developing methods for integration and implementation of a gender perspective in all policy areas (MIEC 1999, 2001a). At the regional level, Sweden's twenty-one county administrative boards are responsible for coordinating national and local policies. Since 1995, there has been a regional expert on gender equality issues in each of the counties. The main task of these experts is to promote mainstreaming of a gender perspective into all policy fields and support efforts to achieve equality between women and men in their regions. County councils and local authorities do not have a specific organization for gender equality matters, but the work of both in this field has been extended in recent years and now encompasses not only staff policy issues but also the content of local and regional government undertakings.

To support this overall strategy, a number of measures have been taken to integrate a gender perspective into every policy area. First, all official statistics are required to be broken down by sex. Making gender discrimination visible is essential to the success of equality efforts. For that reason, the Swedish government decided in 1994 that all individually based official statistics were to be disaggregated along gender lines unless there were special reasons for not doing so (Statistics Sweden 2002, 2004). Second, gender training has been a central pillar of mainstreaming (Government of Sweden 2005; Woodford-Berger 2004). Since 1994, the government has been providing basic training in gender equality studies for ministers, state secretaries, press secretaries, political advisors, heads and staff of ministries, heads and secretaries of central government committees, and commissions of inquiry. Third, all government commissions of inquiry have been instructed to include a gender impact dimension in their research studies.

Although all these components are also in place in Mexico, their impact has been different. For example, despite the fact that statistics are disaggregated by sex, they seldom inform public policy or make inequality visible. Although gender training is an ongoing activity since 1998, it is limited to junior and middle civil servants. To date, no Minister has undergone gender training, and there is a lot of confusion around what gender means in practice. At the local level, Oaxaca is the exception, and has held courses for the governor and senior staff. In Chihuahua and Puebla, which have to some extent followed Oaxaca's example, gender training remains limited to staff who have very little decision-making power.

In Sweden, a great deal of attention has been paid to the issue of management. According to the ministry responsible for gender mainstreaming, "Management's attitude is crucial. If the organization really wants to change its norms and values, it has to work with the three dimensions of the normative model: intention, knowledge and supportive structures" (MIEC 2001b, 22). Working at managerial levels is especially important for creating an empowering environment, in which lower level staff feel safe and confident in promoting change along policy lines.

There have also been efforts to develop methods for the systematic review and analysis of the influence of women and men in particular operations. One of the most widely used is the "3R method" which focuses on issues of representation, resources, and rights, and has primarily been used by local authorities to review and analyse the distribution of power from a gender perspective, the role of gender in the organisation, and gender standards within different municipal activities.

Finally, an aspect of leadership that is less explored pertains to the role that men and their leadership play in gender mainstreaming and empowerment.

The Swedish government has taken a variety of steps to bring men in since the mid-1980s. Besides granting funds to several county councils to support projects on men and equality, the government also initiated a two-year project starting in June 1999 to identify obstacles to men's involvement in work to promote gender equality, and to identify the necessary measures to attract men to such work. The project's final report summarised the efforts of the past twenty years to involve men in gender-equality issues and made a number of recommendations to the government centring around developing a "new masculinity" and a new gender policy (Government of Sweden 2005).

Accountability

Accountability is achieved in the Swedish system both by internal processes of reporting and evaluation and also by an external machinery in the form of the ombudsman. In terms of internal accountability to gender equality goals, ministries are required to state in their annual reports what work had been completed in this field and what further efforts are planned. The issue is also raised in the annual discussions between ministry heads and the heads of agencies, demonstrating the importance the ministry attaches to good results in this field (MIEC 2001a). Additionally, all government-appointed investigatory bodies are required to consider gender equality implications in their reports.

As far as external accountability is concerned, the Equal Opportunity Ombudsman (Jämställdhetsombudsmannen, JämO) is an independent government authority set up when the first Equal Opportunities Act came into force in 1980. Its primary task is to ensure compliance with the Equal Opportunities Act and portions of the Equal Treatment of Students at Universities Act. The ombudsman can represent employees or students in disputes regarding alleged violations of the ban on gender discrimination. The Equal Opportunities Commission (Jämställdhetsnämnden) is a government authority which—following an application by the Equal Opportunities Ombudsman or a union, and under penalty of a fine—can order compliance with the requirements set forth in the Equal Opportunities Act concerning active measures to be taken by the employers.

However, Woodford-Berger (2004) warns that the challenge of accountability goes beyond introducing tools for gender mainstreaming into planning and reporting systems. She argues that it also lies in maintaining a constructive dialogue with those who should be allies. Not taking into account different kinds of alliances and cooperational arrangements between and among various categories of women and men comprises nothing less than a denial of the many lessons that have been learned over the years. In the case of Sweden, the strongest alliances have been with the longstanding feminist movement, female and male professionals working in key areas such as health, education, or labour policy, and a continuous and constructive dialogue with women and men. In the case of Oaxaca, Mexico, strategic alliances with government officials proved to be a successful entry point to gender training. However, this is only one side of the coin. In the absence of alliances with the feminist movement and the constituency of women and men, it is unlikely that gender mainstreaming will have positive outcomes. One lesson to glean from Sweden is that accountability, consensus, and representation have been key in the challenge of institutionalising equality.

CONCLUSIONS

Analysing gender mainstreaming strategies in Mexico and Sweden has yielded insights into why in some countries gender mainstreaming promotes gender equality more steadily than in others. Despite evident differences between the two countries, both had machineries that were strong, politically well-positioned, and endowed with sufficient resources. In the last decade, both nations adopted gender mainstreaming as their main strategy for achieving equality.

Nevertheless, the way in which gender mainstreaming has been implemented and translated into outcomes has been very different. It seems that gender mainstreaming in Sweden, despite being top-down and centrally orchestrated, was successful because aspirations for gender equality had already been institutionalised and could be aligned with general, cultural ideas of social justice and equality. In Mexico, by contrast, it seems that gender inequality, along with other forms of inequality, is deeply embedded in the social structure.

In Sweden, institutions, policy processes, and outcomes are embedded in a common agreement to see them as a public good, and positive changes take place through clear channels. In the case of Mexico, policy processes are weak and often contradictory as different sets of interests compete to shape distributional outcomes and defend privilege. Nevertheless, major changes have taken place in gender relations which have had very little to do with policy intent. The sweeping changes in gender roles during the structural adjustment years in Mexico are an example of this (Beneria 1991; Chant 1991, 1997). More recently, the changes in *machismo* identities and gender roles through the Internet and globalisation (Gutmann 1996, 1997; Cos-Montiel 2001; Cos-Montiel and Rosado 2002) are proof that some emerging forces are outside the scope of the Mexican state (at least initially) and are providing a place where men and women can interact, explore, and grow.

If state institutions foster and reinforce a very unfair and vicious culture, then men and women turn to arenas located outside the formal institutional domain to gain freedom. These arenas provide areas for growth and exploration without the hindrances and constraints of messy institutional procedures. For example, if bureaucratic procedures make formal income-generating activities very complicated for women, then informal market activities or work in the garment industry provide them with a means for making an income, sometimes with desirable effects in terms of empowerment.

This reminds us that gender mainstreaming is not the only way to achieve positive outcomes. As Beall and Todes (2004) point out, equally important are the political and policy conditions and particularly the historical legacy of women's struggle. While in Sweden, women (and some men) have a long tradition of organized struggle, in Mexico this struggle is much more dispersed (Lamas 1997). Mexican feminist groups may have relied too much on setting up a national machinery to promote gender interests, to the neglect of creating a political constituency at the grassroots level.

This chapter has suggested is that it is crucial to assess carefully the institutional/cultural environment in which gender mainstreaming will take place. While gender mainstreaming seems to "fit" well in the institutional scaffolding of Sweden (Stark 2005), that may not be the case in other contexts. This has been partly recognised in an evaluation of gender mainstreaming by SIDA that noted that "in Nicaragua, cultural resistance, or the absence of a public discussion on gender equality as a challenge to conservative political and religious movements was a constraint to gender mainstreaming" (Mikkelsen et al. 2002, xiv). For Swedish development policy, it might be useful to support different gender mainstreaming approaches according to different cultural contexts. As institutional arrangements play such an important role in the success or failure of gender mainstreaming strategies, it would be important to take a strategic approach in determining which ones to support.

Deploying highly complex gender mainstreaming strategies, such as the integration of gender issues in all policies, can prove to be extremely complicated in very intricate bureaucracies, as the Mexican experience shows, where changes that affect any public management—let alone gender mainstreaming—are very difficult to implement. Institutional development thus is a crucial investment that should not be overlooked.

In Mexico, a great deal more attention needs to be paid to complex institutional factors such as endemic bureaucratic procedures, highly authoritarian managerial styles, and punishment/reward political appointments that result in very high staff turnover rates and impede capacity building. Granting a gender machinery resources and importance is not enough to integrate a gender perspective successfully. In the absence of strong leadership, knowledge, and assertiveness, resources—both financial and human—can be wasted on projects that go nowhere, thus eroding prospects for gender analysis in the eyes of important development partners. On the other hand, machineries like the Institute for Oaxacan Women have proved to be more successful in bringing gender concerns into public policy through strong leadership, a process approach, and steady capacity building. In terms of entry points for mainstreaming, the disadvantage of a top-down management style in some developing countries can be turned into an advantage if the decision to integrate gender is made at the top. The Oaxacan experience shows that a top-down approach initially had very good results, as there was widespread compliance with the governor's instructions—even by otherwise reluctant partners, such as senior staff (Reyes 2004; Escudero 2004). However, eventually this top-down approach should merely be a stepping stone to a more participatory one likely to include more women and have more widespread empowerment outcomes.

It is important to remember that the struggle of gender equality in Mexico, as in Sweden, began with grassroots women and their organizations. As the international community has taken up gender mainstreaming, it has become increasingly complex, technical, and bureaucratic. Yet the conditions which gave rise to feminist activism remain largely intact. The most disadvantaged women in Mexico continue to live in very harsh conditions. They are excluded from participation in the very processes which are intended to improve their lives. If gender advocates and feminist activists are to learn anything from the slow progress of gender mainstreaming, it is the importance of improving the governance structures of these efforts so that they become a vehicle for democratic participation by *all* women.

NOTES

1. Moser 1989; Kabeer 1994, 2000; Beall 1998; Levy 1996.
2. For further details see Reyes, 2004; Escudero, 2004.
3. Sweden ranks second in both the Human Development and Gender-related Development Indexes.

REFERENCES

Abercrombie, Nicholas, Stephen Hill, and Bryan Turner. 1988. *Dictionary of sociology*. London: Penguin.

Beall, Jo. 1998. Trickle down or rising tide? Lessons on mainstreaming gender policy from Colombia and South Africa. *Social Policy and Administration* 32(5):513–35.

Beall, Jo, and Alison Todes. 2004. Headlines and head-space: Challenging gender planning orthodoxy in area-based urban development. In *Repositioning feminisms in development*, eds. Andrea Cornwall, Elizabeth Harrison, and Ann Whitehead. Special issue, *IDS Bulletin* 35(4), October.

Beneria, Lourdes. 1991. Structural adjustment, the labour market and the household: The case of Mexico. In *Towards social adjustment, labour market issues in structural adjustment*, eds. G. Standing and V. Tokman, 1–30. Geneva: International Labour Organization.

Boserup, Ester. 1970. *Woman's role in economic development*. London: Allen & Unwin.

Chant, Sylvia. 1991. *Women and survival in Mexican cities: Perspectives on gender, labour and low income households*. Manchester: Manchester University Press.

Chant, Sylvia. 1997. *Women-headed households, diversity and dynamics in the developing world*. Basingstoke: Macmillan Press.

Comisión Nacional de la Mujer (CONMUJER) [National Commission for Women]. 2000. *Programa nacional de la mujer, alianza para la igualdad 1995–2000: Realizaciones y retos.* Policy Report. Secretaría de Gobernación, México.

Cos-Montiel, Francisco. 2001. The effects of globalisation on child farm workers in Mexico. In *Children in a globalising world*, ed. N. del Río, 15–38. Mexico: UNICEF-UAM.

Cos-Montiel, Francisco. 2003. The empress' new clothes: Lessons from gender mainstreaming in México. México: *Debate Feminista* 14:211–260, October 28, 2003. Mexico City: Debate Feminista.

Cos-Montiel, Francisco, and J. Rosado. 2002. *Efectos de la liberación comercial sobre las actividades económicas de hombres y mujeres en México [The effects of trade liberation on men and women's economic activities].* Red de Género y Comercio, Capítulo Latinoamericano. Montevideo, Uruguay: Latin American Chapter of the International Trade and Gender Network.

Cunningham, Wendy, and Francisco Cos-Montiel. 2002. Crossroads of gender and culture: Impediments to economic development in Oaxaca, Chiapas, and Guerrero. In *A development agenda for the south of Mexico*, ed. M. Giugale. Washington, DC: World Bank.

Diario Oficial de la Federación [Official Journal of the Federation]. 2001. *Ley que crea al instituto nacional de las mujeres.* México: Secretaría de Gobernación.

DiMaggio, Paul, and Walter Powell. 1991. *The new institutionalism in organization analysis.* Chicago: University of Chicago Press.

Escudero, Alejandro. 2004. *Apre(h)ender género: Modelo de especialización del sector público [Learning gender: A model for the public sector]*, México: Instituto de la Mujer Oaxaqueña.

Goetz, Anne Marie. 1992. Gender and administration. *IDS Bulletin* 23(4): 6–17.

Goetz, Anne Marie. 1997. *Getting institutions right for women.* London: Zed Books.

Goetz, Anne Marie. 2004. Reinvigorating autonomous feminist spaces. In *Repositioning feminisms in development*, eds. Andrea Cornwall, Elizabeth Harrison, and Ann Whitehead. Special issue, *IDS Bulletin* 35(4), October.

González, Román. 2003. *Improvisación y cuatismo en el inmujeres [INMUJERES: Improvising with the "buddies"].* México: Proceso.

Government of Sweden. 2005. *Moving ahead: The organization of gender equality work in Sweden.* Stockholm: Swedish Government Offices.

Gutmann, Matthew. 1996 *The meanings of macho: Being a man in Mexico City.* Berkeley: University of California Press.

Gutmann, Matthew. 1997. *The ethnographic (g)ambit: Women and the negotiation of masculinity in Mexico City.* Berkeley: University of California Press.

Hall, Peter, and Rosemary Taylor. 1996. Political science and the three new institutionalisms. Paper presented at the MPIFG Scientific Advisory Board's meeting, May 9, Harvard University, Cambridge, US.

Hassim, Shireen. 2000. *Engendering the political agenda: The role of the state, women's organization and the international community.* Dominican Republic: INSTRAW.

Hofbauer, Helena. 2002. The Mexican gender budget initiative: Diverse levels of collaboration. In *Gender budgets make more cents: Country studies and good practice*, eds. D. Budlender and G. Hewitt. London: Commonwealth Secretariat.

Instituto Nacional de las Mujeres (INMUJERES). 2001. *Programa nacional para la igualdad de oportunidades y no discriminación contra las mujeres [National program for equal opportunity and to avoid discrimination against women].* Policy Report. México: INMUJERES.

Instituto Nacional de las Mujeres (INMUJERES). 2002. *Género y equidad* [Gender and equality], México: INMUJERES.

Jackson, Cecile, and Ruth Pearson. 1998. *Feminist visions of development: Gender analysis and policy.* London: Routledge.

Jahan, Rounaq. 1995. *The elusive agenda: Mainstreaming women in development.* London: University Press and Zed Books.

Kabeer, Naila. 1994. *Reversed realities, gender hierarchies in development thought.* London: Verso.

Kabeer, Naila. 2004. Globalization, labour standards and women's rights: Dilemmas of collective (in)action in an inderdependent world. *Feminist Economic* 10(1):3–6.

Kanji, Nazneen. 2003. *Mind the gap: Mainstreaming gender and participation in development.* London: International Institute for Environment and Development (IIED).

Lamas, Marta. 1997. The Mexican feminist movement and public policymaking. In *Women's movements and public policy in Europe, Latin America, and the Caribbean: The triangle for empowerment,* eds. G. Lycklamma à Nijeholt and S. Nieringa, 113–126. New York: Garland.

Lamas, Marta. 2005. *Personal communication.* May 12, 2004.

Levy, Caren. 1992. Gender and environment: The challenge of cross-cutting issues in development policy and practice. *Environment and Urbanization.* 4(1):134–49.

Levy, Caren. 1996. The process of institutionalising gender in policy and planning: The web of institutionalisation. Working Paper 74, Development Planning Unit,, UCL, London.

Lewis, Jane, and Gertrud Åström. 1992. Equality, difference and state welfare: Labour market and family policies in Sweden. *Feminist Studies* 18(1), Spring.

Meyer, John, and Brian Rowan. 1977. Institutionalized organizations: Formal structure as myth and ceremony. *American Journal of Sociology 83*:340–63.

Meyer, John, and Richard W. Scott. 1983. *Organizational environments: Ritual and rationality.* Beverly Hills, CA: Sage.

Mikkelsen, Britha, Ted Freeman, and Bonnie Keller. 2002. *Mainstreaming gender equality: Sida's support for the promotion of gender equality in partner countries.* Stockholm: Sida.

Ministry for Industry, Employment and Communications (MIEC). 1999. *Gender mainstreaming in Sweden.* Stockholm: MIEC.

Ministry for Industry, Employment and Communications (MIEC). 2001a. *Swedish government policy on gender equality: Into the 21st century.* Stockholm: MIEC.

Ministry for Industry, Employment and Communications (MIEC). 2001b. *Just progress! Applying gender mainstreaming in Sweden.* Stockholm: MIEC.

Molina, Natacha. 1997. Women's struggle for equality and citizenship in Chile. In *Women's movements and public policy in Europe, Latin America, and the Caribbean: The triangle for empowerment,* eds. G. Lycklama à Nijeholt et al, 127–140. New York: Garland.

Molyneux, Maxine. 2004. The chimera of success. *IDS Bulletin* 35(4):1–140.

Monsiváis, Carlos. 1997. *Mexican postcards.* New York: Verso.

Moser, Caroline. 1989. The impact of structural adjustment at the micro-level: Low-income women and their households in Guayaquil, Ecuador. In *Invisible adjustment* (Vol. 2), eds. UNICEF. New York: UNICEF, Americas and Caribbean Regional Office.

Mukhopadhyay, Maitryee. 2004. Mainstreaming gender or "streaming" gender away: Feminsts marooned in the development business. *IDS Bulletin* 35(4):95–103.

Murison, Sarah. 2001. Issues in gender mainstreaming. Paper presented at the International Brainstorming Workshop on Gender Mainstreaming and Equal Opportunity Policies, National Institute for Women, México.

Paz, Octavio. 1954. *El laberinto de la Soledad.* México: Fondo de Cultura Económica.

Poniatowska, Elena. 2004. El escándalo del INMUJERES: Burla a los ciudadanos [The INMUJERES scandal: Deceiving the citizens]. *La Jornada*, 1 de febrero, 2–7. México.

Rabo, Annika. 1997. Gender equality policy in post-welfare Sweden. In *Anthropology of policy: Critical perspectives in governance and power*, eds. C. Shore and and S. Wright, 97–143. London: Routledge.

Razavi, Shahra, and Carol Miller. 1995. From WID to GAD: Conceptual shifts in the women and development discourse. UNRISD Occasional Paper No. 1 for Fourth World Conference on Women, Beijing. Geneva: UNRISD.

Reyes, Norma. 2004. *Tres años de políticas públicas sensibles al género* [*The years of gender sensitive policy*]. Informe Institucional. Oaxaca: Instituto de la Mujer Oaxaqueña.

Rothstein, Bo. 1990. Marxism, institutional analysis and working-class power: The Swedish case. *Politics and Society* 18:317–45.

Rothstein, Bo. 1991. State structure and variations in corporatism: The Swedish case. *Scandinavian Political Studies* 14(2).

Secretaría de Gobernación [Secretariat of the Interior]. 1996. *Programa Nacional de la Mujer 1995–2000*. México: Alianza para la Igualdad.

SIDA (Swedish Internation Development Cooperation Agency). 1996. *Mainstreaming: Concept, Strategies and Methodologies—A Think Piece*. Stockholm: SIDA.

Sistema Nacional de Información Municipal [National System for Municipal Information]. 2003. Policy Report. Secretaría de Gobernación [Secretariat of the Interior], México.

Standing, Hilary. 2004 Gender, myth and fable: The perils of mainstreaming in sector bureaucracies. *IDS Bulletin* 35(4):82–88.

Stark, Agneta. 2005. *Personal communication*.

Statistics Sweden. 2002. *Women and Sweden, facts and figures*. Stockhlom: Statistics Sweden.

Statistics Sweden 2004. *Women and Sweden, facts and figures*. Stockhlom: Statistics Sweden.

Subrahmanian, Ramya. 2004. Making sense of gender on shifting institutional contexts: some reflections on gender mainstreaming. In *Repositioning feminisms in development*, eds. Andrea Cornwall, Elizabeth Harrison, and Ann Whitehead. Special issue, *IDS Bulletin* 35(4), October.

United Nations. 1995. *Beijing declaration and platform of action of the Fourth International Conference on Women 1995*. http://www.un.org/womenwatch/daw/beijing/platform/ (accessed February 17, 2004).

United Nations Development Programme. 2004. *Human development report 2004*. New York: Oxford University Press.

Waylen, Georgina. 1997. Gender, feminism and the state: An overview. In *Gender, politics and the state*, eds. Vicky Randall and Georgina Waylen. London: Routledge.

Woodford-Berger, Prudence. 2004. Gender mainstreaming: What is it (about) and should we continue doing it? In *Repositioning feminisms in development*, eds. Andrea Cornwall, Elizabeth Harrison, and Ann Whitehead. Special issue, *IDS Bulletin* 35(4), October.

World Bank. 2001. *Engendering development: Through gender equality in rights, resources, and voice*. Policy research report. Washington, DC: World Bank.

11 Don't Disturb the Men
A Viable Gender-Equality Strategy?

Agneta Stark

INTRODUCTION

Is there anything in particular that Swedish and Norwegian readers may learn from *Reversing the Gaze*, the project presented in this book, and if so, what? The question may seem rather peculiar, coming so late in the book. Naturally, Nordic decision makers, policy makers, researchers, and interested persons can learn a great deal from the rich and comprehensive studies presented here. I now intend to address some issues relating to content, but above all issues relating to starting points and working methods, as well as the experiences and conclusions that can be drawn primarily by readers from the Nordic countries.

Swedish gender equality policy is a controversial issue in Sweden, which at times surprises foreign observers. However, the contested area is defined differently than in other European countries with a similar level of economic development. For example, few Swedish politicians would question paid parental leave[1] in itself, which is long by international standards. The controversial element is whether additional days should be reserved for one of the parents or whether parental leave should constitute an individual work-related right, much like the right to paid holidays, and be divided equally between parents without allowing them the possibility to transfer days between themselves.

This discussion may seem strange to European readers in countries where parental leave is considered a women's issue and where, in comparison with Sweden, leave is short, or long but unpaid. For authors from countries where paid work only provides a negligible degree of social security and the social insurance systems are extremely limited, the issue may hardly be visible. The Swedish gender-equality debate is rightly based on national conditions, as is the case in other countries. To an external observer, the debate may seem to concentrate on rather fine nuances within what in international terms is a high degree of national consensus.

GENDER ISSUES UNDER DEBATE

Some issues relevant to gender have been at the centre of the Swedish debate during the period in which *Reversing the Gaze* has been written. The selection of themes is my own, and is by necessity influenced by my own gender research about paid and unpaid work in international comparison. For Nordic readers, the themes may serve as a reminder; for other readers, they may provide a flavour of a sometimes intensive public discussion influencing policy makers. In Sweden, as in other countries, important policy changes, which influence women and men differently—often to the disadvantage of women—are not analysed for their gender effects. Indeed, often changes are motivated by reasons not connected to gender at all, and negative effects for women come as a by-product. Mainstreaming gender is meant to help policy makers notice such possible effects, but may still be overlooked.

The welfare system and its components are much criticised in the Nordic countries, as in most other European countries. One set of reasons is connected to the European Union. Residing in Sweden used to be the basis for individual entitlements to social benefits such as child allowance, basic pension, and so on. After Sweden joined the European Union in 1995, minimum qualification periods of residence were introduced, replacing the straightforward citizenship/residence rule; full minimum pension now requires a qualification period of 40 years of residence in Sweden after the age of 25. With shorter qualification periods, the benefits are reduced proportionally. The rationale behind this rule is that a migrant brings her right to pension to Sweden from her earlier country of residence, and that benefits will be combined. However, as most countries do not have basic pension rights on individual bases for all residents, this rationale is illusionary for many migrants, especially for migrant women.[2]

Financial concerns have been taken as departure points for domestic debates on welfare systems in both Norway and Sweden. A few themes are: ageing populations, low birth rates, possible immediate use of funds from oil production or saving them for later (Norway), long-term sustainability of both welfare systems and high tax regimes in a globalised economy, as well as a political debate about economic efficiency, incentives for economic growth, and incentives for increasing labour market participation.

The picture is, however, diverse. Some parts of welfare systems in Sweden are strengthened while others are cut back simultaneously. Popular support for many parts of these systems, and widespread protests against cutbacks, have in Sweden been regarded by conservative or neo-liberal opinion makers as indicators of "welfare clientelism," of unhealthy dependence on too-generous services, and of the adverse long-term effects on people of too much security.[3] At the same time, politician—regardless of party affiliation—have found it difficult to ration access to public health care or to close hospitals or schools, due to strong views of the electorate that welfare systems are of highest priority.

GENDER, WOMEN, AND MEN

Gender research, relevant for discussions of gender equality has, for very good reasons, to a great extent targeted women—for instance, women's work—and highlighted neglected aspects of it, such as household work and unpaid work, and it has also discussed women's problems in labour markets. The contribution of Nagy in this book is part of this research tradition and illustrates its relevance. There is also quite a large body of non-gender research where the reasons why women take up paid work at all are studied, especially the reasons for married women to engage in paid work.[4] The question why unmarried and married men participate in the labour market at all, and why their work shows a comparatively standardised pattern[5] irrespective of age, class, race, economic position, and so forth, has been addressed very briefly or not at all. An important aspect of gender equality related to different types of work thus appears under-researched. The phenomenon of male behaviour as a "human norm" from which women are regarded as deviating, fits results of gender research in many social sciences, indicating, illustrating, analysing, and conceptualising women's subordination in many areas.

Most research on gender and equality in the Nordic countries is concentrated on the situation for women or the effects for women. This is also true for gender analyses of family roles, bargaining and power within families, relations to children, care for family members, and others. However, a comparatively new and growing body of research in Norway and Sweden focuses on men, masculinity, and male roles. Parts, but certainly not all, of this research are classified by its authors as feminist, while the relationship between it and feminism remains a contested issue. It is, however, clear that it has grown out of feminist gender researchers' work.

At a political level, some hotly debated topics during the project period in Sweden have concerned men and masculinity. Fatherhood and men's parental leave, including men's suitability as carers for young babies and men's violence against women, have been starting points for strongly contested statements about the roles of women and men in modern Sweden. The availability of gendered statistics and their quite effective dissemination in Sweden has influenced these debates, and has not been questioned. Instead, the statistics have been regarded as a common factual base, and the debaters have argued for different interpretations of it. An example is the fact that Swedish women use over 80 percent of the total parental leave days. Is this a gender-equality issue so that fathers should be encouraged to use more, as claimed by some, or does it prove that gender roles are natural and that women and men are, for good reasons, resisting change on the basis of gender difference? This example serves to illustrate the close and ongoing interaction in Sweden between policy and gender statistics discussed by Akanji. It also supports the argument by Cos-Montiel that gender mainstreaming fits well in some Swedish areas of policy, where there is common agreement to see it as a public good. Parental leave is not questioned, nor is the relevance of gender to the debate about its construction and outcomes. But this example may also fit into the context of consensus highlighted by several of the researchers in the project.

SWEDEN AND NORWAY—SOME CHARACTERISTICS

Differences between Norway and Sweden have at times been discussed among the researchers participating in *Reversing the Gaze*. Are they not too small to be relevant to the project? Are the similarities not overwhelming? The comparison between Iran and Norway made by Razavi in her discussion about maternalism will cast new light on Nordic assumptions about Nordic countries. But it is my experience that many people interested in gender in Sweden know comparatively little about differences between Norway and Sweden. The basic assumption seems to be that the other Nordic countries, as well as many other Western countries, "are very much like Sweden—or perhaps Sweden is a little ahead." Sometimes this view is accompanied by a contrasting one: "Sweden is perhaps ahead but also sadly lagging behind other countries—we have in fact not come very far."

A characteristic of Nordic welfare systems and societal organization is that such entitlements are basically individual, rather than marriage- or family-based. Diane Sainsbury (1996) explores the history of the Swedish welfare systems' bases of entitlement, comparing the Netherlands, Sweden, the United Kingdom, and the United States. She also compares welfare retrenchment during the final decade of the twentieth century in these countries.

In a study of the Nordic countries Sainsbury (1999) asks, "Do variations outweigh commonalities, undermining the clustering of the countries into a single welfare state regime?" , 76). She then constructs and applies the concept of a "gender policy regime" and attributes a number of characteristics to three types of regimes: male breadwinner, separate gender roles, and individual earner-carer. Four underlying dimensions are identified:

- whether rights are individualised or familialised;
- the degree to which a gendered differentiation in entitlement based on the traditional division of labour between men and women exists;
- the scope of state responsibility of caring tasks;
- women's and men's equal access to paid work.

Sainsbury characterises Norway under the heading "privileging men as providers and women as caregivers," stressing that the principle of care has exerted a stronger influence on Norwegian policy than on the other Nordic countries. Universal child allowances, maternity grants, and tax relief for working mothers are strong instruments, while publicly organized childcare and expansion of parental leave had lagged behind. Norway stands out in the Nordic context by not encouraging mothers to become workers.

Sweden, under "transforming gender differentiation in social rights," is characterised by labour market policy, parental insurance, and increased public responsibility for childcare. Sweden comes closer to the individual earner-carer regime.

It is well known that in the Nordic countries, high proportions of women and men participate in the labour market, the distribution of income is comparatively equal, and the levels of poverty are relatively low. The fact that the Nordic labour markets are gender-organized does not in itself distinguish them from markets in other industrialised countries. But the high degree of occupational segregation based on gender in the Nordic labour markets may be regarded as a paradox, especially as the gender-related pay gap in these countries is comparatively small.

Richard Anker (1998) connects theories of sex segregation of labour markets with detailed time-series census and labour force survey data from 41 countries and areas around the world. Some of his main conclusions are: occupational segregation by sex is very extensive in every country; male-dominated occupations are much more common than female-dominated occupations; "female" occupations tend to be less valued, receiving lower pay; levels of segregation by sex differ greatly across regions, with the Asia/Pacific region having the lowest average and Middle East/North Africa the highest; within the OECD, North America has the lowest average level of sex segregation and the Scandinavian countries the highest one; and occupational segregation by sex is not related to socioeconomic development.

Melkas and Anker (1998) explore the Nordic labour market sex-segregation paradox, using detailed census data available in Finland, Norway, and Sweden for a large number of occupations, and using occupation classifications that allow comparisons. The three countries have both high proportions of women and men in the labour market and well-developed welfare state structures. In all of them, the welfare state and service sectors now provide very substantial labour markets for women. But the countries also differ. In Finland, women already participated in the labour market to a large extent before the development of the welfare state. In Sweden, which has the most developed welfare state, the increase in women's paid work coincided with the welfare state development, and in Norway it occurred after important welfare state development had taken place.

Nordic countries are typical of the Organisation for Economic Co-operation and Development (OECD) countries in that men generally work in male-dominated occupations, rather than in gender-mixed occupations. What is unique to the Nordic countries is the extent to which both women and men work in gender-dominated occupations, a characteristic that does not apply to women in OECD countries in general. Thus, the relatively high amount of occupational segregation by sex in the Nordic countries stems mainly from the large size of the female-dominated occupation groups.

However, the number of male-dominated occupations decreased sharply in the 1970s and 1980s, as did the percentage of men working in such occupations. "Men are clearly moving in the direction of losing their privileged position of having so many exclusively 'male' occupations, but there is still a long way to go" (Melkas and Anker 1998, 53).

Not all factors relevant to analysis of occupational segregation by sex are to be found inside or close to the labour market. Since pay differentials in Nordic countries are lower than in many other parts of the world, the price paid by Nordic women for the segregation is lower than it could be in labour markets with higher pay differentials. The Nordic welfare states' provision of services may also be wider and more accessible to women and men at all income levels. Thus, income levels have less influence on standards of living than they would have were such services market-based and paid at full cost or market price by the user. One example is access to high-quality childcare at low cost to parents. Another is publicly organized home help for the elderly, available to and used by old women and men of all income levels.

Scholars often ask how strongly occupational segregation in the Nordic countries is connected to monetisation of what has historically been regarded as typical household work—childcare, care of frail elderly or handicapped persons, and so on. In these countries, a proportion of such work has developed into paid, often professional work. Melkas and Anker conclude that this monetisation is important but does not alone account for the Nordic countries' higher segregation by sex. They also point out that segregation has fallen faster during the last two decades in the Nordic countries than in almost all other industrialised countries. To some extent, they support the view that women have had to transition gradually into paid work. When women entered female-dominated occupations as a first step, this entry may have been more acceptable to society as a whole (meaning mainly to men). But they see the present segregation by sex as an unacceptable state and conclude: "In the Nordic countries, it is time to strive vigorously for ways to achieve the next step on the road to equal opportunities, by having much greater integration of men and women across occupations" (1998, 99).

Such integration cannot be accomplished by women changing labour market behaviour alone, but would also demand considerable change in such behaviour from men.

SOME COMMENTS ON THE PROCESS AND RESULTS OF *REVERSING THE GAZE*

Researchers in this book call attention to and are surprised by the fact that policies adopted in the area of gender equality are actually implemented in Sweden, and that the expectation that they be implemented is so widespread.

They point out that in Sweden, it is considered natural that once a decision on a gender equality policy is taken, it will also be implemented at all levels, and there is a mechanism to ensure that this happens. If the decision is not implemented, it arouses attention and results in criticism in the media and elsewhere. Contrary to a perception common in the Nordic countries, many southern countries do have policies that are both well conceived and wisely constructed. But they are not always implemented, or else implementation is only partial or very slow. For those who find this difficult to understand, it should be enough in the Swedish context to refer to the problems of wage discrimination and sexual violence against women. Everyone agrees with the principle that women and men should receive equal pay for work of equal value, and that violence against women is a major social problem. But there is still a long way to go from that point to reaching agreement on actions that actually deal with the problem. And there have been few tangible changes during recent decades.

But in spite of everything, adopted policies are generally implemented. Why? What has caused this to become the natural chain of events? This is one of the questions that I, as a researcher and gender-equality activist, take with me from the project *Reversing the Gaze*—and also the expectation that further reflection on this theme might lead to greater understanding of Swedish shortcomings concerning violence and equal wages.

Reversing the gaze means that researchers, with starting points and experiences from various disciplines and countries, pose questions about Sweden and, to a certain extent, Norway. It is not an unusual situation; many conferences and seminars are held where invited researchers from different countries comment on Scandinavian reports on social phenomena. What is unusual about the project is that so many researchers from southern countries have themselves chosen their approaches and theoretical frameworks, and that the starting point is not Scandinavian presentations of problems or areas at issue, but rather the researchers' own. As we have not had resources to translate much material within the project, the researchers' had to restrict themselves almost exclusively to material published in English. In the process of searching for relevant material, it became clear that much Nordic research and important parts of debates among Nordic researchers are not available in English and thus seem targeted mainly at a Nordic audience. At the same time, references to research from outside the Nordic countries, with a heavy bias toward research published in English, are common in Nordic researchers' work. This asymmetry could be interpreted as an indication that Nordic gender research tends to choose themes from and for a Nordic research agenda rather than from research topics and angles of interest to researchers from other parts of the world. A certain level of introversion could perhaps be traced in disseminating strategies in parts of Nordic gender research.

During the project, *Reversing the Gaze* has attracted an extraordinary amount of interest compared to the numerous other research projects in which I have participated. Researchers, officials responsible for gender equality, journalists, and actors in the women's movement have all posed questions and expressed interest in learning more. I have taken part in or listened to many discussions dealing with what the project could produce and what results could be hoped for.

Some of the issues and starting points that the participants in reference groups and discussion forums wished the authors to address were clear. Here are a few examples, selected from various phases of the project.

Sweden is not as well developed when it comes to gender equality as is often said to be the case—the project needs to be given a Southern perspective that points out shortcomings in Sweden. In particular, focus should be given to weaknesses in Nordic gender-equality efforts.

Disparities among the Nordic countries are important—the countries are different. Therefore, more Nordic countries, particularly Finland, should be included.

- Regional disparities within the Nordic countries are of importance.
- The study should be based on economics.
- Ethnicity should be taken into consideration.
- Masculinity and the role of men in gender equality efforts are significant.

On a number of occasions during the course of the project, people who heard of it have expressed concern that the foreign researchers would not choose the "right problems" or perceive "real difficulties." In my capacity as a Swedish participant in *Reversing the Gaze*, they felt that I should guide the foreign researchers. By the "right problems" they often meant problems that have been focused on in Sweden or in the European Union. In addition, there have been what are often vaguely expressed wishes that the foreign researchers would express a certain type of criticism toward Swedish gender-equality efforts and its results, or lack of them.

I do not interpret this as a lack of confidence in the foreign researchers and their ability, but rather as a legitimate expectation that contributions provided by the project may be used to support or oppose suggestions that are put forward in the Swedish and Nordic debates. But it also reflects a sense of real confidence in the perception that the "right problems" are those that generally have already been identified in Sweden: in this country we know where the problems lie and what needs to be solved. It is not uncommon that the desire for a certain amount of "Sweden-bashing" is expressed—finally, the truth about shortcomings in Swedish gender equality will be presented in an exhaustive and well-substantiated format! In this case, the results obtained by the foreign researchers have mainly been viewed in a national context.

In addition, there is another aspect that may be worth considering. Representing an activity—to any degree—which is subject to external examination is no simple matter. Swedish participants and others interested in the project *Reversing the Gaze* have, for the most part, not been responsible for the Swedish gender-equality policy and its implementation, but they are involved and knowledgeable in the area. They have devoted a part of their professional lives to it. They want the project to lead to progress and to be useful. They want to avoid what they view as dead ends or wrong turns. This situation can be compared with the one that arises when aid agencies in Sweden or other countries analyse the situation in a country where aid projects focusing on gender equality are being considered. An external consultant comes and describes, analyses, and provides advice. A power relationship develops, which in the case of "gender equality in Sweden" is fairly unusual: it is more common that Swedish actors give advice to actors from other countries than the other way around. External advice and viewpoints are desired, but it has to be the "right advice" and "relevant viewpoints."

A similar feeling that analyses and advice presented by foreign experts are irrelevant in a national context has almost certainly arisen among actors in countries receiving development assistance on many occasions. "What it feels like to be commented upon" could be one important lesson to be drawn from this exercise. Another is the reaction "but this is much more complex—the author has oversimplified and also misunderstood some crucial aspects." I believe that readers associated with Swedish aid could make some interesting observations of their own reactions to the contributions to *Reversing the Gaze*.

Religion is discussed in several of the contributions to this book. It is an area conspicuously absent in present Swedish gender-policy debate—a fact that has come up in some project discussions. This requires a more elaborate comment: religion related to gender is certainly debated but almost exclusively as an issue related to new Swedes and immigration. For instance, it has been claimed that immigrants' religious beliefs prevent them from sharing the Swedish views on gender equality, especially concerning violence, and in the media representatives of immigrant groups are often requested to react against it. Swedish-born men's violence against or aggressive control of women close to them is very rarely connected in the same way to any religious belief, nor are representatives expected to explain or act.

The impact of the Swedish Protestant Church, until recently the state church and still today the religion to which the Swedish ruling King or Queen must belong, is in Sweden mainly seen as history and perhaps as a part of a broad cultural context. It is true that Sweden is considered to be a secularised society, with few people regularly attending church service, and most only attending ceremonies like funerals or weddings.[6] However, there are good reasons to examine the important assumptions, highlighted by several researchers in this project, about sameness, consensus, and homogeneity related to the historic and present role of religion in Swedish society.

POWER ISSUES—A SWEDISH DILEMMA?

From a Swedish perspective, the most controversial contribution to the book is undoubtedly Subrahmanian's chapter dealing with Sweden's policy on prostitution. Her premise is based on the view that prostitution exists and will continue to exist, and that the interests of prostitutes to practice their profession under relatively secure forms constitute an important gender issue. In this she questions the basis for the Swedish ban on purchasing sexual services. But Subrahmanian's chapter also contains what to me is an important lesson not directly concerned with the view of prostitution, something I hope the author's message—which a Swedish public will perceive as provocative—does not hide from readers. She maintains that in Sweden, explicit focus was given to issues on the gender equality agenda concerning the two important areas of violence and power at a relatively late date. In countries that have experienced a struggle for independence, issues of this kind have instead tended to initiate the discussion of gender equality. During a struggle for freedom, human rights issues have been driven by both women and men, and in the independent states gender equality has come to be expressed as civil and political rights, focusing on power issues.

The pragmatic attitude that has characterised the Swedish gender-equality discussion has instead focused on such issues as the labour market, where women have been needed in the labour force. However, power issues connected to the labour market—equal wages is a clear example—have been difficult to deal with, and the debate on suitable working methods to solve them is taking place with widely different starting points. Sexual violence against women is an even clearer example of an unsolved power issue—its scope is debated, court decisions against perpetrators are contested, and proposals for action plans often remain on paper. There is a heated debate in Sweden between those who feel that men as a group have a responsibility to take action against this kind of violence and those who support the view that normal men have nothing to do with deviant behaviour such as physical abuse. In Sweden, issues of violence and power have long been in the periphery. While this may have allowed progress in other areas which appeared less controversial or where conflicts between women as a group and men as a group have not been emphasised, it has also come at a price. Issues that specifically deal with power remain unsolved and have come to be regarded as notoriously difficult.

PART-TIME WORK—A STRATEGIC ISSUE FOR
SOLVING OR AVOIDING GENDER CONFLICTS?

To illustrate this point, let us consider part-time work. The issue of women's' part-time work has been debated extensively during the time in which *this book* has been written. Do women work too much part-time, how can women be encouraged to increase their weekly work-hours and why is it that female-dominated occupations are more often organized as part-time work? Sales assistants' work hours in large shopping centres are illustrative: the women selling textiles work part-time, while the men selling electronics in the same shopping centre with standardised opening hours work full-time. The logical question "why do men work full-time?" is extremely rare. Instead, women's behaviour is problematised, and an array of prescriptions for changing women is presented.

It is well known that concepts such as "full-time" and "part-time" have been defined differently in different countries, or even in different sectors in the same country. For a long time, in some sectors in most countries, work that is considered particularly trying has had a shorter full-time norm than the prevalent one in that sector and country, and this has not changed the definition of full-time work. Examples of this phenomenon are underground mining, work that involves exposure to radiation, heat or cold, etc. Part-time work differs greatly in length. Differences have led to the use of two concepts, "short part-time" and "long part-time," in international comparisons. Short part-time work means 1–19 hours per week. Long part-time work means working hours from 20 up to the lower limit of full-time work.

In Sweden, part-time work is nationally defined as 1–34 working hours per week, and full-time as 35 hours or more. Sweden is generally viewed as having a large proportion of part-time work, especially among women. An internationally large percentage of these part-time women workers work from 30 to 34 hours. Compared to the total number of women employees, the proportion of those who work between 30 and 34 hours is larger in Sweden than in the OECD countries that were part of a special study (van Bastelaer et al. 1997). In other countries, shorter part-time hours were much more common, and consequently Swedish part-time women workers work long hours when seen in an international perspective.

In 1999, the OECD used the suggested 30-hour limit for the first time, in the publication *Employment Outlook* (1999). The change had been implemented by the OECD on the basis of the report described above. Using these redefined data, Norway in 1998 had 36 percent women in part-time work, Sweden had 22 percent, and Finland had 13, ranking them, respectively, as numbers 8, 19, and 26 out of 29 OECD countries. The OECD average was 26 percent. (Stark and Regnér 2002, 35–40). In an international perspective, then, Swedish women's work hours do not seem to be deviating from the gendered norms in other industrialised countries.

Why then all the discussion? What is the problem? In my own view, the lack of sufficient labour market income for many women is one real problem. This need not necessarily be the result of fewer working hours—there are many highly paid jobs which even for long part-time work would provide a reasonable standard of living. But Swedish part-timers work in jobs with low pay, even for full-time work. The other problem is, as I see it, a reluctance to face important power issues.

There is some consensus among gender researchers that the entry of women on the formal labour market has occurred without much adaptation of male work patterns, formally or informally. Fathers of young children do participate considerably more in unpaid childcare and in daily activities like shopping for food. But most men still perform much less household work than women, even when both a woman and a man in the same household are in full-time paid work. It might be said that women have been allowed to take up paid work on the condition that men's traditional life patterns are not affected too much. In this light, part-time work is a solution that allows women labour market participation without creating too much need for change.

This again can be seen as addressing—or not addressing—one gender power issue related to the labour market but also to the structure of family life and to unpaid care issues. The strategy, for it is a strategy, may with at least some truth be labelled: "Do not disturb the men."

The Swedish attempts to have both women and men, parents or not, participate in the labour market has resulted in time structuring their daily lives in new ways. Lack of time, stress, and fatigue is over and over again reported, especially among parents of young children. Allowances for care for sick children (with no maximum number of days), parental leave for mothers and fathers, and the right to part-time work until the youngest child is eight years old doe not alleviate the daily struggle for time for working parents. The hardest hit are solo mothers with young children. High absenteeism—with sick pay—for women, for mothers of young children but also for women over 55 years, has attracted much public attention. Partly this is a consequence of high labour force participation rates for women and men 55–64 years old, in an international comparison. Higher demands on the labour market play a role. But the basic reasons are still much debated, as are possible remedies. Again, discussing possible power issues could provide new views in a Swedish perspective.

Attention has been called to some unsolved power issues in the Swedish Inquiry on Gender Equality Policy (Swedish Government Official Reports 2005, 66). The inquiry proposes a new overall objective for Swedish gender equality policy: "Women and men are to have the same power to shape society and their own lives." In addition, four new targets are proposed:

- active citizenship;
- paid jobs that provide lifelong economic independence;
- care without subordination ; unpaid care is to be shared equally;
- physical integrity: men's violence against women must stop.

The problems are clearly analysed, and some remedies are proposed. However, the study's reception seems to indicate that policy makers are not prepared to initiate a thorough debate on gender and power. Instead, details are used to highlight remedies seen as unrealistic or too radical and problems that may or may not really exist. It appears that Sweden may suffer from a systematic difficulty with seeing and addressing gendered power.

FINAL COMMENTS

Women in Sweden and Norway changed their life-patterns in many ways during the last half of the twentieth century. Swedish and Norwegian men can be said to share the burden or opportunity of bread winning more equally with women than in many other countries. To some extent, men also participate in unpaid care work for young children. However, they have adapted their working lives to the new situation much less than have women. Women combine paid and unpaid work, as do women in large parts of the world, but they have a larger share of labour market income than in many other countries. They are better represented in political life, but not in high decision-making positions in private enterprise. At the same time, absenteeism from work among women is at a record level. Time is regarded as a severe constraint, and stress levels are high. Childcare is not generally seen as a difficult problem, while conditions for those who care—unpaid or paid ——for the frail elderly are regarded as increasingly problematic. Some elderly experience lack of care, loneliness, and depression, while others express deep satisfaction with their care and their lives. In a Nordic perspective, these are some of the main issues on the gender agenda. But this is not the agenda outlined by the authors of this book.

Participating in *Reversing the Gaze* has provided me with ample and at times exhausting opportunities to learn more about gender policy and gender research in many countries, not least my own. Translating and explaining Nordic and Swedish customs, characteristics and peculiarities, statistics, theories, and organizations in such a way as to provide context but not conclusion has been very difficult, but also a rich learning experience.

In discussions about it the project, Nordic gender researchers, policy makers, and activists have reflected on Nordic gender equality in a broader context, and also in a personal context. I have listened to intense discussions about what problems they thought the project should address and how they wanted it to progress. This does not occur in most research projects— in my experience, results attract interest once a project is well on its way or nearly finished, and advice from nonparticipants outside of seminars on how to define problems or perspectives are not common. After careful reflection, I have come to think that *Reversing the Gaze* has offered a projection screen onto which committed and active Nordic people have projected their own visions and dreams for a gender equal or feminist society. What progress has been made, and what are their frustrations? When the gaze was reversed, they may have hoped that their views of advancements and especially of disappointments would come into focus, but more clearly and sharply than before.

Another personal reflection that I bring out of this project concerns the long Nordic history of pragmatism that the researchers in this book have highlighted. Progress by slow and pragmatic negotiations has been an important strategy within Nordic gender policy and practice, with obvious advantages and good results. It could now be time to learn from people in other parts of the world for which conflict in gender issues has been a main strategy—not necessarily the strategy of their choice, but chosen because conflict has been a crucial part of their struggle for independence and self-determination and has been a strategy open to them. Their experience in handling, using, and also in dissolving conflict could now help Nordic feminists and gender-policy makers to rethink strategies in their search for ways forward.

The analyses and arguments presented by authors in *Reversing the Gaze* offer the opportunity to understand some of the reasons why certain gender equality problems in Sweden and the Nordic countries have been easier or less controversial to deal with, while others have been labelled as complicated or politically difficult to manage. The hopes for concrete policy advice to Swedish or Nordic decision makers may not be fulfilled. The question "what did we do wrong?" is generally not answered. The researchers in this volume are not normative in any simple sense. Instead, they give some answers to the more complex question "what did we do, and what did we not do?" They do provide the reader with ample material for reflection over shortcomings and progress, differences and similarities. They invite the reader to active reading and most importantly to active conclusions.

NOTES

1. Parental leave in Sweden 2005 consists of 13 months with 90 percent of the wage up to an upper limit: two months reserved for the mother, two for the father, and nine that the parents can divide between themselves as they wish. Ten extra days for the father are granted after the child's birth. In addition, there are three months with fixed, low pay. The system is tax-financed. Of all users of parental insurance in 2003, 57 percent were mothers and 43 percent were fathers. Mothers used 83 percent of the number of days, and fathers 17 percent (not including the 10 days for the father after the child's birth).
2. There are rules for refugees, formally classified as such by the United Nations, that will provide better pensions. But these form a tiny proportion of all immigrants, the majority of whom will receive extremely low pensions and will be depending on strictly means-tested social assistance.
3. This could be compared to discussions in the United Kingdom about the "nanny state."
4. It is relevant to point out here that there is an even larger body of research that—without explicitly restricting itself to male work—treats male work only, and draws conclusions on "work" and "people" rather than to "men," thus overgeneralising. A random example of how men are treated as an implicit norm in work research is provided in the book *The Concept of Work. Ancient, Medieval and Modern* by Herbert Applebaum (1992) who, in his introduction, 21 chapters, and summary—in total 590 pages, treats only men and men's

work, with one exception: a 20-page chapter "Women and Work in the Medieval Ages." In the index, the words "women" and "female" are listed, while "men" or "male" are not, except in one entry: "male and female work, medieval villages."

5. Men all over the world show less variation in paid work hours than do women, and men with different economical and social backgrounds seem to have remarkably similar patterns of paid work over their life spans, while women as a group vary and adapt their paid work hours to different circumstances. For an overview, see, for instance, UNDP (1995).

6. Perhaps significantly, statistics over religious activities are difficult to find and appear incomplete.

REFERENCES

Anker, Richard. 1998. *Gender and jobs: Sex segregation of occupations in the world.* Geneva: International Labour Office.

Applebaum, Herbert. 1992. *The concept of work: Ancient, medieval and modern.* Albany: State University of New York Press.

Melkas, Helinä, and Richard Anker. 1998. *Gender equality and occupational segregation in Nordic labour markets.* Geneva: International Labour Office.

Organisation for Economic Co-operation and Development (OECD). 1999. *Employment outlook.* Paris: OECD.

Sainsbury, Diane. 1996. *Gender, equality and welfare states.* Cambridge: Cambridge University Press.

Sainsbury, Diane (ed.). 1999. *Gender and welfare state regimes.* Oxford: Oxford University Press.

Stark, Agneta, and Åsa Regnér. 2002. *In whose hands? Work, gender, ageing and care in three EU-countries.* Linkoping: Department of Gender Studies, Linkoping University.

Swedish Government Official Reports. 2005. *The power to shape society and one's own life—New targets for gender equality policy.* Stockholm: Swedish Government Printing Office.

United Nations Development Programme (UNDP). 1995. *Human development report 1995.* New York: Oxford University Press.

van Bastelaer, Alain, Georges Lemaître, and Pascel Marianna. 1997. *The definitions of part-time work for the purpose of international comparisons.* Paris: Organisation for Economic Co-operation and Development (OECD).

12 Passion, Pragmatism, and the Politics of Advocacy

The Nordic Experience Through a "Gender and Development" Lens

Naila Kabeer

INTRODUCTION

The idea of comparing Nordic and developing country approaches to gender equality appeared initially to be an unlikely task. Most of the countries represented in this volume have very little in common with the Nordic countries or indeed with each other. Nevertheless, the contributions to this volume suggest that there *are* lessons to be drawn. Broadly, these discussions suggest that the lessons relate not so much to the precise policies and instruments put to work in Norway and Sweden, but to the processes that led to the adoption of these policies and instruments, the tactics and strategies that were used to drive these processes, together with a better understanding of the enabling conditions that allowed them to bear fruit. And it is the early history of these processes, their inception at a time when Nordic countries were still poor and underdeveloped, that is of particular interest to today's developing countries.

The literature suggests that Norway and Sweden represent somewhat differing pathways to similar gender equality outcomes. In particular, it suggests that feminist struggles in Norway were driven by a discourse of "difference" that demanded attention to the specific qualities and contributions of women, while those in Sweden revolved around a discourse of "equality" that stressed women's capacity to make as valuable a contribution to the public good as men. However, regardless of these differences in approach, the very concrete achievements on gender equality reported in both countries stand in marked contrast to the experiences of many developing countries, which are often characterised by a phenomenon that can be described as one of the hardy perennials in the field of gender and development: the gap between what policy makers *say* and what they *do* or, to use Longwe's colourful metaphor, "the evaporation of gender policy in the patriarchal cooking pot" (Longwe 1997).

Political leaders in the South routinely sign on to various international conventions and declarations in support of gender equality, intersperse their speeches with references to their commitment to women's advancement, pass laws aimed at overturning long-standing forms of discrimination, and formulate policies with the apparent goal of acting on these intentions. However, they also routinely fail to follow through. The experience of the "gender mainstreaming" agenda, which sought to strengthen the mechanisms through which gender equality goals were pursued within national and international policymaking structures, has, according to current evaluations, revealed the persistence of structural problems, which give rise to a depressing picture of unstable histories and uneven performances.

The Nordic experience of pursuing gender-equality goals, in contrast, suggests a track record of commitments to gender equality both made *and* honoured. Although Norway and Sweden officially adopted a "gender mainstreaming" approach in the 1990s as a means of systematising their efforts in this field, their actual achievements predate this development by several decades. This suggests that the explanation for Nordic achievements must be sought in the realm of the wider political culture as well as in the actual policies and instruments that gave rise to these outcomes.

At the same time, a close reading of the literature also reveals some limitations to the Nordic achievements. Once we shift our gaze to what has failed to change—or changed very slowly—it becomes possible to discern certain commonalities in the underlying structures of gender inequality in Nordic and developing countries. These give rise to similarities in the dilemmas and debates that characterise the quest for gender justice in different parts of the world: how to reconcile recognition of gender difference with claims for gender equality; whether to work within mainstream institutions and risk co-optation or to remain outside and risk marginalisation; and how to promote gender equality in a context of diversity.

This chapter attempts to carry out an analysis of both of these sets of circumstances. It builds on the insights provided by the various contributions to this book, exploring some of the factors that help to explain the remarkable progress on gender equality reported in Norway and Sweden and what it tells us about what can be achieved by the collective efforts of women as a socially subordinate group in society.[1] It uses this analysis to reflect on some of the debates and dilemmas that are current in the gender-and-development field. The chapter ends by touching on persisting—and emerging—forms of gender discrimination in the Nordic context and what they tell us about the limitations of Nordic approaches.

NORDIC APPROACHES TO GENDER EQUALITY

Enabling Conditions in Comparative Perspective

Certain distinctive features of Swedish and Norwegian cultural and political life appear to have set the stage for Nordic approaches to gender equality, creating "enabling conditions" for the achievement of concrete goals. One is the foundational status given to the value of equality within Nordic culture. Graubard (1986) talks about the "passion for equality" in the Nordic context, while Eduards suggests that "Equity and equality are probably the most basic values in Swedish—and Nordic—political culture" (1991, 169). The premium placed on equality reflects the historical evolution of the social structures of the Nordic countries as well as the political balance of power that characterised them for much of the twentieth century.

According to Kuhnle and Hort (2003), the Nordic countries were generally characterised by "relatively egalitarian pre-industrial social structures,", populations that were small and culturally homogenous and class differences that were modest in relation to other countries in Europe. In both countries, the efforts of the labour movement and popular organizations, supported by benevolent and philanthropic associations, shaped social provisioning and ensured early commitment to egalitarian policies anchored in principles of universalism and social solidarity. And in both countries, social democratic parties of the working class achieved ascendancy in the 1930s and held power, off and on, for much of the rest of the century.

There is widespread agreement that the spirit of egalitarianism that infused the construction of a universalist welfare state in the two countries reflected the hegemony of social democratic values. The Scandinavian metaphor for the welfare state as the "people's home," explicitly introduced into political discourse by Per Albin Hansson in 1928, spells out the social democratic vision of society:

> The home's foundation is community and concern. The good home does not know privilege or the feeling of being slighted. . . . In the good home, equality, considerateness, co-operation and helpfulness hold sway. Applied to the great people's and citizens' home this should mean the demolition of all social and economic ranks which now divide citizens into privileged and slighted, into rich and poor, propertied and impoverished, exploiters and exploited (cited in Gould 2001, 22).

The value given to equality within Nordic culture does not have an equivalent in most other OECD countries.[2] It is even less in evidence in many of the countries represented in this volume. Only Hungary came close in its socialist period. South Africa, Argentina, and Mexico continue to have some of the most unequal distributions of income in the world. The Indian caste system was founded on the principle of inequality, as was the apartheid system in South Africa. Pakistan is divided by strong ethno-linguistic differences and religious sectarianism. Ethnic differences have led to civil war in Nigeria and continue to fragment the experience of rights and citizenship. In Mexico, the long oppression of indigenous groups has led to their armed struggle against a mestizo-dominated state in pursuit of rights and recognition, while in Argentina, the indigenous population was all but wiped out by European immigrants. Building a sense of citizenship and solidarity on these fractured and divided polities remains a central challenge in the project of nation-building in these countries.

A second enabling feature of the Nordic context —and one which contrasts strongly with the contemporary experience of developing countries— lies in the conditions under which the foundations of the welfare state were established. Much of the work involved in constructing the "women-friendly" welfare states in the two countries was undertaken in the so-called "golden age" of post-war industrial growth in much of Europe—a period when nation-states had the capacity to undertake Keynesian-style demand management of their economies, entailing high levels of public intervention and expenditure, in order to maintain full employment.

In contrast, many developing countries were just beginning to emerge from an extended history of colonialism during the post-war period, with highly centralised states evolved to defend colonial rule. Many have been ruled by military dictatorships and other forms of autocratic government over much of the past half century, and many relied heavily on foreign aid and remain highly aid-dependent today. All of them, as a result of indebtedness to the IMF/World Bank, have had to adopt neo-liberal policy conditionalities that require them to observe fiscal discipline, deregulate their markets, and open up their economies to global competition. They are thus attempting to combine social and economic development in an era when globalisation places severe limits on the options available to nation-states.

A third striking aspect of the political culture in Norway and Sweden is its pragmatism, and the value given to consensus and cooperation in the policy process. Pragmatism refers here to a political culture of decisionmaking that values "co-operation and broad-based political solutions rather than confrontation" (Eduards 1991,169). The adoption of a system of proportional representation from the very outset of democratic elections in these countries may have contributed to this culture, since it generally rules out governments based on absolute majorities and requires dominant parties to build coalitions in order to rule (Gould 2001). However, we must also factor in the rationalist planning tradition that has evolved in these countries and that sets them apart from other countries with a PR system. Sweden's approach to rational planning, in particular, is regarded as exceptional, going further than others in the region in its desire and ability to impose "a social construction of reality" (Bradley 1996, 34). From the earliest years of its ascendancy, the Social Democratic party adopted an approach to planning that sought to combine scientific analysis and democratic process in its efforts to bring about social change.

Contemporary accounts of policymaking in Sweden and Norway confirm the strength of the legacy of consensus and compromise embodied in their corporate approach to policymaking. Halsaa (1998) observes that Norway's "corporate system of extensive negotiations and co-operation between labour, capital and the state" (p. 168) has contributed to a responsible opposition, enabling minority governments in Norway to survive for relatively long periods of time. In Sweden, the consensual approach is operationalised through procedures including independent investigation commissions, widespread consultation, and a considerable emphasis on empirical research (Gould 2001; Gillberg 2000). Commissions are expected to carry out their own investigations or make use of existing studies. Governments continue to finance independent social research in universities and other research organizations often critical of central and local government policies, enabling policy makers as well as the public at large to engage in informed debates (Gould, 2005).

Neutralising Difference: Policy-Driven Approaches to Gender Equality in Sweden

Pragmatism and the search for consensus in the wider policy environment also influenced the trajectory of gender equality advocacy in the Nordic countries, but most notably in Sweden. Sainsbury (1999) observes that women's involvement in the making of the welfare state in Sweden relied on cooperation across class and gender lines, enabled by women working within the party political structures at key moments of Sweden's history who were able to connect a gender-equality agenda with the wider political agenda. In the 1930s, for example—a period of declining fertility rates and high unemployment—these concerns were dealt with in much of Europe through restrictions on family planning methods and on women's right to employment. While demands for similar measures were made in Sweden, it emerged by the end of the 1930s with an anti-discrimination legislation that not only did *not* restrict women's right to work, but also prohibited the firing of women on marital or reproductive grounds.

This remarkable outcome reflected strategic interventions by leading feminists of that period and their allies within the Social Democratic Party. The majority of Social Democratic women in the 1930s recognized that many women had to work for economic survival and, moreover, "viewed work as a basic citizenship right in a political configuration where citizen and worker were bound together" (Hobson and Lindholm, 1997, 488). The ommission set up to look into the issue was deeply influenced by its Subcommittee on Women's Employment, which had leading feminists Alva Myrdal and Kersten Hesselgren among its members. It was also influenced by the arguments made in a book published by Alva and Gunnar Myrdal in 1934 on the population question. They warned that Sweden would become a country of old people if it failed to increase its birth rates, but proposed to address the problem through welfare provisions to persuade couples to have children, endorsing health care provision for mothers and babies, state-funded childcare, and free school lunches. Women's organizations reinforced this message, arguing that if society provoked a conflict between work and marriage, fertility rates would suffer.

Gender advocates of the time thus succeeded in using the "window of opportunity."opened up by population concerns to re-frame them in ways which promoted the rights of mothers (Hobson and Lindholm 1997; Florin and Nilsson 1999). As Alva Myrdal later wrote: "The remarkable thing is that in this crucial moment the population argument was wrenched out of the hands of the anti-feminists and instead used as a new formidable weapon for emancipation ideals. The old debate on married women's right to work was turned into a fight for the working woman's right to marry and have children" (1968, 403).

However, the more radical aspects of the Myrdals' vision of gender equality did not find their way into the policy agenda until another "policy window of opportunity" opened up decades later, in the 1960s. The opportunity this time lay in the emergence of labour shortages, which resulted from the combination of fertility decline and rapid economic growth that characterized post-war Sweden. The choice was between encouraging immigration or persuading women to increase their labour force participation. The strategy of gender advocates was to argue for the latter, a position that won favour with the unions (Jensen and Mahon 1993).

Women, including married women, had already begun entering the labour market in unprecedented numbers by the late 1950s, and the public sector—in the process of expanding the welfare state—was a significant employer. Many women were strategically located within the party and the bureaucracy and in a position to link their arguments for gender equality with the wider policy debates, using a linguistic strategy in which certain prestige words recurred frequently: ". . . long-term commissions and industrial growth, the labour market, gender roles, equality, development, gender equality, welfare and the good of the child. Much was said about children (Florin and Nilsson, 1999, 30). In 1975 alone, there were fifteen investigations by government with "children" in the title. At a time where ties between women and family were loosening, the focus was on the welfare of children.

But it was, in particular, the resonance of their vision with the everyday lives of women that explained their effectiveness. Various studies had highlighted the importance of paid work to women as a continuous thread in Swedish social life. A survey conducted by the Housewives' Association in 1937 had shown that most housewives who had worked before marriage wished to maintain contact with working life for the express purpose of being able to return to it when the children had grown up (Florin and Nilsson 1999, 33). In 1953, a Gallup Poll carried out on behalf of the Social Democratic Association found that 61 percent of women working at home were not happy with one or several jobs they carried out within the household, while 63 percent of those in gainful employment reported they were happy with their work (Jensen and Mahon 1993).

A vision of equality between the sexes that focused on work thus appeared to speak to the interests of much of the female population in Sweden, but particularly to working class women. It thus served to mobilise support across a wide range of constituencies. Women cooperated with women across party lines, and they also cooperated with men who were considered vital allies if women were to make progress from an "inferior position" (Florin and Nilsson, 1999, 32). This required tactical compromises: "many unholy alliances were formed between groups with equality ideologies and the employers' need of a labour force" (Florin and Nilsson, 1999,68). Feminists opted for a "gender-neutral" language that avoided attention to "difference" and argued instead for equality of access to paid work for both men and women premised on a more equal gender division of unpaid domestic labour. As one of the protagonists of this period explained: "We avoided feminist concepts, we didn't want to get caught in that trap . . . it wasn't a question of the struggle for women's rights in the ordinary sense but of a struggle for jobs that needed to be done and that women wanted" (Florin and Nilsson, 1999, 32).

Sexual politics was also underplayed in this search for broad-based support: "Few women or women's organizations took up the issue of sexual emancipation in the sixties. For those involved in the gender debate, it seems to have been an important strategic choice. The debate on equality and sexuality were clearly to be kept apart, otherwise older people in the parties and organizations would be alienated" (Florin and Nilsson, 1999, 42). Instead, advocates focused their demands on the extension of childcare, vocational training for women, upgrading of work traditionally done by women, and individual taxation.

This pragmatic stance won widespread support, including support from the National Board of Labour, from the trade unions, and from representatives in industry and commerce. It also succeeded in gaining major benefits. By the late seventies, the rapid expansion in public day-care places meant these had overtaken child allowances as the most important element of public expenditure. Separate taxation was introduced in 1971, making it more favourable for women to work than for her partner to earn additional income. In 1974, a new scheme of parental insurance offered women compensation for loss of market earnings rather than flat-rate maternity benefits. Men were also offered the same 90 percent replacement of earnings if they chose to care for children. Parents were entitled to leave of six months to be taken before the child reached age four, together with a ten-days-per-year child sick leave entitlement available until the child reached age ten. This has increased over time.

Celebrating Difference: Movement-Led Approaches to Gender Equality in Norway

The early history of Norway, including the history of its feminist struggles, provides a number of contrasts to Sweden and some paradoxes. Norway experienced a slower transition from agrarian to industrial society, a later demographic transition, a greater persistence of religious values, and the later incorporation of women into the labour market. Women were less well integrated into the unions and the political parties and more likely to organize in single-sex associations (Hagemann 2002). Much feminist activity took place outside political parties and established networks. Despite this, Norwegian women gained many of their rights earlier than the rest of Scandinavia, including Sweden. The high levels of political mobilisation by women's organizations in the struggles for national independence from Sweden was an important factor in this (Hagemann 2002).

Another contrast with Sweden was that the struggle for women's rights in Norway was characterised by clashes between women of socialist and non-socialist persuasions over the meaning and justification for gender equality and women's rights, reproducing within the women's movement the more polarised class-based politics of the country (Sainsbury 1999). The influence of traditional values meant that a striking feature of many of these early women's organisations was the politics of "equal worth": recognition of gender differences in roles and the need to give equal value to women's unpaid domestic labour (Sainsbury 1999). "Equal rights" women's organizations also existed, but they were weakened by divisions between mainly socialist women, who tended to prioritise the class struggle, and liberal middle-class women's organisations, who emphasised their special grievances as women, but often failed to acknowledge the relevance of class (Halsaa, 1998).

Equal rights feminism also had little resonance with the main party of the working class. The Labour Party was, and remained until the 1960s, firmly entrenched in a maternalist politics of women's place. In the late 1920s, it passed legislation to curtail employment opportunities for married women. In 1953 it presented an ambitious programme for housewives, including holiday relief, rationalisation of housework, and stand-ins in case of illness. Unpaid housework was given an economic status, and housewives were named as "workers." The 1960s saw a further resurgence of feminist activism around a revitalised "politics of difference," with both traditional women's organisations and women from the far left fighting for recognition of the unpaid work of housewives and mothers in tax and social security systems. However, they remained divided on support for childcare and on whether day care should be interpreted as relief for home-based mothers or as a service for employed ones (Leira 1992, 131).

Where the "politics of difference" did unify feminists was in the demand for political representation (Skjeie, 1991). Women within and outside political parties came together at the end of the 1960s, arguing that men could not represent women's interests and values. Quotas were used as a positive discrimination measure far more widely in Norway than in Sweden: in politics, education, and the labour market. Quotas were also introduced into the corporate structures of government, its public committees, boards, and councils, but here, implementation was discretionary, providing, as Halsaa puts it, an example of how "potentially effective measures end up being largely symbolic" (1998, 177).

Convergence in the Nordic Context

Norwegian feminists thus started out with a politics of difference to argue for equal rewards for paid and unpaid work, while Swedish feminists organized around a politics of equality that sought to equalise the gender division of labour at work and in the home. However, differences in approaches have become less significant over time, partly reflecting efforts at harmonisation by the Nordic Council of Ministers. In addition, while women entered the labour market in large numbers later in Norway than in Sweden, in both countries an "interactive process of increases in women's employment and improvements in parental leave legislation and childcare services" has led to considerable convergence in supports to working mothers (Sörensen and Bergqvist 2002).

Feminists in the two countries have moved over time toward "gender-recognition" strategies, which tried to address the particular obstacles that women encountered in achieving public equality: greater scope for positive discrimination, gender equality training programmes, public child and elderly care to ease women's burden in the household. There is now increasing attention to what Kjeldstad (2001) calls "the gender reconstruction approach," which views active policies to change the male role, with particular attention to fatherhood, as a precondition of substantive equality. The Nordic Council of Ministers in 1995 agreed that "the distribution of the work load between women and men in the family and society must be changed" (cited in Kjeldstad: p. 77). Norway was among the first to act, debating the role of fathers not only their duties but also their rights to be with, and care for, their children. The father's quota was introduced in 1993 in Norway and 1995 in Sweden. In contrast to former regulations, where parental leave was partly reserved for mothers and the rest split between parents on a voluntary basis, the father' quota is "fatherhood by gentle force." If the father does not take it, it is forfeited.

These efforts are having a gradual pay-off. At the level of attitudes, surveys show that Swedish men have become more open over time to the idea that they should participate in unpaid work, while both mothers and fathers in Norway are far more likely to subscribe to the idea that both women and men should contribute equally to the household than social norms suggest (Ellingsæter, 1998). More practically, Norwegian and Swedish fathers of the 1990s spent more time with their children than those of the 1970s. They were more likely to use their quota of parental leave, and many reported strengthened relationships with children and more equal share of housework and childcare.

DISCURSIVE STRATEGIES AND THE POLITICS OF LOCATION: COMPARATIVE PERSPECTIVES

The Politics of Location in the Nordic Context

An important lesson that feminists in different parts of the world can draw from each other's experiences relates to the resources and strategies that women as a subordinate group within a society can bring to bear in pressing their claims for rights and recognition. Analysis of the Nordic experience offers lessons from a context in which these efforts have been relatively successful. It highlights, in particular, the significance of the discursive strategies that feminists in these countries deployed in order to articulate their claims. It also points to the politics of location: how feminists position themselves, or are positioned, in relation to structures of power influences the kind of discourses that they utilize to articulate their demands.

The discourses through which women pressed their claims clearly differed between Norway and Sweden. It is also evident that difference partly reflected the positioning of those making the demands in relation to the state and other mainstream institutions. In Sweden, feminist discourses sought to link claims for gender equality to national concerns with economic growth and labour shortage. The choice of this discursive strategy, including the compromises and silences it entailed, reflected the fact that many of the influential gender advocates making them were located within the structures of the state and mainstream political parties and had a particular understanding of what was likely to advance gender equality within these structures. Their privileged position within the system schooled them in the kind of language that would help to connect their demands to the larger political agenda and hence mobilise support beyond their immediate constituency.

The pragmatism that marked the Swedish approach to gender equality, and the absence of the anger and passion that has characterised feminist movements in many other parts of the world, has led some authors to refer to the Swedish experience as a "conservative" (Lindholm 1991) or a "bloodless revolution" (Florin and Nilsson 1999), a "feminism without feminists" (Gelb 1989). The women's movement in Norway, on the other hand, has been described as "a great deal more angry and confrontational" than the Swedish (Bradley 1996). According to Halsaa (1998):

> The women's movement in the 1970s was radical, proud and provocative. Feminists refused to be conceived of as second-rate, sexual objects. The most dedicated challenged journalists, refused to be examined by male doctors, sabotaged beauty contests and burned their bras. In place of living up to male standards, they called for positive re-evaluations of so-called 'female values'. (p. 171).

The longer period of exclusion from state structures and party leadership of Norwegian feminists and their greater reliance on autonomous women's organizations is likely to explain this difference. At the same time, the difference should not be overstated. Though positioned outside the state to a greater extent than feminist actors in Sweden, feminist groups in Norway worked closely with the state. It was the close relationship between feminist mobilisation and state responsiveness in the Norwegian context that led Hernes (1987) to coin the phrase "state feminism." And we see evidence of Norwegian feminist pragmatism in the strategies used to appeal for cross-party support for the claim that women were in the best position to represent women's common concerns. Arguments were framed in terms of the "conflicting interests of women and men" to appeal to the left parties and in terms of the "complementarity of the resources" that women and men brought to politics, in order to appeal to conservatives (Skjeie, 1991).

Swedish and Norwegian women's movements thus each made efforts to find strategies that would win them allies beyond their immediate ranks, from women from other political parties and walks of life but also, very importantly, from men. They were also willing to engage with the state, from within as well as from the outside. This willingness appeared to reflect the high levels of trust in the state that appears to be a long-established tenet of political culture in these countries (Eduards, 1991; Gould, 2005).

Gender, Development, and the Politics of Location

This level of trust is missing from most of the developing country contexts discussed in this volume. Many were, and some continue to be, ruled by repressive political regimes, and democracy still has very shallow roots. In any case, the distance between state and citizen is being overshadowed by the gradual relocation of major aspects of policy decisionmaking from the state to global financial institutions, expanding the terrain of feminist struggle.

What are the arguments for a pragmatic engagement with national and international agencies in this different set of circumstances? As Molyneux (2004) points out, many feminists from these countries maintain an arms-length, and often oppositional, distance from the state and international agencies, fearing any form of engagement as *in itself* an abandonment of feminist struggle. She notes that the introduction to a recent collection of articles expresses the concern that efforts at gender mainstreaming are "an expression of women's integration into hegemonic patriarchal institutions where they are reduced to a lobbying group, an appendix without influence" (Braig and Wolte 2002, 6).

For others, however, an important reason to engage with mainstream national and international agencies is that they command critical resources and make decisions that have a direct impact on women's lives in terms of health, reproduction, education, and work. The early critiques of mainstream concepts and practices from a feminist perspective helped to leverage open important spaces within these agencies within which feminist advocacy could have, and has had, considerable influence.

At the same time, increasing engagement with the state and other official agencies of development has given rise to debates about the *terms* of engagement. The stance taken by gender advocates within mainstream development institutions has, perhaps necessarily, been the most pragmatic. Their challenge has been to find ways of presenting arguments in favour of gender equality that are likely to win sufficient support from their generally more powerful colleagues to leverage resources that can help to advance women's rights and well-being. Many seek to do so by basing their advocacy efforts on "win–win" scenarios that cast the relationship between mainstream development goals and the goal of gender equality in terms of positive synergies rather than negative trade-offs.

These instrumentalist arguments, in which gender equality is presented as a means to other ends, has drawn criticism from other feminists, generally working on the "outside," who believe that gender equality should be argued for on intrinsic grounds, as an end in its own right. Their arguments are summed up in Razavi: "Entering the mainstream entails making alliances and compromises, and modifying agenda and language. . . . Some feminists have argued that the "game is not worth the candle"; in other words, what is lost in the process of assimilation has been so central to the feminist agenda that there seems to be little reason to pursue the same strategies any further (Razavi 1997, 1112).

Critics of instrumentalism argue for an "intrinsic" approach to gender advocacy, in which gender equality is constituted as an end in itself. As Taylor puts it, "For feminists and those who advocate gender justice women should not be seen as instruments of development, but as people who have the right to secure their own development. . . . women's development is important because they are citizens in their own right . . . who require resources and opportunities to fulfil their human potential" (2004, 27). According to Jackson, attempts to "mainstream" gender have led to the de-politicisation of gender advocacy and the reduction of women to the status of a resource to meet other development goals, "a position that is not always consistent with gender interests" (1996, 501).

Such forms of advocacy, which stress gender justice as a basis for holding policymakers to account for their actions, provide an important counter to narrow instrumentalism, reminding policy makers that gender inequalities are a matter of social injustice and a violation of human rights, regardless of how they relate to mainstream concerns about poverty reduction or economic growth. However, a blanket dismissal of the strategic potential of instrumentalism fails to understand how discursive politics play out in bureaucratic structures where feminists must compete with other interest groups pressing their own claims. It also fails to understand the limits to what can be achieved through bureaucracies. Feminists who engage with the structures of policymaking have to deal with the "rules of the game" within different institutions, the mandates these define, and the cultures they generate in terms of language, procedures, and behaviour (Kardam 1993). These contexts shape which issues are likely to be heard, which are transformed into policy and which are subsequently acted on.

A major problem with certain kinds of feminist discourses within the international development context has been what Standing (2004) describes as a tendency to construct binary oppositions and to attach moral hierarchies to them. This gives rise to a discursive absolutism which ranks certain discourses as "right" and others as "wrong": equity is posed in opposition to growth; intrinsic arguments in opposition to instrumental; and strategic gender interests in opposition to women's practical needs. These dichotomies, however, are rarely based on evidence as to which set of discourses have been more effective in advancing women claims and translating them into concrete measures. Nor is it evident that they have to stand in opposition to each other. Policy support for women's paid and unpaid work can be argued for on the grounds of economic growth, and certainly on the grounds of a more equitable growth path, just as the neglect of women's needs can be argued against in terms of the knock-on effects on family and the wider community as well as women themselves (Boserup 1970; Palmer 1991; Elson 1998a, 1998b). Nor does the relationship between practical needs and strategic interests need to be cast as a static dichotomy: addressing strategic gender interests can pave the way for greater responsiveness to women's practical needs, just as women's practical needs can be met in ways that open up the possibility of tacking their strategic interests (Kabeer 1994, 2005).

Reflections on the past thirty years of the difficulties faced by gender-and-development advocates in getting their message heard suggest the need to locate advocacy efforts within a better empirical understanding of the relationship between growth, equity, and gender justice in different empirical contexts. They also suggest that a *strategic* pragmatism, combining a vision of gender justice with critical assessment of what gains can be won and at what costs given institutional constraints, may be a more effective strategy for gender advocates who engage with policy makers than the pursuit of intrinsic arguments, regardless of who is listening.

In addition, however, feminists seeking to push for gender equality through bureaucratic means may need to be more modest in their expectations of what they can hope to gain in the short term (Subrahmanian 2004). The possibility for the grassroots mobilisation that provided crucial political support to the endeavours of Nordic femocrats and their allies may not exist, or may exist very unevenly, in many developing countries. In their absence, bureaucrats within mainstream agencies, whether national or international, are unlikely to act in ways that will bring about the social transformations that feminist activists would like to see. But given their critical role in the practical interpretation of policies, bureaucrats can be motivated to act in ways that make a concrete difference to the lives and well-being of women on the ground (Standing 2004). They may even be motivated to take actions that have the effect, intended or otherwise, of creating conditions that enable women to mobilise in the future.[3] The relationship between women's collective action and the policy process does not have to be a one-way street.

THE DISCURSIVE "POSITIONING" OF WOMEN: DOMESTIC VERSUS EMPLOYED MOTHERS

A second set of questions raised by our comparison of Norwegian and Swedish discursive strategies concerns the practical possibilities that these engendered, the concrete difference it made to women's lives. For Nordic feminists, a key concept driving their claims-making efforts was that of "women's autonomy," women's ability to maintain themselves and their children with some degree of economic independence from men through paid work or public support. Some, like Hobson, argued that entry into the labour market lessened economic dependence on husbands for many women and strengthened their bargaining power within the family. It allowed others to exercise the basic civil right of leaving an oppressive relationship, "literally to vote with their feet" (Hobson, 1990). Others, like Lewis (1997), are more cautious about the emancipatory potential of paid work. Along with women's right to do paid work and, by extension, their right not to engage in unpaid work, they argue for their right *not* to engage in paid work and, by extension, their right to do unpaid work (see also Land and Rose, 1985).

These differences in political position play out in the different demands made by Swedish and Norwegian feminists, with the former seeking greater equality in the gender division of labour at work and at home while the latter sought to valorise difference through the social recognition and remuneration of women's unpaid domestic work. While each on its own appears to ignore the other dimension of women's life experiences, in reality, women's organizations and advocates in each context made imaginative use of the discursive resources available to them to expand the received boundaries of the concept of "motherhood," in one case, and the identity of the "worker" in the other. In each case, they were able to renegotiate the meanings of these concepts and to lay claim to new rights and resources for women as a result.

Nevertheless, discourses have material effects, effects which can be traced in the evidence of "path dependence" which marks the historical trajectories of the welfare state in the two countries. Along with the later onset of urbanisation, industrialisation, and fertility decline in Norway, the strength of the values of domestic motherhood explains why Norwegian women entered the labour market much later than women in Sweden. It also explains the subsequent absence of any attempt by the state to pioneer new models of motherhood to address the incompatibility between women's paid and unpaid work, leaving them to rely to a far greater extent on privatised and informal child-care arrangements (Leira, 1993). It was not until the mid-1980s that their demands as workers began to be taken up in the form of improvements in parental leave and child-care provision. Moreover, despite considerable convergence between Norway and Sweden in recent years in terms of female labour force participation, fertility rates, child-care provision, paternity leave, and political representation, Norwegian social policies continue to display a greater differentiation of gender roles compared to the dual earner-carer model promoted in Sweden. If, as a number of authors have argued, we take the economic status of solo mothers as a measure of the extent to which the search for economic autonomy to which feminists in both countries aspired, the greater poverty of these households in Norway relative to Sweden (Sainsbury, 1999; Kilkey and Bradshaw, 1999) suggests that the citizen-worker model, combining individual taxation, childcare provision and parental leave may offer women a better exit option from unhappy marriages or relationships than the citizen-mother model.

Stepping back from these accounts, it is important to point out that the different advocacy discourses that were used to such powerful effect in the two countries were not plucked out of thin air: they reflected significant aspects of social reality in the two contexts and hence resonated with their wider constituencies. At the same time, they sought to reconstruct this social reality in ways that promoted the interests of their constituencies. It is also significant that in both contexts, women's entry into the workforce preceded the provision of social measures in support of working women (Leira, 2002). The public provision of childcare and other supports to the working mothers appeared to be an effect of women's entry into paid work, generating pressure for public care, rather than the other way around (Sorensen and Bergqvist, 2002).

Motherhood, Paid Work, and Collective Action in Developing Countries

How does this politics of claims-making in the Nordic context resonate with experiences in developing country contexts? Given the deep entrenchment of male breadwinner ideologies in most of the countries we are dealing with, it is not surprising that maternalism has been the more acceptable and more frequently encountered discourse on women's issues, both in the policy-making domain and in wider society. Consequently, the Norwegian experience, with its history of the resourceful re-imagining of the meaning of motherhood, appears to have a more immediate relevance for feminist struggles in these societies. However, there are few examples of the kind of radical maternalism that allowed Norwegian women to move beyond the "given" limits of their domestic roles through, in their case, the demands for a universal state allowance in recognition of their care work.

One example is provided by Razavi's discussion of post-revolutionary Iran (this volume). She notes the instrumentalist use made of Islamic idiom and law by Islamist feminists to promote notions of "republican motherhood" articulated through "a careful balancing of "entitlements" and "duties'" (this volume). This has not only given them a language to speak to those in power but also a language that has "narrative fidelity" (Snow and Benford, 1992) for women from lower income and traditionalist backgrounds in a way that the narratives offered by secular feminists did not. Despite their marginal presence in Parliament, Islamist feminists were successful in reversing the negative stance taken by the Islamic state in relation to child custody and quotas for women in university and in promoting new policies, such as index-linked maintenance payments to wives in the event of divorce.

However, there were limits to what Islamist discourses of motherhood were able to achieve, even within the sphere of the domestic. Women's right to maintenance in the event of divorce as compensation for the housework she performed during marriage was recognized by the state, but its payment was left to the discretion of the husband. Furthermore, the rationale for the payment lay in a particular interpretation of the Islamic legal code, according to which, apart from sexual services, a wife was not obliged to do any form of housework, or even suckle her own babies, within the marital home. Thus, compensation reflected a view of gender roles in which women provide sexual services in return for complete dependence on husbands for all their living requirements (Moghadam, 2006).

Other examples of radicalised maternal politics come from Latin America and are touched on in Jelin's contribution. As she notes, decades of brutal repression in the Latin American region gave rise to maternalist politics as a powerful rallying cry against human rights violations. Conceptions of motherhood and its location in the private domain were dramatically challenged in these mobilisations for human rights by mothers in Chile, Nicaragua, Brazil, and Argentina (Stromquist, 1993). The best known were the Mothers of the Plaza de Mayo in Argentina, who demonstrated for 10 years in central Buenos Aires for information about their "disappeared" children and grandchildren. While it was the fate of their own children that took them into the public domain, they became the symbolic mothers of *all* disappeared children, translating their personal grief into the demands of citizens for justice. For many observers, their acts represented a reconstruction of female citizenship through the redefinition of women's domestic role in public terms.

However, Latin American feminists have also had to struggle with the dangers of "essentialisation" that can come with collective identities based on "natural" or "innate" qualities associated with motherhood. As de Volo (2004) points out, the Mothers of Matagalpa in Nicaragua have seen themselves as more deserving of state support than, for instance, the fathers of the fallen because of their knowledge and experience of giving birth and raising children. Generalised political discourses based on maternal identity also operate to establish hierarchies *between* women: mothers of the fallen who failed to mobilise were portrayed as "uncaring" along with women without children. In addition, Jelin argues that this form of maternalist politics has also been associated with a circumscribed view of political agency. The extension of familial metaphors into the struggle for human rights divides political mobilisation into those who are directly affected by personal and private injustice and those who mobilise without any personal ties and gives familial identities greater legitimacy in the public struggle for rights than citizenship and political concerns.

A less radical, and perhaps more typical, form of maternalist discourse is to be found in the South African context. Hassim (this volume) suggests that the struggles of the established women's organizations for recognition of women as a distinct disadvantaged constituency were largely divorced during the anti-apartheid movement from the redistributive struggles of poorer working women and that this continues today. Not surprisingly, it has been through the default option of a maternalist politics, which interpreted women's rights primarily through their gender-specific roles as mothers and wives, that the most significant gains have been made. However, the narrow definition given to maternalism within mainstream politics has had correspondingly limited implications for women's resource claims: "in South Africa, . . . the emphasis on the *cultural value* of caring in social welfare policy is not accompanied by a recognition of the *work* of caring" (this volume). This is despite the fact that women's caring responsibilities, which have increased in the context of a HIV/AIDS pandemic, curtails their access to the public sphere in terms of both economic as well as political participation.

In general, there are good reasons why many feminists working in development have shied away from a reliance on maternalist arguments. They echo the point made by Ellingsæter in her discussion of the Norwegian context: "The choice between employment and care takes place in a context of cultural values. If a formal right to care is instituted in an environment with a sense of strong cultural duty to care for women, only women will exercise the right to care, locking themselves into a caring role" (1999, 121). The early experiences in the women and development field with welfarist projects that focused primarily on women's caring role and failed to recognize its economic dimensions, have left behind a lingering fear that maternalism may not constitute a strong enough base from which to argue for adequate and independent resources for women.

There are additional concerns in those parts of the world where women's ability to gain employment is subject to powerful cultural restrictions and where a maternalist politics would serve to legitimate these restrictions. As Moghadam points out in the context of the Middle East: "The masculine nature of the labour force and the predominance of the discourse of motherhood is surely why MENA feminists tend not to engage in a maternalist politics or advocate for policies pertaining to women's care work" (2005, 104).

Unlike Europe, where "the highly unequal distribution of unpaid work and especially caring labour underlies much of the inequality found in employment and reproduced in social security" (ILR 2000, 115), she suggests that the main issue in Middle Eastern countries like Iran is the highly unequal distribution of paid work, along with explicitly discriminatory family laws, that underlies the gender inequalities found in the region.

The question, then, is to what extent paid work has offered a more promising route than domestic motherhood for women in developing countries to make their claims as workers, as citizens, *and* as mothers. This question is becoming increasingly prominent in the gender-and-development literature as a result of the recent phase of globalisation and the widespread "feminisation" of the labour force that has accompanied it. Many more women, including many more married women, are now in paid work across the world, but find themselves concentrated in the informal economy with little social or legal protection. Debates about domestic versus working motherhood have become increasingly irrelevant for the vast majority of poorer women, who have no choice but to work for a living.[4] However, views differ as to whether their increasing entry into paid work has been exploitative or empowering.

On one hand, studies have invoked the image of the "global sweatshop" to draw attention to the exploitative conditions under which women workers have been incorporated into paid work under globalisation, as well as to the intensification of women's workloads, with additional responsibilities for earning superimposed on unchanged gendered responsibilities in domestic work (Ross 1997; Elson 1999; Pearson 2004; Greenhalgh 1991). On the other hand, while acknowledging the exploitative nature of a great deal of paid work for women, studies from contexts as varied as Latin America, the Middle East, and Asia have pointed to its positive effects on women's bargaining power within the family, their greater control over their life choices (including the "right to vote with their feet'), and a greater sense of self-confidence and self-worth (Kabeer 2000; Wolf 1992; Chant and McIlwaine 1995; Eraydin and Erendil 1999; Guzman and Todaro 2001; Wilson 1991; Davin 2004).

There is clearly no automatic relationship between women's entry into paid work and their capacity to claim their rights as workers, mothers, or citizens: a democratic space within civil society for such action to occur is an important precondition, along with the willingness on the part of organised groups to work with women workers around their priorities. Nevertheless, the visible growth of a range of different kinds of grassroots collective action on the part of women in various forms of paid work suggests that shared interests associated with economic activity offer a potential for collective action that domestic activities have failed to provide on an equivalent scale.

The Central American Network of Women in Solidarity with Maquila Workers, for example, has taken the current realities of the lives of women workers, and the existing political and economic conditions, as the starting point for a strategy of gradual improvement. Mendez (2002) calls this a strategy of "radical reformism" or "self-contained radicalism": it acknowledges institutional constraints and seeks to work for change within them. Such a negotiating stance clearly has its limitations, but it reflects a perspective that distinguishes between what is desirable and what is possible in situations of extreme poverty.

There has also been increasing attention to the informal economy, where the vast majority of women workers in the developing countries are located. The Self Employed Women's Association in India, which works with both self-employed and wage workers in the informal economy, is perhaps the best known example. It seeks to combine developmental activities with collective bargaining, and has beenadmitted into the International Confederation of Free Trade Unions. It continues to face resistance from national trade unions in its struggles for recognition in national bargaining efforts, but its presence has had the effect of motivating sections of the trade union movement in India to pay greater attention to workers in the informal economy, including the founding of a non-partisan trade union. Similar trends are to be seen as a result of the work of the Independent Garment Workers Union and of Working Women in Bangladesh (Kabeer and Mahmud 2004) and the Self-Employed Women's Union in South Africa (Horn 2002).

There has also been increasing mobilisation among some of the most exploited sections of the informal economy: domestic workers (Selcuk, 2004; 2005). In Brazil, the Union of Women Domestic Employees, which has been organising since the 1960s, was recognized as a trade union in 1989 and as an affiliate of the Central Workers Union in 1992. The support of the latter has allowed it to reach out to many more workers. In Namibia, the National and Domestic Allied Workers' Union was established in 1990 and had unionised a third of the domestic workers in the country within a few years. However, the low earnings of its members means that it continues to face financial difficulties (Selcuk 2005). In Hong Kong, more than 2,500 organizations and associations are working with migrant and domestic workers, although only three are registered as unions.

In India, the Mahila Milan is a federation of another category of women workers who are difficult to organize: those who have migrated from the countryside in search of work and have made their homes on the pavements and in slums. As members of Mahila Milan, women engage in various forms of collective action to improve access to credit and urban infrastructure, particularly housing and sanitation. A critical feature of their approach is a determined nonpartisanship, unusual in a context where most grassroots organizations, including trade unions, are affiliated to political parties and rely on their clout to advance their cause. At the same time, as Mitlin and Patel (2005) point out, poor people in pursuit of improvements in their shelter and livelihoods do not have the choice of disengaging from the state: they have to deal with it continuously in its various guises. Appadurai calls their approach a "politics of patience"; it entails accommodation, negotiation, and long-term pressure on the state rather than critique and confrontation: "this pragmatic style is grounded in a complex political vision about means, ends and styles that is not entirely utilitarian or functional. It is based on a series of ideas about the transformation of the conditions of poverty by the poor in the long run . . . a logic of patience, of cumulative victories and long-term asset building . . . is wired into every aspect of the activities . . ." (Appadurai , 2002, 29).

There are also a number of quantitative findings that support the view that paid work offers the basis for transformative action. Cross-country regression analysis in a study by Cueva (2004, cited in UNRISD, 2005), which took the right to abortion on demand as an indicator of women's reproductive rights, found that women's participation in the economy, along with their participation in politics, was a significant variable in explaining the recognition of this right. Seguino reports that women's greater participation in paid work may result in a greater predisposition on the part of women—and men—to challenge the status quo. She uses a number of rounds of World Values survey data in the 1990s for both developed and developing countries to explore the effects of women's entry into paid work on gender norms and stereotypes. Her findings suggest that increases in the share of women in the labour market led to a decline in the percentage of women—as well as men—who adhered to traditional norms about gender. These results held regardless of the rate of economic growth in a country and regardless of region. She concludes: "Policies that enable women to combine work with care responsibility thus appear to be a fruitful avenue to promoting still greater improvement not only in well-being but in hastening the dismantling of restrictive norms and stereotypes that inhibit women and give men justification for their superior material and social status" (2006, 19).

Finally, Chhibber (2002), who also used the World Values Survey to examine data on women's political activity, found that while political participation rates varied across the world, female employment, along with membership of associations, were among the factors that led to higher levels of political participation, while identification with domestic roles led to lower levels.

BACK TO BASIC VALUES: THE UNFINISHED REVOLUTION IN GENDER EQUALITY

The Limits to the Social Democratic Imagination

The discussion has focused so far on some of the factors that help to explain the considerable progress made on gender equality in the Nordic context. However, while these changes have indeed constituted "something of a bloodless revolution", it is also an unfinished, or rather an "ongoing," revolution. Alongside evidence of progress on some key dimensions of gender equality, the literature also highlights evidence that the pace of change on other dimensions has been far slower, suggesting the persistence of male dominance in some key spheres of Nordic society.

For instance, along with the highest levels of labour force participation among OECD countries, Nordic women also operate within some of its most gender-segregated labour markets (Melkas and Anker, 2001). Women tend to be found primarily in the public sector and in "caring" occupations that extend their domestic roles into the public domain. Markets are also vertically segregated. There are very few women in the upper echelons of public and private bureaucracies, in finance and banking, or in the top levels of trade unions and academic institutions. In Norway, a recent survey of leadership positions in different sectors of society concluded that 85 percent of such positions were held by men, varying from 60to 65 percent in party politics and 98 percent in private business (Skjeie, 2005).

Women are more likely to be found in part-time work than men, and gender wage disparities, while small when the focus is on full-time work, are considerably larger when part-time work is included. Although women and men work roughly the same number of hours a day, more of women's time is unpaid than men's (Gould 2001,114). And while gender disparity between paid and unpaid work appears to have decreased between 1990 and 2000 in Sweden, the costs of attempting to combine work and care hits certain sections hard. Lack of time, stress, and fatigue is over and over again reported, especially among parents of young children. A comparison of statistics from the Little Book in Sweden (discussed in the chapter by Akanji) shows that, from a position of reporting lower levels of long-term, stress-related illness than men in 1975, women reported higher susceptibility to such illness than men in 2002. The stresses for men associated with living up to the traditional male-breadwinner model appears to have been overtaken by the stresses for women of managing the "mother-carer model.".

Some version of these inequalities is, of course, prevalent in most countries of the world. Nevertheless, their persistence in the Nordic context is particularly striking in the light of the determined efforts on the part of the state to bring about a radical change in gender relations and the variety of different strategies pursued by feminists in the two countries. They suggest a certain resilience in the underlying structures of patriarchal constraints that mediate these strategies and help to determine their limits.

For those working in gender and development, a concern with male power brings us into familiar territory. And while patriarchal power may take infinitely variable forms in different cultures and social formations, the privileged status of men and the subordinate status of women remain its defining core. Agneta Stark (this volume) suggests that the "subtext" to Nordic approaches to gender equality can be summarised as "don't disturb the men." Clearly what "disturbs men" is likely to vary across cultures. To understand how male privilege is defined, defended—and disturbed—in the Nordic context, we need to return once again to the wider political struggle for the welfare state that provided the context in which the struggle for gender equality was fought.

The welfare state in the Scandinavian context, as we noted earlier, was a product of the social democratic imagination that both defined the scope and set the parameters within which feminist strategies have been framed. While the language of equality drew on the discourse of social solidarity, it was, first and foremost, a discourse of class solidarity. This provided the cultural medium through which male power had worked in the Nordic context and hence the forms it took.

Social democratic values explain the resolutely gender neutral formulation of policies for equality taken, particularly in the Swedish context. One effect of this was that all gender-specific measures were implicitly characterised as equally suspect and potentially threatening to gender equality (Ruggie 1984, 243). Thus, while the "private" arena of reproduction—the right to abortion, family planning, illegitimate births, and so on—had been the subject of state intervention for much of the twentieth century, given concerns about declining population, other aspects of body politics received less attention. According to Elman (1995), the welfare state promoted women's rights as workers and mothers, but issues that affected women *as women*, regardless of these roles, were largely overlooked. Eduards (1992) identifies the difficulties that feminists faced in getting domestic violence recognized and acted on as an expression of male power.

Skjeie (2006) suggests that an implicit "duty to yield" clause operated in official gender equality rhetoric so that where gender equality appeared to conflict with other values of state policy, equality measures were put on hold. As examples, she cites the limited scope of equal pay regulation in Norway in the face of trade union resistance to any regulation that impeded the right to collective negotiations as well as the failure to afford CEDAW the same legal status as other human rights conventions in Norwegian legislation. Gelb (1989, 175) makes a similar point in relation to the belated recognition of rape and domestic violence in Sweden relative to other European countries: ". . . the special interests of women have been subordinated to the general good . . . qualitative gender issues tend to be ignored in an agenda that defines equality in economic terms."

For feminists in developing countries, therefore, an appreciation of the persistence of gender inequality in the Nordic context, and of the forms that they take, provides a different perspective on what *has* been achieved. It suggests that, in the face of the complex and multidimensional nature of power relations between men and women, there is unlikely to be a single "win–win" strategy: each course of action, whether imposed by circumstances or adopted on strategic grounds, will have trade-offs that cannot always be known in advance. Feminist strategies for making claims have therefore had to evolve on the basis of lessons learned and gains made.

Gender Equality and the Challenge of Diversity

There is one further aspect of contemporary social reality in the Nordic context that contributes to the unfinished nature of the revolution in gender relations. This relates to the challenge of dealing with issues of gender equality in the face of the diversity that is becoming an increasing feature of society in both Norway and Sweden. Scandinavian countries have been characterised for much of their history by a relative cultural homogeneity. Immigrants up until the 1960s came primarily from the Nordic region or from other European countries. This began to change with waves of refugee migration from the 1970s onwards, which brought populations from the Middle East, Africa, and Asia, as well as from Eastern Europe. As the Nordic countries have become increasingly diverse, inequalities are opening up between these more "culturally distant" migrants and the rest of the population (de los Reyes, 2000). The picture emerging is one of high unemployment, low incomes, marked segregation in housing patterns, and a widespread view associating criminality with immigrants. As Knocke notes (1991), women from migrant groups are more likely to be marginalised from the labour market or confined to the lower levels of the work hierarchy than the rest of the female population.

The disadvantaged position of immigrant men, and even more so of immigrant women, raises questions about the purported neutrality of the welfare state between different kinds of workers. When access to entitlements is closely bound up with access to paid work, welfare distribution is likely to reproduce the inequalities of the labour market (Hammarstedt, 2001). There are attempts in the Nordic literature to explain these gaps in terms of the cultural competencies necessary to operate in local labour markets, measured by such variables as the geographical distance of the immigrants' place of origin, their ability to speak Swedish or Norwegian, and their ability to pronounce it correctly. However, as studies from Sweden show, the gaps persist regardless of how long culturally distant immigrants have lived in Sweden, and even for those who were adopted into Swedish families. Straightforward prejudice toward even the *appearance* of cultural difference clearly has a role to play. To paraphrase Longva (2003), the "passion for equality" within Nordic culture appears to be premised on an underlying "antipathy to difference."

Culturalist explanations also feature in the public discourses about family, sexuality, and personal life. Gender equality has become a key marker in delineating the boundary between Nordic and "other" cultures. Immigrant men are seen to be more patriarchal and misogynist than Nordic men and hence immigrant women more oppressed than Nordic women. This view has been reinforced by the occurrence of a number of well-publicised honour killings among certain immigrant communities in Norway and Sweden. The most widely publicised of these was the murder of Fadime Sahindal who was killed by her father, after a known history of threats to do so, because she had defied his will regarding her choice of partner and lifestyle.

The incident generated a highly polarised debate between a number of well-known feminists. The position taken by Gudrun Schyman, Chair of the Socialist Party, was that Fadime's death represented patriarchal power at its worst and had little to do with ethnicity or culture. Yvonne Hirdman, on the other hand, argued that it had everything to do with ethnicity and culture. Fadime had spent her life contesting her father's culture and trying to become a part of Swedish culture. The Swedish gender system was something to be defended and be proud of.

As Bredström (2003) argues, debates such as these serve to construct, perpetuate, and racialise "absolute differences" between Swedes and immigrants. Patriarchy has been made synonymous with immigrant culture, and what "disturbs immigrant men" has become a key focus of popular discourse: "When white men kill, rape or batter their women, this is never attributed to Swedish culture and the same can be said to apply to any other expression of sexism in Swedish society" (Bredström 2003, 4).

Such representations serve to ignore, however, the mutability of culture as a set of beliefs and practices that are negotiated and transformed through interactions with others. They also shift attention away from wider issues of racism within Nordic society that are likely to permeate these interactions. In doing so, they place immigrant women who do not necessarily share mainstream views about their culture in a difficult position, forcing them to choose between fighting for their rights as individuals and fighting for the rights of their communities (Lundström, 2003). In the statement that Fadime Sahindal made before the Swedish Parliament in 2001, some two months before her death, she spoke of her regret at her estrangement from her family in her struggle for her individual rights but added that it could have been prevented if her family had received the support they needed to integrate into Swedish society.

These debates have served to highlight what Kuovo (2004) calls the "epistemological blind spots" in Nordic feminism. It is evident that feminists in the Nordic context have long dealt with gender inequalities in terms of categorical differences between men and women, categories that cut across the class-based categories of capital and labour. Exemplifying this form of theorizing is the work of Hirdman (1988, cited in Woodford-Berger, 2004), who posits the existence of an intractable, hierarchical power order based on the separation of the two sexes and the primacy of men as the norm by which all human behaviour is valued and evaluated. Based on these two opposing and seemingly mutually exclusive categories of "women" and "men," Hirdman's work has played an important role in naming gender as a power relationship in Sweden in contrast to the more neutral formulations of earlier times. At the same time, it represents a form of theorizing that has problems incorporating inequalities of race/ethnicity and, more particularly, the intersections between gender, class, and race. As a result, there is very little feminist work that has taken on the reality of power differences between *women* (or, for that matter, men) from different social categories: research on gender has tended to take the perspective of Nordic women, while research on ethnicity has focused on immigrant men (Hägerström 2003). Women from immigrant communities either do not feature in these studies at all or feature as passive, victimised, and trapped in their cultures. This partial understanding of class, gender, and ethnicity has led to fragmented knowledge that does not recognize how different forms of power relate to each other: "reducing power to partial categories makes us blind to the interplay between different forms of superiority and subordination" (Hägerström 2003, 4).

There have been many critiques of this essentialised view of "the gender order" by both Nordic anthropologists as well as ethnic minority women living in Nordic countries. Longva points to the absence of feminist solidarity across ethnic boundaries in Norway despite the country's generous support to gender equality projects in developing countries. As she notes, the limited participation by feminists in debates around immigration is true of feminists occupying central positions in the gender equality machinery of the state bureaucracy as well as of independent feminist organizations.

Woodford-Berger's (2004) analysis of the analytical framework used for gender training within the Swedish government points out how it draws on dominant theorisations of gender in the Nordic context, particularly the work of Hirdman, and suggests that it may be extending the "epistemological blindspots" associated with this form of theorising to its international gender mainstreaming work. While such approaches may have played an important role in naming male power during a period of Nordic history when there was shared understanding and experience of gender inequality, they do little to open up analysis to the diversity of ways in which patriarchy is organised across the world, and among the different cultural groups who make up Nordic societies today.

CONCLUSION: PASSION, PRAGMATISM, AND THE POLITICS OF SOLIDARITY

It is evident from a reading of the literature that the struggles for gender equality in the Nordic context were made somewhat easier by the broader political culture in which equality was given a foundational status. However, the analysis in this chapter also draws attention to the role played by women's collective action within, as well as with, the state. In particular, it highlights the importance of finding discursive strategies that connected feminist goals and visions not only with the concerns of policy makers but also, very importantly, with those of grassroots women whose capacity to mobilise was critical to translating discursive strategies first into policies and then into practical outcomes. This grassroots mobilisation took a variety of forms. In Norway, we saw that women's activism was more visible because it took the form of autonomous organisations including housewives' associations, temperance societies, public health associations, and equal rights organizations. In Sweden, women's greater integration into mainstream structures made them less visible—hence the claim that it had feminism without feminists—but also more pervasive.

However, gender inequalities have not disappeared in the Nordic countries. If anything, the successive efforts to tackle gender inequality have rendered its roots in male power and privilege increasingly visible. As Eduards puts it, ". . . once the days of public patriarchy grew numbered, men became more obvious as those individually and collectively responsible for the discrimination of women" (1992, 99). It may be that the Nordic reputation for being the most gender equal societies in the world, a view given official recognition by the UN's GDI and GEM rankings, has made it more difficult for feminists in these countries to voice their dissent with the prevailing consensus.

Nevertheless, there is evidence that a number of feminists have therefore begun to question some of the basic assumptions of Nordic feminism. In the Swedish context, Eduards (1991) has pointed to what she sees as the limits to the dominant political culture, with its orientation toward consensus and compromise, for future feminist struggles. Writing about the Norwegian context, Skjeie and Teigen (2003) question the value of instrumentalism (the utility of gender equality) in a neo-liberal era when arguments for gender equality based on women's contribution to the public good are being recast in the discourse of private competitiveness and profit. This greater impatience on the part of some Nordic feminists suggests a desire for a more passionate—and less pragmatic—politics in the future, a greater reluctance to observe the duty to yield, and a greater willingness to mobilise around forms of inequality that cannot be subsumed within the hegemonic social democratic framework.

Woodford-Berger also argues for a more passionate politics but from a somewhat different perspective. She suggests that the consensus orientation of the political culture closes off the space to explore the possibilities of conflicts, differences, and inequalities *between* women—and between men—and hence the shared forms of oppression that might unite men and women from marginalised ethnic minorities against totalising articulations of gender equality: "we need to go beyond the 'consensus' processes that dry up dialogue and leave us unable to explore, let alone debate, commonalities in our concerns and the complexity of difference . . ." (2004, 70).

As Mouffe has argued (2000), the privileged value attached to reason, moderation, and consensus as the basis of political culture can overlook the role of passion and emotions in creating some of the identities and affiliations that matter most to people in the course of their lives. Such identities and affiliations are necessarily based on notions of "them" and "us," but they are not singular, unified, bounded, or fixed. It is essential, therefore, to open up discursive spaces that allow the expression and articulation of the diverse ways in which women and men identify themselves and form alliances: these may be family or workplace affiliations, along religious, cultural, and ethnic lines, or the myriad of other ways in which people come together in the course of their lives. It is by multiplying various configurations of them/us relationships within a society that potential antagonisms around constructions of identity can be defused and passions channelled into clearly differentiated political positions offering a choice between real alternatives, the essence of democratic politics.

From the Nordic perspective, therefore, there seems to be a case for giving greater importance to passion in a political culture that has prided itself on keeping passion out of politics. However, in those parts of the world where patriarchal power and privilege are exercised in far more overt ways than are evident in the Nordic context, the possibilities for pursuing dispassionate gender-neutral approaches to gender equality have been far fewer. Women have organised in these countries as workers, as mothers, and as citizens but also very often explicitly *as women*, because it is as women that they see themselves as oppressed, regardless of the roles they assume in public or private life. The state has generally been positioned as the enemy in these struggles, an expression of patriarchal power and dedicated to its defence, rather than an ally to pressure and persuade.

However, there is also evidence of a more pragmatic politics gaining ground among groups and organisations in developing country contexts for a variety of different reasons: the need to work across clearly recognized differences, to exploit promising windows of opportunity, to mobilise support beyond immediate constituencies, or to tailor strategies for change to a pace that does not expose already vulnerable groups to further risk. We find evidence of this in the "politics of patience" and "radical reformism" espoused by some of the organisations that work directly with women from low-income households.

We also find it within the feminist movement itself in the willingness to put aside ideological differences in the interests of practical gains. As Sen points out, the acceptance of women's rights as human rights within the international development agenda can be seen not as co-optation by the state, as some women's groups have argued, but as a victory for the feminist movement whose efforts it represents: "If knowledge is power, then changing the terrain of discourse is the first but very important step. It makes it possible to fight on the ground of one's choosing" (2004, 13). These hard-won gains were due in no small measure to the ability of feminists from different countries or different political leanings to work through their differences and to develop common positions around common goals.

The need to put aside differences in the face of a common enemy has also led to the emergence of a "pragmatic feminism" in the context of post-

Revolutionary Iran (Paidar, 2001). For secular feminists, many espousing socialist principles and universal rights, and Islamist feminists, working for women's rights within a religious framework, feminism and Islam were seen as diametrically opposed with little scope for dialogue or cooperation. However, over the difficult decades following the Islamic Revolution both sides have begun to develop more diversified self-definitions which allow for greater possibilities for working with each other. In a context where Islamic hardliners had begun abrogating women's most fundamental rights, and male reformers were interested only in a "gender-blind" concept of democracy, this willingness to cooperate emerged as political necessity rather than theoretical luxury.

Paidar's description of pragmatic feminism in the Iranian context has relevance to a broader politics of feminist solidarity: "pragmatic feminism is about creating an enabling and empowering environment in which each category of feminism can be supported and encouraged to stretch its own boundaries and bring out its own potential rather than corner the other's feminism into entrenched positions . . . (it) advocates collaboration across feminisms, irrespective of their perceived limitations, on gender issues where interests meet and collaboration can yield results" (2001, 37).

The grassroots mobilisation by women that helped to translate gender advocacy in the Nordic contexts into concrete policy outcomes is present only unevenly, if at all, in many developing countries. Feminist advocacy at national and international levels has been strong enough to make discursive gains in the policy domain in many of these countries but not strong enough to see these through to concrete outcomes. If feminists are to mobilise grassroots constituencies for gender equality, they will have to find a way to forge a politics of solidarity that can combine both passion and pragmatism. Passion motivates the struggle for justice, whatever form it might take, and provides the kind of courage that allowed the Mothers of the Plaza de Mayo to confront a repressive military regime in Argentina and women from lower-income traditionalist households to come out against the autocratic Pahlavi regime in support of Khomeini. Passion offers a politics of hope, a belief that an alternative world, free from injustice, is possible, essential if young women with their lives ahead of them are to be attracted to feminist politics.

Yet passion stems from beliefs and values, and it is clear that even among feminists, beliefs and values are not uniform. Passion becomes a divisive force when these beliefs and values harden into an unwillingness to respect difference. It is here that a strategic pragmatism, built perhaps on visions and dreams but concerned with the practical consequences of different courses of action, can provide the foundation for a more viable politics of solidarity: "To build something," as Amitav Ghosh puts it, "is not the same as dreaming of building it: building is always a matter of well-chosen compromises" (2004, 277).

272 *Kabeer*

NOTES

1. Like the rest of the book, it draws exclusively on publications in the English language and hence misses out on the rich body of literature in Norwegian and Swedish.
2. In Anglo-American cultures, for instance, freedom and individual choice tend to be assigned a higher value than, and often opposed to, equality.
3. Possible examples are interventions that promote girls' education, for instance, a factor which has proved important in both Norway and Iran (Razavi, this volume) in creating higher expectations on the part of women, as well as reservations for women in local government, which in India was a top-down policy rather than the product of grassroots mobilisation but which has increased women's political participation at the grassroots level (Kapadia 2002).
4. In any case, maternal allowances are rarely large enough to address the income needs of women from poorer households in either Nordic or developing country contexts. Historically, in Norway, poorer working-class women were rarely able to stay at home as a result of maternal allowances. More recently, evidence shows that while most parents claimed the "cash for care" allowance introduced in 1998 as an alternative to use of public child-care facilities, very few reduced their time in paid work. The ratio of "stay-at-home" mothers actually decreased (Ellingsæter, 2003, cited in Nagy, this volume). In Mexico, many of the women recipients of the widely studied "conditional cash transfer programme," which can be seen as a form of maternal allowance with conditions attached, expressed assistance in obtaining paid work since maternal allowances, in Mexico as much as in Norway, are seldom large enough to address the income needs of women from poorer households (Adato et al. 2000).

REFERENCES

Adato, Michelle, Bénédicte de la Briere, Dubravka Mindek, and Agnes Quisumbing. 2000. *Final report: The impact of PROGRESA on women's status and intra-household relations*. Washington, DC: International Food Policy Research Institute.
Appadurai, Arjun. 2002. Deep democracy: Urban governmentality and the horizon of politics. *Public Culture* 14(1):21–47.
Boserup, Ester. 1970. *Women's role in economic development*. New York: St. Martin's Press.
Bradley, David. 1996. *Family law and political culture: Scandinavian law in comparative perspective*. London: Sweet and Maxwell.
Braig, Marian, and Sonja Wolte. 2002. *Common ground or mutual exclusion Women's movements and international relations*. London: Zed Books.
Bredström, Anna. 2003. *Gendered racism and the production of cultural difference: Media representations and the production of identity work among "immigrant" youth in contemporary Sweden*. Paper presented at the fifth Feminist Research Conference, "Gender and Power in the New Europe," Lund University, August 20–24.
Chant, Sylvia, and Cathy McIlwaine. 1995. *Women of a lesser cost: Female labour, foreign exchange and Philippine Development*. London: Pluto Press.
Chhibber, Pradeep. 2002. Why are some women politically active? The household, public space, and political participation in India. *International Journal of Comparative Sociology* 43(3–5):409–29.

Cueva, Hanny. 2004. *Women in politics: What difference does it make? An empirical assessment of the case of abortion laws.* Master's thesis, Institute of Development Studies, Sussex.

Davin, Della. 2004. The impact of export-oriented manufacturing on the welfare entitlements of Chinese women workers. In *Globalisation, export-oriented employment and social policy*, eds. Shahra Razavi, Ruth Pearson, and Caroline Danloy, 67–90. Basingstoke: Palgrave Macmillan.

De los Reyes, Paulina. 2000. Diversity at work: Paradoxes, possibilities and problems in the Swedish discourse on diversity. *Economic and Industrial Democracy* 21:253–66.

De Volo, Lorraine Bayard. 2004. Mobilizing mothers for war: Cross-national framing strategies in Nicaragua's Contra War. *Gender & Society* 18(6):715–34.

Eduards, Maud. 1991. The Swedish gender model: Productivity, pragmatism and paternalism. *West European Politics* 14(3):166–81.

Eduards, Maud. 1992. Against the rules of the game: On the importance of women's collective actions. In *Rethinking change: Current Swedish feminist research*, eds. M. Eduards, I. Elgquivst-Saltzman, E. Lundgren, C. Sjoblad, E. Sundin, and U. Wikander, 83–104. Uppsala: Swedish Science Press.

Ellingsæter, Anne Lise. 1998. Dual breadwinner societies: Provider models in the Scandinavian welfare states. *Acta Sociologica*, 4(1):59–73.

Ellingsæter, Anne Lise. 1999. Women's right to work: The interplay of state, market and women's agency *Nora: Nordic Journal of Women's Studies* 7(2–3):129–33.

Ellingsæter, Anne Lise. 2003. The complexity of family policy reform: The case of Norway. *European Societies* 5(4):419–43.

Elman, Amy. 1995. The state's equality for women: Sweden's equality ombudsman. In *Comparative state feminism*, eds. D.M. Stetson and A. Mazur, 237–253. London: Sage.

Elson, Diane. 1998a. Talking to the boys: Gender and economic growth models. In *Feminist visions of development: Gender, analysis and policy*, eds. Cecile Jackson and Ruth Pearson, 155–170. London: Routledge.

Elson, Diane. 1998b. The economic, the political and the domestic: Businesses, states and households in the organization of production. *New Political Economy* 3(2):189–208.

Elson, Diane. 1999. Labor markets as gendered institutions: Equality, efficiency and empowerment issues. *World Development* 27(3):611–27.

Eraydin, Ayda, and Asuman Erendil. 1999. The role of female labour in industrial restructuring: New production processes and labour market relations in the Istanbul clothing industry. *Gender, Place and Culture* 6(3):259–72.

Florin, Christina, and Bengt Nilsson. 1999. Something in the nature of a bloodless revolution: How new gender relations became gender equality policy in Sweden in the 1960s and 1970s. In *State policy and gender system in the two German states and Sweden 1945–1989*, ed. R. Torstendahl, 11–77. Uppsala: Opuscula Historica Upsaliensia.

Gelb, Joyce. 1989. *Feminism and politics: A comparative perspective.* Berkeley: University of California Press.

Ghosh, Amitav. 2004. *The hungry tide.* New Delhi: Ravi Dayal Publishers.

Gillberg, Minna. 2000. Making women count in Sweden. In *Making women count: Integrating gender into law and policy-making*, eds. Fiona Beverage, Sue Nott, and K. Stephens, 131–162. Aldershot: Ashgate.

Gould, Arthur. 2001. *Developments in Swedish social policy: Resisting Dionysus.* Basingstoke: Palgrave.

Gould, Arthur. 2005. Resisting post modernity: Swedish social policy in the 1990s. *Social Work and Society* 3(2):72–84.

Graubard, Stephen R. 1986. *Norden: The passion for equality.* Oslo: Norwegian University Press.

Greenhalgh, Susan. 1991. *Women in informal enterprise: Empowerment or exploitation.* Research Division Working Paper No. 33, Population Council, New York.

Guzman, Virginia, and Rosalie Todaro. 2001. *Notes on gender and the global economy.* Santiago: Centro de Studios de la Muter.

Hagemann, Grow. 2002. Citizenship and social order: Gender politics in twentieth-century Norway and Sweden. *Women's History Review* 11(3):417–29.

Hägerström, Jeannette. 2003. *Perspectives on race/ethnicity and class in feminism (in an educational context).* Paper presented at the fifth European Feminist Research Conference, "Gender and Power in the New Europe," University of Lund, August 20–24.

Halsaa, Beatrice. 1998. A strategic partnership for women's policies in Norway. In *Women's movements and public policy in Europe, Latin America, and the Caribbean,* ed. Generate Lycklama à Nijeholt, Virginia Vargas, and Saki Wiring. New York and London: Garland Publications.

Hammarstedt, Mats. 2001. Disposable income differences between immigrants and natives in Sweden. *Journal of International Social Welfare* 10:117–26.

Hernes, Helga Maria. 1987. *Welfare state and woman power: Essays in state feminism.* Oslo: Norwegian University Press.

Hirdman, Yvonne. 1988. Genussystemet—reflexionerkring kvinnors sociala underordning. In *Kvinnoretenskaplig tidskrfit* 3:49–63.

Hirdman, Yvonne. 1998. State policy and gender contracts: The Swedish experience. In *Women, work, and the family in Europe,* eds. Drew et al. London: Routledge.

Hobson, Barbara. 1990. No exit, no voice: Women's economic dependency and the welfare state. *Acta Sociologica* 33(3):236–50.

Hobson, Barbara, and Marika Lindholm. 1997. Collective identities, women's power resources, and the making of welfare states. *Theory and Society* 26(4), August, 475–508.

Horn, Pat. 2002. *Voice regulation and the informal economy* (draft). Paper presented at the Informal Consultation on Reconceptualising Work, ILO, Geneva, December 12–13.

International Labour Review (ILR). 2000. Introduction: Social policy and social protection. *International Labour Review* 139(2):113–17.

Jackson, Cecile. 1996. Rescuing gender from the poverty trap. *World Development* 24(3):489–504.

Jensen, Jane, and Rianne Mahon. 1993. Representing solidarity: Class, gender and the crisis in social-democratic Sweden. *New Left Review* 201:76–100.

Kabeer , Naila. 1994. *Reversed realities: Gender hierarchies in development thought.* London:Verso Press.

Kabeer, Naila. 2000. *The power to choose: Bangladeshi women and labour market decisions in London and Dhaka.* London: Verso.

Kabeer, Naila. 2005. *Mainstreaming gender equality and poverty reduction in the Millennium Development Goals.* Ottawa: IDRC; and London: Commonwealth Secretariat.

Kabeer, Naila, and Mahmud, Simeen. 2004. Globalization, gender and poverty: Bangladeshi women workers in export and local markets. *Journal of International Development* 16(1):93–109.

Kapadia, Karin (ed). 2002. *The violence of development: The politics of identity, gender and social inequalities in India.* New Delhi: Kali for Women; and London: Zed Press.

Kardam, Nüket. 1993. *Bringing women in: Women's issues in international development programs.* Boulder, CO: Lynne Rienner Publishers.

Kilkey, Majella, and Jonathan Bradshaw. 1999. Lone mothers, economic well-being and policies. In *Gender and welfare state regimes*, ed. Diane Sainsbury. Oxford: Oxford University Press.

Kjeldstad, Randi. 2001. Gender politics and gender equality. In *Nordic welfare states in the European context*, ed. M. Kautto, 66–97. London: Routledge.

Knocke, Wuokko. 1991. Women immigrants: What is the problem? *Economic and Industrial Policy* 12(4):469–86.

Kouvo, Sari. 2004. Equality through human rights: Nordic and international feminist perspectives on rights. In *Nordic equality at a crossroads*, eds. E. Svensson, A. Pylkkanen, and J. Niemi-Kiesilamen, 219–233. Aldershot: Ashgate.

Kuhnle, Stein, and Sven Hort. 2003. *The developmental welfare state in Scandinavia: Lessons to the developing world*. UNRISD Project: Social policy in a development context. Geneva: UNRISD.

Land, Hilary, and Hilary Rose. 1985. Compulsory altruism for some or an altruistic society for all. In *In defence of welfare*, eds. P. Bean, J. Ferris and D. Whynes, 74–96. London: Tavistock.

Leira, Arnlaug. 1992. *Welfare states and working mothers: The Scandinavian experience*. Cambridge: Cambridge University Press.

Leira, Arnlaug. 1993. The woman friendly welfare state? The case of Norway and Sweden. In *Women and social policies in Europe: Work, family and the state*, ed. J. Lewis, 49–71. Aldershot: Elgar.

Leira, Arnlaug. 2002. Updating the "gender contract"? Childcare reforms in the Nordic countries in the 1990s. *Nora: Nordic Journal of Women's Studies* 10(2):81–89.

Lewis, Jane. 1997. Gender and welfare regimes: Further thoughts. *Social Politics* 4(2):160–77.

Lindholm, Marika. 1991. Swedish feminism, 1835–1945: A conservative revolution. *The Journal of Historical Sociology* 4(2):121–42.

Longva, Anh Nga. 2003. The trouble with difference: Gender, ethnicity and Norwegian social democracy. *Comparative Social Research* 22:153–75.

Longwe, Sara Hlupekile. 1997. The evaporation of gender policies in the patriarchal cooking pot. *Development in Practice* 7(2):148–56.

Lundström, Katrin. 2003. We are the others: Negotiating gender identity within racialised and gendered discourses among young women with Latin American backgrounds in Sweden. Paper presented at the fifth European Reminist Research Conference, "Gender and Power in the New Europe," University of Lund, August 20–24.

Melkas, Helina, and Richard Anker. 2001. Occupational segregation by sex in Nordic countries: An empirical investigation. In *Women, gender and work. What is equality and how do we get there?*, ed. M. F. Loutfi. Geneva: ILO.

Mendez, Jennifer Bickham. 2002. Creating alternatives from a gender perspective: Transnational organizing for Maquila workers' rights in Central America. In *Women's activism and globalization: Linking local struggles and transnational politics*, eds. Nancy A. Naples and Manisha Desai, 121–141. London: Routledge.

Mitlin, Diane, and Sheila Patel. 2005. *Re-interpreting the rights-based approach— A grassroots perspective on rights and development*. GPRG-WPS-022, Global Poverty Research Group, Economic and Social Research Council, United Kingdom.

Moghadam, Valentine M. 2006. Maternalist policies versus women's economic citizenship? Gendered social policy in Iran. In *Gender and social policy in a global context: Uncovering the gendered structure of "the social,"* eds. S. Razavi and S. Hassim, 87–108. Basingstoke: Palgrave Macmillan Press.

Molyneux, Maxine. 2004. The chimera of success. In *Repositioning feminisms in development*, eds. Andrea Cornwall, Elizabeth Harrison, and Ann Whitehead. Special issue, *IDS Bulletin* 35(4).

Mouffe, Chantal. 2000. Politics and passions: The stakes of democracy. *Ethical Perspectives* 7(2/3):146–50.

Mulinari, Diana, and Anders Neergaard. 2002. "Black skull consciousness": The new Swedish working class. *Race and Class* 46(3):55–72.

Myrdal Alva. 1968. *Nation and family: The Swedish experiment in democratic family and population policy*. New York: Harper and Brothers.

Myrdal, A., and G. Myrdal. 1934. *Kris i befolkningsfragan*. Stockholm: Bonniers.

Paidar, Parvin. 2001. Gender of democracy: The encounter between feminism and reformism in contemporary Iran. *Democracy, Governance and Human Rights*. Paper No. 6, UNRISD, Geneva.

Palmer, Ingrid. 1991. *Gender and population in the adjustment of African economies*. Geneva: ILO.

Pearson, Ruth. 2004. Women, work and empowerment in a global era. In *Repositioning feminisms in development*, eds. Andrea Cornwall, Elizabeth Harrison, and Ann Whitehead. Special issue, *IDS Bulletin* 35(4),

Razavi, Shahra. 1997. Fitting gender into development institutions. *World Development* 25(7):1111–1125.

Ross, Andrew (ed.). 1997. *Fashion, free trade and the rights of garment workers*. London: Verso.

Ruggie, Mary. 1984. *The state and working women: A comparative study of Britain and Sweden*. Princeton NJ: Princeton University Press.

Sainsbury, Diane. 1999. Gender and social democratic welfare states. In *Gender and welfare state regimes*, ed. Diane Sainsbury. Oxford: Oxford University Press.

Seguino, Stephanie. 2006. *Plus Ca Change? Evidence on global trends in gender norms and stereotypes*. GEM-IWG Working Paper Series 06-2 (June) www.econ.utah.edu (accessed September 19, 2007).

Selcuk, Fatma Selcuk. 2004. Labour organisations in the informal sector. *South-East Europe Review* 3:93–106.

Selcuk, Fatma Selcuk. 2005. Dressing the wound: Organising informal sector workers. *Monthly Review* 57(1) www.monthlyreview.org/0505selcuk.htm (accessed October 1, 2007).

Sen, Gita. 2004. The relationship of research to activism in the making of policy: Lessons from gender and development. Paper presented at conference on *Social Knowledge and International Policy Making: Exploring the Linkages*, UNRISD, Geneva, April 20–21.

Skjeie, Hege. 1991. The uneven advance of Norwegian women. *New Left Review* 187:79–102.

Skjeie, Hege. 2005. Gender equality: On travel metaphors and duties to yield. In *Women's citizenship and political rights*, eds. Anne Maria Holli, Sirkku Hellsten, and Krassimira Daskalova, 86–104. Basingstoke: Palgrave Macmillan.

Skjeie, H., and M. Teigen. 2003. *Menn i mellom. Mannsdominans og likestillingspolitikk*. Oslo: Gyldendal Akadmisk.

Snow, David A., and Robert D. Benford. 1992. Master frames and cycles of protest. In *Frontiers in social movement theory*, eds. A. D. Morris and C. M. Mueller, 133–155. New Haven, CT: Yale University.

Sörensen. Kerstin. and Christina Bergqvist. 2002. *Gender and the social democratic welfare regime: A comparison of gender-equality friendly policies in Sweden and Norway. Work Life in Transition 2002:05*. Stockholm, Arbetslivsinstitutet.

Standing, Hilary. 2004. Gender, myth and fables: The perils of mainstreaming in sector bureaucracies. In *Repositioning feminisms in development*, eds. Andrea Cornwall, Elizabeth Harrison, and Ann Whitehead. Special issue, *IDS Bulletin* 35(4).

Stromquist, Nelly. 1993. The political experience of women: Linking micro and macro democracies. *La Educacion* 37(116):541–59.

Subrahmanian Ramya. 2004. Making sense of gender in shifting institutional contexts: Some reflections on gender mainstreaming. In *Repositioning feminisms in development*, eds. Andrea Cornwall, Elizabeth Harrison, and Ann Whitehead. Special issue, *IDS Bulletin* 35(4),:89–96.

Taylor, Viviene. 2004. Social security and gender justice. In *Proceedings of the Gender and Social Security Seminar*, Centre for Applied Legal Studies. Johannesburg: University of Witwatersrand.

UNRISD. 2005. *Gender equality: Striving for justice in an unequal world*. Geneva: UNRISD.

Wilson, Fiona. 1991. *Sweaters: Gender, class and workshop-based industry in Mexico*. Basingstoke: Macmillan Press.

Wolf, Diana L. 1992. *Factory daughters: Gender, household dynamics and rural industrialisation in Java*. Berkeley: University of California Press.

Woodford-Berger, Prudence. 2004. Gender mainstream: What is it (about) and should we continue doing it?. In *Repositioning feminisms in development*, eds. Andrea Cornwall, Elizabeth Harrison, and Ann Whitehead. Special issue, *IDS Bulletin* 35(4).

Contributors

EDITORS

Agneta Stark is President of Dalarna University, Sweden. Her research focuses gender aspects of paid and unpaid work and international comparisons of work and living standards. In 2002 she was Marie-Jahoda Gastprofessorin für Internationale Frauenforschung in Ruhr-Universität, Bochum Germany. In 2004 she was made Doctor Honoris Causa by Karlstad University for her contributions to economic gender research and dissemination of such research to the public. Recent publications include the article "Warm Hands in Cold Age" in the book with the same title co-edited by Nancy Folbre, Lois Shaw and Agneta Stark, Routledge 2006. She is on the Editorial Board of *Feminist Economics*, and on the Board of Directors of the International Association for Feminist Economics.

Naila Kabeer is a Professorial Fellow at the Institute of Development Studies, Sussex. She was Kersten Hesselgren Visiting Professor at the Center for Global Gender Studies at the Department of Peace and Development Research Göteborg University 2004–2005. She is a social economist and works primarily on poverty, gender, and social policy issues. She has worked extensively in South and South East Asia. Her areas of specialisation are gender, poverty; population, labour markets and livelihoods. She has worked with a range of governments, NGOs and multilateral agencies on practical ways of integrating gender and social analysis in policy and planning. She has authored a number of books, including 'Reversed Realities: gender hierarchies in development thought' (1994) and 'The power to choose: Bangladeshi women and labour supply decisions in London and Dhaka'. She has also co-edited several books including most recently 'Inclusive citizenship: meanings and expressions' (2005). She is currently convening the theme of women and paid work as part of the Research Consortium Centre on Pathways to women's empowerment at the IDS.

Edda Magnus completed a Masters in Gender and Development from the Institute of Development Studies, Sussex University in 2002. She has worked on a number of projects relating to the gendered aspects of social policy and the labour market for, among others, the Department for International Development in the UK and Princeton University. Since the conclusion of her work on 'Reversing the Gaze' she has been employed as an attaché, with a focus on human rights and humanitarian issues, at Iceland's Permanent Mission to the United Nations in Geneva.

CONTRIBUTORS

Haris Gazdar is an economist working as a Senior Researcher with the Collective for Social Science Research in Karachi. His research interests include poverty, public action, schooling, gender and patriarchy, and political economy. He has worked as a Research Associate at the Asia Research Centre of the London School of Economics where he was involved in a research project on universal basic education in Pakistan, with a focus on the political economy of public service delivery. He has developed a combination of qualitative and quantitative research tools for his work on poverty and social marginalization in Pakistan. Besides Pakistan he has published on poverty and social policy issues with respect to India and Iraq. He combines consulting work with academic pursuits and is currently editing a volume on structural constraints to poverty reduction, and another one on bonded labour in Pakistan.

Elizabeth Jelin is Senior Researcher (Investigadora Superior) at CONICET (National Council of Scientific Research, Argentina). She is Director of the Doctoral Program in the Social Sciences developed jointly at the Universidad Nacional de General Sarmiento (UNGS) and the Instituto de Desarollo Económico y Social IDES. She is the author of numerous publications. Among the more recent ones, *State Repression and the Labors of Memory* (Univ. of Minnesota Press, 2003), and editor of several volumes in the series "Memorias de la represión" published by SIGLO XXI EDITORES in Madrid and Buenos Aires. She is also the author and editor of *Más allá de la nación: las escalas múltiples de los movimientos sociales* (Buenos Aires: Libros del Zorzal, 2003) and of *Pan y afectos. La transformación de las familias* (Buenos Aires: Fondo de Cultura Económica, 1998). Her research interests are in human rights, the family, citizenship, and social movements.

Shahra Razavi is Research Coordinator at the United Nations Research Institute for Social Development (UNRISD), Geneva. Her current areas of research are gender, social policy and care, and religion, politics and gender equality. Her most recent books include *Gender and Social Policy in a Global Context: Uncovering the Gendered Structure of 'the Social'* (edited with Shireen Hassim), Palgrave 2006; *Agrarian Change, Gender and Land Rights* (Special Issue of *Journal of Agrarian Change*) Blackwell 2003; *Gender Justice, Development and Rights* (edited with Maxine Molyneux) Oxford University Press 2002.

Beáta Nagy is an associate professor at the *Corvinus University of Budapest in the Institute of Sociology and Social Policy*. Her main research field is gender and work – especially management, organisations and entrepreneurs. She received her PhD in sociology in 1996. Recently she carried out investigations on companies' equal opportunity policies, and the gender awareness of local governments. She is the co-director of the newly established *Gender and Cultural Centre* at her home university. She was the co-editor of the book series Artemis, produced by the publishing house Csokonai (Hungary), which deals with gender issues. Since 2004 she is the Hungarian expert in the Network of Experts in Employment, Social Inclusion and Gender Equality (European Commission).

Ramya Subrahmanian is a Research Fellow at the Institute of Development Studies, University of Sussex, working on social policy and gender issues. Her particular focus is on primary education, and the intersections between livelihoods, poverty and household strategies for investing in education. She also works on issues of social exclusion in relation to education and health service delivery. She is the co-editor with Naila Kabeer of *Institutions, Relations and Outcomes: A Framework and Case Studies for Gender-Aware Planning* (Kali for Women 1999; Zed 2000) and with Naila Kabeer and Geetha Nambissan of *Needs versus Rights: Child Labour and the Right to Education in South Asia* (Sage 2003).

Seema Arora-Jonsson received her doctorate from the Swedish University of Agricultural Sciences for the dissertation, *Unsettling the Order, Gendered Subjects and Grassroots Activism*. Her research includes studying the micro-politics of power in defining resource management and local development, importantly how notions of women's empowerment and gender equality are intimately tied up with these processes. She studies the roles played by community members, researchers like herself and by development workers in defining resource management and local development. One ambition in her work has been to be of use to those with whom she works and she is concerned with questions of participatory research and reflexivity. At present Seema is a research fellow at the Centre for Gender Research at Uppsala University and will begin as Assistant Professor at the Department for Urban and Rural Studies at the Swedish University of Agricultural Sciences in Uppsala this summer.

Shireen Hassim is Associate Professor in Political Studies at the University of the Witwatersrand in Johannesburg, South Africa. She is co-editor (with Anne Marie Goetz) of *No Shortcuts to Power: African Women in Politics and Policy-Making* (Zed Books, 2003). She has written extensively on the South African women's movement, including *Women's Organizations and Democracy in South Africa: Contesting Authority* (University of Wisconsin Press, November 2006). She is co-editor, with Shahra Razavi, of *Gender and Social Policy in Global Context: Uncovering the Gendered Structure of the 'Social'* (Palgrave, 2006). She is a member of the editorial boards of a number of international journals. She has published widely in the areas of feminist politics, political institutions and social policy.

Bola Akanji is an Associate Research Professor at the Nigerian Institute of Social and Economic Research in Ibadan. She has her Ph.D in Agricultural Economics and has done extensive research on agricultural and broad economic policy issues in Nigeria, mostly from a gender perspective. Her major research interests are labour, agricultural markets and policy studies and gender and macro-policy interactions. From a multidisciplinary view point, her gender research and consulting have covered areas such as poverty reduction strategies, structural adjustment policies or economic reforms, national and regional economic policies and globalization. Her current interests and activities are in engendering national policies, budgets and national statistics. She has consulted for UNIFEM, OXFAM, UN.ECA, World Bank, IDRC and numerous national NGOs in Nigeria. She is a Fellow of the Salzburg Seminar in Austria and a member of the International Working Group on Gender and Macroeconomics (IWG-GEM), based at the University of Utah, Salt Lake City, USA and also a member of the African Finance and Economics Association (AFEA).

Francisco Cos-Montiel is a social policy-maker specialising in gender, poverty and institutional development. He was born and brought up in Mexico and has considerable work experience there; other countries of interest include Sweden, South Africa and India. He has occupied positions such as Director General of the Gender Planning Unit of the Government of Mexico and has been a consultant for the World Bank, UNDP, UNIFEM and the Pan American Health Organisation. In 2005 he received the Gender Professional Award from the International Development Research Center (IDRC).

Index

For Product Safety Concerns and Information please contact our EU
representative GPSR@taylorandfrancis.com
Taylor & Francis Verlag GmbH, Kaufingerstraße 24, 80331 München, Germany